Curing
Violence

CURING VIOLENCE

EDITED BY

MARK I. WALLACE

AND

THEOPHUS H. SMITH

SONOMA, CALIFORNIA
POLEBRIDGE PRESS
1994

Theophus H. Smith's essay, "King and the Black Religious Quest to Cure Racism," previously appeared in *Conjuring Culture* (Oxford University Press, 1994).

Library of Congress Cataloging-in-Publication Data

Curing violence / edited by Mark I. Wallace and Theophus H. Smith.
    p.   cm. — (Forum fascicles)
    Includes bibliographical references (pp.   ) and index.
    ISBN 0-944344-43-7 : $27.95
    1. Violence—Religious aspects. 2. Girard, René, 1923- .
3. Scapegoat. I. Wallace, Mark I., 1956- . II. Smith, Theophus
Harold. III. Series.
    BL65.V55C87   1994
    291.5'697—dc20   93-48828
                                                                 CIP

Cover illustration by John McDonough

Printed in the United States of America

10   9   8   7   6   5   4   3   2   1

Contents

3. Contemporary Issues

Contributors

Gil Baile is Director of The Florilegia Institute, Sonoma, CA.

B. Robert Bater is Professor of Religion at Queen's University, Kingston, Ontario.

Robert G. Hamerton-Kelly is Senior Research Scholar at the Center for International Security and Arms Control, Stanford University, CA.

Robert W. Hough is Associate Professor of Religion at Central Michigan University, Mt. Pleasant, MI.

Cheryl Kirk-Duggan is Assistant Professor of Religion at Meredith College, Raleigh, NC.

Stuart Lasine is Associate Professor of Religion at Wichita State University, Wichita, KS.

Charles Mabee is Director of the Urban Development Program at Ecumenical Theological Center, Detroit, MI.

Edward McMahon is Research Associate in the Department of Religion at Texas Christian University, Fort Worth, TX.

Charles D. Orzech is Assistant Professor of Religious Studies at the University of North Carolina, Greensboro, NC.

William Schweiker is Assistant Professor of Theology and Ethics at the University of Chicago Divinity School, Chicago, IL.

Chris Shea is Associate Professor of Classics at Ball State University, Muncie, IN.

Theophus H. (Thee) Smith is Associate Professor of Religion at Emory University, Atlanta, GA.

Tod D. Swanson is Assistant Professor of Religious Studies at Arizona State University, Tempe, AZ.

Mark I. Wallace is Assistant Professor of Religion at Swarthmore College, Swarthmore, PA.

James G. Williams is Professor of Religion at Syracuse University, Syracuse, NY.

René Girard
A Selective Bibliography

Prepared by Mark I. Wallace

This abbreviated bibliography includes books, articles, recent reviews, and some varia by Girard. It omits interviews, reprints, excerpts, non-English translations, and works about Girard. For a complete primary and secondary bibliography on Girard until 1986, see *To Honor René Girard*, ed. Alphonse Juilland (Stanford French and Italian Studies 34; Saratoga, CA: Anma Libri, 1986). For the relevant secondary literature from the mid-1980s to the present, see "The Bulletin of the Colloquium on Violence & Religion," c/o Wolfgang Palaver, Institut für Moraltheologie und Gesellschaftslehre, Universität Innsbruck, Karl-Rahner-Platz 3, A-6020, Innsbruck, Austria.

Books

Ed., *Proust: A Collection of Critical Essays*. New York: Prentice Hall, 1962.

Dostoïevski: du double à l'unité. Paris: Plon, 1963.

Deceit, Desire, and the Novel: Self and Other in Literary Structure. Trans. Yvonne Freccero. Baltimore: The Johns Hopkins University Press, 1965. Originally published as *Mesonge romantique et vérité romanesque*. Paris: Grasset, 1961.

Critique dans un souterrain. Lausanne: L'Age d'Homme, 1976.

Violence and the Sacred. Trans. Patrick Gregory. Baltimore: The Johns Hopkins University Press, 1977. Originally published as *La violence et le sacré*. Paris: Grasset, 1972.

"To Double Business Bound": Essays on Literature, Mimesis, and Anthropology. Baltimore: The Johns Hopkins University Press, 1978.

The Scapegoat. Trans. Yvonne Frecerro. Baltimore: The Johns Hopkins University Press, 1986. Originally published as *Le bouc émissaire*. Paris: Grasset, 1982.

Things Hidden Since the Foundation of the World with Jean-Michel Ourgoulian and Guy Lefort. Trans. Stephen Bann and Michael Metteer. Stanford: Stanford University Press, 1987. Originally published as *Des choses cachées depuis la fondation du monde*. Paris: Grasset, 1978.

Job: The Victim of His People. Trans. Yvonne Frecerro. Stanford: Stanford University Press, 1987. Originally published as *La route antique des hommes pervers*. Paris: Grasset, 1985.

A Theater of Envy: William Shakespeare. New York: Oxford University Press, 1991.

Contributions to Collective Works

"Duc de Saint-Simon." Pp. 336–41 in *A Critical Bibliography of French Literature* 3. Ed. D. C. Cabeen and J. Brody. Syracuse: Syracuse University Press, 1947.

"General Studies on the Novel." Pp. 125–29 in *A Critical Bibliography of French Literature* 3. Ed. D. C. Cabeen and J. Brody. Syracuse: Syracuse University Press, 1947.

"A propos de Jean-Paul Sartre: la notion de rupture en critique littéraire." Pp. 223–41 in *Chemins actuels de la critique.* Ed. G. Poulet. Paris: Plon, 1967.

"La notion de structure en critique littéraire." Pp. 61–73 in *Quatre conférences sur la nouvelle critique.* Turin: Societa Editrice Internationale, 1968.

"Explication de texte de Jean-Paul Sartre." Pp. 175–91 in *Explication de textes II.* Ed. Jean Sareil. New York: Prentice-Hall, 1970.

"Introduction to 'De la folie.'" Pp. 59–64 in *L'esprit moderne dans la littérature française.* Ed. Reinhard Kuhn. Oxford: Oxford University Press, 1972.

"Differentiation and Undifferentiation in Lévi-Strauss and Current Critical Theory." Pp. 111–36 in *Directions for Criticism.* Ed. Murray Krieger and L. S. Dembo. Madison: University of Wisconsin Press, 1977.

"Narcissism: The Freudian Myth Demythified by Proust." Pp. 293–311 in *Psycho-analysis, Creativity, and Literature.* Ed. Alan Roland. New York: Columbia University Press, 1978.

"'To Entrap the Wisest': A Reading of *The Merchant of Venice.*" Pp. 100–19 in *Literature and Society.* Ed. Edward W. Saïd. Baltimore: The Johns Hopkins University Press, 1980.

"Comedies of Errors: Plautus-Shakespeare-Molière." Pp. 68–86 in *American Criticism in the Post-Structuralist Age.* Ed. Ira Konigsberg. University of Michigan Press, 1981.

"La contingence dans les affaires humaines: 'Débat Castoriadis-René Girard.'" Pp. 331–52 in *L'auto-organisation: de la physique au politique.* Ed. Paul Dumouchel and Jean-Pierre Dupuy. Paris: Seuil, 1983.

"La danse de Salom." Pp. 365–71 in *L'auto–organisation: de la physique au politique.* Ed. Paul Dumouchel and Jean-Pierre Dupuy. Paris: Seuil, 1983.

"Mythos und Gegenmythos: Zu Kleists 'Das Erdbeben in Chili.'" Pp. 130–48 in *Positionen der Literaturwissenschaft.* Ed. David E. Wellbery. Munich: Beck, 1985.

"Le Meurtre fondateur dans la pensée de Nietzsche." Pp. 597–613 in *Violence et vérité: autour de René Girard.* Ed. Paul Dumouchel. Paris: Grasset, 1985.

"The Politics of Desire in Troilus and Cressida." Pp. 188–209 in *Shakespeare and the Question of Theory.* Ed. Patricia Parker and Geoffrey Hartman. London: Methuen, 1985.

"Bottom's One-Man Show." Pp. 99–122 in *The Current in Criticism.* Ed. Clayton Koelb and Virgil Lokke. West Lafayette, Ind.: Purdue University Press, 1987.

"Generative Scapegoating." Pp. 73–105 in *Violent Origins: Walter Burkert, René Girard, and Jonathan Z. Smith on Ritual Killing and Cultural Formation.* Ed. Robert G. Hamerton-Kelly. Standord: Stanford University Press, 1987.

"Der tragische Konflikt." Pp. 62–76 in *Das Tabu der Gewalt.* Innsbruck: Hildegard Fässler, 1987.

"Des pestes médiévales au SIDA: le danger des extrapolations abusives." Pp. 138–46 in the *Proceedings of a Symposium on AIDS, June 20–21, 1987*. Annecy: Fondation Marcel Mérieux, 1987.

"Jealousy in *The Winter's Tale*." Pp. 39–62 in *Alphonse Juilland: D'une passion l'autre*. Ed. Brigitte Cazelles and René Girard. Saratoga: Anma Libri, 1987.

"Nietzsche and Contradiction." Pp. 53–65 in *Nietzsche in Italy*. Ed. Thomas Harrison. Saratoga: Anma Libri, 1988.

"Theory and Its Terrors." Pp. 225–54 in *The Limits of Theory*. Ed. Thomas Kavanagh Stanford: Stanford University Press, 1989.

Articles

"L'homme et le cosmos dans *L'Espoir* et *Les Noyers de l'Altenburg* d'André Malraux." *Publication of the Modern Language Association* 68 (1953): 49–55.

"Les réflections sur l'art dans les romans de Malraux." *Modern Language Notes* 68 (1953): 544–46.

"Le règne animal dans les romans de Malraux." *French Review* 26 (1953): 261–67.

"The Role of Eroticism in Malraux's Fictions." *Yale French Studies* 11 (1953): 49–58.

"L'histoire dans l'oeuvre de Saint-John Perse." *Romantic Review* 44 (1953): 47–55.

"Marriage in Avignon in the Second Half of the Fifteenth Century." *Speculum* 28 (1953): 485–98.

"Franz Kafka et ses critiques." *Symposium* 7 (1953): 34–44.

"Valéry et Stendhal." *Publication of the Modern Language Association* 69 (1954): 347–57.

"André Suarès et les autres." *Cahiers du Sud* 42.329 (1955): 14–18.

"Existentialism and Criticism." *Yale French Studies* 16 (1956): 45–52.

"Situation du poète américain." *Cahiers du Sud* 42.336 (1956): 196–202.

"Saint-Simon et la critique." *French Review* 29 (1956): 389–94.

"Winds and Poetic Experience." *The Berkeley Review* 1 (Winter 1956): 46–52.

"Où va le roman?" *French Review* 30 (1957): 201–06.

"Man, Myth and Malraux." *Yale French Studies* 18 (1957): 55–62.

"Voltaire and Classical Historiography." *The American Magazine of the French Legion of Honor* 24 (1958): 151–60.

"Tocqueville and Stendhal." *The American Magazine of the French Legion of Honor* 31 (1960): 73–83.

"Pride and Passion in the Contemporary Novel." *Yale French Studies* 24 (1960): 3–10.

"Memoirs of a Dutiful Existentialist." *Yale French Studies* 27 (1961): 41–47.

"De Dante à la sociologie du roman." *Revue Belge de Sociologie* (1963): 263–69.

"Marivaudage and Hypocrisy." *The American Magazine of the French Legion of Honor* 34 (1963): 163–74.

"Des formes aux structures, en littérature et ailleurs." *Modern Language Notes* 78 (December 1963): 504–19.

"Racine, poète de la gloire." *Critique* 20 (June 1964): 484–506.

"Camus's Stranger Retried." *Publication of the Modern Language Association* 79 (December 1964): 519–33.

"Monstres et demi-dieux dans l'oeuvre de Hugo." *Symposium* 29 (1965): 50–57.

"De l'expérience romanesque au mythe oedipien." *Critique* 21 (November 1965): 899–924.

"Réflexions critiques sur les recherches littéraires." *Modern Language Notes* 81 (1966): 307–24.

"Symétrie et dissymétrie dans le mythe d'Oedipe." *Critique* 24 (January 1968): 99–135.

"Dionysos et la genèse violente du sacré." *Poétique* 3 (1970): 266–81.

"Une analyse d'*Oedipe roi*." *Critique Sociologique et Critique Psychanaytique* [Institut de Sociologie. Université Libre de Bruxelles] (1970): 127–63.

"Myth and Ritual in *A Midsummer Night's Dream*." *Harry F. Camp Memorial Lectures* [Stanford University] (November 1972): 1–17.

"Perilous Balance: A Comic Hypothesis." *Modern Language Notes* 87 (December 1972): 811–26.

"Vers une définition systématique du sacré." *Liberté* [Montreal] 16 (July 1973): 58–74.

Lévi-Strauss, Frye, Derrida and Shakespearean Criticism." *Diacritics* 3 (Fall 1973): 34–38.

"Discussion avec René Girard." *Esprit* 429 (November 1973): 528–63.

"The Plague in Literature and Myth." *Texas Studies* 15 (1974): 833–50.

"Les malédictions contre les Pharisiens et la révélation évangélique." *Bulletin du Centre Protestant d'Etudes* [Geneva] (1975): 5–29.

"French Theories of Fictions, 1947–1974." *The Bucknell Review 21* (Spring 1976): 117–26.

"Differentiation and Undifferentiation in Lévi-Strauss and Current Critical Theory." *Contemporary Literature* 17 (Summer 1976): 404–29.

"Superman in the Underground: Strategies of Madness–Nietzsche, Wagner and Dostoevsky." *Modern Language Notes* 91 (1976): 1161–85.

"Violence and Representation in the Mythical Text." *Modern Language Notes* 92 (1977): 922–44.

"Mimesis and Violence: Perspectives in Cultural Criticism." *Berkshire Review* 14 (1979): 9–19.

"Rite, travail, science." *Critique* 380 (January 1979): 20–34.

"Peter's Denial and the Question of Mimesis." *Notre Dame English Journal* 14 (Summer 1982): 177–89.

"Le démolisseur de l'Olympe." *Le Nouvel Observateur* (February 4, 1983): 70–75.

"Un prétexte pour régler les comptes." *Le Nouvel Observateur* (February 26, 1983): 67.

"Esprit de concurrence: des vertus inaltérables." *Le Point* (May 9, 1983): 80.

"Job et le bouc émissaire." *Bulletin du Centre Protestant d'Etudes* [Geneva] 35 (November 1983): 3–33.

"Culture 'primitive,' giudaismo, cristianismo." *La pena di morte del mondo* [Italy: Marietti. Casale Monferrato] (1983): 75–86.

"Dionysus versus the Crucified." *Modern Language Notes* 99 (1984): 816–35.

"Scandal and the Dance: Salome in the Gospel of Mark." *New Literay History* 15 (Winter 1984): 311–24.

"Hamlet's Dull Revenge." *Stanford Literature Review* 1 (Fall 1984): 159–200.

"Exorciser la violence." *Le Figaro* (April 15, 1985): 2.

"The Bible Is Not a Myth." *Literature and Belief* 4 (Autumn 1985): 7–15.

"La Différence Franco-Américaine." *L'Expansion* [special issue entitled "Demain la France"] (October-November 1985): 275-81.

"Violence et réciprocité." *Les Cahiers de l'IPC* 2 [special issue entitled "L'Acte de violence"] (November 1985): 53-88.

"'The Ancient Trail Trodden by the Wicked': Job as Scapegoat." *Semeia: An Experimental Journal for Biblical Criticism* 33 (December 1985): 13-41.

"What is the Question?" *The Stanford Magazine* 14 (Winter 1986): 60.

"Dieu et l'esprit moderne." *L'Express* (April 11, 1986): 36-38.

"Quelques clés des désordres collectifs." *Le Figaro* (May 9-10, 1987): 18.

"Violence et société." *Revue des Deux Mondes* 12 (December 1988): 91-8.

"La mythologie et sa déconstruction dans 'L'Anneau du Niebelung." *Cahiers du CREA* 12 (December 1988): 57-201.

"Love Delights in Praises: A Reading of *The Two Gentlemen of Verona*." *Philosophy and Literature* (Autumn 1989): 231-47.

"'Génie et démons du christianisme,' in *Fanastisme : la menace religieuse*." *Le Nouvel Observateur* (October 5-11, 1989): 20.

"'Tis Not So Sweet Now As It Was Before: Orsino and Olivia in *Twelfth Night*." *Stanford Literature Review* 7 (1990).

"*Do You Love Him Because I Do!* Mimetic Interaction in Shakespeare's Comedies." *Helios* 17 [special issue on *René Girard and Western Literature*] (Spring 1990): 89-108.

"Croyez-vous vous-même à votre propre théorie?" *La Règle du Jeu* 1 (May 1990): 254-77.

"Love and Hate in *Yvain*." *Recherches et Rencontres* 1 (1990): 249-62.

"The Crime and Conversion of Leontes in *The Winter's Tale*." *Religion & Literature* (October 1990): 193-219.

Reviews (since 1972)

"Système du délire." Review of *L'anti-Oedipe*, by Gilles Deleuze. *Critique* 28 (November 1972): 957-96.

Review of *Ce que je crois*, by André Chouraqui. *Le Nouvel Observateur* (May 7, 1979): 84-85.

"Vers une nouvelle anthropologie." Review of *Les jeux du désir*, by Georges-Hubert de Radkowski. *Le Monde* (May 10, 1980): 2.

"Derrière la modestie de l'approche, un projet vaste se dessine." Review of *Histoires du temps*, by Jacques Attali. *Le Matin* (December 27, 1982).

Review of *Le 19e siècle à travers les âges*, by Philippe Muray. *Commentaire* 27 (Autumn 1984): 613-16.

"Le jeu des secrets interdits." Review of Milan Kundera. *Le Nouvel Observateur* (November 21-27, 1986): 102-03.

"Serres, le philosophe en marche." Review of *Statues*, by Michel Serres. *Le Figaro Littéraire* (December 7, 1987): 3-4.

"Des chiffres et des hommes." Review of *Métamorphoses de la Valeur*, by Georges-Hubert de Radkowski. *L'Express* (May 13-19, 1988): 186.

Introductions, Prefaces, and Postfaces

"Tiresias and the Critic." Introduction to *The Languages of Criticism and the Sciences of Man.* Ed. Richard Macksey and Eugenio Donato. Pp. 15–21. Baltimore: The Johns Hopkins University Press, 1970.

Preface to *Structures romanesques et vision sociale chez G. de Maupassant*, by Charles Castella. Pp. i-v. Lausanne: L'Age de l'Homme, 1973.

Preface to *Mimesis Conflictiva*, by Cesáreo Bandera. Pp. 9–18. Madrid: Gredos, 1975.

Postface to *L'enfer des choses: René Girard et la logique de l'économie*, by Paul Dumouchel and Jean-Pierre Dupuy. Pp. 257–64. Paris: Seuil, 1979.

Preface to Stanford *French Review* 7 [special issue on "La Foule"] (Summer 1983): 117.

Preface to *The Secret Sharers: Studies in Contemporary Fictions*, by Bruce Bassoff. Pp. ix-xv. New York: AMS Press, 1983.

Abbreviations

Deceit

Deceit, Desire, and the Novel

Double
Business

*"To Double Business Bound": Essays on Literature,
Mimesis, and Anthropology*

Job

Job: The Victim of His People

Proust

Proust: A Collection of Critical Essays

Scapegoat

The Scapegoat

Things
Hidden

*Things Hidden Since
the Foundation of the World*

Violence and
the Sacred

Violence and the Sacred

Violent
Origins

*Violent Origins: Walter Burkert, René Girard, and
Jonathan Z. Smith on Ritual Killing and Social Formation*

Acknowledgments

Our thanks to Swarthmore College students Alex Vishio, Erin Sawyer, and Sean Latham for assisting in preparing the manuscript; to Margaret Tompkins at Stanford University for help with the bibliography; to Swarthmore College, Emory University, and the American Academy of Religion for grant support that enabled our work on this book; and to Bob Funk, Char Matejovksy, Ben Wheeler and the other staff members of Polebridge Press for their skill and professionalism in bringing this project to completion.

Religion as Cure or Religion as Structure of Violence?

Mark I. Wallace and Theophus H. Smith

O. Introduction

Why does religion sometimes appear to be the "cure" for social violence, and yet also and at the same time its cause? This question provides the entree to this book's common concern with the relevance of René Girard's writings for the study of religion. Girard argues that the foundation and unity of all culture and religion occurs in the interaction between desire and violence. The basic human drive to own or imitate what the other person has or is–what Girard calls "mimetic desire"–inevitably threatens to tear apart a society by fomenting unchecked rivalry between individuals and groups. Eventually, however, this threat is contained by the society's invention of a "scapegoat" who is said to be the cause of its problems, even while the society denies the violence that results from imitation and rivalry. Convenient scapegoats are those individuals (for example, Jesus, Martin Luther King, Jr.) or groups (Jews in medieval Europe, persons with AIDS) that are marginal and different to a society's sense of order, and hence deemed to be a "threat" to its collective identity. Since violence toward the outsider initially checks the corrosion of mimetic rivalry by reuniting, at least temporarily, warring factions under a common vision (the unanimity of the lynch mob), such violence is a permanent fixture of all world cultures. Over time this violence becomes routinized in different forms of ritual sacrifice, and the cultus renews its common life through the regular imputation of the cause of its problems to a random scapegoat.

This pessimistic thesis is balanced by Girard's recovery of the God of Victims who in the Bible (and other sacred texts) advocates on behalf of the scapegoats who are unjustly accused of creating social chaos. This God makes common cause with the Hebrew prophets and Jesus by encouraging nonviolent opposition to the destructive political and religious interests that threaten to destroy the innocent. The God of Victims desires love and justice rather than sacrifice and burnt offerings. Girard then concludes that a nonviolent and nonsacrificial understanding of the Sacred contains critical moral and spiritual resources for responding to the needs of oppressed communities in today's world. And herein lies the paradox of the Girardian project: religion is simultaneously criticized as the cultural medium for collective violence and is valorized as the antidote for healing such violence.

While using Girard's thesis as their underlying point of departure, the authors of this volume compose a diverse group: biblical scholars, historians and anthropologists of religion, theologians, and humanists of various disciplines. Within this range of backgrounds we have worked together to render the contents of the book internally integrated and mutually illuminating. At different points in the late 1980s we met together as members of the Bible, Narrative, and American Culture Seminar of the Westar Institute to discuss the import of Girard's work in religious studies and to plan the contents of the volume.[1] In this seminar we benefitted from cross-disciplinary exchange and the participation of Girard himself, whose critical comments on early drafts of these chapters proved enormously helpful, even when not included in the final versions. We dedicate this volume to René Girard in gratitude for his regular and spirited participation in our seminar meetings in Sonoma.

Since the publication of *Violence and the Sacred* in 1972 and *The Scapegoat* ten years later, Girard's theory of religion and violence has received increasing attention. Along with scholars in literary and history criticism–Girard's original disciplines–specialists in other fields such as anthropology, psychology, and biblical studies have provided introductory and critical commentary on his thought. This book offers the first multiauthor assessment of the usefulness of Girard's theory for religious studies, and is not designed to be an addition to the number of critical introductions to Girard already available. The virtue of these chapters lies elsewhere.

Our distinguishing task has been to struggle with the topic of the relationship between religion and violence, and to do so by way of Girard's thought. We believe this is one of the most compelling problems of our time and, indeed, of all previous history and the foreseeable future. We want the reader to discern the warrants for pursuing this problem, not as a specialized concern, but as one of the few single topics that focus many of the major issues of contemporary experience. In the interests of coherence and brevity, however, we have been forced to limit our scope, with the result that certain areas in culture and art, religion and science, and history and politics have been left out of our account. The reader will notice, for example, that while feminist, Mesoamerican, Buddhist, and African-American sources are used in the following chapters, the book's authors are predominantly North American and Western and their focus falls primarily on the religions and scriptures of Christianity and Judaism. Notwithstanding these limitations, we have labored

---

1 Westar Institute is a scholarly organization based in Sonoma, California, founded by New Testament scholar Robert W. Funk; it meets twice yearly and is most noted, among its other activities, for the research on the historical Jesus of its Jesus Seminar.

to provide a sufficient diversity of perspectives on the problem of religion and violence vis-à-vis Girard's interests. If more studies are needed in order to complete the project launched by this one, then–to paraphrase Mao Tse-tung–"Let a thousand books follow!"

An implicit but highly consequential aspect of the project was most often represented in seminar discussions by our chair, Charles Mabee. Mabee often pointed out that one of the major consequences of Girardian theory for the human sciences is the centrality it accords religion as a phenomenon, and religious studies as a discipline. In Girard's work religion scholars may have found (if not conclusively, then at least indications toward) a "field theory" of religion that intrinsically correlates the other disciplines of the academy within its sphere of competence and explanatory power. Few thinkers since the time of the early architects of modern social thought (Durkheim, Marx, Weber) have taken as seriously as Girard the role of religion in the formation and maintenance of human society. In spite of the current trend toward more specialized research within the liberal arts, Girard's "maximalist postulate" concerning the relation of religion and culture marks the return of grand theory to the academy.[2]

1. Works by Girard

René Girard is the Andrew B. Hammond Professor of French Language, Literature and Civilization at Stanford University. He is a native French thinker whose theory of ritual sacrifice and "the scapegoat" has distinguished him among scholars in a wide variety of disciplines. Among religion scholars he is best known for his claim that "generative violence" or violence as the "primitive sacred" best explains the deep structures of religion and culture from the prehistory of the human species to the present. After writing a dissertation in modern history, he began his scholarly career as a literary critic and theorist focusing on the phenomena of mimesis (imitation), desire, and mimetic rivalry in the novel. What he discovered there led him to expand his literary critique in order to include the fields of anthropology, psychology, history of religions, and biblical criticism.

Girard's major works in English translation date from 1962 with *Proust: A Collection of Critical Essays*, and 1966 with *Deceit, Desire and the Novel: Self and Other in Literary Structure*. These seminal works were followed in 1977 with *Violence and the Sacred*, his first major application of the mimetic theory to anthropology, myth, and religion, and in 1978 by *"To Double Business Bound": Essays on Literature, Mimesis, and Anthropology*. In the mid-1980s three books were translated and published in quick succession. What they

---

2 See Wallace, "Postmodern Biblicism," 312–15; Williams, "The Innocent Victim," 320–26; cf. Skinner, *The Return of Grand Theory in the Human Sciences*.

have in common is Girard's "discovery" of the Christian gospels as definitive for exposing, demystifying, and destabilizing the "scapegoat mechanism" in human culture. 1986 featured *The Scapegoat*, and in 1987, first *Job: the Victim of His People*, and then Girard's most comprehensive statement to date, *Things Hidden Since the Foundation of the World*, respectively. In 1991 he published his major treatment of Shakespeare, *A Theater of Envy: William Shakespeare*, which includes important comparisons between mimesis in the gospels and Shakespeare's writings.

The English language commentaries and critical reviews on Girard's work include six books and five special journal issues. The first major journal issue was published by *Diacritics* (8) in Spring, 1978. It includes an article by Girard's colleagues, Jean-Michel Oughourlian and Guy Lefort, on "Psychotic Structure and Girard's Doubles," as well as a sharply critical piece by Hayden White, "Ethnological 'Lie' and Mythical 'Truth.'" The same year witnessed a discussion on Girard in the *Modern Language Association Newsletter* (93). The *Diacritics* and *MLAN* issues were followed in 1979 by a special issue on "Culture and Violence" in the *Berkshire Review* (14). Among other contributors to that issue, F. T. Griffiths discusses Girard and the Greeks; Elizabeth Traube takes up incest and mythology in Girard's anthropology; Rafael Fernandez examines the "iconography of violence" in nineteenth- and twentieth-century art; and John Pemberton III reviews Girard's theory of sacred kingship in Africa, with specific reference to the Yoruba people. The fourth special journal issue is the only religious studies periodical devoted to Girard's work. In December 1985, *Semeia* (33) published an issue on "René Girard and Biblical Criticism." Edited and introduced by Andrew J. McKenna, the *Semeia* issue includes Girard criticism focused on biblical figures such as Jonah (Sandor Goodhart), Paul (Eric Gans; Robert G. Hamerton-Kelly), Jesus (Raymund Schwager; Burton Mack), and Job (Baruch Levine). A fifth journal issue, *Helios* (17), Spring 1990, surveys Girard's literary theory and includes an article by McKenna on "Biblical Structuralism: Testing the Victimary Hypothesis."

In addition to these journal issues, Raymund Schwager and James G. Williams have published in English book-length religious studies treatments of Girard's work with special reference to his interpretation of the Bible. Translated and published in 1987 (German edition, 1978), Schwager's book is *Must there Be Scapegoats? Violence and Redemption in the Bible*. Williams's volume is entitled *The Bible, Violence, and The Sacred: Liberation from the Myth of Sanctioned Violence*, published in 1991. These works were preceded by a sixtieth birthday festschrift edited by Alphonse Juilland in 1986, *To Honor René Girard*, which includes a comprehensive bibliography of Girard's writings and Girard criticism up to that publication year. Beginning in 1991 and covering the period of the mid-1980s to the present, a more recent bibliography has been provided by "The Bulletin of the Colloquium on Violence

& Religion"; under the editorship of Wolfgang Palaver of Innsbruck, this bulletin now serves as a clearing house for all secondary literature on Girard.

In 1987 and 1988, respectively, Stanford University published two works of Girard commentary and criticism: *Violent Origins: Ritual Killing and Cultural Formation*, edited by Robert G. Hamerton-Kelly and including an introduction by Burton Mack, commentary by Renato Rosaldo, and essays and discussions by Walter Burkert, René Girard, and Jonathan Z. Smith; and *Violence and Truth: On the Work of René Girard*, edited by Paul Dumouchel. The Dumouchel volume includes, among others, articles by Schwager on Girard's theology, Sandor Goodhart on Girard and the biblical Joseph cycle, Frederuic Delarge on the status of the gospels in Girard, and Lucien Scubla on the nature of Christianity and religion in Girard's project. Most recently, McKenna authored in 1992 *Violence and Difference: Girard, Derrida, and Deconstruction*, which juxtaposes Girard's mimetic theory and Derridean deconstruction with occasional reference to biblical hermeneutics.

It is evident that none of these books or journal issues attempts a representative range of religious studies issues. The present book is the first cohesive treatment of Girard's theory by a broad spectrum of religion scholars, with interests extending from hermeneutic theory and the history of religions, to biblical-exegetical and theological-ethical considerations. It fills a gap in the current literature, both in Girard criticism and in religious studies, by calling attention to the challenge of his work to contemporary approaches in religion, ethics, and theology.

2. Book Format

The proposed format divides the book into three sections, with individual chapters ranging in approach from explication to criticism. Part 1 comprises the two inaugural chapters that provide general theoretical perspectives on Girard's work in religious studies. Part 2 consists of three chapters on historical applications of his theory in relation to classical and biblical studies. The great majority of chapters fall into Part 3, which is devoted to contemporary issues, some of which apply the Girardian theory, some of which are critical of the theory, and some of which do both.

2.1 Theoretical perspectives

Chapter 1, "Religion and the Thought of René Girard: An Introduction" by Robert G. Hamerton-Kelly, surveys Girard's work with special reference to the notion of desire, the surrogate victim mechanism, the nature of ritual and founding myths, and the role of the Bible in "demythifying" the victimage mechanism. Chapter 2, "Religion and the Philosophers of Mimesis" by William Schweiker, evaluates Girard's use of mimesis as a foundational concept and critically compares it with the role of mimesis in the works of hermeneutic theorists Hans-Georg Gadamer and Paul Ricoeur.

2.2 Historical perspectives

Chapter 3, "Sacrificial Violence in Homer's *Iliad*" by Gil Bailie, studies the power of Girard's theory of mimetic rivalry within the narrative contours of one of the founding texts of western literature, the *Iliad*. Chapter 4, "'Steadfast Love and Not Sacrifice': A Nonsacrificial Reading of the Hebrew Scriptures" by James G. Williams, contrasts sacrificial and nonsacrificial readings of the Hebrew Bible in order to uncover and evaluate the structures of sacred violence within Israel's cultus. Chapter 5, "Before the Law: Un/rivaling the Old Testament," by Charles Mabee, argues that Christians and Jews are rival communities of biblical interpretation but need not be.

2.3. Contemporary perspectives

Chapter 6, "An Ungodly Resemblance: Colonial Violence and Inca Analogies to Christianity" by Tod Swanson, challenges Girard's valorization of the Christian gospels as anti-persecution texts *par excellence*, by reference to traditional religions in South America and their revelatory power vis-à-vis the history of Christian violence. Chapter 7, "'Provoked Suicide' and the Victim's Behavior: The Case of the Vietnamese Self-Immolators" by Charles D. Orzech, examines the cogency of Girard's theory as applied to nonwestern religions; the theory is assessed with reference to the self-immolation of Buddhist monks as ritual efforts to end the Vietnam war. Chapter 8, "'You Will Reap Just What You Sow': The Vietnam War Poetry of Donald G. Kemp" by Robert W. Hough, is concerned with some of the same historical events as Orzech's piece. The war poetry of a Vietnam veteran is examined for its display of scapegoating processes operating in American society and civil religion–processes that blame the veterans for the failure of the war effort and that still require rites of healing and transformation.

Chapter 9, "Violence, Religion, Law: A Girardian Analysis" by Edward McMahon, studies both the mitigation *and the mediation* of scapegoating processes in institutions of law and justice, with attention to modern "sacrificial crises" (particularly in totalitarian states) that lead to the collapse of law, a regression to the "primitive sacred," and the compelling need for counter-processes in national and international affairs. Chapter 10, "Levite Violence, Fratricide, and Sacrifice in the Bible and Later Revolutionary Rhetoric" by Stuart Lasine, is a study of the uses and abuses of biblical narrative with reference to Mosaic law and the levitical codes sanctioning priestly violence. This dynamic is then examined in relation to political rhetoric from the French revolution to the Stalinist purges and as ameliorated by lesser known traditions of rabbinic dissent.

Chapter 11, "King and the Black Religious Quest to Cure Racism" by Theophus H. Smith, studies the nonviolent activism of Dr. Martin Luther King, Jr. in relation to its spiritual and ritual foundations in an Afro-Christian tradition of countering ethnic victimization, transforming the victimizer, and realizing the vision of a "beloved community" (King). Chapter 12, "Victims on Violence: 'Different Voices' and Girard" by Chris Shea, surveys counter-Girardian criticism in terms of women's experience, providing alternative views of fundamental human anthropology. Chapter 13, "Gender, Violence, and Transformation in Alice Walker's *The Color Purple*" by Cheryl Kirk-Duggan, examines gender violence against the background of ethnic violence, internalized by Afro-American men and misdirected against Afro-American women, in the context of Alice Walker's novel and its culminating triumph over victimage. And chapter 14, "Apocalyptic Religion in Christian Fundamentalism" by B. Robert Bater, studies Girard's contention in *Things Hidden* that the threat of nuclear holocaust renders our global situation "objectively apocalyptic." This thesis is explicated in relation to fundamentalist Christianity and the problem it represents: how to counter modern sacrificial processes seek nuclear cataclysm in a final effort to vindicate and restore the primitive sacred.

3. Girard and the *Pharmakon*

In what ways do religious traditions alternately foment and sacralize violence and sacrifice, on the one hand, and serve as a check against the spread of violence, on the other? Already in the biblical gospels–in the accounts of the life, death and resurrection of Jesus–we find the churches' problem of understanding the relationship between violence and the sacred. Using Girard's terms, we discover embedded in the Christian scriptures a particular form of the more general problem facing all theistic religions. This is the problem of discerning which is the true God: the God invoked by persecutors as the guarantor of sacrificial violence or the God who saves victims as the liberator of the oppressed?[3] Regardless of specific issues and particular events in subsequent church history, this issue–as a critical issue for Christians and other religious communities–is narratively prefigured in the gospels by the collusion of all institutional powers, religious and civil, in the crucifixion of Jesus.

Too often, however, the most prominent, narrative feature of Christian action in church history has been a sustained repetition of the victimization set forth in the gospel story. The churches' practice or praxis (recall here the Greek title of the book of Acts: *Praxis* of the Apostles) bears a pathological continuity with its sacred texts–specifically, those passages that malign and condemn unbelievers and heretics. At first, the New Testament rhetoric of condemnation was largely impotent because Christians were themselves the

---

3 Girard similarly contrasts the "God of persecutors" and the "God of victims" in *Job*. Also compare Cone's black liberation theology, *God of the Oppressed*.

victims of persecution for three centuries. Yet the rhetoric turned lethal following church empowerment under Constantine in the fourth century. As bearers of the new state religion of the Roman empire, Christians began a fateful, but all-too-familiar, transition from the role of victims to that of victimizers. Immediately upon the new alignment with state power there commenced Christian persecution of outcast groups: notably the official persecution of Jews following Constantine's death, but also the violent suppression of Christian schismatics, the Donatists of Roman North Africa, under the theologian Augustine.

We need not and cannot rehearse here the long and bloody "trail trodden by the wicked" (Job 22:15) that extends from the Crusades and the Inquisition in the Middle Ages, to the eighteenth- and nineteenth-century mis-alliance of the "Bible and the bullet" on the mission fields of the third world. Let us simply acknowledge the persistence, since Constantine, of Christian patterns in which victims turn victimizers–patterns that have intensified rather than dissipated in the case of the churches' anti-Judaism and anti-Semitism.[4] Indeed, so ironic is specifically Christian oppression of innocent victims that its recurrence seems more than incidental. The historical patterns appear all-too-literally "true" to the gospel story. In that story religious and political powers combine to murder a victim who is ostensibly the accursed of God, but who also bears peculiar marks of identification with—and reclamation by—a God of victims.

In Girard's perspective the structure of Christian violence is consistent with the sacralization of violence that characterizes all religious cultures since human prehistory. He calls this identification or equation–the equation of violence as the sacred–the "primitive sacred" of the human species. According to Girard, the ritual structuring of violence emerges in human prehistory as a prophylaxis against unstructured forms of violence: the virulent, contagious, reciprocal violence in which every group in a community is turned against every other group without means of resolution. To prevent that ultimate catastrophe early hominids devised sacrificial rituals that cathartically released conflictual passions and reestablished communal harmony by the unanimous action of the many against the one victim: a kind of "fighting fire with fire" as the best expedient available to the earliest societies lacking institutions of law and order to mediate such conflicts. On this view the collective church appears merely as one among many other religious institutions that have structured rites of victimization–and typically, like these other institutions, the church invokes the name of "God" as the supreme sanction for its violence. It

---

4 Accordingly, Nazism has been treated as a German *Christian* phenomenon, however aberrant, by correlating its political-economic and its folk religious elements. See Barth, et al. "The Barmen Declaration," 148–51.

is evident from Girard's perspective that no immunity from scapegoating or sacrificial violence obtains for Christians; there is no immunity due simply to their avowed allegiance to Jesus. Rather, violent Christians betray the gospel message of a God who *saves* rather than destroys victims (so consider the Latin *salvus*, to "save" or "heal," and the derivative terms "salvation" and "safe"). On the one hand, we might suppose, Christians are constitutionally predisposed toward *nonviolence as the sacred* by virtue of their founding identification with Jesus as the premier emissary of a God who saves victims. On the contrary, Christian communities seem as much at risk as their co-religionists for regressing to the so-called primitive sacred. They chronically forget or occlude the model of their sacred exemplar, and collude with profane powers to reconstitute Jesus as the God of persecutors.

Otherwise stated, Christian traditions of oppression chronically replicate the tragic climax of the gospel story–its sacrificial rather than its salvific import, first by the creation of new victims, and then by covering-up that miscreation. As Girard's analysis brilliantly exposes, by masking the truth that their own victimizing of others is a misconstrual of the gospel, a malpractice in "doing the truth," Christian communities exhibit the crowning feature of their captivity to the primitive sacred. For a fundamental aspect of the "sacrificial mechanism" is the requirement that its operation remain opaque rather than transparent to its agents. Occlusion of the malevolence (the bad will) impelling the bloody process is necessary in order that its "cathartic quotient"–its efficacy for achieving group unanimity and resolving conflictual desires–be as strong as possible. Such occlusion is most efficacious precisely by the expedient of claiming that God requires victimization in the performance of believers' obedience or holiness. In the name of their God, Christians, acting compulsively under false allegiance to the primitive sacred, displace the God who saves with the God who persecutes.

The benefit of Girardian theory in this connection is its extraordinary analytic and explanatory power. The forces underlying Christian captivity to primal rites of sacrificial violence and scapegoating are rendered utterly transparent. Such overt betrayal of the gospel no longer remains "the great incomprehensible" of western history and culture. The supreme irony, or even mystery, of the Christian millennia–that the putative religion of undeserved love, radical forgiveness, and universal salvation should repeatedly provide the supreme sanction for social domination and violence–becomes starkly intelligible. In this regard Girard's fundamental anthropology of mimetic desire, leading to conflict and sacrificial crises, encompasses Christian humanity as well. Indeed, theologically motivated efforts to thwart or otherwise attenuate sacrificial mechanisms in culture can produce the opposite result of intensifying Christians' own primal need for violent satisfaction of conflictual desire. Thus there obtains no Christian immunity from the anthropological rigor of "acquisitive mimesis" and conflictual desire, because Christians and their communities remain fundamentally human–their claims to salvation or conversion or transcendence notwithstanding.

That Girard's anthropology appears radically secularist . In this regard the explanatory clarity it provides for illuminating Christian violence exacts too high a price–too high for traditional communities and their theologies. Certain theological claims–for example, that "in Christ" believers receive and experience a saved and redeemed human nature–become proportionately nonsensical as Girard's theory gains its analytic force. Such irony, then, provokes the question whether such putative claims as a "new humanity in Christ" must be excluded categorically from the purview of Girard's theory. Otherwise stated, must the theory be articulated with such non-dialectical rigidity that it excludes a priori alternative data evincing a nonviolent sacred? Could the theory be advanced in an exploratory manner, as a heuristic for elucidating the truly antiviolent character of the biblical witness? Could the Girardian theory be understood as a counterpoint to the secularist's compelling but one-dimensional data concerning the impotence of Christians' claims concerning human transformation? In this regard the Girardian hypothesis is inadequate even for the one counter-indication that Girard himself wants to emphasize: the Christian gospels as anti-persecution texts *par excellence*. But this introduction is not the place to examine that particular data and its Girardian uses. Instead, and in general, what is suggested here is the value of a heuristic treatment of the problem of "violence and the sacred," one that allows for the counter-evidence of its opposite: the evidence of certain Christian traditions in which *nonviolence* configures the sacred.

In relation to violence, religion in Girard's thought is like Plato's *pharmakon*: it is both disease and cure, poison and remedy. As editors of this volume our hope is that this double understanding of the nature of religion can provide the reader with resources for uncovering and perhaps dismantling some of the systematic distortions that lie at the base of our common forms of life and cultural institutions. If "curing violence" is a type of soulcraft or spiritual discipline that is right for our time, then the wager of this book is that Girard's antisacrificial proposal can aid and empower the enactment of this discipline.

The Editors
Mark I. Wallace
Theophus H. Smith

PART ONE:
Theoretical Perspectives

Religion and the Thought of René Girard

AN INTRODUCTION

Robert G. Hamerton-Kelly

... Thou dost stone my heart
And makest me call what I intend to do,
A murder, which I thought a sacrifice.
Othello, Act 5, 2

"La vie monte aux orages sur l'aile du refus."
St. John Perse, *Pluies* 6.

Abstract

This introductory essay examines the overall theory of René Girard concerning the role of religion and violence in the formation of human culture. It begins with Girard's notion of mimetic "desire," that is, the fundamental human orientation toward possessing what another person considers worthy of desire. This "desire for desire" is mimetic because it imitates the desire of a model. It is also conflictual because it inevitably results in violence as the imitator and the model both converge on the same desired object. This conflict leads to Girard's second major insight concerning the role of the "surrogate victim mechanism." The outbreak of violent mimesis is checked in primordial and modern societies by the community's spontaneous ascription of the cause of violence to an innocent victim. By transferring its hostilities to a vulnerable substitute the community doubly valorizes the victim as both the origin of its initial divisions and the source of its newly found unity. The essay shows how this victim mechanism generates and shapes the community's understandings of the Sacred, religious prohibitions, ritual behaviors, vengeful acts, and founding myths. The essay concludes with some attention to the role of the Bible in "demythifying" the victim mechanism. The Bible is the "essential" counterwitness to the hunger for scapegoats because it exposes the lie that the victim is to blame for the community's collective violence.

The modern quest for an understanding of human desire can be traced to Hegel's *The Phenomenology of Mind* (1807).[1] Freud made the strategies of desire central to psychoanalysis, and Sartre to the project of Existentialism. The nature of desire was a major concern of French thought after the second world war and in the context of that concern René Girard, who had been influenced by Sartre, turned his attention to the nature of desire. Since he is not a philosopher but a literary critic he did not pursue his project in conversation with these philosophers, but was oriented to the problematic of desire by the general trend of thought.

He was alerted to the triangular nature of desire by the Anselmo and Lothario episode in Don Quixote, where Anselmo urges Lothario to seduce his fiancée. To explain this Girard followed the evidence of literary and ethnological texts to the Bible, where he claims to have found the answer plainly set forth. Beginning with triangular desire he elaborated a theory of the Sacred that explains the role of religious institutions in the generation of culture and provides a hermeneutical theory to interpret both religious texts and cultural formations.

It is a poststructuralist theory in the sense that it assumes the gains of structuralism, precisely the insight that there are generative patterns or structures beneath the surface of the texts that supercede the intention of the author and control the actions of the agent without the agent's conscious collaboration. Something speaks in the text that transcends the consciousness of the author and leads one to the depths not just of the author's unconscious but of the culture itself. The generative energetics and mechanics of culture can be discovered by those who penetrate its disguises. That energy is violence and that mechanism is the Sacred.

We shall present a straightforward account of the theory with some preliminary critical evaluation. We cannot evaluate the literary and ethnological evidence exhaustively, and in any case the best test of its validity is the pragmatic one: use it and see how it succeeds or fails in elucidating the phenomena.[2] It is a working hypothesis to be tested by its heuristic power. The energetics of the system might be called "generative scapegoating"[3] and the mechanics the "founding mechanism."

The hypothesis has two dominant and closely related parts: mimesis and the surrogate victim.[4] Girard develops it in a series of books published during the

1 See Butler, *Subjects of Desire.*
2 For examples see, Hamerton-Kelly, "A Girardian Interpretation of Paul," and "Sacred Violence and the Curse of the Law."
3 The best composite statement of the theory is *Things Hidden*, 3–138. Mack gives a brief account in "Introduction: Religion and Ritual," in Hamerton-Kelly, *Violent Origins*, 1–70. See also Girard's chapter "Generative Scapegoating," in *Violent Origins* and the discussion of it (73–145); See also Webb, *Philosophers of Consciousness*, 183–225.
4 Dupuy, *Ordres et Desordres*, 125, identifies the two; mimesis is the inclusive category of which surrogate victimage is one form amongst others.

last twenty years, and it is necessary to follow this development from book to book if one is to grasp the theory. To each of the major moments in the theory there corresponds a major book. *Deceit, Desire and the Novel* (1961, E.T. 1965) expounds mimetic desire, the starting point of the theory; *Violence and the Sacred* (1972, E.T. 1977) expounds the role of sacrifice and the surrogate victim in the formation of culture; *Things Hidden from the Foundation of the World* (1978, E.T. 1987) applies both parts to the interpretation of anthropology, psychology, and the Bible; *The Scapegoat* (1982, E.T. 1986) summarizes and defends the category of the surrogate victim and applies the theory to further texts of persecution and texts from the gospels; and *Job, the Victim of his People* (1985, E.T. 1987) uses it to give a new interpretation of the book of Job. His latest book, *A Theater of Envy: William Shakespeare* (1991) is a brilliant demonstration of the critical power of mimetic theory to interpret poetry and drama.

The starting point of the theory is something Girard calls mimesis. He begins the analysis of mimesis in *Deceit, Desire and the Novel*, by treating mimetic desire. In *Things Hidden*, however, he speaks less of desire and more of acquisitive and conflictual mimesis. We shall focus our discussion on these two works, with some attention to *Violence and the Sacred*.

1. Acquisitive Mimesis[5]

1.1

Desire is mimetic in the sense that it imitates desire, that is, it copies the other's volitional orientation to an object and not the outward form of his actions.

The model of desire is the "mediator." All the great novelists understand this fact "intuitively and concretely, through their art."[6] Don Quixote, for instance, ". . . has surrendered to Amadis the individual's fundamental prerogative: he no longer chooses the objects of his own desire—Amadis must choose for him. This model, Amadis, is the mediator of desire."[7] Madame Bovary desires through the heroines of the second-rate fiction she reads, and one of Stendahl's vaniteux "will desire any object as long as it is already desired by another person whom he admires."[8] Proust's snob is the prisoner of those he wishes to be like, and their disdain of him lashes his admiration of them to greater intensity. Such characters suffer from "mimetic desire" and can only

---

5 The best introduction to this part of the discussion is found in Books 1 and 3 of *Things Hidden*; see also Kaptein and Tijmes, *De Ander als Model en Obstakel*, and Atlan and Dupuy, "Mimesis and Social Morphogenesis."

6 Girard, *Deceit*, 3.

7 Girard, *Deceit*, 1.

8 Girard, *Deceit*, 6.

value objects that others already value. The configuration of desire is therefore triangular. It runs from the subject through the mediator to the object.

1.2 External Mediation

The angles at the base of the triangle can be large or small; the larger they are the farther the distance between the plane of the subject and the plane of the mediator, and vice versa. When the distance is relatively far the relationship between the subject and the mediator is one of pure imitation untrammeled by rivalry; Girard calls this the state of external mediation.

1.3 Internal Mediation

When the distance is relatively near the relationship is one of mimetic rivalry; Girard calls this internal mediation.

1.4 Transcendence

The triangularity of desire means that human being is structured with reference to transcendence; human desire is mediated desire, it comes from without not from within. The state of mimetic rivalry is the pathology of a "deviated transcendence," of a desire that should be aroused from a truly transcendent spiritual source but instead is aroused by the immanent neighbor. The biblical name for this is idolatry, and its antidote is faith in the unseen God.

1.5 Mimetic Rivalry

As the plane of the mediator approaches the plane of the subject-object rivalry grows with an intensity inversely proportionate to the diminishing distance.

1.6 The model/obstacle

As the plane of the model approaches the plane of the subject-object the model turns into an obstacle. The subject is thus sado-masochistically related to the model/obstacle. He/she needs the model to certify the value of the object and he/she wishes to destroy it because it impedes access. Desire, therefore, always loves the thing it hates, hates the thing it loves, and needs the stumbling block to hurt it because in the obstruction lies the value. Prohibition therefore stimulates desire because it signifies that the prohibitor desires the prohibited object. Prohibition belongs within the dynamics of the model/obstacle situation.

1.7 Metaphysical Desire

In the situation of mimetic rivalry the object becomes progressively less important. The rivals focus chiefly on each other in a struggle for the being that they mistakenly assume each other has. This is the stage at which the Hegelian analysis of human relationship as the struggle for recognition becomes pertinent. Schwager refers us to Hegel's idea that desire desires the desire of the other.[9] For Girard, however, desire is imitative and acquisitive; it does not desire the desire of the other as such but imitates the other's desire for an object.[10] Only as the mimesis progresses towards conflict does desire begin to lose sight of the object and to focus on the other with the extreme outcome of the mimetic crisis in which the object is lost altogether. Thus it becomes the desire not merely to possess what the other desires but to possess the being of the other, to be the other.

1.8 Substitution

Since the object is now unimportant several substitutes can serve as the excuse for metaphysical competition, hence the frequent incommensurateness between the trivial cause and the passion of conflict. For the same reason violence can easily substitute one object for another. The model/obstacle loosens the attachment of both to the object.

1.9

Not all acquisitive motivation is mimetic. There is a difference between needs and desires. Needs are the biological requirements of the organism and certain rudimentary psychic requirements like infantile interaction with parents, while desires are culturally mediated wants. The major part of human acquisitiveness is, however, mimetic, provoked and defined by the pull of the acquisitive actions and intentions of the other. The phrase "mimetic desire" is, therefore, a tautology: desire is mimetic acquisitiveness, and it can be more or less rivalrous depending on the distance between the planes of the subject and the mediator.[11] This is why Schwager draws the distinction between natural needs and desire in terms of the specificity of the former and the generality of the latter; the desire that is subject to mimesis is "that fundamental desire that forms and defines the total behavior of the human being," which is to be distinguished from hunger or the need for sleep.[12] This fundamental human desire is characteristically cultural.

---

9 Schwager, *Must there be Scapegoats?* 35–40.

10 Schwager, *Must there be Scapegoats?* 35–37; Dupuy, *Ordres et Desordres*, 133, distinguishes Girard's position as "un desir *selon l'Autre*" from Hegel's as "un desir *du desir de l'Autre*."

11 "Desire is what happens to human relationships when there is no longer any kind of resolution through the victim. . . . Desire is the mimetic crisis in itself: it is acute mimetic rivalry with the other which occurs in all the circumstances which we call 'private,' ranging from eroticism to professional or intellectual ambition" (Girard, *Things Hidden*, 288). "We might well decide to use the word desire only in circumstances where the misunderstood mechanism of mimetic rivalry has imbued what was previously just an appetite or need with this ontological or metaphysical dimension" (Girard, *Things Hidden*, 296).

12 Schwager, *Must there be Scapegoats?* 235, n.9.

1.10 Mimetic desire is rooted in phylogeny

Girard first recognized mimetic desire in European novels, Greek tragedies, and certain ethnological sources, and then expanded the insight into a fundamental anthropology and ethology. The question of human nature remains alive and is to be asked and answered in the "domain . . .of the origin and genesis of signifying systems," which in the life sciences is the process of "hominization".[13]

Thus it is a theory of origins that links current human relations with traditional societies and animal behavior. The basic premise is that all human behavior is learned and all learning is based on imitation. This capacity for imitation is shared by human beings with the higher apes; there is a developmental connection between animal mimicry and human imitation, and the point of hominization might be plotted with reference to the change in this activity. Animal mimicry is also acquisitive and goes through the same process of escalating rivalry as human mimesis. However, animals have instinctual braking mechanisms that prevent the rivalry from becoming group-destroying violence. The weaker animal surrenders and patterns of dominance are established; subordinate animals now imitate dominant ones in non-competitive areas, without acquisitiveness. Their mimesis is closely tied to the object and does not develop the metaphysical dimension of a struggle for being expressed by intangibles like prestige.

The human capacity for metaphysical desire might be correlated with the growth of the brain and the extraordinary length of infantile dependency. Humans have more mimetic energy than animals and press the rivalry to the point where the object disappears and the rivalry becomes metaphysical and murderous.

2. Conflictual Mimesis

Thus the moment of hominization occurs with the disappearance of the contested objects in the midst of conflict. In Girard's terms, acquisitive mimesis becomes conflictual mimesis. The rivals are model/obstacles to each other in a struggle not for an object but for recognition or prestige.

2.1 Monstrous Doubles and the Sacrificial Crisis

The rivals come to resemble each other more and more, the differences between them are progressively erased and they eventually become doubles. What started as a one-way imitation becomes a two-way imitation, each copying the desire of the other until they are identical. The appearance of doubles in a text, the erasure of difference, as for instance in the characters of Dionysus and Pentheus in Euripides' Bacchae, is a sign that mimetic desire has reached this crisis stage. Distinctions are blurred, animals and humans melt together

13 Girard, *Things Hidden*, 6–7.

into monsters and violence reigns in confusion. This stage of the erasure of differences is the "sacrificial crisis" and can be seen in the texts wherever distinctions are blurred and one can no longer tell the difference between the sexes or between humans and animals.

Mimetic desire is infectious on the group level; we catch it from one another. Fashion, the arms race, and the markets are driven by mimesis. The market defines in large measure our likes and dislikes; it is a network of bondage to one another's imagined wants, an essentially fantastic web of servitude to the phantoms of desire. Mimesis thus generates violence in groups through the competition for objects and for prestige. Unless this violence can be contained it will make culture impossible. In traditional societies it was contained by means of the Sacred.

The violence thus generated converges upon a victim.

> If acquisitive mimesis divides by leading two or more individuals to converge on one and the same object with a view to appropriating it, conflictual mimesis will inevitably unify by leading two or more individuals to converge on one and the same adversary that all wish to strike down.[14]

We have arrived at the second fundamental human characteristic upon which all culture is based, the surrogate victim mechanism.

3. The Surrogate Victim

The banal "French triangle" is the clue that leads to the discovery of mimetic desire; the equally banal tendency to transfer blame to others leads to the surrogate victim. These characteristic human behaviors are omnipresent and require no special insight to see. Girard shows that they are common because they represent fundamental truths about human nature—are traces of the founding mechanism—and that we have made them banal by our inattention to their significance. It is a strength rather than a weakness of the theory that it is founded on facts that we usually consider banal.

3.1
The surrogate victim is a spontaneous psychological mechanism.[15] It can be observed synchronically in the everyday tendency to make scapegoats bear the brunt of violence that cannot be vented on the self or on a target that can avenge itself. In the diachronic development of humankind it is the same as the conflictual mimesis that happens when the rivals converge no longer on

14 Girard, *Things Hidden*, 26.
15 Girard uses the term "surrogate victim" only for the spontaneous psychological mechanism by which we transfer violence to a victim, and not for ritual transference (*Things Hidden*, 33). His essay "Generative Scapegoating" in *Violent Origins* is the best explanation of the surrogate victim mechanism.

the object that divides them but on the victim that unites them. The most significant other clue to its existence is religion, that is, the primitive Sacred in its manifestations of prohibition, ritual, and myth. In taking the institutions of religion this seriously Girard stands in the tradition of Durkheim, especially as it is represented by the English school of Social Anthropology, pioneered for religion by Jane Harrison and the Cambridge school of Greek historians.[16]

We have seen that mimetic rivalry in its advanced stages can easily change the object. Violence has the capacity to substitute one object for another. There are two factors at work in this substitution: one is the obscuring of the object in the advanced stages of mimetic rivalry, the detachment of the rivalrous energy from any particular objective focus by its progressive submersion in the subjective conflict between the rivals; the other is the spontaneous agreement of the mutually intimidated rivals to transfer the hostility to a vulnerable substitute. This is formally a rediscovery of the object, now as something to be destroyed rather than possessed. The conflict reaches the point at which the rivals, now doubles, find that they share the desire to destroy each other, but since they are mutually intimidated and identical, they rediscover the object pole as the target of the desire to destroy, and deflect the destructive energy from one another onto a substitute. Thus the surrogate victim appears from within the process of mimetic rivalry as the temporary resting place of desire. From this we see that the mechanism of the surrogate victim is psychological in both an individual and a social sense, and that the two dimensions cannot be separated; it is a socio-psychological mechanism.

We might imagine the originary scene as follows: In the beginning the primal horde was wracked by mimetic violence. This violence increased until it reached a crisis point at which the surrogate victim mechanism spontaneously generated from within the system "kicked in." This was the point of hominization.

This spontaneous generation from within the system was the result of the following events: First one pair of rivals then another rediscovered the object pole of the mimetic triangle in the substitute target for their murderous rage at one another. Some might have discovered it spontaneously; most would have discovered it by imitating the discoverers. Mimesis broke out in a new form, acquisitive mimesis that had become conflictual mimesis now returns to its original form but at a different level, uniting rather than dividing the community, as all rushed to co-operate mimetically in the killing of the victim. Thus unanimous victimage played the same role in human community as the

---

16 See Turner, *The Greek Heritage*, 116–34, cited by Henrichs, "Loss of Self, Suffering, Violence," 207–8. Henrichs describes the Cambridge school as "a small circle of historians of Greek religion at the turn of the century who transformed Greek myth and tragedy into a blood-drenched hunting ground for cannibals and ritual murderers and who saw a human substitute for the dying Dionysus in each tragic hero on the Attic stage." J.G.Frazer of *The Golden Bough* fame, Jane Harrison's teacher, was an important influence behind the school.

surrender of the weaker animal plays in the establishment of dominance patterns among the higher animals.[17] It is the cultural counterpart of animal dominance patterns.

Gazing at the corpse the mob's stupefaction turns to awe as it realizes that it has just experienced its first moment of unanimity. This reconciliation must have come after a mimetic crisis so severe that the sudden resolution at the expense of a single victim seemed like a miracle. "The experience of a supremely evil and then beneficent being, whose appearance and disappearance are punctuated by collective murder, cannot fail to be literally *gripping*."[18]

4. The Double Transference

Thus occurs the primal misunderstanding: the group misidentifies the causes of its unanimity. The cause of peace is in fact mimetic rivalry in the members of the group and the surrogate victim mechanism that it activates, but they think it is the victim. The victim is at most a catalyst and at least only the passive object of the mechanism; he or she is not the cause. The mob, however, makes the victim the cause, and by so doing obscures its own violence from itself and transfers it to the victim. The first illusion is ". . .the illusion of the supremely active and all-powerful victim";[19] it makes the victim a god, placing him or her above the group as both the transcendent source of order and the repository of disordering violence.

4.1 *The Nature of the Double Transference*

The mob transfers its own violence to the victim by the simple misattribution of the cause of unanimity. This is the critical step, according to the theory, and it occurred spontaneously when violence reached a certain level of intensity in the group. Violence was not repressed and cast off into the unconscious, but rather it was detached by being transferred to the victim who becomes, as a result, the god.[20] Now the victim/god is the processor of bad violence into good violence, the violence of disorder into the violence of order. Thus the victim/god is the personification and reification of the mob's violence through the victim. "Violence is the heart and secret soul of the Sacred".[21]

The transference is double because the mob's violence has two parts: mimetic rivalry and surrogate victimage. The former causes disorder while the latter restores order. The victim, in fact, is merely the target and catalyst of the

17 Girard, *Violent Origins*, 129.
18 Girard, *Things Hidden*, 28 (italics added).
19 Girard, *Things Hidden*, 52.
20 Girard, *Violence and the Sacred*, 136.
21 Girard, *Violence and the Sacred*, 31.

latter; as an active cause, however, he or she signifies full double-sided violence. Thus the mob attributes mimetic rivalry and surrogate victimage to the victim, and makes him into the sign of the two valences that correspond to these two stages of human violence. The double founding mechanism now operates through the victim; he is full of mimesis that demands to be appeased by victims. Thus we transfer to the victim not only our mimetic violence but also our deflecting mechanism; in theological language, we make him bear both our sins and the sin of making him bear our sins. It is not we who demand victims; it is he!

4.2

The double transference makes the victim the transcendent signifier. The cadaver is the first object of a non-instinctual attention because of the miraculous peace that attends the victim's death. The cadaver is the sign of peace and the mob seeks to perpetuate that peace by repeating the sign; hence the imperative of ritual. The cadaver signifies the violence that led to the killing; it is the signifier and the violence of the mob is the signified. But now the signals are crossed; the cadaver has been made to signify the non-violence of the group and the violence of the victim.

The victim signifies by the logic of the exception, of the "short straw," or "the odd man out." Structuralist topology demands at least two signs at the beginning because signs only signify with reference to each other; the logic of the victim differentiates by means of the one who stands out from the many, the exception, "the odd man out." The mob and the victim are thus the two poles of the first act of signification.[22]

Since the victim determines human behavior not by means of "what really happened" but through the interpretation that the community transfers to him and that he in turn represents to them, to interpret culture is to decode the double transference. To decode the double transference is to read ". . .all the actual and potential meaning the community confers onto the victim and, through its intermediacy, onto all things."[23] The interpretation of the Sacred is therefore the beginning of the interpretation of culture.

All of culture, then, comes from the surrogate victim by way of this double transference. He is made both the cause and the cure of mimetic disorder (bad violence) and of surrogate-victim order (good violence). His living must have caused disorder if his dying brought order. For this reason the victim becomes a god, and in that form reflects these two misunderstandings as the imperatives for prohibition, ritual, and myth.

22 Girard, *Violence and the Sacred*, 100–101.
23 Girard, *Things Hidden*, 103.

5. The Products of the Double Transference

The victim processes bad violence into good, disorder into order. Violence passes from the mob, through the victim, and back to the mob. It leaves as violence and returns as hominization, religion, and culture. It leaves as undifferentiation and returns as differentiation. Thus the double transference transforms the victim into the Sacred and through the Sacred generates prohibition, ritual, and myth, the fundamental principles of culture.

5.1 The Sacred

The center of the Sacred is the victim-become-god-by-the-double-transference (4.2). The double transference gives the Sacred a double valency of threat and promise corresponding to mimesis and surrogate victimage respectively. Threat takes the form of prohibition and promise the form of ritual. The two valencies represent the two forms of violence, bad violence that disrupts order and good violence that establishes it. The Sacred is, therefore, essentially violence.

The Sacred is the transcendental pole of primitive religion. It has been understood either as an invention of the superstitious mind to provide prescientific explanations, or a mysterious real presence apprehended in the religious attitude. Girard tells us that it is a mendacious representation of human violence; it is ". . .the sum of human assumptions resulting from collective transferences focused on a reconciliatory victim at the conclusion of a mimetic crisis".[24]

The element of "the overwhelming" defines the Sacred; it includes the experience of tempests, fires, and plagues, but its primary content is violence understood, like these catastrophes, as being outside of normal human control.

Religious thought conceives of a malevolent quasi-substance polarized around the Sacred.[25] This quasi-substance of the Sacred is the violence of the primordial murder transformed by the lie of the double transference into the sanction of cultural order. The polluting power of the holy, and the prestige of kings, priests, and mythic heroes, is, therefore, unacknowledged violence. It pollutes and confuses precisely because it is unacknowledged. All institutions and their hierarchies are fundamentally sacred structures of organized violence.

The Sacred engenders or destroys cultural structures, but is not itself present in the structures;[26] they are the result of human restraint, a rational response to an irrational threat. Fear is the motivating power of the Sacred.

Through the Sacred the double transference generates prohibition, ritual, and myth as the building blocks of cultural order. They are dynamics of the

24 Girard, *Things Hidden*, 42.
25 Girard, *Things Hidden*, 48.
26 Girard, *Violence and the Sacred*, 241–2.

Sacred rather than conscious or unconscious functional strategies of the group. The interdiction of mimicry, or the ritual regulation of vengeance, for instance, are not primarily unconscious judgments of a functional kind but rather responses to and representations of the valences of the Sacred.

5.2 Prohibition

Prohibition corresponds to the mimetic rivalry pole of the double transference and the negative valency of the Sacred. It aims to prevent mimesis. Mimetic conflict is the common denominator of prohibitions, and they all have an antimimetic character.[27] They generally pertain to objects that the community cannot divide peacefully: women, food, weapons, and the best places to live. The prohibition, therefore, derives primarily from the mimetic-rivalry element in the Sacred.

As a dynamic of the Sacred the common denominator of all prohibitions is fear of mimetic rivalry transfigured by the detour through the Sacred into the fear of the return of the victim to avenge his death or, finally, the fear of the vengeance of the god.[28] Having been the catalyst of conflictual mimesis that united the group the victim becomes the sign of prohibition on anything that can disrupt that unity.

The vengeful god appears as the terrible model-obstacle. The god is represented by monsters; it attracts and repels; it confers prestige, the mimetic essence of rivalry; and it is acquisitive, possessing certain persons, places, and things exclusively. The possessions of the god are prohibited to humans; prohibition, therefore, represents the model-obstacle transformed by the Sacred into a threat. Fear of vengeance is the subjective pole of the prohibition.

The first prohibition and the first differentiation are the same. The transfigured victim is not to be approached, not to be touched, not to be possessed; it occupies a place beyond reach and a line of distinction is drawn between it and every other place. Thus the first prohibition and the first differentiation are the same; they are the distinction between the victim and the group, the Sacred and the profane. This distinction and fundamental prohibition is the essence both of religion and of the law. Therefore, prohibition, although principally correlated with the negative pole of the Sacred, is correlated in a secondary way with ritual, the positive pole, through the distinction between the Sacred and the profane. The prohibited Sacred place is the place of ritual sacrifice from which the energy of order emanates. Prohibition guards the sacrality of ritual.

The two imperatives of prohibition and ritual are curiously contradictory. Prohibition in essence means that one should not repeat any aspect of the crisis, while ritual requires that one repeat the whole thing with great care. Prohibition interdicts mimicry, contact with former antagonists, acquisitive

---

27 Girard, *Violence and the Sacred*, 14 and 19.
28 Girard, *Violence and the Sacred*, 76.

gestures towards the objects that caused rivalry, and anything that may reactivate the crisis; ritual deliberately reactivates it, organizes orgies of transgression, and immolates new victims in ways that are thought to repeat the original action.

5.3 Ritual[29]

Ritual corresponds to the surrogate victim pole of the double transference and the positive valency of the Sacred. The primary form of ritual is blood sacrifice.[30] Girard sees this theory of ritual as corroboration of the intuition that ". . . there is a relation between the forms of ritual and the universal human tendency to transfer anxiety and conflict on to arbitrary victims".[31] It is an attempt to repeat the transference of violence onto the surrogate victim under controlled circumstances, and so renew the power of pacification of the original murder. It is generated by the positive valency of the Sacred while prohibition is generated by the negative.

Girard's theory of sacrifice is only one among several.[32] It traces its lineage from Robertson Smith's postulate that the earliest form of religion was a belief in a theriomorphic ancestor with which the tribe had a blood relationship and which they consumed periodically in a ritual communal meal to assimilate the power of the ancestor. Freud took this theory as the starting point for his own proposal that the murder of the father by the sons for the purpose of gaining access to the monopolized women lies at the dawn of religion. Adolf Jensen's theory that sacrifice is a re-enactment of the killing of a primordial divine being from whose body came forth the plants useful for food also belongs to the same family, insofar as it sees sacrifice as the ritual of a killing that in the beginning brought advantages essential to the founding of culture. For Girard sacrifice is "a mechanism for diverting violence" that operates by substitution; it is the principal form of ritual and it performs a vital social function by representing the founding mechanism.

Girard stands in the Durkheimian tradition, which sees religion as the primary expression of the power that forms society, and ritual as the essence of religion. For Girard the Sacred is itself a product of society. The social crisis of violence is prior to the Sacred and to ritual and myth. Girard, therefore, breaks

---

29 Doty, *Mythography*, is a good account of the state of the discussion in myth and ritual studies.
30 Smith, in Hamerton-Kelly, *Violent Origins*, 202–5, reminds us of the argument that blood sacrifice is not part of the earliest strata of culture but only emerges at the stage of nomadic animal herding. He admits that the evidence is tenuous and difficult to assess. Given that fact, and our general epistemological situation of having to read evidence in the light of our theories (cf. Quine and Ullian, *The Web of Belief*) we see no reason to abandon Girard's claim that blood sacrifice is the first cultural act. Clearly there can be no hard evidence for this. It must remain a theoretical postulate.
31 Girard, *Things Hidden*, 131.
32 For a convenient treatment of current theories see, Joseph Henninger, "Sacrifice," in *The Encyclopedia of Religion*, Vol. 12, pp. 544–57; for Girard's theory of sacrifice, see *Violence and the Sacred*, 1–67.

with the exchange-of-gifts theory of sacrifice (do ut des) for the sake of a theory of substitution that arises logically out of his theory.

A major alternative view, represented in our time by Eliade, sees religion as a response to the experience of the Sacred as ontologically prior to the human individual or society.[33] Myth rather than ritual is the essence of religion, and both of them are human responses to the manifestation of the Sacred. The word precedes the deed and myth goes before ritual.

Like the prohibition (cf. 5.2), sacrifice can also be correlated, in a secondary way, with the other, mimetic pole of the Sacred. Mimetic conflict appears through the Sacred as the "vengeful fury of the divinity,"[34] and this fury has to be appeased.

The interpretation of sacrifice as appeasement of the wrath of the god is the essence of the sacrificial lie. The victim actually recalls the god in his or her role of the surrogate victim, and should, therefore, represent the violence of the offerer. The double transference, however, reverses the order and makes the victim represent the offerer as victim of the god rather than the god as victim of the offerer. The murderer thus appears as the murdered, the persecutor as the persecuted. Sacrifice conceals the fact that the offerer is violent and imputes the violence to the god, pretending that the vengeance deflected onto the substitute is divine and not human. Sacrifice, therefore, reverses the direction of the original action identifying the victim as the executioner and the executioner as the victim.

Sacrifice is therefore the deflection of violence from one target onto another. As part of the double transference it is the avoidance of responsibility for violence. It is prophylactic. It prevents disorder by removing violence that might otherwise be directed at a member of the group and set the spiral of revenge spinning. It is a device for channeling violence out of the group.

The impact of these moves on the general conception of religion is to place ritual, whose primary and generative form is sacrifice, at the center of the general description, and to see religion as the product of social forces and the filter through which those forces pass to generate culture. In this sense, it represents the triumph of Durkheim over Freud and Eliade.

5.4 Rules of Ritual Purity

Sacrifice renews the therapeutic effect of the deflecting mechanism by providing a ritual core to which the violence is attracted and from which it flows out again in proper channels.[35] These channels are the rules of ritual

---

33 Eliade, *The Sacred and the Profane.*
34 Girard, *Things Hidden*, 14.
35 Doty, *Mythography*, 141, "By ritual retelling of the Creative Acts (*gesta*), the society believes it can make present once again the powerfully creative dynamics of that primal period and so recharge the energies of the present."

purity that keep the various parts and persons of society in their "proper" places. The essential ingredient in all ritual pollution is violence.

5.4.1 Contravention of the rules causes pollution and the polluting agent is not dirt but violence. "Dirt" is a rationalization of violence. In these matters biblical scholars usually invoke the authority of Mary Douglas, and her designation of dirt as that which is out of its proper place.[36] This is too rationalistic a definition and, besides, it begs an important question. It does not explain how or why the notion of a "proper" place came about at all. It assumes that the logical order of thought can be attributed univocally to the order of society. Such attribution is at best metaphorical and at worst anthropomorphic.

The "proper" place is any place that is so located as not to cause unnecessary rivalry. Thus the proper place of family members in the subsequent generation is another family, because siblings are too close to each other to avoid mimetic rivalry; and so the laws of incest are part of the sacrificial strategy to inhibit and channel violence. The incest taboo functions sacrificially in two ways: it drives out those who are drivable, that is, those who are weak and least likely to be able to defend themselves, and it prescribes the limits of proximity of family members. Brides, therefore, were victims before they were commodities. Incest pollutes because it breaches the dikes against mimetic rivalry and lets violence flow outside sacrificial channels.

5.5 Priests, Kings, and Heroes

Hyam Maccoby calls attention to the figure of the "Sacred Executioner."[37] The double valency of the sacred victim is also in the executioner; he is the source of both bane and blessing. In him the status of victim is extended to a living member of the group, who by that action becomes a liminal figure. He is the priest, a figure who, along with the king and the mythic hero, is especially associated with the Sacred and therefore regarded with deep ambivalence. These figures represent the "beyond" at the center of society. Their precincts are the forbidden cities, temples, places of sacrifice, where violence is processed into power. Prestige and all the other intangibles of authority that cling to them is the quasi-substance of violence that congeals around the victim. Every king, priest, and hero, therefore, is the victim and the god, an institution for the processing of violence from bad to good.[38]

As the incarnate Sacred, the king is feared and adored, and his perch is always precarious; the oscillation from god to victim takes place suddenly, as many a politician can attest. The shift from adoration to execration usually happens in a mimetic crisis when the community needs to engage the founding mechanism again. Only the double valency of the Sacred can explain the

---

36 Douglas, *Purity and Danger.*
37 Maccoby, *The Sacred Executioner.*
38 Girard, *Violence and the Sacred,* 104–8.

gyrations of political attitude and the extraordinary power of the leader for good and for ill.

The rituals of kingship show the working of the founding mechanism. In the beginning the king was probably the victim whose period of preparation stretched until he had so much prestige that the community could no longer kill him. He was originally ". . . a victim with a suspended sentence."[39] Kingship rituals often include the king's transgression of especially strong taboos in a moment of ritual chaos that is reduced to order by his enthronement, thus enacting the transformation of violence through the death of the victim, and presenting enthronement as the ritual equivalent of sacrifice.

The king is the living god, and the god is the dead king; the king represents the presence of Sacred power in this world, while the god represents its presence in the "beyond"; the king is correlated with the moment before the death, in which the chosen victim shares the prestige of violence while still alive, while the god is correlated with the moment after the death in which the violence is located in the "beyond." Thus the polysemousness of the surrogate victim resolution presents now one resource then another for the cultural process.[40]

5.6 Vengeance

Vengeance is mimetic violence. The principals imitate each other's violent acts. It is a ritual of reciprocity, and poses an insoluble problem for the normal economic interpretation of reciprocity,[41] because it is a reciprocity not of gain but of loss. It is the classic instance of the absurd notion that two wrongs make a right, and so cannot be based on a rational calculation of advantage. Vengeance is a phenomenon of the Sacred.

Girard deals with the subject in connection with sacrifice. Violence must be appeased: ". . .if left unappeased, violence will accumulate until it overflows its confines and floods the surrounding area."[42] The acting out of violence that this appeasement demands calls forth reciprocal violence (vengeance), and so unless a way can be found to express violence without vengeance there can be no appeasement.

Sacrifice is the way to express violence without vengeance by deflecting the violence from its target onto a victim that cannot retaliate and has no one to avenge him. Sacrifice, therefore, is primarily intended to prevent vengeance by providing ritual channels for conducting violence out of the group (cf. 4.2). It functions apotropaically on behalf of the whole community, but when it fails the society falls into a crisis of vengeance, of violence provoking counterviolence, culminating in the disorder of the sacrificial crisis.

39 Girard, *Things Hidden*, 52–53.
40 Girard, *Things Hidden*, 57.
41 The sociology developed by Hubert and Mauss in conjunction with Durkheim is called the sociology of reciprocity. See Mack, in Hamerton-Kelly, *Violent Origins*, 1–2.
42 Girard, *Violence and the Sacred*, 10.

The sacrificial deflection ruse can be seen clearly at work in the way some primitives deal with an actual case of vengeance. Girard has observed that among the Chukci the fear of reciprocal violence is so great that they do not allow vengeance to be taken on the one who commits the outrage, but rather on someone else belonging to his cognizant group. In this way they seek to avoid a symmetry that could become an endless reciprocity.[43] This device of deflection onto an innocent victim is the essence of sacrifice, it is the ruse by which violence is tricked into missing its target. Mimetic desire controls the back-and-forth of violence between the poles of vengeance; the one copies the desire for vengeance of the other. The sacrificial deflection interdicts this oscillation.

Clearly, such a move is unsatisfactory to a mind used to the rational concept of guilt and punishment, because it results in two random victims and two killers infected by violence, and it violates the canon of individual responsibility. Nevertheless, it makes perfect sense because it protects the groups in question from falling into a spiral of reciprocal violence. It breaks the symmetry so that the clash is never between violence and violence, that is, between the avenger and the murderer, but always between violence and a victim. Because the victim comes from outside the interchange he can draw off the violent energy and carry it away from the groups. In this way the current of violence is broken, and the power fizzles dangerously but fruitlessly into the social space made for it by the surrogate victim. The two infected persons are kept from contacting one another and so the possibility of an epidemic of violence is reduced.

A more advanced form of the sacrificial solution is the judicial system. Theoretically, law as the regulator of reciprocity is rationally rather than ritually controlled vengeance. The judicial system is a development of the sacrificial control of violence. The violence operating in the judicial system is the "good violence" of the sacrificial order itself. The law represents this order of "good violence," in the form of a controlled reciprocity, which is, in fact, the energy of mimetic desire running in the channels carved for it by sacrifice.

The initial form of those channels was ritual, as one can see from the stages of the development of law, both logical and actual. Law is the third logical stage of vengeance, in the sequence, 1) uncontrolled vengeance, 2) ritually controlled vengeance, and 3) law (rationally controlled vengeance). Raymond Verdier, the editor of the most thorough recent examination of the phenomenon of vengeance,[44] calls level two "the vindicatory system" (le systeme vindicatoire), by which he indicates that most primitive societies had pre-

---

43 Girard, *Violence and the Sacred*, 17–28.
44 Verdier, *La Vengeance*, vols. 1 and 2, La Vengeance dans les societes extra occidentales; Vol 3 ed. Verdier and Poly, Vengeance, pouvoirs et ideologies dans quelques civilisations de l'Antiquite; Vol 4, ed. Courtois, La vengeance dans la pensee occidentale. This reference is to Verdier's introductory essay in vol. 1, 13–42.

legal, ritual, devices for confining vengeance. He sees this as a refutation of Girard's claim that primitive society was subject to the danger of limitless revenge before they discovered the sacrificial mechanism; but his view in fact confirms Girard, in that the ritual vindicatory system is precisely the sacrificial mechanism.[45] The vindicatory system is in fact a subset of sacrifice.

Courtois confirms Girard's reading when he notes that the vindicatory system is animated by a strictly retributive idea of justice centered on the victim, not on the perpetrator; the evil to be remedied is that of the situation of the victim.[46] Girard explains this as a result of the idea that the victim is ritually impure, which in turn means that he is the repository of bad violence. He has been contaminated by a violence that has overflowed its ritual channels, and the action that has to be taken at this point seeks to return that violence to its proper channels. This remedial action is usually sacrificial.

Thus vengeance is an instance of mimetic violence in human groups, and its control by deflection is a manifestation of the working of the sacrificial system. The deflection of avenging violence onto someone other than the perpetrator is the surrogate victim mechanism at work on the level of human relations. It is the logical precursor of law and shows how law and the sacrificial system are genetically related through the Sacred. Law is the myth of vengeance. Violent reciprocity is first ritualized and then rationalized, mythically transformed into law, and so hiding its violent origin.

5.7 Myths

Mythology is the narrative counterpart of prohibition and ritual, generated by the same mendacious energies of the Sacred. "Myths are the retrospective transfiguration of sacrificial crises, the reinterpretation of these crises in the light of the cultural order that has arisen from them."[47] "Mythological elaboration is an unconscious process based on the surrogate victim and nourished by the presence of violence."[48] Myth like ritual represents the founding murder from the point of view of the murderers; only the murderers can make a murder appear as a good thing.

Both Levi-Strauss and Girard see mythology as a representation of the birth and development of differential thought. They also share the conviction that the passage from undifferentiation to differentiation through a "driving out" is a constant structure in myths. Levi-Strauss interprets the "driving out" as the expression of the logic of elimination and exclusion by which the mind disencumbers a congested field of perception to make space for differential thought. Mythic thought represents this differentiating process metaphorically, but because it is incapable of sufficient abstraction it confuses the process of thought with the process of history and reifies the players.

45 Anspach, "Penser la vengeance," 103–11.
46 Verdier, La Vengeance, 4:32.
47 Girard, Violence and the Sacred, 64.
48 Girard, Violence and the Sacred, 136.

Levi-Strauss' topological interpretation leaves some critical points unaccounted for. Firstly, one might ask why the generation of something as antiseptic as his immaculately conceived differential thought should so frequently be represented by a violent expulsion. Secondly, if the expulsion is for the purpose of disencumbering a field the expelled must come from within that field; in the myths the victim comes both from within and from without. Thirdly, his topology cannot account for the conjunction of the chief elements in the structure. Fourthly, it cannot account for the fact that the eliminated fragment at first bears a negative connotation and then a positive connotation.

Only the surrogate victim mechanism accounts for all the important phenomena. Girard does not simply display the same inability for abstract thought as Levi-Strauss attributes to the myths and confuse the representations with their referents. He does not infer the communal murder from its representation. Rather he offers it as a better explanation of the phenomena that both he and Levi-Strauss observe. Minimally these are: the negative connotation of the eliminated fragment, the positive connotation of the elimination as such, and the collective nature of the expulsion. It is precisely the conjunction of these three that the topology cannot explain, while the hypothesis of an actual communal murder can.

A full Girardian account of the structure of myth has the following features: the theme of undifferentiation; accusations; collective violence; the founding or re-founding of culture; the accusation against the mythic hero taken as an incontestable fact.[49] He also speaks of the "stereotypes" of persecution as loss of differences, crimes that eliminate differences, the marks of the victim on the alleged authors of the crimes, and the violence itself.[50]

The accusations are transformed into facts because the tellers of the story are the accusers themselves. Mythology's ". . . real project is that of recalling the crises and the founding murder, the sequences in the realm of events that have constituted or reconstituted the cultural order,"[51] and it is always a project of the killers rather than the victim. Therefore, demythification consists in retelling the story from the point of view of the victim, exposing the lie, and revealing the founding mechanism.

Myths have been demythified in the process of history; the great Greek tragedians took the process part of the way, and the Bible brought it to a decisive climax. The Bible is the ". . .essential if not exclusive cause of the dynamic . . ." that sustains Girard's program. Historically, it is the fountainhead of the unprecedented and unparalleled progress of Western civilization away from ritual and myth. The desacralization of culture is the gift of the Bible; we now know the founding mechanism and so can decipher the myths.

49 Girard, *Things Hidden*, 119.
50 Girard, *The Scapegoat*, 24.
51 Girard, *Things Hidden*, 120.

5.8 Texts of Persecution

On a spectrum from thorough misrepresentation to complete disclosure, myth stands close to the former pole. With the decay of the sacrificial order texts come into being that are nearer the midpoint of the spectrum. Girard calls these "texts of persecution." They are especially helpful for identifying the victimage mechanism since in them it is partially revealed. Texts about the persecution of Jews or witches, for instance, betray their mendacity clearly; they accuse their victims of incredible crimes, and although the texts accept those accusations we know them to be false. We also know the victims and their sufferings to be real. Thus we have an instance of the founding mechanism working before our eyes.[52] The mimetic crisis of violence generates the need for victims, who are accused of incredible crimes and executed, and as a result order returns to the community.

6. The Term "Scapegoat"

The term "scapegoat" is the counterpart in the realm of ritual to the text of persecution in the realm of mythology. In modern usage it designates both a ritual and a more or less unconscious and spontaneous socio-psychological act. It is a technical term in ethnology for a ritual and a term in common usage for a psychological act. It is half-way between the pole of concealment and the pole of complete disclosure. Thus the correlation between psychology and ritual has been inscribed in the language; the Girardian theory has been hidden in plain view for centuries. The psychological precedes the ritual meaning of the term in that the surrogate victim mechanism is the cause, not the result, of ritual. Therefore, the scapegoat is not a mere metaphor for an inconsequential psychological phenomenon, but a ritualization of a spontaneous impulse. The "savage mind's" strange idea that guilt can be transferred from one person to another like a physical burden is not the result of an inability to reason, but, on the contrary, a cunning act of rationalization by means of ritual.

7. Critical Evaluation

Girard's proposal enriches the discussion of the theory of religion and shows that what is at stake could be of momentous importance for religious studies because it gives religion a place of preeminence within the human sciences. That fact alone provokes criticism and even hostility, not least because of Girard's rather polemical mode of discourse and his perhaps too hasty claim that it is a "scientific" theory in the traditional sense of an empirical science that produces falsifiable hypotheses.

---

52 Girard, *The Scapegoat*, 1–44.

Girard has always presented his theory as a working hypothesis, and if that claim is located within the context of an essentially analytic rather than positivistic understanding of the methodology of the human sciences, it loses most of its provocation. It might then be called an heuristic model, which is an accepted category in that context, to be tested by its analytic power on the raw material to be interpreted.

Other objections are lodged against his reading of the anthropological evidence and involve the crisis of self-understanding in the field of anthropology itself. It is a limitation endemic to interdisciplinary research that one inherits the controversies of the disciplines one draws upon without being able to adjudicate them; nevertheless a cross-disciplinary synthesis can be construed in certain cases as corroborative. We believe that this is the case here. (For instance, the extraordinary hermeneutical power of sacrifice might be construed as an admonition to anthropologists to pay more attention to that category. It is not sufficient to undermine the theory to point out that sacrifice is not high on the agenda of current anthropology).

Another provocation is Girard's claim that the founding mechanism is revealed unequivocally in the Bible. This is construed as an attempt to vindicate the truth of Biblical revelation scientifically. There are passages in his work that are reasonably construed as making that claim and it is a claim that can be publicly adjudicated by responsible exegesis. In any case, he does not claim that all of the Bible is equally revelatory in this regard, but recognizes that the biblical texts are themselves "texts in travail" between myth and Gospel, between the cover-up and the unveiling of the mechanism. The Cross, however, is a prima facie indication of the possible validity of the claim that the Bible discloses sacred violence unequivocally.

Girard's interpretation of mythology has also been called into question by those who argue that not all myths are ideologies of violence told to conceal the founding mechanism. This is a legitimate question that once again can only be answered by an exhaustive analysis of the mythological corpus. To date there is enough evidence to support his claim but not to put it beyond doubt. The investigation is difficult because the interpretation of mythical transformations takes place within the context of rival theories of the generating mechanisms. The likelihood of an interpretation must be assessed as part of the whole schema of generation, and that involves us in a form of the hermeneutical circle. Given this epistemological predicament, exacerbated by the exigencies of reader response, we probably cannot escape the hermeneutical drift of a sociology of knowledge, and so must regard Girard's reading as one among many, and appeal once again to its relative heuristic efficacy.

In the end, therefore, we propose the theory of the founding mechanism as a hermeneutical theory of texts and culture. It should be set to work on the rich material that we have hitherto been able to organize historically and phenomenologically, but have been unable to appropriate for the task of self-understanding in a time that is characterized by nothing so much as systemic violence. Indeed, the possibility of limitless violence that commands the intentionality of our time in the paradox of nuclear deterrence commends a theory that puts violence at the center of its explanation of the human enterprise.

What sort of civilization is it whose dominant meaning is cultural suicide, in the sense of our cultural intentionality, as expressed in our willingness to threaten mutual and assured destruction? Girard enables us to approach an intellectually responsible answer to that challenge to our rationality and that question about our sanity, and to restate the religious imperative as that of self-knowledge and self-restraint rather than primitive self-deception and chauvinist rage.

Religion and the Philosophers of Mimesis

William Schweiker

Abstract

This essay examines the distinctive contribution of René Girard to the interpretation of religion through a comparison of his work with the thought of Hans-Georg Gadamer and Paul Ricoeur. Each of these thinkers retrieves and rehabilitates the concept of mimesis as central to their interpretation theories. The essay, therefore, probes their understandings of mimesis and the points of similarity and difference between their positions. In contrast to Gadamer, Girard's theory of religion explores the connection between the literary or textual dimension of religion and its social practices. Girard also addresses the problem of violence in religious discourse through the idea of mimesis in a way not explored in Ricoeur's account of narrative mimesis. Having isolated the similarities and differences between Girard, Gadamer, and Ricoeur, the essay concludes with suggestions for the study of religion.

* * *

"Mythology and religious cults form systems of representation necessarily untrue to their own genesis."[1]

This essay explores René Girard's approach to the study of religion. The distinctiveness of Girard's work, I hope to show, is that he links an analysis of desire and ritual action with a theory of religious myths. This enables Girard to examine not only the beliefs, myths, and symbols of religions, but also the social practices–especially sacrifice–which ground but are also legitimated by those beliefs, myths, and symbols. The importance of his theory comes to light in contrast to other theories of interpretation. For the purpose of this essay, I will compare Girard's thought to the work of Hans-Georg Gadamer and Paul Ricoeur, two theorists who have made singular contributions to hermeneutical inquiry. This comparison is possible, and, I believe, helpful, because each thinker develops his theory of interpretation around the idea of mimesis.

---

1 Girard, "Mimesis and Violence," 14.

These theorists find in the idea of mimesis resources for exploring the meaning and truth of myths, symbols, rituals, and narratives. Mimesis provides then an apt point of comparison. Thus, I will examine the work of these philosophers of mimesis in order to isolate Girard's specific contrubition to interpreting religion.[2]

As a first step in the inquiry, we must know something about the history and use of the term mimesis itself. This is so because Girard develops his theory of religion through a novel account of this rather old idea. Indeed, his theory of mimesis draws together diverse strands of reflection on this idea, strands that are found in ancient Greek cult, Plato, and Aristotle's *Poetics*.

1. From Ritual to Reflection

The Greek term *mimesis* is usually translated by the English word "imitation." For the English speaker, imitation connotes the idea of "copying" or "representation." An imitation is a copy of some original. This common understanding of mimesis is what Girard wants to challenge. His challenge is possible because the idea of mimesis actually arose in Dionysian cultic worship and also ancient mime and thus with ritual, dramatic performance.[3] Mimesis originally meant something like "presentation" or "ex-pression" in mime, drama and cult. Through the cultic action, the god Dionysius was believed to be present. In the voiceless action of the mime, some story is expressed and presented; it is enacted. Girard wants to reclaim this ancient ritualistic and dramatic idea of mimesis. But in order to understand Girard's work, we must also grapple with the philosophical uses of the idea, especially in classical thought. What do I mean?

Plato was the first thinker to use the idea of mimesis in a philosophical sense. He used the term mimesis not to speak about dramatic or cultic action, but to think about visual and conceptual images. Indeed, our understanding of "imitation" as "copying" merely demonstrates the power of Plato's theory of mimesis on Western thought. But what exactly did Plato mean by mimesis? In the *Republic*, he spoke of the artist as a maker of images. These images are thrice removed from the truth. The painting of a chair, for instance, is an imitation of the artist's idea, his or her concept of the chair, which, in turn, is an imitation of the true "idea" or "form" of what the artist seeks to represent or imitate. The use or making of images signals a difference between what is imitated and the imitation. Mimesis was important for Plato, then, because it implied a theory of truth. Truth, in his view, is the right correspondence between a sign (an image, word, text, painting) and its referent, that which the

---

2 Cf. Schweiker, "Beyond Imitation" and "Sacrifice, Interpretation and the Sacred."
3 Cf. Auerbach, *Mimesis*; Boyd, *The Function of Mimesis and Its Decline*; Koller, *Die Mimesis in Antike*; Morrison, *The Mimetic Tradition of Reform in the West*; and Sörböm, *Mimesis and Art*.

"sign" is about. But of course the "sign" can never be the "thing;" the painting of the chair is never the chair, even if we can mistake a painting for the real thing. Because of the possibility of error, Plato was suspicious of all forms of imitation. They seem to entail a falsehood and thus can deceive us. Imitations are not the way to truth.

On reaching this conclusion Plato articulated a basic problem for Western thought. It is a problem Girard's theory of interpretation explicitly addresses. How, if at all, can something be truthfully known by means of what is seemingly untrue and unreal? How can I know a chair by means of what is not a chair, but is, rather, a painting of an artist's conception of a chair? More profoundly, how can I communicate truthfully about anything when the words I use are not the things about which I am speaking, but are themselves open to ambiguity and can even be used in deceptive ways? Plato thought that any use of imitation to grasp the truth was ultimately impossible. For him, the height of wisdom is immediate, intuitive perception of the forms (the good, true, and beautiful) of reality unencumbered by imitations. Knowledge is a matter of vision; it is not reached through the interpretation of imitations.

Plato's theory of mimesis is not the only one to shape Western philosophy or Girard's work. Aristotle sought to counter Plato's critique of art and mimesis by reclaiming the meaning of mimesis within the context of drama. In the *Poetics*, Aristotle speaks about how the poet organizes a sequence of actions in a drama into a coherent narrative whole, a plot (*mythos*), that purports to be an imitation, a mimesis, of human action. This suggests that the plot of a drama provides insight into how different kinds of persons will act in varying situations. Given this, Aristotle insisted that we do learn something from artistic imitations. The drama is not life, of course. Yet it can still provide insight into how different kinds of persons act in different situations. As James Redfield notes, by reasoning out a plot with all its twists and turns of fate an audience exercises its ability to think about the practical life.[4] We learn about how real characters act by seeing their actions imitated on the stage.

Aristotle made another claim about poetic mimesis, and specifically about tragedy. He argued that by reasoning out a plot the audience undergoes a purging, a *catharsis*, of its pity and fear evoked by the tragic fate of the characters. *Catharsis* is therefore a way of speaking about the resolution of the plot's tension within the work itself and the emotional relation of the audience to this resolution. As we will see, Girard claims that ritual sacrifices purge the community of uncontrolled violence and thereby restore social order. And Ricoeur argues that it is precisely through our feelings that we are able to enter into what a text is trying to present to us.

What does this historical background to the idea of mimesis mean for the study of religion? The strand of thought initiated by Plato and Aristotle, despite their differences, requires that the interpreter of religion explore a

---

4 Redfield, *Nature and Culture in the* Iliad.

tradition's or a community's "representations" (myths, symbols, and ideas) relative to human action and feeling. But the fact that mimesis had its origins in cultic and dramatic action is also important. How are we to understand the relation between "representations" and social practices, like rituals and dramas? As we will see, Gadamer draws on Plato and Aristotle but returns to the primitive roots of mimesis in performative action. His central concern is with language and human understanding through the act of interpretation as a kind of mimetic action. Ricoeur, for his part, recovers Aristotle's claims about plot (*mythos*) and *catharsis*. He is concerned with understanding human action through mimetic narrative. Girard's unique contribution to interpretation theory is to link a theory of religious symbols and myths with a theory of ritual action. In doing so, he develops an account of religion and also addresses the question of the truth of religious systems. With this historical background in mind, we can turn to Girard's novel interpretation of mimesis and religion.

2. Mimesis, Violence, and Transcendence

Girard's notion of mimesis is central to his theory of religion, fundamental anthropology, and critique of modernity. Through the idea of mimesis he develops an insight of Heraclitus: "Strife is the father and king of all. Some it makes gods, others men; some slaves, and others free."[5] More pointedly, Girard believes that violence is the core of cultural life. His theory of mimesis and religion is an attempt to explicate this astonishing claim.

The origin of violence in human society is desire arising out of the attempt of two or more persons to appropriate the same "object." As Girard notes, when "any gesture of appropriation is imitated it simply means that two hands will reach for the same object simultaneously: conflict cannot fail to result."[6]

Girard is concerned with the act of appropriation driven by desire which leads to conflict. What is more, he claims that desire for appropriation is not self-actuated or evoked simply by what is desired. We cannot properly understand human desire only by appealing to some person who "wants" something. We must see how desire itself is produced in persons. And desire is produced, according to Girard, by a "rival" who possess the object, whatever it happens to be, or reaches for it. Mimesis is precisely to desire to appropriate what another has.

Girard's thesis about desire challenges many modern assumptions about persons as autonomous subjects who decided what they want. If desire were in fact "object centered," that we simply find some object desireable and seek it, then conflict would be accidental, the unfortunate outcome of two or more persons happening to seek to appropriate the same thing. Similarly, if desire is

---

5 Cf. Valadier, "Bouc émissaire," 88.
6 Girard, *Double*, 201.

understood simply in terms of subjective "wants," then conflict also would be contingent on these wants. Violence hardly seems to be accidental in this way. Girard holds that desire originates in an imitative relation between persons. The rival is not only an obstacle to the appropriation of the object that I want, but also mediates the desire for that object. All desire is therefore self-deceptive because it is modeled on what the rival has even though I believe that my desires are simply my personal "wants." In a mimetic relation, I am deceived about my own desires! This also means that desire can shift between "objects" insofar as desire is mediated by a rival. If the rival desires something else, so too will anyone in conflict with that rival. The possibility of this shift in what is desired is crucial to Girard's theory of religion. How so?

Girard seeks to explore the relation between subject, the rival, and the object desired. This triangle of desire means that two persons now desire to appropriate the same thing and have become undifferentiated in that desire. The denial of the social and personal differences between individuals is, according to Girard, the condition for violence. Violence happens when two rivals seek the same thing and are defined by this one desire. The basic problem of any society is to divert the outbreak of violence, which, if it does transpire, can spread like a disease through the social order. For Girard, religion is one response to this social crisis, an answer that is mimetic in character. Religion does so by shifting the desire from the disputed object to an ostensible victim or scapegoat which is sacrificed, under divine sanction, in order to restore social coherence. Religion diverts desire from a contested object to a scapegoat which can be sacrificed in order to stop the violence between rivals.

In order to understand this claim we must look closer at Girard's idea of mimesis. Clearly, he has modified the Platonic notion of mimesis as realistic representation. That "conception of imitation–which goes back to Plato and marks the whole Occidental tradition–masks the fact that imitation is more originally the desire for the appropriation of that which the other possesses."[7] The mimetic desire to appropriate something held by another, and not the disparity between artifact and its referent, is the true meaning of mimesis. Mimetic desire is a clue to the origins of cultural conflict. Strife is lord and father of all, as Heraclitus said, and he rules, according to Girard, through mimetic processes.

Mimetic desire always threatens to reach a crisis level and thereby engulf the social whole in endless rivalry and violence. Girard admits that animals have instinctive mechanisms that abort the complete breakdown of their communities. Humans do not. In one of his most fundamental claims, Girard explains why this is the case. "The reason is that he (i.e., the human) desires

---

7 Troisfontaines, "L'identité du social," 73.

being, something he himself lacks and which some other person seems to possess."[8] Because human beings are radically finite, we desire whatever seems to possess the fullness of being. Mimetic desire exposes the condition of the human, a *lack* of being, which gives rise to the desire for appropriation of any object we believe will help to complete our existence.

Thus, a mimetic crisis arises from the effacement of differences between persons through rivalry for some object of desire. The root of this possibility is the human awareness of its own finitude. If the crisis is not answered, it leads to violence. In order to stop the crisis what is required is an act of "good" violence that ends the disruption by imputing the cause of the social breakdown to a suitable victim, to a scapegoat. This sacrificial act, in other words, is the mimesis of the social crisis, but one which resolves the crisis by shifting desire to a third object and then destroying that object, the scapegoat. Sacrifice is, then, "the resolution and conclusion of ritual because a collective murder or expulsion resolves the mimetic crisis that ritual mimics."[9] In Girard's theory the distinction between "good" violence (sacrifice) and "bad" socially destructive violence turns on the power of sacrifice to engender social solidarity.

Sacrificial ritual controls the spread of violence by means of a violent act against its ostensible cause represented in a scapegoat. Sacrifice is mimetic in that it is driven by desire while shifting this desire to the victim, itself an imitation of the triangular desire. Yet here too there is deception; appearance and reality are confused. At "the height of the sacrificial crisis man's desires are focused on one thing only: violence."[10] The scapegoat is a mimetic substitute for the true cause of violence. This leads to the odd fact that the victim is both venerated as a savior and despised as the cause of social conflict. The victim attracts and repels the community in much the same way as does the Holy.[11]

How is this shift of desire to the "victim" possible? In order to answer this question, Girard makes another claim crucial to his theory that relates to the long history of reflection on mimesis. He argues that the "transformation of the real into the unreal is part of the process by which man conceals from himself the human origin of his own violence by attributing it to the gods."[12] That is, "real" violence in the social order is transformed into the violence of sacrifice thereby concealing the true origin of the social crisis. I will call this process a "mimetic transformation." By means of this mimetic transformation, the violence that arises from the human lack of being is itself negated. Religion must be understood as a form of mimetic transformation. As the quota-

---

8 Girard, *Violence and the Sacred*, 146.
9 Girard, "Mimesis and Violence," 11.
10 Girard, *Violence and the Sacred*, 145.
11 Cf. Otto, *The Idea of the Holy*.
12 Girard, *Violence and the Sacred*, 161.

tion that begins this essay notes, if religion is to be socially effective, it must, ironically, be untrue to its genesis. Let me explain this point.

Religion attempts to cure violence through mimetic processes and the "good" violence of sacrifice. In order for a religion to fulfill its social function, the participants "do not and must not comprehend the true role of the sacrificial act." How is this possible? Girard continues: "The theological basis of the sacrifice has a crucial role in fostering this misunderstanding. It is the god who supposedly demands victims; he alone, in principle, savors the smoke from the altars and requisitions the slaughtered flesh."[13] Religious myths conceal their origins in human violence and sacrifice through a mimetic transformation. Myths provide an illusory answer to the cause of violence by appealing to the gods as having commanded the sacrifice. A system of mythical representations and ritual actions must be untrue to its origins if it is to fulfill its social function. In fact, Girard insists that religion "in its broadest sense, then, must be another term for the obscurity that surrounds man's efforts to defend himself by curative and preventative means against his own violence."[14]

We have isolated three levels of Girard's interpretation of religion and mimesis.[15] First, there the loss of differences between rivals that arises in mimetic desire and eventuates in a social crisis. Mimesis at this level is a way of thinking and speaking about the generative power of culture in the desire for appropriation. Next is the illusion of sacred difference in the sacrificial mechanism. Mimetic substitution and transformation is needed if the ritual practice is to meet its social function. The victim is the imitation of the desire for violence and the sacrificial act is legitimated by appeal to theological warrants which mimetically conceal their origins. And, last, there is for Girard the real difference between violence and love. Through this complex analysis, Girard claims to have isolated the unity of all rituals and even the foundation of society.

How is it possible for Girard to make this claim about the religious foundations of society, especially when religious traditions conspire to conceal their true origins? To answer this question we have to explore the perspective from which Girard hopes to dispel religious illusion. And in order to understand this, we must begin where he does. Against Plato, Girard sides with the poets, that is, with dramatic mimesis. In doing so, he links his mimetic theory of ritual action with a theory of literature.

Augmenting Aristotle's understanding of drama, Girard argues that with the Greek tragedians "conflict is now transferred to a purely verbal plane, transforming itself into a true tragic dialogue."[16] That is, with the develop-

13 Girard, *Violence and the Sacred*, 7.
14 Girard, *Violence and the Sacred*, 23.
15 Cf. Dumouchel, "Différences et paradoxes," 215–224.
16 Girard, *Violence and the Sacred*, 45.

ment of tragic drama actual social conflict is transformed into artistic form. This is a second mimetic transformation basic to Girard's theory of interpretation. And it means that one can explore literature in order to uncover the social processes a work of art presupposes. Unlike some social theorists, Girard turns to forms of discourse and literature in order to understand social life. How is it, he asks, that Western societies have overcome sacrifical action? Girard thinks that literature is important in this development. Indeed, he claims that for the West it is the novel which unmasks false transcendence and the machinery of desire.

In his first major work, Girard argued that "repudiation of a human mediator and renunciation of deviated transcendence inevitably call for symbols of vertical transcendency whether the author is Christian or not."[17] Girard holds that in the Jewish and Christian scriptures, particularly in the figure of Jesus, we find the decisive unmasking of religion and violence in the name of the innocent victim and the God of non-violent love.[18] These texts bespeak a different form of transcendence than that of the sacred; they overturn rather than legitimate the processes of social violence and victimage. The Bible provides, then, the standpoint from which Girard's theory seeks to uncover and cure violence. This is because the Bible sides *with the victim*, especially in the anti-mimetic act of the Christ. It thereby provides insight into violence and culture. The mere presence of the Bible in Western culture is the condition *sine qua non* for our advance beyond sacrificial social forms, an achievement he believes grasped by great novelists. The novelist levels her or his criticism of culture based on the anti-mimetic shape of the Gospel's proclamation of the innocent victim. In a similar way, Girard's own theory is meant to extend and deepen the criticism of violence in our culture by providing the means to understand the mechanisms of violence. In order to do so, he too draws on biblical texts.

Girard's theory uncovers the roots of religion and culture in mimetic desire which effaces social difference and leads to violence. Mimesis is crucial for explaining culture and the legitimation of social practice through myth and beliefs about the gods. Yet we have also seen that the anti-mimetic claims of the Bible and its vision of the God of non-violent love provide a perspective from which to criticize and thus overcome social oppression. At issue is the difference between bad transcendence in religion and the "vertical" transcendence found in the Bible. Through this distinction Girard believes he has isolated not only the meaning of religious systems, but also the truth of the biblical message.

Girard's interpretation of religion is developed through this novel account of mimesis. His theory bridges the analysis of social action and the place and

17 Girard, *Deceit*, 312.
18 Cf. Gans, "Sacred Texts in Secular Culture."

significance of literary works in our culture. But this is not the only way mimesis is being used in current theories of interpretation. If we are to understand the full importance of Girard's theory, it will be helpful to contrast it with other positions, especially the work of Gadamer and Ricoeur.

3. Mimesis, Play, and Understanding

Gadamer's interest is not in explaining religion; he hopes to provide a philosophical account of human understanding. For Gadamer, genuine understanding is always reached through an act of interpretation. We do not immediately know what a text, event, or experience means; we must interpret in order to understand. How are we to think about the activity of interpretation? Gadamer begins by arguing that the act of interpretation has analogies to human play. That is, Gadamer begins his theory of interpretation with cooperative action and not strife, as Girard does.

Play is a to-and-fro movement between participants, the throwing of a ball between children, for instance. What is more, the point of the play is simply the play itself. Play is then "really limited to presenting itself. Thus its mode of being is self-presentation."[19] Gadamer explores play action finding that it is an activity that presents itself; this activity of presentation, we saw above, was one of the root meaning of mimesis. There is no purpose to the play but the play itself; it is a self-contained activity. According to Gadamer, this also means that play appropriates the participants into its action. We lose ourselves in the activity; we become absorbed by the action and it is as if we are as much being played as we are playing. Gadamer notes that it "is the play that is played irrelevant of whether or not there is a subject who plays."[20]

In genuine play, the activity itself takes over; the purpose of the play is the activity itself rather than the personalities involved. It is through the movement of a drama, for instance, that the participants come to some awareness of themselves *as* actors and the plot itself is presented. This suggests that we know ourselves *as* ones who participate in various kinds of activity. Gadamer is interested in this analogy between play and the activity of interpretation through which we understand anything at all. Interpretation, he argues, is the most basic activity of human being in the world. It is a to-and-fro relation between interpreter and what is being interpreted in which the subject matter under consideration is the dominant concern and not the personality of the interpreter. Interpretation is the activity through which we come to understand something. How is this related to mimesis?

Gadamer uses the idea of mimesis to develop the analogy between play and intrepretation. First, the play-action, as we have seen, simply presents itself.

19 Gadamer, *Truth and Method*, 97.
20 Gadamer, *Truth and Method*, 93.

The being of the play is in its being played. Sophocles's *Antigone* only exists when it is being performed. Otherwise it awaits to be brought to life. Yet in noting this about Sophocles's dramatic work we have actually introduced the idea of mimesis in a way similar to Girard's move from ritual to literary tragedy. *Antigone* is a particular form of human play. It is a drama, after all. In it human action has been given structure and form by the script. Human action has been transformed into a dramatic representation with a script and plot which can be re-enacted again and again. This is an example of what I have called mimetic transformation. For Gadamer, this transformation happens at the level of the text.

Gadamer argues that this "transformation into figuration" is the true meaning of mimesis. This transformation that takes place through the production of a literary work is a leap into the true in the sense that through it human action is raised to a level beyond the actual moment of action in a way that can be understood. In a drama, for instance, the fleeting character of human action is given a certain ideality which opens it to the possibility of being understood in other times and places. *Antigone* gives form to a time-bound sequence of events so that we, centuries after Sophocles, can encounter the story. For Gadamer, mimesis is a transformation which allows us to see the truth of something rather than, as with Girard, a way to conceal what is really the case.

Thus, Gadamer uses play as his clue for speaking of what it means to engage in the activity of interpretation. He has also used mimesis to specify the transformation into an understandable form of the reality of something, say the actions of the character Antigone. And through mimetic figuration in a text, drama, or work of art a time-bound action breaks beyond itself in the possibility for understanding. Through figuration, play action is presented for someone, for an audience. *Antigone* allows specific human actions to be seen and understood by others. We grasp the meaning of an ancient work of art through the interpretation of the work itself. We can enter, as it were, the work through our interpretive action. Yet if this is the case, are we not forced to ask Girard's question? Must we not examine the relation between this performance and what is being performed, its referent, and ask if it is true?

This question takes us one step deeper into Gadamer's work. He notes that mimesis and "presentation are not merely a copied repetition, but a recognition of the essence. Because they are not merely repetition, but a bringing-forth, the spectator is involved in them."[21] The work of art, in other words, allows us to recognize the essence of something, say the character of human tragedy in the play *Antigone*. And as interpreters we are involved in the bringing forth of the recognition of something which is basic to any truthful claim about it. This means that by seeking to interpret any work of art or any event an audience is called into a special form of mimetic action. That form of mimetic action is the act of interpretation. Through interpretation the inter-

21 Gadamer, *Truth and Method*, 103.

preter's own understanding and the view of life presented in the text melt into each other, as it were, thereby overcoming the distance between them. The event of truth, for Gadamer, is precisely this fusion or melting between the interpreter and the work which discloses something about human life and forms understanding around its "object."

We have then a double mimesis in Gadamer's thought: the subject matter in question comes to some figurative appearance in the work of art; the audience enters into the drama of understanding through interpretation.[22] Interpretation is, in other words, the mimetic action of the interpreter. It is a back-and-forth movement of dialogical interaction with the text. Through this movement, Gadamer insists, something is presented (the meaning of the text) in such a way that the interpreter participates in what is presented, that is, understands it. Mimesis provides the means to describe the work of art or the written text as well as the event of understanding through interpretation. What does all of this mean for religion?

Gadamer insists that "the form in which religious texts speak is myth. . . . Myth means a tale conveyed and to be verified by nothing else than the act of telling it."[23] Gadamer is concerned, then, with *myth* rather than sacrificial processes. He treats myths like texts which are to be interpreted in order to understand their "truth." Myths do not tell us something about social existence, as Girard insists. Rather, myths are occasions for understanding something about the human condition. Myth is also verified not by recourse to its ostensible origins in social processes, as it is for Girard. We do not find out the truth or untruth of a myth by exploring its social grounds and purpose. In Gadamer's words, a myth is verified by "nothing else than the act of telling it." But what is the truth of a religious myth? Gadamer argues that religions speak about the human belonging to the total scheme of things when that scheme is taken as luminous with the holy. Religion is about the human place in reality and not an answer to a specific social problem. The meaning of religion must be approached through the study of particular religious myths and the tales they tell about human existence and the holy. And this means, we should note, that the truth of a religious myth is independent of its social origins. A myth can be the occasion for understanding something about the human condition in relation to the holy irrespective of the social conditions which gave rise to that myth. This is a point of grave difference between Gadamer's hermeneutic and Girard's theory of religion.

One would expect Gadamer to argue that Christianity also speaks by means of myths about the meaning of the whole of what is and the human place in it. Yet he says that the "general character of the mythic tradition stands in striking contrast to that of Christianity."[24] The authors of the New Testament

---

22 Cf. Weinsheimer, *Gadamer's Hermeneutics*.
23 Gadamer, "Religious and Poetic Speaking," 92.
24 Gadamer, "Religious and Poetic Speaking," 95.

were not mythic poets, but witnesses to the event of Christ. In other words, Christianity is non-mythic in character! Its concern is "faith." Given this, theology, for Gadamer, has "the special task of making acceptable what seems to be fundamentally incomprehensible: that faith is not the product of a believer's merit but an act of grace."[25] And this is, Gadamer thinks, the truth of faith. Faith is the connection, we might say, between the interpreter and what is presented in the New Testament texts, that is, the witness to the event of Christ.

What is not clear in Gadamer's argument is how the truth of faith, understood in this rather Protestant way, is related to the mythic discourse of religions. It is this question that Girard has tried to answer. But in order to do so, Girard has had to chart the connection between myth and ritual, that is, the connection between the linguistic dimension of a religion and the social practices it entails. In other words, Girard's theory of mimesis and religion seeks emancipation from the violence masked by religion. Gadamer's hermeneutic, however, centers on the understanding of "representations" which escape their time-bound character. Girard clarifies, in a way Gadamer does not, the connection between literary works and the dynamics of social actions. This enables Girard to provide an interpretation of religious systems of meaning with respect to actual social existence and violence.

Girard is not the only one to explore the connection between action and text through mimesis. Paul Ricoeur has attempted to articulate this connection in his theory of narrative. If we are to grasp fully the distinctiveness of Girard's theory, we must also compare it with the work of Ricoeur.

4. Mimesis, Time and Hope

Ricoeur's interpretation theory specifies a claim about human existence similar to the fundamental claim we isolated in Girard's work.[26] Ricoeur argues that human beings in their very existence are a duality seeking unity. We are finite and yet free creatures. We are mortal and yet can in some measure transcend our finitude through imagination and freedom. We know that we are finite and in this knowledge transcend brute finitiude. Given this, we seek some unity in our lives. This unity must affirm and not deny the duality of our existence; it cannot be a matter of asserting that we are only finite creatures or that we are really minds trapped in bodies. How are we then to understand the unity of our existence? Ricoeur argues that we come to understand ourselves by interpreting symbols, metaphors and narratives which protray the human condition. How is this an answer to the human dilemma? In order to see this, we have to grasp how we are involved in the act of interpretation.

25 Gadamer, "Religious and Poetic Speaking," 97.
26 Cf. Van Den Hengel, *The Home of Meaning.*

Ricoeur develops a theory of the imagination to carry out his analysis of linguistic forms.[27] In doing so, he speaks of the reproductive and productive imagination. By reproductive imagination he means the power of mind to grasp a unity of meaning with respect to literal claims and their referents. For instance, we make sense of the metaphoric sentence "my love is a rose" by relating the predicate (rose) and subject (my love) through the temporal verb. In this act, we reproduce a perception of the reality to which the sentence refers, roses and lovers. But that is not all. Meaning is produced through a unifying act of the imagination which brings diverse elements (lovers and roses) into relation through a temporal verb. This suggests that time, represented in the verb, is the context of meaning and that the production of meaning is through the unifying act of the imagination. The importance of this insight will become apparent in Ricoeur's theory of narrative.

However, we must first see that the structure of the metaphoric sentence entails its own negation as a literal claim. Lovers are not literally roses. The sentence is not simply an image of something real but absent and to which we have access independent of the image. We might perceive lovers and roses as things in the world, but we only understand lovers *as* roses through the metaphoric image. As Plato first saw, this "raises the problem of the *unreal* as distinct from the mere absence of the *real*."[28]

The metaphor of lovers as roses is not simply a report of what is absent—that is, some absent real lover who is actually a rose! Rather, the metaphor suggests how something that is literally unreal (lovers as roses) can provide insight into what is real–actual lovers. The productive imagination is the human capacity correlate to this metaphorical power of language. In bringing together the dimensions of a metaphoric sentence the imagination helps produce its fictive referent. The productive imagination grasps the possibility that lovers are like roses.

It is the productive imagination that enables us to grasp the meaning disclosed by a literary text. Yet it is through our affections, our feelings, that we enter that vision of reality. I am moved by the metaphor of rose-like lovers at the level of feeling and affection. Ricoeur does not mean feeling in any sentimental sense; it is, rather, a personal commitment to make something one's own. In genuinely understanding the metaphor of lovers as roses I am committed to make this insight my own, and, perhaps, even be changed by it. This "feeling," or commitment, is much like Aristotle's notion of *catharsis*, especially in the appropriation of narratives. It is not a sensation, but part of the reasoning out of the work and making its meaning one's own.

This account of the power of metaphor to open new ways of understanding life, the work of the imagination in this process, and also the role of feeling are

---

27 Cf. Ricoeur, "The Metaphorical Process."
28 Ricoeur, "Can Fictional Narratives Be True?" 9.

all basic to Ricoeur's interpretation of mimesis. He uses the concept of mimesis in order to explore the relation between narrative and the meaning of human action and human temporality. Mimesis relates then to the question of time and meaning we isolated above but with respect to metaphor. How does Ricoeur speak of mimesis?

Any narrative construal of human life and time draws its intelligibility from our preunderstanding of the order of action: structural attributes that distinguish action from natural motion; the symbolic mediation of human action in rules and norms for behavior; and, the temporal character of action. This prefigured understanding of narrated time provides the anchoring of narratives in the literal world of human conduct. Ricoeur calls the prefigured but intelligible order of action "Mimesis I." It is what the reproductive imagination can and must grasp if we are to understand any narrative. Any narrative–whether in a religious myth or the simple stories we tell about ourselves–is only intelligible because it relies on features of human action.

The meaning of a narrative is not limited to these features of action. A narrative also configures actions into a meaningful whole. After all, when we tell a story we bring a sequence of actions into some coherent relation. This unifying act, as we have seen, is productive of meaning. "Mimesis II," as Ricoeur calls it, is this unifying act in the structure of the plot (*mythos*); the plot brings together discordant events and actions, synthesizing them into a meaningful unity. This is a creative act, an act of the imagination, in which the narrator provides unity to events.[29] By doing so, the narrative is open to interpretation, to the possibility that it will be understood by others.

The reception of narrative by the interpreter is called "Mimesis III." The event of understanding, then, is the intersection of the text (Mimesis II) and the lived world of the interpreter (Mimesis I). In this way the unreal (the narrated action) potentially refigures the real (our practical lives) and thereby returns to what we already possess in our actual lives. A fictive narrative has then the same dynamic as a metaphor: what is literally unreal (the story) can provide insight into what is real (human life). More specifically, narrative, like metaphor, makes possible an understanding of our temporal existence. The meaningfulness of human time, Ricoeur claims, is bound to the imaginative act of figuration relative to our experience of time. But what is that experience?

Returning to the anthropological point I noted earlier, the human *is*, for Ricoeur, a duality seeking unity. In the present context we must ask, what is the duality of human existence in terms of temporal experience? The duality is that human existence in time is oriented towards some finite end, death, even as we can anticipate another transcendent finality (eternity) by means of the capacity of freedom and the imagination to reach beyond finitude. How can

29 Cf. Ricoeur, "Erzählung, Metapher und Interpretationstheorie."

narrative help to render productive this clash between death and eternity in our existence without trying to escape it through denial or illusion? Ricoeur attempts two interrelated answers to this question, one at the level of narrative and the other in religious discourse.

In his work *Time and Narrative*, Ricoeur explores how narrative renders productive three unsolvable problems, or *aporias*, that mark human temporal experience. The first aporia concerns the unity of personal identity within the temporal diversity of actions. Through the act of narrating a life or interpreting narratives, we understand ourselves as the subject of our actions; we gain a "narrative identity" and thereby we understand ourselves as the subject of diverse actions. The aporia remains, however. We sense a tension between the unity of own identity and the diversity of our actions in time. But while not resolved, the aporia has been rendered productive through narrative identity and our act of narration. We can always say "who" we are by narrating what we have done and lived through.

The second aporia of temporality is closely related to the first; it has to do with the unity of history. Can we speak of there being "one" history? From what vantage point could we speak of its unity? Here too understanding is won not by resolving the aporia, but by rendering it practically productive. Ricoeur argues that we achieve this through the imaginative idea of one history and human solidarity which serves as an ideal to guide thought and action. The idea of human solidarity, like that of narrative identity, constitutes a moral and political task. We ought to work for human solidarity. Thus narrative provides a practical, not theoretical, answer to the unity of history.

However, time itself remains inscrutable. We cannot really say what time "is," since, as we have seen above, time is the condition and context for all meaning. This exposes the limit of our ability to answer the duality of our own existence, that we are oriented towards death and yet can anticipate eternity. How then are we to make sense of our temporal lives? The third aporia is between our search for meaning and the inscrutability of time. It is rendered productive by driving us back to the practical tasks of working for some personal identity and human solidarity. Narratives do not simply symbolize something prior to experience or chronicle factual events. Instead, they configure the limits of our ability to comprehend the temporal constitution of our lives.

One answer to the duality of our existence is then through narrative itself. The act of narrating our temporal experience establishes a practical agenda for life and also provides some means for us to understand our lives. However, this is not a complete answer to the problem of human temporality. We have not yet addressed the question of "feeling," or commitment, basic to understanding. Religious discourse becomes relevant at this point. Religious myths, symbols, and narratives open up a vision of the human situation. They tell us about death and eternity, but also, and more importantly, about the grounds of hope. Religious symbols and myths exceed what we can know in the strict sense. But this does not mean, in Ricoeur's judgment, that they are beyond rational interpretation. Why is this the case?

According to Ricoeur, the human drive for wholeness within the paradox of our lives as finite freedom means that we cannot answer the question of our own existence. In the face of the anxiety and guilt that surround life, we cannot, in other words, constitute the grounds of hope for wholeness. Insofar as we do hope, Ricoeur holds that our lives rest on some affirmation of being that is a response to something other than ourselves. As he puts it, "In the end I do not know what man is. My confession to myself is that man is instituted by the word, that is, by a language which is less spoken *by* man than spoken *to* man. . . . Is not The Good News the instigation of the possibility of man by a creative word?"[30]

By exploring religious symbols and myths, Ricoeur seeks to show how they disclose this "Word" about human possibility and evoke an affirmation of being amidst human fault, the experience of evil, and our sense of incompleteness. Such myths and symbols are testimonies to this affirmation of being. More than this the philosopher *qua* philosopher cannot say: here we are at the limits of knowledge. But we also see that religious discourse can speak meaningfully to human beings.

For Ricoeur, mimesis is, then, a way to speak of the semantics of narrative and its capacity to render discordant events into a whole. By interpreting narrative, we have a way to understand the radical trajectory of human action and time as well as a means to address the aporias of lived temporality. Religious discourse, whether in symbols, metaphors or narratives, articulate the grounds of hope and thus open new ways of living in the world. Yet what remains unclear, it would seem, is why the human drive for wholeness, born of a lack of being in human existence, does not lead to violence, as Girard contends that it does. And if this is a possibility, which, empirically is certainly the case, then a theory of narrative and religion must answer not only the problem of the grounds of hope but also the spread of violence through the social order.[31] Girard's theory, as we have seen, attempts precisely this task.

5. Mimesis and the Study of Religion

It is now possible to isolate the distinctiveness of Girard's theory of mimesis and religion by comparing it with the other hermeneutical positions we have explored. We have seen that Girard's account of mimesis enables him to draw the connection between social action and literary texts in ways Gadamer does not explore. Indeed, Gadamer's idea of mimetic transformation means that the

---

30 Ricoeur, "The Language of Faith," 237–238.
31 Ricoeur does address the problem of violence, but not with attention to social practices, as Girard does. Cf. Klemm and Schweiker, *Meanings in Texts and Actions.*

work of art escapes its historical and social context and acheives a certain level of ideality. What is more, Girard's theory of religion can specify the connection and yet distinction between Christianity and religious violence without Gadamer's appeal to a Protestant notion of faith. The truth of a particular religion, in this case Christianity, is determined by how it answers a problem common to all religions–the dilemma of social existence–rather than how the interpreter understands the significance of those religious beliefs for herself or himself. In this respect, Girard provides a more comprehensive theory of religion than Gadamer does. This is based on Girard's idea of mimesis. He understands mimesis not only at the level of play action and the literary text, but also through ritual, social action. Girard's theory of mimesis enables him to explore in a comprehensive way the totality of a religious system.

We have seen that Ricoeur draws the connection between text and action through the idea of mimesis. In this respect, Ricoeur's narrative theory might enrich and deepen Girard's understanding of the novel in Western culture and also the biblical texts themselves. Showing that to be the case is beyond the scope of this chapter. I have argued, however, that the similarities and differences between Girard and Ricoeur run deeper than might first be expected. Each of these thinkers grounds his interpretation theory in a similar claim about human existence, that human beings experience their finitude. For Ricoeur, the hermeneutical task is a response to that problem; it is a response to the drive for wholeness in human life. According to Girard, religion and the anti-mimetic message of the Bible are responses to the human lack of being. The difficulty, then, for Girard is not how to answer the possible hopelessness and meaninglessness of existence. The problem is much more how to cure violence.

Attention to the problem of violence would seem to be required by any theory that begins with the anthropological claim Girard and Ricoeur share. The reason for this is simple. If Girard is correct about human desire, there is no reason to believe that hope itself, or the object of hope, cannot instigate mimetic rivalry. And given that possibility, the answer to the human dilemma must expose the mechanism of violence. In this respect, Girard's theory does not negate Ricoeur's concern with the question of hope. It does, however, provide the means to examine other and more violent possibilities that arise out of the character of human existence.

We have, then, specified the distinctiveness of Girard's theory of interpretation with respect to other options in contemporary hermeneutics. Given that fact, what insights can we draw from this discussion? In ending our inquiry, I want to return to the idea of mimesis and make two points. The first is quite simple. The idea of mimesis has enabled us to compare and contrast major hermeneutical theories. This is important, I suggest, since one difficulty facing religious studies is how to relate the various approaches to the study of religion in a coherent fashion. One result of our inquiry is that the idea of mimesis is a way to do so. What awaits further work is a more extended engagement between hermeneutical theories around the idea of mimesis. This essay has established the possibility of this enterprise on a number of levels of thought, levels reaching from the theory of language to basic claims about human existence. However, much work still needs to be done.

Second, by focusing on the idea of mimesis the scholar of religion commits herself or himself to the dual task of exploring the meaning of religious symbols, myths, and action and also the question of their truth. And this is because, as Plato first saw, the use of "imitations" raises the question of how we can, if at all, truly understand something, in this case religious discourse and practices, through representations. The thinkers we have explored in this essay address this problem despite their differences. This is why they develop hermeneutical theories. Put differently, the old division between descriptive approaches to the study of religion interested in the meaning of religious discourse and practices as opposed to normative theories which try to assert the truth of one religion must be reconsidered in the context of a fully hermeneutical approach to religion.

In a word, the study of religion is an interpretive enterprise. And this suggests that the study of religion can be seen as part of the wider enterprise of trying to understand the human condition. Reclaiming mimesis as a complex concept able to bridge hermeneutical theories allows us to consider anew the importance of religious inquiry into the whole domain of culture (Girard), the experience of truth (Gadamer), and the affirmation of existence (Ricoeur). So understood, the study of religion contributes to the basic task of the human sciences: the examination of life and how we should live.

6. Conclusion

In this essay I have examined the work of Girard, Gadamer, and Ricoeur and what they contribute to religious studies. Exploring the concept of mimesis has also allowed us to consider theories of interpretation which seek to explore the meaning and truth of religious actions and myths, the topics, we should recall, found in the passage by Girard that begins this chapter. In the end this much seems clear: the mimetic dynamic Girard isolates in the religions has much to tell us about the questions which actually beset us. For is it not the case that we too ask about the truth of systems which form and transform the fragile and complex shape of our world and our lives?

PART TWO:
Historical
Applications

Sacrificial Violence
in Homer's Iliad

Gil Bailie

Abstract

The following essay is a reflection on Homer's *Iliad* undertaken in light of René Girard's premises concerning the role of mimesis in the formation, maintenance and dissolution of cultural structures. In the introductory and concluding comments, and in brief allusions in the body of the essay, reference is made to biblical texts and themes which echo the concerns with which the poet of the *Iliad* is preoccupied. The essay argues that Homer has described in remarkable detail a world strikingly similar to the one Girard's theory predicts, and that Homer's fleeting and inchoate glimpses of an alternative to the prevailing sacrificial violence trace a trajectory which, were it drawn further out, would intersect the trajectory traced by the biblical psalmists and prophets, and conclude in the gospels.

0. Introduction

War is one of the handful of overtly sacrificial institutions ("capital punishment" being another) that has managed to preserve its social legitimacy into our time despite growing and welcome indications of a weakening of its mythos. Coming to terms with that institutionalized ritual may constitute the maturation crisis for our epoch. As specifically modern as that crisis seems, it was made modern more by our awareness of it and by the destructive power of our weapons than by any change in its perennial dynamism. Dealing though it does with so ancient and so stylized a war, Homer's *Iliad* lays bare the anthropological dynamics of collective violence with astonishing insight. As abundant as are Homer's insights into the nature of violence, however, the task of harvesting the insights and thematizing them remains incomplete. We are in a better position to take up this task than were the ancients for whom the epic was composed, for we are heirs—grudging or grateful—of a religious traditon whose historical effect has been to undermine the very myths from whose grip Homer was able to partially extricate himself. As the bloody history of the 20th century demonstrates so clearly, we ourselves are far from being emancicated from the myths of righteous violence. And yet the violence of our time, in addition to being a social and physical fact, has become a moral and cultural dilemma precisely because the myths that once so routinely immunized it from moral scrutiny are less and less able to do so. Centuries of exposure to the demythologzing power of the biblical revelation has deprived our world of its justifying myths and thrown it into crisis, but, at the same time, it has made it possible for us to recognize and decipher earlier—even ancient—texts whose perspective is, at least rudimentally, post-mythological.

Though there is some logic to the critical conventions that place Homer and the Christian gospels in distinct literary pigeonholes, keeping either pigeonholed is no easy task, and given the crisis in which we now find ourselves, continued attempts to do so may be counterproductive. Homer's brilliant poetic analysis of the violent impulse and the gospel's revelation of the matrix of violence, culture and religion cannot, and should not, be isolated from one another. Nor should either be excluded from our increasingly urgent attempts to comprehend the upsurge of violence that is rapidly becoming the defining phenomenon of our age.

The intellectual tradition has only infrequently tolerated the kind of joint-venture between the classical and Christian dispensations herein undertaken, and the prevailing attitude toward such a collaboration is still decidedly skeptical. In this volume we have perhaps more license for such a project, inasmuch as this collection of essays has in large measure been provoked by the work of René Girard, a man whose writings presuppose the applicability of Christian texts to non-Christian literary and cultural data. In any case, Homer's epics, long regarded as Greek "old testament" in a symbolic sense, might now be so regarded in the more familiar sense. A more adroit and less chronological appreciation of what is "old" and what is "new" testament may be helpful in assessing texts from a Girardian perspective. Tomorrow morning's newspaper, for instance, will very likely be "old testament" in its grudging and hand-wringing acceptance of the logic of necessary violence. It will probably be more "old testament" than, say, Deutero-Isaiah, which is part of the Old Testament canon. Tomorrow's newspaper may even be more "old testament" than Book Twenty-four of Homer's *Iliad*. What distinguishes "old" from "new" testament may eventually come to be measured, not chronologically, but by the ability of a piece of literature to rend the veil of the cult of sacrificial violence (Matt 27: 51–53) and awaken the reader from the narcosis of its justifying myth. "There is," Girard has written, "a first and essential diversity of literary texts . . . distributed along something like an axis of dissimulation/ revelation."[1]

---

1 Girard, *"To Double Business Bound,"* 221–22.

Even by this definition, Homer's *Iliad* falls considerably short of the biblical prophets and the gospels, but it can nevertheless be read anthropologically as an "old testament" anticipation of them. This is so for two reasons: first, the *Iliad* is better understood, all things being equal, by someone who has grasped the gospel message than by someone who has not; and, secondly, its structural inconclusiveness and reticence anticipates the gospels and, in some haunting sense, awaits them. All of this implies a willingness to read the text informed by understandings that are both exterior and posterior to it, something even a nonspecialist recognizes as critical deviance.

> It is a commonplace to observe that the meaning of a poem may wholly escape paraphrase. It is not quite so commonplace to observe that the meaning of a poem may be something larger than its author's conscious purpose, and something remote from its origins.[2]

When all is said and done, the appropriate question is: what does the text of the *Iliad* mean? The answer must be that it means the deepest thing we can honestly imagine it to mean. If—our imaginations made acute by exposure to the gospels—we find meaning in the *Iliad* that Homer might not have found, he would be the last to begrudge us the discovery. And if a passing familiarity with the gospels makes more insights into the poem possible, it would be folly to rule them out of order for reasons having to do with literary discontinuity.

1. The Mythic Background

Homer presupposes, though he does not explicitly allude to, the mythological origins of the Trojan war. Our concern with the genesis of violence and the mythos in which it is camouflaged, warrants a word or two about those origins. The conflict begins when Eris, the goddess of strife, is not invited to the wedding of Peleus, a mortal, and Thetis, a goddess, the father and mother of Akhilleus. Immediately, we have an insight into origins: conflict arises from the attempt to avoid conflict. Peace, peace, we humans are wont to say, but there is no peace. Eris, so shunned, retaliates by tossing a golden apple over the wall into the midst of the celebrants. Attached to the apple are the words: "for the fairest." Instantly, the three most prominent goddesses claim the apple, and Paris, the young prince of Troy, is chosen to arbitrate the matter. In a scene that has an illuminating, if not strictly parallel, counterpart in the wilderness temptations in the synoptic gospels, the goddesses bid for his consideration: Hera offers him royal greatness, Athena offers wisdom and glory in war, and Aphrodite, the loveliest woman in the world. This Olympian course in mimetic desire finds a willing pupil. Paris chooses Aphrodite. Hera and Athena, offended by his choice, become the archenemies of both Paris

2 T. S. Eliot, *On Poetry and Poets*, 22.

and Troy. For her part, Aphrodite now has to deal with the slight complication: the most beautiful woman in the world, Helen, is already married to Menelaos, king of Sparta. The perfect triangle is configured. Menelaos serves as the mediator of Paris' desire and as the obstacle to its satisfaction. Thus the emotional agitations of desire and rivalry can be unleashed and mutually exacerbated. Aphrodite arranges the seduction-abduction by virtue of which Helen is taken to Troy. Here is the prehistory of war: a reference to *mimetic desire* and *mimetic rivalry* that could not possibly be more explicit. The whole of the *Iliad* is permeated by the interweavings of mimetic *desire* and mimetic *rivalry* and mimetic *violence*, but these related dynamics are already perfectly clear even in its mythological background.

One reason, perhaps, that Homer felt no need to recapitulate these mythological origins is that he has chosen to unpack the mimetic dilemma in some detail in Book One of his epic. The poem opens:

> Anger be now your song, immortal one,
> Akhilleus's anger, doomed and ruinous,
> that caused the Akhaians loss on bitter loss
> and crowded brave souls into the undergloom,
> leaving so many dead men—carrion
> for dogs and birds; and the will of Zeus was done.
> Begin it when the two men first contending
> broke with one another—
>   the Lord Marshal
> Agamemnon, Atreus' son, and Prince Akhilleus. (1:1–7)[3]

The poem is first set in motion by rivalries born of mimetic desire. To the desire and rivalry between the three goddesses, and the desire and rivalry between Paris and Menelaos, is now added the mimetic desire of both Akhilleus and Agamemnon for Briseis, a concubine given to Akhilleus as part of the spoils of war. Remarkably and undeniably, the poet has chosen conflictual mimesis as the dramatic engine of his narration. Everywhere one turns, one finds mimetic entanglements replicating mimetically. The poem begins with just such a replicating episode. Those who flew to Troy on the wings of righteous indignation, determined to punish Helen's abductors, find the vile behavior of their rivals so mimetically compelling they decide to punish it by replicating it. It is left to old Nestor in Book Two to make the irony unavoidably clear.

> Therefore let no man press for our return
> before he beds down with some Trojan wife,
> to avenge the struggles and the groans of Helen. (2:354–56)

---

3 The Robert Fitzgerald translation is used throughout.

This is a glaring instance of the gravitational power of what we might call the *mimetic vortex*. Even those whose initial response to the mimetic conflict is outrage at its injustice and illegitimacy are soon enough seduced into the reciprocal logic by which it breeds and spreads its contagion. If history, already drowning in a surfeit of instances, needed additional literary confirmation of the mirror imaging that occurs in advanced stages of intense rivalry, this would be one of them.

2. The Poem

2.1 A Plague of Rivalry

The poem opens with a plague sent by Apollo in response to Agamemnon's arrogant rebuff to a priest of Apollo who had asked that his daughter, taken by Agamemnon in a war raid, be returned. Forced to relinquish this girl in order to end the plague, Agamemnon takes Akhilleus' concubine in her place. Homer has done something both simple and astounding. He has recapitulated within the Argive confederacy the mirror image of the conflict at the heart of the Trojan war itself. Put another way, we could say that the Akhaian camp has fallen prey to the historical mimeticism, whereby the social pattern that has given rise to a conflict reproduces itself within any social unit that becomes predominately defined by the conflict. Ironically, the rivalry that first consolidates a social unit by providing it with an adversary eventually infects that social unit with the same rivalry, now manifested *within* the social unit and between its members. Shakespeare's Enobarbus put the matter well in speaking of the alliance between Caesar and Antony:

> . . . that which is the strength of their amity shall
> prove the immediate author of their variance.[4]

And so it has in the Argive camp on the plains of Troy. Thus Homer has put into play from the very beginning the device of parallel plot lines which were later to supply Shakespeare with such creative suggestiveness. The crisis that is the Trojan war and the irruption of mutual hostility within the Greek camp are nearly perfect replicas of each other. Each will be worked by the poet as he sees fit, but Homer seems more concerned initially with the conflict between Akhilleus and Agamemnon and its threat to the fragile Argive confederation.[5]

The first unavoidable indication of the crisis, as in the Exodus story and in Sophocles' *Oedipus Tyrannus*, is the outbreak of a plague. We might regard as crucial the moment when a physical dislocation or catastrophe becomes recog-

---

4 Shakespeare, *Antony and Cleopatra*, act 2. sc. 6, lines 155–57.
5 For a parallel, see Stuart Lasine's discussion below of the Korah rebellion; "Levite Violence, Fratricide and Sacrifice in the Bible and Later Revolutionary Rhetoric".

nized as a "plague." The very use of this word may be one of the more tangible symptoms of what Girard terms the *sacrificial crisis*. The word "plague" still carries a vestige of the shudder of dreadful numinosity which was no doubt its most prominent feature for archaic societies. The use of the word indicates that some physical disruption has begun to threaten the essential cultural fabric, setting in motion an effort to locate the disrupting agent, a move that leads inexorably toward the ritual sacrifices upon which the social harmony was first based and upon which it is periodically reconstituted. The social order put in jeopardy by the "plague" is one that maintains social harmony by dissolving what mimetic violence it can in sacrificial rituals, and by redirecting what violence it cannot dissolve outward onto nontribal victims. Again, Homer's poem corroborates Girard's analysis. In the midst of the ravages of the plague, Akhilleus rises to question why Apollo might be sending such disaster on the Argives.

> Has he some quarrel with us for a failure
> in vows or hekatombs? Would mutton burned
> or smoking goat flesh make him lift the plague? (1:65–67)

The first supposition that comes to Akhilleus' mind is that the rituals of animal sacrifice (vestiges and veiled reenactments of foundational human sacrifices) have failed in some way to keep the otherwise menacing gods propitiated. As the Hebrew texts amply indicate, the failure of animal sacrifices—however it may be theologized—indicates that the substitution of animal for human victims has insufficiently achieved what Girard calls the "quotient of cathartic potential" necessary for the renewal of social harmony.[6] Such failures ominously presage or coincide with social crises. And indeed there is ample evidence of just such a failure of the sacrificial cult, most prominently perhaps in Book Two when Agamemnon, with his captains assembled around him, sacrifices a fatted ox to Zeus and prays for quick victory over Troy. The text says:

> But Zeus would not accomplish these desires.
> He took the ox, but added woe on woe. (2:419–20)

It is this failure of the sacrificial cult to renew the cultural consensus that is the backdrop for the social disintegration represented by the hostility between Akhilleus and Agamemnon. Reminiscent again of *Oedipus*, the seer who is asked to divine the hidden malady at the heart of the Argive social and military disarray finds that the tribal leader has offended a god. This accusation gives rise to a fierce confrontation between Agamemnon and Akhilleus over the

---

6 Girard, *Violence and the Sacred*, 272.

slave girl Briseis. Homer quickly telescopes the development from mimetic desire to mimetic rivalry to mimetic violence, interrupting the latter only by the intervention of Athena, who prevents Akhilleus from killing Agamemnon and tells him to nurse his grievance and quit the war.

Though it all moves with dazzling speed, no essential feature of either the *mimetic rivalry* or the *crisis of distinctions* is omitted. Of the many nuances Homer provides for the understanding of such a crisis, two are worth mentioning in passing. Akhilleus articulates his challenge to Agamemnon's leadership clearly in terms of a mimetic rivalry.

> I have seen more action
> hand to hand in those assaults than you have,
> but when the time for sharing comes, the greater
> share is always yours. Worn out with battle
> I carry off some trifle to my ships. (1:165–68)

Here, as so often, the incipient feature of an emerging crisis of distinctions is the cry for social equity. Though justice may be the principle on which Akhilleus officially stands, it is unmistakably clear from the larger text that the deep-seated resentment he harbors toward Agamemnon is the product of mimetic desire and rivalry. Though the complaint is made in terms of material possessions, the true rivalry between Akhilleus and Agamemnon is for preeminence within the tribe, a rivalry which is, as we shall mention below, the archetypal rivalry between two distinct types of leadership. Achilleus' lamentations over social inequities are noticeably weighted in favor of his own fortunes. Cause might be found for questioning his high-sounding rhetoric even before we begin to wrestle with the cultural conundrums. As it does here in the case of Akhilleus, the principle of justice frequently gives the outcropping of mimetic rivalry its social legitimacy. This is in no way to gainsay the cry for justice in an unjust world, but rather to recognize that such a cry can be a symptom of the collapse of cultural norms, the measurable deviation from which first makes injustice palpable. Archaic societies institutionalize social inequality and absolutize social barriers precisely to keep social resentments from arising. It is worth noting in passing that traditional societies avoid social equality "like the plague" precisely because they know from bitter experience that they do not have the cultural resources for keeping an egalitarian society civil. Shakespeare never tired of demonstrating how short the half-life of social equality and how quickly it decays into mimetic rivalry. What we need Shakespeare to show us, traditional societies knew in their viscera. They found it less taxing to believe their own hierarchial fictions than to live amid the perils of social undifferentiation. Homer and Shakespeare turned some of the same social paradoxes into literary masterpieces. Akhilleus' resentment at Agamemnon's privilege indicates that the war has begun to dissolve the cultural distinctions that kept social inequalities from giving rise to resentments. He is demanding equality because he is being caught up in the mimetic rivalry born of equality. Akhilleus may have correctly assessed the arrogance of Agamemnon's leadership, but in his turn, Agamemnon correctly assesses the longstanding mimetic resentment behind Akhilleus' demand for justice.

> No officer
> is hateful to my sight as you are, none
> given like to faction, as to battle— (1:176–77)

What is driving the rebellion is a swelling of mimetic rivalry beyond the considerable arena which Homeric society provided for its legitimate operation. Once the hostility spread beyond such an arena, cultural forms may be swept away by it, leaving the social order bereft of a source of authority weighty enough to call things to order again. Such a state of affairs can spiral into social chaos and trigger a sacrificial crisis.

2.2 The Staff of Cultural Authority

Hardly has Akhilleus first raised his voice against the injustice of Agamemnon's leadership than he demonstrates where his outburst is leading. As he speaks to the assembly, he takes the staff in hand according to custom. The staff is the express emblem of social order and consensus. When someone begins to call into question the social conventions for which the staff is symbolic, as Akhilleus does here, the sacred power of the staff itself wanes. Akhilleus says of it:

> But here is what I say: my oath upon it
> by this great staff: look: leaf or shoot
> it cannot sprout again, once lopped away
> from the log it left behind in the timbered hills;
> it cannot flower, peeled of bark and leaves;
> instead, Akhaian officers in council
> take it in hand by turns, when they observe
> by the will of Zeus due order in debate. (1:233–39)

The conflict between Akhilleus and Agamemnon is that between the authority of natural strength, on one hand, and cultural or bestowed authority, on the other, with Akhilleus possessing the former and Agamemnon the latter. Both these authorities are based on violence, the violence of cultural authority being only slightly more sublimated into cultural structures than the violence of raw physical power. It is the business of primitive religion to sublimate some especially remarkable violence into cultural forms in such a way that it remains metaphysically pre-eminent with respect to even those forces that are physically superior to it. Characteristically, Homer skillfully exploits the paradoxes which the familiar convolutions of culture exist to suppress. Akhilleus swears by the staff while at the same time remarking on the diminution of its natural vitality necessitated by its conversion into the token of cultural authority. Akhilleus, personifying a paramount physical force, is disparaging the cultural token by recourse to which something other than physical prowess is given social pre-eminence. Finally he concludes his speech by declaring his intention to withdraw from the battle. It all ends with a gesture of crucial significance.

> He hurled the staff, studded with golden nails,
> before him on the ground. (1:245–46)

By defiantly throwing the staff to the ground, Akhilleus manifestly displays his contempt for the cultural structures it symbolizes. His hurling of the staff to the ground announces a full-blown crisis in the Argive confederacy.

Before we leave this richly symbolic image, however, we must pause long enough to note how nuanced is Homer's insight into the social function of the staff. In Book Two Agamemnon again has the staff in hand, but he is no longer holding it with authority; he is leaning on it! In this revealing posture, he fabricates an ill-conceived deception. He has arranged that, as he suggests a retreat from Troy, his captains will urge that the war be carried on. His purpose is to awaken new enthusiasm for the battle. The ploy fails. He gambles that the centripetal forces in the make-up of the Akhaian confederation are still stronger than the centrifugal ones on which the poem has been focusing attention. He is wrong. With Agamemnon ridiculously trying to support himself by leaning on the staff, the troops, whom he had hoped to rally with his dissembling speech, dash toward the ships. Odysseus tries to salvage the cultural enterprise.

> . . . wheeling
> close to the silent figure of Agamemnon
> [he] relieved him of his great dynastic staff,
> then ran toward the ships. (2:185–87)

Odysseus here demonstrates that as cultural standards dissolve, a point is reached beyond which every attempt to reestablish those standards succeeds only in further compromising them. Having just snatched the staff from Agamemnon, he tries to rally the retreating troops by saying:

> "Let there be one commander, one authority,
> holding his royal staff and precedence
> from Zeus, the son of crooked-minded Kronos:
> one to command the rest."

> So he himself
> in his commanding way went through the army. (2:204–7)

Odysseus is doubly caught in a double bind. He who just usurped the commander's authority must now argue against usurpation. In this he brings to light one of history's glaring contradictions. But the problem is, of course, a much deeper one, as his use of the epithet "son of crooked-minded Kronos" suggests. By using it, Odysseus has unwittingly acknowledged the fate of all cultures based on a founding murder. His appeal to order is made in the name of the now-reigning rebel: Zeus, whose ascension to power required the violent overthrow of his Agamemnon-like father. With the epithet about Crooked-minded Kronos, Odysseus lets a Homeric ray of light pierce the cultural illusions which make possible the distinction between good and bad revolutionary violence.

On his way to the ships, Odysseus uses the staff as a club to whip the common soldiers into obedience. Homer creates the figure of Thersites in order to drive home the point. Since the less conscious a person is, the more unsophisticated tends to be his mimetic behavior, the common soldiers, like Thersites, are given to mob reactions and to blatant mimicry. Thersites copies the model of Akhilleus and berates Agamemnon. That he feels free to do so is another clue to the weakening of the cultural distinctions. In quelling this rebellious outbreak, Odysseus, unable to salvage enough of the staff's cultural authority, uses the staff as a bludgeon. Unable to use the bludgeon on Thersites' mimetic model, he uses it on Akhilleus' shameless mimic. The use of the staff as a club is symbolically devastating. This is nothing more than the latent truth about the staff having to surface in response to a social crisis.

> At this he struck [Thersites] sharply with his staff
> on ribs and shoulders. The poor devil quailed,
> and a welling tear fell from his eyes. A scarlet
> welt, raised by the golden-studded staff,
> sprang out from his back. Then, cowering down
> in fear and pain, he blinked like an imbecile
> and wiped his tears upon his arms.
>   The soldiers,
> for all their irritation, fell to laughing
> at the man's disarray. (2:265–70)

Here is the staff revealing its true character, a revelation made possible by its failing aura and its waning power. The gavel is revealed to be a bludgeon which can, during periods of social calm, achieve its effects symbolically, but which, in a social crisis, reverts to its cruder form. By disclosing the violent source of cultural authority, this episode reenacts in miniature the scapegoat ritual upon which cultural resuscitation must depend once the cultural functionaries have lost the ability to renew allegiances by manipulating the society's ritual apparatus with enough finesse. The soldiers' unanimous laughter of derision at the now despised Thersites supplies the social pandemonium with its momentary scapegoat and reintroduces just that minimum of cultural distinction needed to reconvene, for the time being, a consensus.[7]

2.3 The Will-To-Revenge

Since this collapse of cultural distinctions is the backdrop for the central concern of Homer's poem, we have postponed until now a discussion of that concern. Homer leaves no doubt as to what that concern is.

> Anger be now your song, immortal one,
> Akhilleus' anger, doomed and ruinous
> that caused the Akhaians loss on bitter loss. . . . (1:1-3)

The poem can instruct us about cultural history and the institution of war at the heart of cultural history because it is a poem about "anger" and its roots. Often translated as wrath, the Greek word is *menis*. We can only give proper scope to what is after all the scope of the poem if we see this word as referring to the source of the violent contagion. In this respect it is best to understand *menis* to mean the *will-to-revenge*. Homer's Akhilleus is the incarnation of such a revengeful will. This will-to-revenge is at the confluence of many psychological, social, cultural and metabolic streams, but to feel the heart of Akhilleus' tragedy we must let Homer call our attention to at least one of these sources. Caught up in his wrath toward Agamemnon, Akhilleus wavers.

> A pain like grief weighed on the son of Peleus,
> and in his shaggy chest this way and that
> the passion of his heart ran: should he draw
> longsword from hip, stand off the rest, and kill
> in single combat the great son of Atreus,
> or hold his rage in check and give it time? (1:188-94)

Akhilleus' name has as its likely etymological roots the Greek words for grief (*echoes*) and grieved (*ekache*). He virtually personifies the impulse to turn grief into grievance, to convert, so to speak, heartbreak into proto-violence, remorse into revenge. Conversions in the opposite direction gave rise to the New Testament. To the extent that Simone Weil is correct in asserting that the false god turns suffering into violence and the true God turns violence into suffering, Akhilleus is the high priest of the false one. If he cannot turn his emotional angst into immediate violence, he will, at Athena's bidding, nurse the grudge until his vengefulness completely eclipses the offense which first gave rise to it. Moving counter to this, the poem seems to be searching for a

---

7 For a biblical parallel, see Stuart Lasine's discussion below of the role of Phineas in the restoration of order in Numbers 25; "Levite Violence".

load of grief that will finally overwhelm Akhilleus' impressive ability to turn it into grievance.

The crisis in the Argive camp is that the focus of Akhilleus' will-to-revenge has shifted from his Trojan enemies to his fellow Akhaians and their leader. The social forces and, half-consciously, Akhilleus himself, begin to grope for a way to redirect that vengeful violence away from the in-group, where it has already begun to destroy the cultural consensus, and toward the out-group, who can be expended with no internal Akhaian consequences. In this, Akhilleus is the opposite of Hamlet. Hamlet has the corpse and the ghost of his murdered father as provocation to revenge, and yet his grief overrides his grievance. Unlike Hamlet, Akhilleus has, as yet, no grievance against the Trojans with which to override the one he has with Agamemnon and his fellow Greeks. Neither he nor his comrades will be able to redirect his colossal will-to-avenge outward toward "legitimate" cultural foes until such an overriding grievance is brought into play. However vaguely understood, only something akin to Girard's "interdividual psychology" can account for how the Akhaian social organism seems to now grope for ways of stirring Akhilleus into action against the Trojans. This occurs as Akhilleus sulks in his hut, steeping in his own constrained violence.

> Walking here lonely and strange now, I must find
> A grave to prod my wrath
> Back to its just devotions. . . .[8]

The stalemate within the Akhaian camp remains as the war with the Trojans takes its several turns. Homer makes the symbolic preparation for the sacrificial resolution in Book Nine, when the emissaries from the main Akhaian camp come to Akhilleus' hut to offer gifts in return for his renewed participation in the war. The embassy fails to placate Akhilleus, but what will eventually achieve the resolution is hauntingly alluded to. As the meal is prepared and set before the assembled leaders, the one whose sacrificial death will begin the reconciliation of Argive forces is chosen to perform the token sacrifice that prefigures his own fate.

> Meanwhile Patroklos, like a god in firelight,
> made the hearth blaze up. . . .
>   Akhilleus served the meat.
> He took his place then opposite Odysseus,
> back to the other wall, and told
> Patroklos to make offering to the gods.
> This he did with meat tossed in the fire. (9:210–11, 217–20)

The consummation of this augury of Patroklos' death begins when Ak-

---

8 James Wright quoted in, Richard Howard, *Alone With America*, 578.

hilleus sees a man wounded whom he thinks to be one of the Argive healers, Makhaon. Akhilleus sends Patroklos to ask Nestor about the wounded man's identity. After plying Patroklos with stories of valor in battle, Nestor suggests that Patroklos don Akhilleus' armor and appear on the battlefield, thus terrorizing the Trojan ranks and giving the Akhaians a respite. Eager to follow Nestor's suggestion, Patroklos hastens towards Akhilleus' hut. On the way there, he finds the wounded Eurypylos who confirms that one of the two Argive healers is wounded. Homer seems to rely on the symbol of the wounded healer as a turning point implying the social attrition of the war is overwhelming the Akhaian capacity to restore and reassert its cultural cause. Whereupon Homer, almost literally, drives his point home. Patroklos takes on the role of healer and performs a healing on Eurypylos, demonstrating with characteristic Homeric genius that he is the one who will now heal that larger social wound with which the poem began. He is to be the *pharmakos*; the one who is both the carrier of the disease (arrayed, as he is soon to be, in the armor of Akhilleus, the man who destroyed the social distinctions) and the healer of it (the victim around whose corpse the new social consensus will begin to convene.) Patroklos' healing of Eurypylos gives Homer another opportunity to hint of things to come.

> [Patroklos] took
> his sheath knife and laid open the man's thigh
> to excise the biting arrow. With warm water
> he washed the black blood flowing from the wound,
> then rubbed between his hands into a powder
> over the wound a bitter yarrow root,
> that dulled all pangs of pain. Now the gash dried
> as the blood and powder clotted. (11:843–47)

Patroklos, in Akhilleus' armor, returns to the battlefield and is eventually killed by Hektor. His death provides the preliminary sacrificial resolution to the divisions within the Akhaian camp. Hektor's killing of Patroklos arouses a rage (*menis*) in Akhilleus, a will-to-revenge, that eclipses the seething rage he feels toward Agamemnon. He enters the war once again. But the social benefits of such a sacrifice can only be consolidated by the sacrifice of the great Trojan warrior, Hektor. Now that Akhilleus' vengeful wrath has been redirected toward Patroklos' killer, everything builds toward the single combat between Akhilleus and Hektor. With considerable help from the gods, Hektor falls and pleads that he be given proper burial, at which Akhilleus brutally scoffs. Akhilleus plunges his spear into Hektor and then

> . . . he pulled his spearhead from the body,
> laying it aside, and stripped
> the bloodstained shield and cuirass from his shoulders.

> Other Akhaians hastened round to see
> Hektor's fine body and his comely face,
> and no one came who did not stab the body.
> Glancing at one another they would say:
> "How Hektor has turned vulnerable, softer
> than when he put the torches to the ships!" (22:367–374)

With impressive economy of stroke, Homer has conflated an account of the founding murder with a ritual reenactment of it. Nor are we asked to wait long for evidence of the social benefits of the mob murder. Akhilleus speaks to the assembled Akhaians who have just shared in this ritual, and he speaks as he has not spoken throughout the poem. The tribal unity has clearly been restored.

> Men of Akhaia, lift a song!
> Down to the ships we go, and take this body,
> our glory. We have beaten Hektor down,
> to whom as to a god the Trojans prayed. (22:391–94)

Singing the equivalent of the Akhaian national anthem, the victimizers now have but one culturally relevant task: to institutionalize the social harmonies this murder has restored. The funeral of Patroklos will provide the opportunity for doing so. "There is no culture without a tomb," writes Girard, "and no tomb without a culture; in the end the tomb is the first and only cultural symbol."[9]

The renewed Akhaian social consensus made possible by the victim's death provides Homer with the dramatic backdrop for his most profound concern. To appreciate what he has done, we must be alert to his preparations. Akhilleus is still consumed with vengeful wrath. His tragedy and his greatness consist in this: the sacrificial ritual fails to completely work on him. As Akhilleus turns in the tangles of his vengeful ire, the shade of Patroklos appears to him and asks to be buried and, more importantly, reminds Akhilleus that he too will shortly be dead. What has been implicit in the famous transfer of Akhilleus' armor, now becomes explicit:

> Thou too, Akhilleus,
> face iron destiny, godlike as thou art,
> to die under the wall of highborn Trojans.
> One more message, one behest, I leave thee:
> not to inter my bones apart from thine
> . . . may the same urn hide our bones. . . . (23:80–83, 91–92)

So, for Akhilleus, the funeral of Patroklos has another meaning. It is his own funeral as well. Two distinct dynamics are occurring. For the Argive col-

---

9 Girard, *Things Hidden*, 83.

lectivity, the funeral of Patroklos is an important part of a larger ritual of social renewal.

> Next he [Akhilleus] drew a circle for a mound
> around the pyre, and laid stones on the line,
> and made a mound of earth. When they had done,
> they were all ready to be gone, but now
> Akhilleus held the troops upon the spot
> and seated them, forming a wide arena. . . . (23:255–58)

Here is the ritual of cultural formation, circled as it must be around the grave of its fallen hero-martyr in the aftermath of the killing of the culprit-victim.[10] What remains to be done is the social consolidation of this new-found cultural consensus, and the Homeric mechanism for that is the funeral games. It is in the games that the new cohesion can be worked out in the glorious heyday of culture: in the brief afterglow of unanimity immediately following the successful blood sacrifice. The games are a rehearsal for the most harmonious phase of social life. In the games, mimetic desire is intentionally aroused by the prizes (and the prestige attached to them) to be awarded to those who successfully compete in the games. The resulting mimetic rivalry is given a formal and socially tolerable outlet, and governed by rules strict enough to prevent the rivalry from slipping over into intratribal conflict. The games represent the return of cultural distinctions that were so notably missing in Book One. Homer reinvokes many of the symbols from Book One in his treatment of the games. Space permits only a brief allusion to them.

In the chariot race, two contestants are competing furiously for second place, Antilokhos and Menelaos. Antilokhos, the young son of Nestor, runs Menelaos' chariot into the gully and comes in second place. Tempers flare. Here we have the mimetic rivalry threatening to overflow its carefully pre-scribed channel. Menelaos, in contesting the outcome, picks up the *staff*, and in that one gesture symbolizes the renewal of social order. Calling a council, Menelaos asks for an impartial judgment and insists that in determining the controversy there be no favors accorded him because of his power and rank. And yet it is his opponent, Antilokhos, who bows to precisely those social distinctions.

> Wait a bit, sir.
> Surely I'm younger far than you, my Lord
> Menelaos; you stand higher in age and rank.
> You know a young man may go out of bounds;

---

10 As Girard notes, these are typically the same victim, regarded as the source of the pollution (*pharmakos*) until the sacrificial murder, and as the source of the healing (*pharmakos*) afterward. The *Iliad* employs two victims to the same effect.

his wits are nimble, but his judgment slight.
Be patient, then. (23:587–91)

Homer is clearly inviting a comparison between this and the controversy in Book One between the younger Akhilleus and the elder Agamemnon. Menelaos rewards Antilokhos' recognition of the cultural distinctions by praising his deference for age and rank and relinquishing the contested prize to him after all. Since it is the desires of others for it that gives such prizes value, now that the rival claimant's desire for it has been renounced, it can be ungrudgingly relinquished to him. Since it was but a token of the social eminence Antilokhos has already conceded to Menelaos, the prize is superfluous.

At the end of Book Twenty-three Homer rounds out the theme of the return of proper social distinctions. Immediately preceding what is to be the final contest, Meriones, an adroit archer, shoots a dove in flight, astonishing everyone. The contest to follow, the javelin throwing contest, pits Meriones, whose prowess Homer has just underscored, against Agamemnon, the commander. As the poem has taken pains to show, it is with regard to just such leaders that the mimetic rivalry can be most socially dangerous. The fragility of all social orders makes it necessary to avoid subjecting the key leadership to constant challenge. Meriones' abilities make it likely that a contest between himself and Agamemnon will result in a socially compromising defeat for Agamemnon. Again, Homer has reconstituted the dynamics of Book One in order to contrast them with what happens here. Now it is Akhilleus, the master of ceremonies and supreme diplomat throughout the games, who intervenes. He speaks to Agamemnon:

> Son of Atreus,
> considering that you excel us all—
> and by so such—in throwing power, I'd say
> that you should simply carry off this prize.
> We'll give the spear, though, to Meriones,
> if you agree. That is what I propose. (23:890–94)

The proposal is diplomatically accepted and a challenge to the commander of the confederation is avoided. But it must be noticed that this is exactly the situation Akhilleus found intolerable in Book One. There he had denounced Agamemnon publicly as one who is spared the rigors of the fight but who nonetheless receives its material rewards.

We can return now to the implications of the funeral of Patroklos for Akhilleus. The more recalcitrant problem that Akhilleus represents is still fundamentally unresolved. The death of Patroklos has concluded the rivalry within the Argive camp. For most, that is the ultimate goal of the elaborate sacrificial ritual of the war, but not for Homer, as we are soon reminded by the grim scene at the beginning of Book Twenty-four. Akhilleus is mutilating the body of Hektor.

Akhilleus
in rage visited indignity on Hektor
day after day. . . . (24:22)

The one who has always been able to turn grief into grievance, remorse into
revenge, is once again trying to make that conversion, but with diminishing
results. He is reenacting the ritual slaughter of Hektor in a vain attempt to
resolve the crisis for himself. Anthropologically, what this scene presents to us
is an intermediate stage—a literary trace of the anthropological missing link—
between the actual killing and its ritual reenactment.

We, in our day, urgently ask, is there no way out of this mad cycle of
reciprocal violence? Our historical circumstance arouses an especially keen
interest in the scene of Akhilleus stabbing again and again the body of his
victim. We might see in this grisly scene a prophecy of the moment when,
habituated to sacrificial rituals that nevertheless have lost their mesmerizing
power, humanity strains to fend off the social and psychological reckoning by
unconvincing repetitions of the sacrifice. It is, ironically, this diminishing
effectiveness that turns the ritual into such a compulsion. It is a compulsion
that calls into question not only this "neurotic" version of it but, by implication, the perfectly normal one as well, the one in Book Twenty-two which
restored the Akhaian confederacy.

2.4 A Homeric Pietá

The field of Homer's interest, and in a sense the poem's special venue, now
turns from the Trojan war and from the fractious Argive confederation to the
heart and mind of Akhilleus. With the Old Testament prophets, Homer would
have that heart of stone turn at last to a heart of flesh, and with Paul of the New
Testament, he would have that persecutorial mind renewed. The mind and
heart of Homer's Akhilleus, of course, is the mind and heart of the human
race, wherein a struggle is under way between the revelatory power of remorse
(compassion and love) and the delusional power of revenge (resentment and
reciprocal violence).

The gods finally find Akhilleus' grim ritual of mutilation intolerable and
intervene to inspire the embassy of Priam to Akhilleus to ransom back the
body of Hektor. The scene that follows is one of the greatest in all of literature.
It is as worthy of humanity's thoughtful attention as anything on the far side of
the gospels.

Homer has made it clear that for Akhilleus the funeral of Patroklos is
Akhilleus' funeral as well. Just as Paul understood himself to have been
baptized into Christ's death, so, more obliquely perhaps, Akhilleus presides
over the funeral of Patroklos, his alter-ego, experiencing something of Meister
Eckhart's injunction to "die before you die." Both of the parties to the supreme
scene in Book Twenty-four, Priam, the old king of Troy and father of the slain

Hektor, and Akhilleus, Hektor's slayer, must prepare for the scene by re-
nouncing the whole paradigmatic construct upon which the heroic code is
based.

In preparation for his ransoming petition, the old king loads the wagon with
the elaborate treasures he will offer Akhilleus. Homer dilates a moment on the
last item because it is a symbol for them all.

> . . . and finally one splendid cup, a gift
> Tracians had made him on an embassy.
> He would not keep this, either—as he cared
> for nothing now but ransoming his son. (24:232–37)

It costs not less than everything. This last trophy is a token of Priam's willingness to exhaust completely his cultural resources for the sake of Hektor's
burial. With this gift and its implications, Priam renounces any hope that,
upon returning, cultural life might be resumed. There is, for Priam, no
tomorrow. It is only in this light that the reader can fully appreciate what
would otherwise seem a strangely inappropriate and gratuitous scene as Priam
leaves the walls of Troy. He pauses there long enough to disinherit, in Lear-
like fashion, his remaining children. It is Homer's way of showing us that
Priam is now spiritually childless. As he leaves Troy, Priam leaves everything
behind him.

Akhilleus, for his part, had begun his own version of this renunciation in
Book Twenty-three as he prepared to preside over the funeral which was
simultaneously his own and Patroklos'. A scene as curious as that of Priam
disinheriting his sons—and having the same effect—precedes the funeral.

> Akhilleus
> turned to another duty now. Apart
> from the pyre he stood and cut the red-gold hair
> that he had grown for the river Sperkheios.
> Gazing over the winedark sea in pain,
> he said: "Sperkheios, Peleus my father's vow
> to you meant nothing, that on my return
> I'd cut my hair as an offering to you . . .
> . . . The old man swore it,
> but you would not fulfill what he desired.
> Now, as I shall not see my fatherland,
> I would confer my hair upon the soldier
> Patroklos." (23:140–51)

On the strictly historical level, Mycenaean warriors took a vow at the outset
of war not to cut, comb or wash their hair until victory had been achieved. By
cutting his hair, Akhilleus is demonstrating to his fellow warriors that he no
longer holds out any hope of participating in a victory or of returning to his

home and his father. In a gesture anticipating the eventual co-interment of
their ashes in the same urn, he places the shorn locks of his hair on Patroklos'
funeral pyre.

> And he closed his dear friend's hands
> upon it, moving all to weep again. (23:152–53)

Like Priam, there is no tomorrow for Akhilleus, if he is to have a home-
coming, if there is going to be a reunion with a father, it will have to be *here
and now*. Both Priam and Akhilleus have for a moment emerged from the
social myth by which their lives and those around them have always been
encompassed. They are free for the time being from the heroic code that
sustains the zeal of its adherents on reassurances of victories and home-
comings. Thus liberated, they are capable of what Paul Ricoeur calls an
"absolute action." Ricoeur puts it this way:

> Absolute actions are senseless for historians, for an absolute action is not under-
> stood as proceeding from antecedents or giving rise to consequences but as the
> uprooting of a free consciousness from its historical conditions.[11]

Such absolute actions, that give rise to no historical consequences, are just
those actions that illumine truths eclipsed by "history" and its sundry mimetic
entanglements. They give rise to no historical consequences because their
kingdom is not of "this world"—that is, the world that only knows how to
make meaning by making "history" and only knows how to make history by
making victims. But such "absolute actions" as Homer sets before us in Book
Twenty-four, show us, on one hand, the comparative shallowness of this sort of
"history" and, on the other, the profound human truth that this history manages to obstruct with its mystifications. Nothing in the standard heroic code
prepared Homer's first listeners for the stunning scene he now orchestrates.

> Priam
> the great king of Troy, passed by the others,
> knelt down, took in his arms Akhilleus' knees,
> and kissed the hands of wrath that killed his sons. (24:476–9)

Priam speaks to Akhilleus, and, making explicit what Homer has anticipated
in the earlier scene, compares himself to Akhilleus' father. He says

> . . . take
> pity on me, remember your own father.
> Think me more pitiful by far, since I
> have brought myself to do what no man else

---

11 Paul Ricoeur, *Essays on Biblical Interpretation*, 152.

> has done before—to lift to my lips the hand
> of one who killed my son. (24:503–6)

If this scene falls short of the gospel's—"forgive them for they now not what they do"—it falls short of little else. Akhilleus, always heretofore able to convert grief into grievance, fails to convert this, and discovers thereby a new world—the existence of which he had never suspected.

> Now in Akhilleus
> the evocation of his father stirred
> new longing, and an ache of grief. He lifted
> the old man's hand and gently put him by.
> Then both were overborne as they remembered:
> the old king huddled at Akhilleus' feet
> wept, and wept for Hektor, killer of men
> while great Akhilleus wept for his own father
> as for Patroklos once again: and sobbing
> filled the room. (24:507–12)

It is precisely this kind of *remembering* that is required. In each other's arms, Priam and Akhilleus remember; and we read this passage and find it difficult to think of a more powerful verb. Finally, Akhilleus' great heart bursts; he discovers a "new longing" and the "ache of grief." It is this that Akhilleus has in common with Paul and Lear and countless others for whom the collapse of mimetic rivalry has revealed the "kingdom" of genuine human compassion. The translation of the New Testament word *metanoia* by the English word "repentance" diminishes, in most respects, the depth of its meaning. As this emotionally revealing passage indicates, however, remembering, *metanoia* and repentance are related, for being "re-minded" and feeling remorse for the brutalities over which the "old mind" presided are two parts of one profound awakening.

In the same way that the greatest "resurrection" text in Luke, the road to Emmaus story, is really a "recognition" story, so here Homer has reserved until the very end a recognition scene of comparable magnitude. Like its Lukan counterpart, it occurs in the context of a shared meal.

> Priam, the heir of Dardanos, gazed long
> in wonder at Akhilleus' form and scale—
> so like the gods in aspect. And Akhilleus
> in his turn gazed in wonder upon Priam,
> royal in visage as in speech. Both men
> in contemplation found rest for their eyes,
> till the old hero, Priam, broke the silence:
> "Make a bed ready for me, son of Thetis. . . ." (24:629–35)

Old Priam says, "make a bed ready for me," as though he had known Akhilleus for a thousand years. Gazing at each other in silence, they have parted the veil for one brief moment. The words "make a bed ready for me" represent the spiritual adoption of Akhilleus by Priam.[12] A fatherless child and a childless father, both with very little longer to live, both caught in historical convulsions that they can only escape for one brief moment, see each other at last. The victor and the vanquished recognize each other. The unmistakable dignity of old Priam, especially as it is inseparable from the outwardly humiliating character of his embassy, endows him with an immense capacity for compromising the cornerstone of the heroic system: that the first shall come first and the last, last. As unforgettably as Lear with the dead Cordelia in his pitiable arms, Priam in his agony, deprived even of his son's lifeless corpse, empties the sack of heroic delusions and enters for one brief and timeless moment into another reality.

Before we can fully savor, much less fully comprehend, this Homeric *Pietá*, however, all is shattered once again. The old familiar world intrudes. This "absolute action" will not be allowed to have historical consequences; it will simply have to sit there in the literary record, along with passages of roughly comparable revelatory power in Sophocles, Deutero-Isaiah, Jeremiah, and Virgil awaiting the hermeneutical key, provided by the gospels, that will render these anticipations into revelation. Both Akhilleus and Priam know that the war will continue, neither has the paradigmatic resources with which to comprehend the experience they have just shared. All that can be conceded is a respite from the fighting of sufficient length to allow for Hektor's funeral services.

Both of the parallel social crises with which the poem began, the war between the Trojans and the Argives, and the intratribal conflict within the Argive camp, return at the end of the poem. In responding to Priam's request for a bed, Akhilleus insists that he sleep outside for otherwise he might be discovered by an Akhaian officer who would report it to Agamemnon. This is no time to get mired in textual details, but we may note that one exists, and that the best solution to it seems to be Fitzgerald's, inasmuch as he translates an unclear phrase at the beginning of Akhilleus' remarks with the phrase "defiant of Agamemnon." With this phrase, and the continued struggle between the wills of Akhilleus and Agamemnon that it portends, Homer brings his poem full circle. With his characteristic economy, he introduces with this one phrase the inevitable next phase of the mimetic rivalry. There is no warrant for assuming that the reconciliation between Agamemnon and Akhilleus, purchased as it was at the price of Patroklos' life, might last, any more

---

12 See Theophus Smith's discussion of "the enemy [as] an intimate in the process of one's ordeal" in "King and the Black Religious Quest to Cure Racism."

than might the somewhat comparable reconciliation between Pilate and Herod in Luke's Gospel. Homer need not depict the renewed hostility in detail, for it will be, as all its historical replicas will be, a variation on the theme that Homer has just thoroughly examined. This interpretation is forced all the more compellingly on us by the fact that the speech which began with this phrase reintroduces the larger, parallel crisis: the war itself. The poem concludes as the truce that was to allow for Hektor's burial is about to be engulfed again in violence.

> The men were quick to raise the death-mound, while in
> every quarter lookouts were posted to ensure against an
> Akhaian surprise attack . . . (24:798–800)

Homer seems to know that the world to which he addresses his epic song is as incapable of assimilating the implications of the earlier Priam and Akhilleus recognition scene as were the two characters themselves. He eclipses that scene with such poignancy that all who have been attentive will ache at its passing. And so the poem ends "realistically," but the reader has perhaps had certain recognitions of his own, in light of which a new criteria for discerning the real from the unreal begins to emerge.

3. The Poet of Legend

Since, in conclusion, I want to turn to the matter of legends which have sprung up around the Homeric epics, perhaps here is the place to address the possibility that the poet himself was one of them. For no telling how long, uncertainties about the origin of the *Iliad* and the *Odyssey* have been summed up by the quip that these poems were written either by Homer or by someone with the same name. Beginning about two hundred years ago, however, a scholarly debate over the authorship of these epics began in earnest. Multiple authorship was argued. It was contended that these poems were polished by the grinding literary tides of oral tradition rather than by the brilliant mind of a single Mycenaean poet. It seems to me one could as easily imagine a hundred mural painters on the scaffolding of the Sistine Chapel busily at work making the legend of Michelangelo plausible. Critical opinion has largely abandoned the idea of multiple authorship.

A more interesting tradition is the legend that Homer was blind. The description in the *Iliad* of the blind bard Demodocus has often been regarded as the poet's self-portrait, and the poet of the Homeric *Hymn to Apollo* describes himself as blind. Without claiming more than legendary status for this tradition, we might regard this piece of folklore as an ally in our attempt to assess this epic and the poet who wrought it. The legend of the poet's blindness, however, is based at least as much on the uniqueness of Homer's *vision* as on explicit textual references to sightlessness.

Among the Neoplatonists, Homer's blindness was thought to epitomize his achieved independence from the allure of the phenomenal world (their symbol for which was Helen). Their reasoning seemed to imply that only one so immunized could have "seen" the Trojan war from outside the delusional (and we would add *mimetic*) structures which fired the partisans with zeal for their cause. Of Helen, as the personification of the spell under which the war was conducted, the late Neoplatonist Proclus wrote:

> It is over this beauty that eternal war rages among souls, until the more intellectual are victorious over the less rational forms of life and return hence to the place from which they came.[13]

As Robert Lamberton comments, "the implication is that it is his beauty that entices souls (i.e., the Greeks) to leave their true home and to enter into a mode of existence for which the war provides the most apt metaphor."[14] One need not share the broader Neoplatonist sentiments to recognize in their insight something akin to Girard's understanding of the etiology of conflict. Their claim that Homer's distinction derives in large part from the fact that he did not confuse *mythos* with *logos* is one with which we, from another perspective, can concur.

Homer has, one can safely argue, remained outside of the paradigm that gave war its justifications, outside the myth in which both his characters and his audience were enclosed. Even if he is writing after the heroic heyday depicted in his epic, in the late Mycenaean cultural world or the successor to it in which Homer might have lived, the cultic routines for convening unanimous war parties would have been considerable. Once activated, these cult rituals conjure into existence a sort of social black hole, a paradigmatic gravitational field capable of drawing virtually the entire community into its vortex.

The processes by which cultural participants were then and are now mentally and emotionally drawn into this highly charged paradigm are largely sensory. Rituals, initiations, and liturgical reenactments drive the compelling myth, so to speak, into the synapses via the sensory apparatus.[15] To the extent that the myth which insures this social uniformity is communicated visually, a sightless person might be, in comparison with his contemporaries, inadequately brought under its spell. A blind Homer would have been less in the grip of the culture's preconceptions and therefore available to experiences and insights inaccessible and unintelligible to those caught up in the myth. Literature abounds with references to blindness as something of a blessing, making

---

13 Quoted in Lamberton, *Homer The Theologian*, 199–200.
14 Lamberton, *Homer The Theologian*, 200.
15 Attempts to break with such dominant paradigms also rely on liturgies and sacraments and rituals that introduce the participant into other and wider fields of awareness. See Theophus Smith's discussion below of counterrituals.

possible *in*-sight. In *King Lear* when Gloucester, blind and stumbling, is pitied by the old man who leads him, Gloucester assures him:

> I stumbled when I saw. Full oft 'tis seen
> Our means secure us, and our mere defects
> Prove our commodities.[16]

With something of this kind of liberation in mind—and, in the West, in response to Paul's injunction to "be not conformed to this age"—the contemplative and mystical traditions have often urged an initial deprivation of sensory stimuli as a precondition for the awakening from the mystifications of the Zeitgeist. Transferring this assessment of things to Homer and his world, one could say that a blind bard is less likely than a sighted one to justify the sacrificial violence, because he is less exposed to the mimetic *spectacles* of desire and rivalry and violence, and less given to the mimetic reflexes they provoke. To employ a New Testament term, we might say that such a one would be less *scandalized* by the display of enthralling cult rituals.

One of the most frequently remarked upon of Homer's peculiarities is that, in his obvious aversion toward the senseless brutalities that he depicts, there isn't the slightest hint of a partisan judgment. Did one not know Homer to be Greek, it would be as likely to conclude from the text that his sympathies were with Troy and Hektor. This characteristic is one of the rarest in human experience. It is rarer still to find it in one who was as preoccupied with the detailed horrors of war as was Homer, and who, in spite of these preoccupations, remained almost sublimely immune to the *mimesis* of violence and its justifying logic.

To see how this relates to the legend of Homer's blindness and, at the same time, to Girard's theoretical work, we can turn to a discussion by Girard of the New Testament term *skandalon*. The term literally means a stumbling block, and it is used in the gospels to refer to a person or situation in the social setting which "trips one up" or as we sometimes hear "pushes one's buttons." The "scandal" is something that draws one into the mimetic vortex, into the spiral of *mimesis* that swirls toward violence. It is the triggering mechanism by which a seemingly autonomous individual or a seemingly heterogeneous social group is, as Erich Neumann put it, *recollectivized*.[17] Reflecting on the New Testament's use of scandalization, Girard writes:

> The indignation caused by scandal is invariably a feverish desire to differentiate between the guilty and the innocent, to allot responsibilities, to unmask the guilty secret without fear or favour and to distribute punishment. The person who is scandalized wants to bring the affair out into the open; he has a burning desire to see the scandal in the clear light of day and pillory the guilty party.[18]

16 Shakespeare, *King Lear*, act 4, sc. 1, lines 22–24.
17 Neumann, *Depth Psychology and a New Ethic*, 70 ff.
18 Girard, *Things Hidden*, 426.

As we have said, one of the most remarkable things about Homer is that his palpable evulsion toward the brutalizing violence he depicts lacks precisely this "desire to differentiate between the guilty and the innocent" and to "pillory the guilty party." He has, in other words, remained unscandalized. Keeping Homer in mind, we might ponder one of the gospel passages dealing with scandalization. It is in Matthew 18:8–9:

> If your hand or foot causes scandal, cut it off and rid yourself of it! Better to come to life maimed or crippled than to be thrown with two hands and two feet into endless conflagration. If your eye is the source of scandal, gouge it out and rid yourself of it! Better to come to life with one eye than be thrown with both into gehenna.

The gospel passage, albeit in Oriental hyperbole, suggests that avoiding scandal and the mimetic vortex into which it draws one, may require sensory deprivation. If one's entire sensory system is credulously attuned to the official and unofficial scandalizations of social life, the gospel passage seems to say, one will end in a place described in the alternative as "the endless conflagration" (my translation) or *gehenna*. So given to mimesis are we humans, and so profoundly mimetic are the spectacles of desire, rivalry, violence, and the orgies of recrimination that follow in their wake, that only by avoiding the sensory input can we hope to avoid the visceral reaction and the logic of collective violence toward which it leads.

So, deviating from the respected divisions of classical and Christian literary canons, we can better comprehend the poet of the *Iliad*, or at least the legend of his blindness, by bringing to bear on Homer's literary uniqueness the New Testament term *skandalon*. The other word that the gospel passage lends to our inquiry is the word *gehenna*. Widely translated as "hell," the term refers to a ravine near Jerusalem used in New Testament times as the garbage dump, from which a stench and the smoke of smoldering fires constantly emanated. The gospel's author has placed "endless conflagration" in a verbal parallel to *gehenna*. The humble use to which the ravine was put may have derived from the fact that in earlier times this valley had been condemned as the place where the bodies of sacrificial victims were burned. The word *gehenna*, in fact, is the Greek translation of the Hebrew for "Ben Hinnom," the valley condemned by Jeremiah for the notorious cult of human sacrifice which periodically reasserted itself there earlier in Israel's history. There is warrant, I believe, for bringing these recessive associations to *gehenna* back into play when grappling with the passage we have quoted. Once we do so, a link can be seen between scandal and the process by which one first condones and then eventually participates in the rituals of human victimization. That link is so fraught with dire consequences that extraordinary measures designed to break the linkage (and made intentionally shocking to underscore the scope of the disaster toward which scandalization leads) would be justified.

The legend of Homer's blindness thus corroborates our assessment of his uniqueness and helps deepen our appreciation not only of his literary achievement, but of the unlikely anthropological nexus from which it almost miraculously emerged. The Christian idiom has it that the "world" must end before the "kingdom" of truth and love can be made manifest. "World" here means "worldview"—the paradigmatic shackles by which one remains lifeless save for the mimetic motivations and the agitations and eventual violence toward which they lead. The poet's penetrating *insight* and his autonomy with respect to the cultural *outlook*, its "worldview," are but two sides of the same coin. Only one "blind" to the seducing phantasmagoria of desire, rivalry and violence would be able to "see" the tragic truth of the human situation. Homer saw it. That he but fleetingly saw defenseless love as finally the only sustainable response to the tragedy, contributes to, rather than detracts from, the pathos, grandeur, and anthropological significance of his poem.

"Steadfast Love and Not Sacrifice"

James G. Williams

Abstract

This essay explores the role of mimesis and sacrifice in the Hebrew Bible against the backdrop of Girard's theory of religion and culture. It argues that while a sacrificial reading of the Bible is possible, a nonsacrificial approach is better able to account for the Bible's distinctiveness. This distinctiveness stems from the biblical witness to the revelation of the God of victims and includes a polemic against sacrifice and violence, especially as that polemic is found in the prophets. Part 1 is an overview of the sacrificial perspective, Part 2 counters this perspective, and Part 3 compares the sacrificial and nonsacrificial readings in order to highlight their points of similarity and difference. The sacrificial perspective holds that occasional violence in the form of sacrifice and warfare is potentially a healthy and redemptive form of cleansing for the people Israel. The nonsacrificial perspective counters that while violence is constitutive of Israel's cultus (that is, its prohibitions, rituals, and myths), it is not the ultimate means by which God desires that Israel renew its common life. Indeed, the violence of cultic origins is criticized already in the cultic narratives. And in the stories of the patriarchs and the pronouncements of the great prophets, God's will is that Israel eventually become disengaged from sacrifice and recommitted to the victims of sacred violence. In sum, a nonsacrificial reading unmasks the structures of cultic violence in Israel's history and discloses the witness to the God who desires love and justice rather than sacrifice and burnt offerings.

For I desire steadfast love and not sacrifice,
the knowledge of God rather than burnt offerings. (Hos 6:6)⋆

And if you had known what this means, "I desire mercy and not sacrifice," you would not have condemned the guiltless. (Matt 12:7)

⋆ All biblical quotations are based on the New Revised Standard Version unless designated as AT, which indicates the author's own translation.

The question of the relation of religion and sacrifice continues to haunt both Jews and Christians who look to the Bible as the primary source of models for faith and practice and professional interpreters who must deal with texts and religious institutions ranging over a wide gamut of history and cultures. Typically, both laypeople and scriptural scholars think "sacrifice" is outmoded, a relic of the past except in the derived spiritual sense of an individual's or a group's willingness to give up certain goods or pleasures for the sake of other people or some higher cause. One result is that the ancient Israelite and Christian struggle with the problem of violence and sacrifice and the revelation of God's rejection of victimage in any form is ignored, passed over lightly, or simply not accepted by those believers and theologians whose traditions legitimate a "sacrificial reading" of the Bible (see below), even though they view ancient institutions of sacrifice as no longer valid.

Another result of this view of sacrifice as outmoded is that we usually do not recognize the structure of sacrifice in our personal and public lives. By "structure of sacrifice" I mean those elements of the underlying social structure that lead to the elimination or expulsion of a victim as these have been identified by René Girard in his theory of religion and culture.[1] If Girard's theory is accepted as interpretively powerful, whether finally "true" or not, the consequence is that the structure of sacrifice, or the "victimage mechanism," as he often puts it, is not only the core element of all ancient religion and culture, but is also addressed in the Bible as the central problem of human existence and continues to be the central problem today.

What I propose in this essay is to offer a nonsacrificial reading of the Hebrew Scriptures. "Nonsacrificial reading" here means an engagement with the texts that views their primary general concern and dynamics as that of disclosing and demystifying the victimage process, which is detrimental to the liberation of victims and the human community intended by the God of love and justice. To accomplish this while trying to be as fair as possible to another view of the Scriptures, I will first present a sacrificial reading of the Bible, whose central theme is regeneration through violence and sacrifice. I will then offer an extensive nonsacrificial reading, after which I will conclude with a brief comparison of the points of agreement and disagreement in sacrificial and nonsacrificial readings of the Bible.

Girard's total theory will be explicated and evaluated in Part I of this volume, which is devoted to theoretical perspectives. Here I will simply give a brief indication of how I understand certain key terms, which will be presupposed and sometimes used in my nonsacrificial reading. Girard argues that violence has its roots in *mimetic desire*. Mimetic desire is the subject's wish or craving to imitate its respected, though sometimes feared model. Against

1 See Robert Hamerton-Kelly, "Religion and the Thought of René Girard: An Introduction," in *Curing Violence*.

Freud, Girard holds that the "Oedipus complex," the drive for sexual possession of the parent of the opposite sex, is Freud's own myth. Where he departs from Freud is Freud's insistence on the *inherent* character of attachment to the parent of the opposite sex. The model (and potential rival) or authoritative rival (and thus implicit model) could be anyone: parent, authority figure, peer, et al. However, he does agree with Freud to the extent that he sees a dynamic structure in human relations in which the subject tends to imitate a model (be it a parent, peer, or whomever) in a fashion that puts the subject in a double-bind.

The mandate of the model, at least as perceived by the subject, is "imitate me!" Yet if one imitated the model completely one would be and have what the model is and has, thus displacing the model as rival. The predicament of mimetic desire, which involves this unconscious process of *mimetic rivalry*, would result in complete social chaos without some means of regulating it.

Human groups are generally not aware of the real sources of conflict and their own mechanisms for dealing with it. Their universal tendency has been to regulate rivalry by arbitrarily choosing a *victim* in order to transfer the community's ills to this person or animal. Since human communities maintain their order through a system of differences, these established differences are threatened by the potential or actual violence within the group that arises from the working of mimetic desire. Both *sacrifice*, the offering of a victim, and any ritual of *scapegoating*, the expulsion of a victim, are both the ritualized repetition of an original convergence upon a victim. Sacrifice and scapegoating are a ritual reversion to chaos (that is, the absence or confusion of appropriate differences) in order to maintain the system of differences. Thus *deification* of the victim is quite common because just as the community's previous ills are ascribed to the victim, so also is the relief of the problems, whatever they are thought to be, once the sacrifice is completed.

1. A Sacrificial Reading of the Biblical Tradition

A sacrificial reading of the biblical tradition stays within the boundaries of the centrality of sacrifice and regeneration through violence. In Christianity for example, those who hold to a doctrine of salvation through the sacrifice of Christ that satisfies a just—and justly angry—God (even if this sacrifice was once and for all), read biblical texts in terms of this central sacrifice. Likewise, Christians as well as Jews who envision a final apocalypse as the destruction of the wicked by a triumphant God or Messiah, tend to see the world and read the Bible sacrificially.

From the standpoint of a sacrificial reading the Bible recounts the revelation of a God who seeks to redeem the world through individuals and a people whom he chooses but who must be tried and purged so that they may be holy and righteous bearers of the divine revelation. It is in the inscrutability of

God's wisdom that certain people are chosen to do his will. The younger son is favored because God chooses him, and he is tranformed into a vessel of God's word (the promises to Abraham) through ordeals which are necessary for preparing anyone to be delivered from the human condition of sin—guilt, meaninglessness, and death.

Part of God's plan according to the Bible is the offering of sacrifice. Sacrifice of animals and produce to God was instituted because of human sin, which must be acknowledged and eliminated by the willingness to offer a victim to God. Sacrifice is an act of giving part of one's life and livelihood, which in turn symbolizes the willingness to surrender everything to God, the true owner and giver of everything.

Likewise, the law (Torah) of Moses is given because of sin. That is, individuals and communities must be regulated, otherwise chaos would break out and threaten the fabric of society. In fact, both sacrifice and the law are God's bulwarks against the sin that would destroy even the chosen people if these institutions were not available as the primary means of maintaining order and directing the group to a right relationship with God.

There is an analogy or symmetry between the experience of chosen individuals and the history of the people Israel. Just as figures like Abraham, Isaac, Jacob, and Moses must undertake arduous journeys and suffer threats to their very existence, so also must the chosen people do the same. Just as the patriarchs and Moses must give up some aspect of themselves, so also the people Israel. Abraham is asked to undergo circumcision and to sacrifice Isaac; Jacob wrestles with the adversary and is injured; Moses is attacked by God in the wilderness and later loses part of his prophetic spirit, which is conferred upon the seventy elders. The people likewise lose many of their number in the retaliation for worshiping the golden calf and for crying out for meat in the wilderness.

Moreover, just as foreigners threaten the existence and welfare of the patriarchal protagonists, so also the people Israel is threatened by foreign nations. There is a sense in which the journeys and dangers of Abraham in Egypt and Gerar, Isaac in Gerar, Jacob in Aram, and Joseph in Egypt prefigure the journey of Israel to Egypt and from Egypt to Canaan. The people of the covenant are continually threatened by the lust of foreign peoples for power and sexual favors and worship of their gods. Israel is always a potential, and sometimes an actual victim of foreigners, although she is temporarily overcome only when she disobeys and turns away from the covenant in order to seek the favor of other gods. However, when Israel returns to her God he rescues and spares her life once more. Israel's existence is assured if she is faithful to the covenant, which involves affirmation and realization of loyalty to the God who leads her, a loyalty that requires proper maintenance of the Torah and the sacrificial cult.

The Torah keeps social conflict and alienation from God to a minimum by offering a voice of authority "in place of God," that is, the divine words spoken and written that the entire community is supposed to know. These words that establish boundaries of acting and relating do not come from any human source (even if Moses is the mediator) or special interest in the community. They apply to all and bind all equally.

If Torah is the word, the reaching out of God to people, then sacrifice is the reaching out of the people to God through the gifts and animal victims that are offered. Sacrifice attests that life belongs to God and so is sacred; thus plants and animals are off limits for human use unless they are redeemed. The blood of animals cannot be eaten nor the blood of humans taken in murder. Life is in the blood, thus taboo to human consumption. This taboo applies to anything living or growing unless it is redeemed.

All forms of life are sacred in that they are reserved for God, their giver and owner. The human community, of which Israel is to be the model, must therefore redeem the life that it obtains. Just as it is necessary to take life in order to live, it is also necessary to give over life in order to live. This "giving over" is brought to its sharpest cultic expression in the interdiction of blood and the offering of the first fruits and the firstborn. These basic patterns of the sacrificial cult are closely related to God's design in eliminating the firstborn son from the inheritance of the promises to Abraham. Ishmael is blessed and becomes the ancestor of many peoples, but he cannot inherit the promises made to Abraham and so cannot be one of God's special chosen ones. Esau's descendants are closely related to the Israelites in that he is the brother of Jacob, but it is Jacob that the God of Abraham chooses to become the recipient of the special blessing. This pattern of the younger son as divinely favored continues in the stories of Joseph and his brothers, Ephraim and Manasseh, Moses and Aaron, Nadab and Abihu, and David and his brothers. It is implied in the story of Samuel, in that the narrative tells of sons and daughters born to Peninnah before Hannah, Samuel's mother, gave birth to Samuel. These stories of the older son or sons who are brothers of Israel's ancestors must have posed a problem for the necessity of exclusion of the foreigner in the sacrificial cult.[2] Deuteronomy 23 represents the compromise of provisional exclusion of the Edomites, who are descendants of Esau according to Israelite tradition, but in the third generation they, with the Egyptians, may be included: "The children of the third generation that are born to them may enter the assembly of the LORD" (Deut 23:8).

The only exception to this pattern of the dominance of the younger son is the story of Cain and Abel. However, God did favor the offering of Abel, so the exception stems from Cain's slaying of his brother. The story evidently discloses that from the beginnings of humankind and civilization human beings have lived in a state of sin, and this sin inevitably results in violence.

2 See Chidester, "Rituals of Exclusion," 681–702.

Since the oldest son normally received the "birthright" and a greater share of the family inheritance, the status of the youngest son must attest to something distinctive in the revelation of God's historical design. In order to overcome the original violence of Cain, some sort of counter-violence is required. The displacement of the firstborn son in the biblical stories is relatively nonviolent by comparison to the offering of an animal victim in the sacrificial cult or the destruction of the enemy in holy war, but all of these phenomena belong to the divine plan whereby significant change and transformation comes about through the surrender of life to God. The logic of this divine plan entails that the threats to Israel from other nations, starting with the ancient oppression in Egypt and continuing through the Babylonian exile and beyond, is part of the sacrificial pattern. I will return to this shortly.

The younger son or brother also, in his turn, becomes a kind of sacrificial victim. In fact, the threats to his existence are more serious and graphic than the ordeals of the older brother. Abraham binds Isaac and places him on the altar in readiness for sacrifice. Jacob is attacked by a divine adversary and injured. Joseph is cast into a pit and sold into slavery, taken to Egypt, and then imprisoned. YHWH attacks Moses in the Sinai wilderness. The truth that these stories represent is that the chosen one, whether an individual or the people, must always undergo an ordeal for the sake of God's mission in the world. Just as the older brother is displaced by the younger brother, so the Israel of the present must be a sacrifice for the Israel and the new world of the future. In the history and tradition of the covenant people, the "older"—whether it be older brother or father or institutions and leaders—cannot be idolized. God liberates his people from human conventions and authorities that they may worship and obey only him.

The logic of this plan of salvation history is likewise that the powerful nations of the world cannot permanently subjugate those whom the Almighty calls to himself and forms for his own. This means that those nations that defeat and subjugate Israel are simply unknowing agents of the transformational process by which God moves history. Israel as chosen is a kind of offering or holocaust to God.

In this sacrificial reading of the biblical tradition, the greater part of the pattern of the chosen one and the chosen people applies to the New Testament writings about the Christ—the difference being that a single figure dominates religious consciousness so that the covenant people of God, the church, while extremely important, is always in principle subordinate to the messianic savior. The Christ may be seen as the firstborn or older brother as Paul states it in Romans, or as the younger, favored son as his relation to John the Baptist intimates in the synoptic Gospels. The Gospel of John radicalizes this relationship in relating that the Baptist witnesses to Jesus as the Lamb of God, an image of the redemptive victim that is reminiscent of the "lamb for a burnt offering" in Gen 22:7–8. The Letter to the Hebrews presents the Christ as simultaneously high priest and sacrificial victim, and the Apocalypse dramatically depicts Jesus as both the Commander of God's armies in the final wars against Satan and the Lamb of God. In other words, from the Christian point of view Jesus as the Christ is the embodiment of the new Israel, the new chosen one and the supreme sacrificial victim in whose transformative work the new Israel, the church, participates and by which it understands its suffering. The church as the Body of Christ is persecuted in the present but will prevail in the end as God brings to consummation his plan of salvation.

Whether one belongs to Israel or the Church, one is called to be constrained by the instruction that God gives his people in order to maintain good order and to love one's neighbor. God's intention is to establish peace, to create harmony out of a world that may seem to be entrapped in chaos and violence. It is unfortunately necessary that those who are given to know the revelation of God must take sides, they must commit themselves zealously to the cause of God, which is simultaneously the cause of his people. As it is inevitable that the favored one undergo an ordeal, so also there will necessarily be a cataclysmic war of judgment before the foes of God are defeated. It is not without reason, in this context, that the psalmist calls on the Lord to pour out his anger on the nations (Ps 79:6), for his "day of wrath" will consume the earth (Zeph 1:14–18), leading to the ultimate transformation of the world. The Apocalypse envisions the Lamb, the Word of God, on a white horse and commanding his armies. And from the great battle that leads to the binding of Satan for one thousand years the birds of the air will feast on the flesh of the dead, "the flesh of horses and their riders—flesh of all, both free and slave, both small and great" (Rev 19:18).

In sum, as it has taken form since the original transgression of Adam and the violent deed of Cain, human history is inevitably permeated with conflict and violence. Even though the consciences and deeds of God's people are to be constituted by love and justice both in this age within covenant community and in the age to come when God will reestablish his creation, it is not possible to accomplish anything in the present world that is health-giving and redemptive short of sacrifice. And the sacrifice required may entail violence. But the violence, whether it be an animal victim offered at the altar, an injury or loss of life through some ordeal, or military battle, is in principle an event which cannot be avoided if a greater good is to be brought about. Thus violence may be righteous if God ordains it in order to redeem the people of God, bring about peace, and destroy idolatry.[3]

2. A Nonsacrificial Reading of the Biblical Tradition

A nonsacrificial reading of the biblical tradition will take into account the same basic patterns that are the basis of a sacrificial reading. However, the

---

3 See chapter 8 of Jewett, *The Captain America Complex.*

starting point of this non-sacrificial reading involves focusing on what is *different* in the biblical tradition; it highlights the *exceptional* that emerges from the common patterns. The necessity of violence and sacrifice, the inevitability of the ordeal of the hero, and the centrality of the divinely favored people in the order of things are universally known and always lead to the same conflict: my/our side versus your side, my/our claims versus your claims, my/our desires versus your desires. Both the devotion of the Canaanites to destruction and the execution of Achan and his family (Joshua 1–7) are presented as necessary and divinely validated due to the rules of holy war, which had been mandated by the God of Israel. Likewise the slaying of those Israelites crying out for meat (Numbers 11) was justified because they lacked trust in God and were fomenting disorder. The point concerning these incidents is that the symbolic order is not questioned and the victim is either the foreigner or the Israelite who has betrayed his own sacred order and therefore deserves the punishment of ultimate exclusion.

A nonsacrificial reading emphasizes the *questioning* of these themes in another dimension of the biblical tradition, which is indeed intertwined with the more common and universal dimension of sacrificial religion and culture. A nonsacrificial reading will point out the extraordinary thing about the Cain and Abel story is not the fratricidal violence. Violence is common in myths of origins, and *enemy brothers* is a pervasive mythical theme.[4] Indeed, as René Girard has pointed out, all three moments or stages of the victimage mechanism in the origin of primitive religion and culture are found in the Books of Moses:

1. Dissolution in conflict, removal of the differences and hierarchies which constitute the community in its wholeness;
2. the *all against one* of collective violence;
3. the development of interdiction and rituals.[5]

Clear signs of the first moment, dissolution in conflict, may be found in the *tohu vavohu* or chaos of the beginning of Genesis, and it is quite clear in the events leading up to the Flood as well as the confusion of the Tower of Babel, the corruption of Sodom and Gomorrah, the hostility of the other sons of Jacob for Joseph, the ten plagues of Egypt, and the rebellions in the Sinai wilderness.

The all against one of collective violence is obvious in the story of Joseph and the Israelites in Egypt. These founding stories end characteristically with an expulsion: Jacob flees to Aram, Joseph is taken to Egypt, Moses has to run away from the king of Egypt (and is later attacked by YHWH). Israel's exodus

4 Girard, *Violence and the Sacred*, 61–63.
5 Girard, *Things Hidden*, 142.

from Egypt is in fact an expulsion, although the narrative presents it as an action commanded by God (Exod 12:29–32). The Garden of Eden tale results in the expulsion of Adam and Eve, but here we see a difference from the ordinary founding myth: "God takes the violence upon himself and founds humanity by driving Adam and Eve far away from him."[6] Likewise different, though very ambiguous, is the struggle of Jacob with the adversary at the Jabbok. It is ambiguous in that it conforms, in one regard, to the ordinary mythic pattern: The adversary, called initially a *man*, is defeated and must leave, and then Jacob refers to him as *God*. In other words, at the formal level this follows the ritual pattern of expulsion of the victim who is then deified. But as the *double* of Jacob that is defeated, the adversary's expulsion does not involve violence upon the community, and the only loss for Jacob is the injury to his thigh (or genitals?). It may well be that an older expulsion story stands somewhere behind the present text, but has been reworked in light of the dawning insight of the Israelite narrators. In other words, even in most of these mythical, sacrificial tales there are elements modifying if not contradicting the element of founding violence. This will be taken up shortly.

But before coming to that let us look at the third moment, the development of interdictions and ritual. The priestly institution of circumcision in Genesis 17 appears to be an interpretation overlying, rationalizing, and to some extent concealing what lies behind it, namely the offering of a victim such as we find in Genesis 22, the Binding of Isaac. The celebration of Passover is connected with the death of the firstborn of Egypt and the slaying of the paschal lamb, which is, in the logic of sacrifice, offered in place of the people themselves. And in the midst of the cultic laws given in the wilderness the oldest two sons of Aaron are mysteriously slain (Lev 10:1–3), an event referred to in the narration of the law of the scapegoat (Leviticus 16). In fact, there is a certain symmetry between the two priests that are "consumed" by the fire and the two goats of sacrifice, one of which is offered on the altar as a sin-offering and the other is sent out into the wilderness to Azazel (see further below).

But again, there are aspects of these interdictions and rituals that modify the usual form of such phenomena. In the Binding of Isaac a ram is offered as a substitute victim. Generations of Jewish interpreters have understood this as an implied prohibition of child sacrifice. In the story of the plagues and Passover the slaying of the Egyptians is confined to the *firstborn*. It is true that the tale of the crossing of the Sea of Reeds has the Egyptians, including the king, engulfed by the waters—the very waters of chaos, the *tehom* (Exod 15:8), that Egypt itself represents. However, the text does not present this destruction as due to the desire of God or Israel for revenge; it occurs rather because the king, once more reneging on his promise to let the Hebrews go, pursues them with his forces.

6 Girard, *Things Hidden*, 142.

As for Leviticus 10, it may partially conceal a founding murder. Notice what Moses says to Aaron after Nadab and Abihu offer an "alien fire" before the Lord and a fire comes from the Lord to devour them:

This is what YHWH spoke: "I will prove myself holy among those near me, and before all the people I will be glorified." (Lev 10:3, AT)

We see here a sequence of death of the two priests and exaltation of God. Behind this sequence may lie the founding murder pattern in which the victim is deified. Here, however, it is concealed and rationalized in terms of the enigmatic guilt of the brothers. The ritual of the two goats in Leviticus 16 then becomes a substitute action whose repetition is to prevent the same thing from happening to the community ever again.

Such glimmers of a movement away from the older and universal mythical pattern begin to come into focus more clearly in the Flood story and the priestly account of creation. In the story of Noah and the great inundation the covenant after the flood is based on God's promise never again to destroy the earth. For the priestly account the covenant with Noah incorporates the prohibition of eating animal blood and shedding human blood. This priestly tradition in Genesis 9 presupposes that in the original state of things human beings were vegetarians (Gen 9:3). The divine covenant stands as a promise and a law that concedes the existence of violence but prohibits its radical expression among human beings. The interdiction of blood is a continual reminder of God's original intention for creation.

And concerning the creation of the world, the priestly account of creation, Genesis 1, relates a founding of the world and humankind in the beginning that takes place without victimage. The priestly story of beginnings in Gen 1–2:4a continues with the genealogy of the descendants of Adam in Genesis 5, and there again no trace of violence is indicated. Cain and Abel are not even acknowledged, as Seth is named as the only son of Adam. The narrative evidently wants us to understand that Seth continues to bear the image of God like his father (Gen 5:3), so the image of God has not been effaced by violence and murder. This point of view makes it difficult to explain why God sent the Flood. The priestly beginning of the Flood account gives only a general and vague comment that the earth was corrupt and filled with violence (Gen 6:11). What we find in chapters one and five of Genesis is very enigmatic by comparison to the Yahwist narrator's specific indication of the confusion and wickedness that emerged from the mating of divine beings with human women (Gen 6:1–8).

These modifications of the victimage mechanism that is found universally in myth and ritual are testimony to the distinctive insights of the *revelation* given to Israel and the church. For a nonsacrificial reading of the biblical tradition this revelation is brought to expression in a number of distinctive stories. To start with the tale of Cain and Abel, it could of course be cited as a typical example of the founding murder. To do that, however, would be to miss the essential fact that *the founding figure who commits the crime is condemned in the narrative* and, even more importantly, *the person slain is innocent.* The voice of God in the narrative condemns Cain for his crime. Cain, the first builder of a city, has desired God's favor, which means he has desired what Abel has: success before God. In his anger and depression—"So Cain was very angry and his countenance fell" / Genesis 4:5(1)—he murders his brother.[7] Cain is marked with a sign that simultaneously protects him and serves as a reminder of the crime. Language as well as "civilization" (which means the state or condition of city existence) begins with Cain. Girard remarks, "I see in this the establishment of a differential system, which serves, as always, to discourage mimetic rivalry and generalized conflict."[8] The attempt to discourage mimetic rivalry and generalized conflict is always present in the institution of sacrifice, and in the legal system in more advanced cultures. What makes the biblical account of the origin of civilization so distinctive is that the founding violence is not concealed or justified, as for example in the comparable myth of Romulus and Remus. Romulus' slaying of his brother Remus is not condemned, and in one version given by Livy it is justified by the latter's refusal to respect the boundary marking the inside and outside of the city. As Girard observes, Cain is, by contrast, presented as a "vulgar murderer," even if his deeds as a founding figure are similar to those of Romulus.[9]

It is in the Joseph story that both the collective character of persecution and the countering of the victimary mechanism become visible. As Girard says,

> From the mythological perspective, the eleven brothers would appear first of all as the passive objects of the violence inflicted by a malevolent hero, then as the recipients of the benefits conferred by this same hero after he has been victimized and deified.[10]

However, there are three ways in which the Joseph story is different from the mythological perspective. First, we must take into account that Genesis 37 in its present form definitely holds the brothers to blame, with a partial exemption of Reuben and Judah. Later, when Joseph is taken into the house of Potiphar, who becomes like a father to him, we see that the wife's accusation of rape against Joseph, comparable in this case to incest, is false. In other

---

7 See Bailie, "Sacrificial Violence in Homer's *Iliad*," in *Curing Violence.*
8 Girard, *Things Hidden*, 146.
9 Girard, *Things Hidden*, 147.
10 Girard, *Things Hidden*, 151–152.

words, the story rehabilitates the victim rather than confirming the charges as in mythical conventions.

Second, when Joseph uses trickery to accuse and arrest his younger brother Benjamin, Judah offers himself in place of the lad, stating in a moving speech that he pledged himself to Jacob for the boy's safety and could not "see the suffering that would come upon my father" (Gen 44:34). The willingness to become a victim as a necessary act in order to achieve the welfare of the community is quite different from the all against one of collective violence and the scapegoating mechanism. In some respects it anticipates the Suffering Servant of Second Isaiah and Jesus as the crucified in the Gospels.

Third and finally, Joseph attempts to nullify the deification process. He forgives his brothers, affirming instead God's hidden design, and attempts to reunify the family by demanding that the brothers bring Jacob and the rest of the clan to Egypt (Gen 45:1–15). Later, after Jacob's death, the brothers fear that Joseph will requite them for earlier deeds. Will the cycle of mimetic rivalry and vengeance continue? They present themselves to him and fall prostrate before him. In a revealing word of reassurance Joseph says,

> "Fear not! *For am I in the place of God?* But as for you, you meant evil against me, but God meant it for good, in order to bring about the preserving of a great people, as it is this day." (Gen 50:19–20, AT)

Joseph's denial that he is in the place of God breaks, in principle, the victimary mechanism. The victim is now not the *sacrifice*, the one made sacred, but their brother—powerful indeed, but not a god. As such, as the brother whose dreams have come true, "he reassured them, speaking kindly to them" (Gen 50:21).

This revelatory, iconoclastic point of view of the Joseph story is related to what I would call the "prophetic" dimension of ancient Israelite religion and culture. I am not contending that these disclosures of the scapegoat mechanism and the attempt to counter it in the Torah all stem from the influence of the great prophets. Rather, from early on in the Israelite tradition there was a nonsacrificial element of faith and vision, a faith and a vision which comes to powerful articulation in prophets like Amos, Hosea, Micah, Isaiah, Jeremiah, and the Second Isaiah.

One can discern this nonsacrificial element in dialectical struggle with mimetic desire, rivalry, sacrifice, and violence within the cult, which I will briefly discuss first before turning to the prophets. It is as though the sacrificial foundations and associations of the cultic institutions were too powerful to be completely dissolved, but they were nonetheless greatly modified. In an illuminating essay, "The Sons of Aaron: The Development of the Scapegoat Ritual in Israel," Gil Bailie has described this process of modification in Exodus and Leviticus. At the conclusion of a survey of the Plague and Passover stories he cites the divine command to redeem the firstborn sons with an animal (Exod 13:13). Noting that this animal sacrifice is presented against the backdrop of human sacrifice, he concludes, "So what the 'passover' is commemorating is the first recorded attempt to launch a cultural enterprise while consciously trying to avoid a founding murder."[11] Of course, the substitute of an animal only defers or—historically—tends to repress the consciousness of the generative sacrificial mechanism, which is not eliminated. This is an ongoing problem. Although avoidance of human victimage is achieved by the use of the animal surrogate, there is still a routinization and institutionalization of violence through the sacrificial mechanism. The prophets would address this problem with radical spiritual insight.

In his further remarks on the texts of Exodus and Leviticus, Bailie clearly recognizes the achievement of Israel's sacrificial cult and its ambiguity concerning the sacrificial mechanism. He notes, concerning Exodus 32, "the candor of the text . . . about the *failure* of the Mosaic attempt" to establish the high ethical demands of Torah and covenant.[12] Indeed, "while the formal institutionalization of the sacrificial cult is found [in Leviticus], this text [Exodus 32] locates its true genesis at the moment of the slaughter of the three thousand."[13] Instead of the usual all against one of collective violence, this episode took the form of the tribe of Levi against "them" who worshiped the calf. As Stuart Lasine points out in this volume, the Levites' act of killing other tribal members is a *sacrifice*, not a just punishment of the guilty.[14] If it were the latter, then why the slaying of only three thousand? Then with the giving of the substitute code (Exodus 34) in place of the ethically oriented decalogue (Exodus 20), Bailie writes that "the biblical exodus ends not with a bang but a whimper: the victory of the sacrificial cult over the Mosaic spirit."[15]

11   Bailie, "Sons of Aaron." It is important for a comparative study of mythology and sacrificial mechanisms to raise the question of an "Egyptian" point of view on Moses and the exodus. In fact, in the Hellenistic period there were Egyptian writers, most notably Manetho and Apion, who did present an Egyptian point of view on Moses and the exodus. From their standpoint the "exodus" is an "expulsion" of a diseased people, in some cases viewed as Egyptians, in other instances said to be aliens; they were the cause of a crisis of some sort (the accounts vary) and were led, according to Manetho, by a renegade Egyptian priest. The texts, which are derived primarily from *Against Apion* by Josephus, are gathered together in Menahem Stern, ed., *Greek and Latin Authors on Jews and Judaism*, 3 vols. This Egyptian perspective basically follows the structure of the Oedipus myth: a crippled or handicapped stranger enters the community during a time of plague and is accused of heinous crimes which have brought about the plague due to divine anger; he is expelled or executed and the ills of the community disappear. See chapter 3 of Williams, *The Bible, Violence, and the Sacred.*
12   Bailie, "Sons of Aaron."
13   Bailie, "Sons of Aaron."
14   Stuart Lasine, "Levite Violence, Fratricide, and Sacrifice in the Bible and Later Revolutionary Rhetoric," in *Curing Violence.*
15   Bailie, "Sons of Aaron."

Bailie then shows that a series of substitutions take place whose purpose is evidently the attempt to repeat or represent the generative event without taking human life in the cult. First was the substitution of an animal for the human firstborn, then the redemption of the firstborn by the Levites in that they stand before the altar in place of all the firstborn of Israel (see Num 3:11–13, 41, 45; 8:16–19 and the essay in this volume by Lasine)—though an animal will actually die in place of the Levite. But there is a primitive "cathartic potential" to the ritual whereby the animal victim dies and the God makes his presence known. We see this, for instance, in Lev 9:22–24:

> Aaron lifted his hands toward the people and blessed them; and he came down after sacrificing the sin offering, the burnt offering, and the offering of well-being. Moses and Aaron entered the tent of meeting; and then came out and blessed the people; and the glory of the LORD appeared to all the people. Fire came out from the LORD and consumed the burnt offering and the fat on the altar; and when all the people saw it, they shouted, and fell on their faces.

The formal elements of the purification of the community in the primitive setting are still quite visible here. (1) The sacrificial victim is offered, in this case a number of animals (Lev 9:3–4). (2) The deity, which at an earlier stage was the apotheosized victim, appears in "glory" or "honor" (*kavod*) and is associated with the fire from the altar. It is likely that one of the really archaic elements of the ritual is represented in the fire: the death of the victim produces the effective presence of the life-giving god. (3) The community is united in the thrill of unanimity produced by the succession of death of the victim and the flaring up of the fire ("they shouted and fell upon their faces").

There is a chronic danger that the repetition of the generative act will overflow its routinized channel. In a narrative that immediately follows Lev 9:22–24, this is exactly what happens in the strange execution of Nadab and Abihu, whose culpability is given only the vaguest explanation in the text (Lev 10:1–2). In this instance a fire comes from YHWH and consumes the two priests rather than animal offerings. To look at it from another angle, it is as though *Nadab and Abihu themselves* are the offerings. *No satisfying reason* is given for their death. (Their offering of "unholy" or "alien fire" reads like a vague rationalization.) One may well suspect that the primitive power of the act of sacrifice reasserts itself in communal violence. It is interesting to observe also, as already indicated, that they were evidently the two older sons of Aaron. The text of Leviticus probably expresses a tradition of the cult that maintains a symmetry of sacrifice of the firstborn and the death of these priests. The cultic tradition, while maintaining its sacrificial base and structure, still loosens it somewhat by using the old sacrificial correlation of firstborn=best as well as symbolic of the whole in order to provide an opening for protesting or revoking the power of older traditions and authorities, which is certainly one of the effects of the various brother stories of Scripture. There is an ambiguity in this, for while the tradition maintains, if opaquely, the generative act of eliminating the victim, it probably also reflects a tendency to side with the younger and weaker.

In the event, the death of the two sons of Aaron is explicitly connected with the slaughter of the two goats and the scapegoat ritual in Leviticus 16, as already indicated. Bailie infers from the text that

> the people who established this ritual actually knew what they were doing! This is both remarkable and foreboding. It is foreboding because this ritual cannot fully operate when those who seek its benefits actually know what they are doing. . . . And so once again we are drawn into the Israelite double-bind.[16]

Bailie points out that the uniqueness of the Hebrew Scriptures is twofold: (1) The cultural formation of the Israelites shows a "decisive effort to avoid human victimage," one that failed over and over again, but which is "historically of supreme importance." (2) In spite of these failures, the pertinent texts "have somehow managed to largely resist the undoubted efforts made by their transmitters and defenders to camouflage and mythologize these failures."[17] Bailie's point about the ability of these texts to resist camouflage and mythologization is evidently closely related to Lasine's conclusion about the rhetoric of the biblical narrators who addressed an audience they assumed to be *related* to the Levites and other biblical personages. Lasine points out that

> this aspect of biblical rhetoric acts as an oblique way of leading readers to acknowledge their own potential to act as scapegoaters. In this sense biblical rhetoric transcends the tendency to scapegoat those we regard as scapegoaters.[18]

This uniqueness of the revelation struggling to make itself known in the cultic texts reaches a new stage of clarity with the great prophets. It may be argued that primitive religion rests on three pillars: mythology, the sacrificial cult, and prohibitions.[19] Mythology could be viewed as the primary narrative and symbolic expression that justified both sacrifice and the obsession with differentiation that lies behind a primitive form of law. If that is so, then the great prophets subverted the primitive, universal foundations of religion and culture that continued to determine Israelite institutions.

Amos (prophesied ca.760–750 B.C.E.) proclaims God's judgment on Israel, but this judgment of military defeat and exile is something Israel brings upon

---

16 Bailie, "Sons of Aaron."
17 Bailie, "Sons of Aaron."
18 Lasine, "Moses."
19 Girard, *Things Hidden*, 154–155.

itself, for Israel *misunderstands its very beginnings.* "Did you bring to me sacrifices and offerings the forty years in the wilderness, O house of Israel?" (Amos 5:25). This rhetorical question concludes a well known oracle in which YHWH says, "I hate, I despise your festivals," spurning the outpourings from the sacrificial cult (5:21–24). It was not, implies Amos, God's command to offer sacrifices in the wilderness. This is a remarkable insight. Amos is the first prophet or spokesperson of any sort in the Scriptural texts who so unambiguously asserts this, although other prophets will reject sacrifice, and one, Ezekiel, sees the sacrificial cult in the wilderness as a kind of punishment of Israel (see below).

What was Israel supposed to do from the beginning? How was it to be constituted? Amos is not too specific about that, although clearly from his standpoint it would have to do with letting "justice roll down like waters, and righteousness like an everflowing stream" (5:24). That is, the constitution of Israel has to do with concern for the victim. Not selling "the righteous for silver, and the needy for a pair of sandals" (2:6), avoiding indiscriminate licentious sex at the cultic shrine, and not drinking in a cultic sanctuary the wine of those who had been taxed or fined—here we see moral and cultic concerns brought together in a vision of justice. Yes, Israel is exceptional among the peoples (3:1–2), but not so exceptional that it can pretend to be the only people that God has cared for and guided to a land of its own (9:7).

It is no wonder then that the high priest expels Amos from the royal sanctuary of Bethel! Even if Amaziah had agreed with Amos' moral concerns and advocated reform, he quite rightly senses that Amos' message subverted the foundations of prevailing Israelite social order. Charity and purification of the cult were not enough for Amos. Israel's very foundations had been misunderstood.

Hosea (prophesied ca.740–720 B.C.E.) implies that Israel was not constituted as a sacrificial cult in the beginning, for in his visions of the renewed "marriage" of YHWH and Israel the relationship will be a tender one of covenant love "as in the days of her youth" (Hos 2:15). This renewed "bride of YHWH" will not have king or sacrificial cult (3:4). Meanwhile, the present judgment on Israel comes on account of its fundamental misunderstanding, its gross lack of "knowledge:"

> For I desire steadfast love and not sacrifice,
> the knowledge of God rather than burnt offerings. (6:6)

Hosea is somewhat clearer than Amos about the mimetic process. Israel goes after her lovers (2:5), the other gods, in imitation of the indigenous cults. The formation of desire by imitation, if its object is a source or authority that represents domination and power, involves yearning to *acquire* the object of the desire imitated. The lack of the knowledge that is the basis of Israel's existence (4:6) results in the absence of faithfulness, kindness, and knowledge of God (4:1–3). The people's "spirit of whoredom" (4:12), a key notion for Hosea, moves them continually to seek satisfaction in the *other* powers, those gods and their rituals who seem not only to promise pleasure and plenty but also, and more fundamentally, an explanation and expiation of sin, guilt, and the ills befalling the human community through an outpouring of sacrifices. "They sacrifice on the tops of the mountains, and make offerings upon the hills" (4:13)—sacrifice after sacrifice.

It is therefore not without accident in Hosea that the divine lament, "I desire steadfast love and not sacrifice," is juxtaposed to God's judgment (6:5) directed against those who have transgressed the covenant and are implicated in murder, robbery, and idolatry (6:8–10).

Since the prophet perceives that desire is formed by imitation, he intuits also that it may be *re-formed* by the mimetic process. Thus his act of purchasing or redeeming an adulterous woman (perhaps Gomer, who had been his wife) and keeping her under a kind of restriction or corrective punishment until the time when the two could be truly husband and wife (3:1–3). So also Israel will be under discipline "without king or prince, without sacrifice or pillar, without ephod or teraphim" until they return to the LORD (3:4–5).

In order to understand Hosea's mimetic act it is necessary to observe that the prophets were performers who dramatically verbalized and enacted their understanding of Israel's situation in order to bring the latter to the point of understanding and transformation. Amos delivers oracles suggested by a plumb line for a wall and a basket of summer fruit (Amos 7:7–9; 8:1–3). Jeremiah refers to a potter's broken vessels and two baskets of figs (Jer 18:1–11; 24). Isaiah and Hosea gave their children's names which were signs of God's judgment (Isa 7:3; 8:1–4; Hos 1). As for dramatic enactments, Hosea married "a wife of whoredom" (Hos 1:2), Isaiah "walked naked and barefoot for three years" (Isa 20:3), Jeremiah buried a loincloth, wore yoke-bars, purchased property, and invited the Rechabites to drink wine (Jer 13:1–11; 28; 32:6–15; 35), and Ezekiel swallowed a scroll, lay bound on his left side and then on his right side, and shaved his hair (Ezek 2:8–3:3; 4:1–5:12)—all as dramatic representations of Israel's situation. Usually the mimesis has to do with God's judgment on Israel, but in some instances it has to do with the promise of Israel's renewal, as in Hosea 3, where the viewers, hearers, or readers are invited to identify with the adulteress who becomes a faithful wife, or in Jeremiah 32, where the prophet's purchase of property is an invitation to live in hope and look to the future in spite of the devastation of exile.

In this volume Theophus Smith comments on the role of black preachers and orators as agents of community therapy through mimesis ("King and the Black Relgious Quest to Cure Racism"). Since ethnic conflict and violence usually originate outside of African-American communities, speakers not only engage in the "cure of souls" within the given congregation or community, but in some instances heed a calling to turn to the larger social order. Such figures, among whom Martin Luther King, Jr. is a preeminent example, appeal to and dramatically represent biblical patterns, particularly the pattern of the Christ in his suffering and transcendence of suffering. Although Israel's prophets are in some respects very different from the African-American Christian patterns of "good" or "healing" mimesis, still the African-American tradition of proclamation and representation stands basically in the prophetic tradition. The object of the good mimesis is to invite the victimizer to identify with the victim and thus be changed from oppressor to neighbor or brother or sister.

In Isaiah (prophesied ca. 745–700 B.C.E.) the connection of sacrifice and violence is made even more explictly than in Hosea and Amos. Although Isaiah's understanding of Israel's origins is a puzzle in some respects, he refers to the once faithful Jerusalem (Isa 1:21), evidently meaning the time of the judges (1:26), and in oracles of judgment he recalls events associated with Joshua and David (28:21; 29:1). His vision of the new age includes a new Davidic king (9:1–7; 11:1–8), but there is no clear evidence that he knew or appealed to the Exodus-Sinai tradition.[20] Likewise unclear is his view of how the sacrificial cult began. None the less he condemns it in no uncertain terms. Those who bring "vain offerings," who think YHWH delights "in the blood of bulls," have hands "full of blood." This image, whether hyperbole or not, pictures mass violence and murder. The prophetic alternative is an ethical exhortation given in a staccato series of brief imperatives:

> Wash, clean up, remove the evil of your deeds
> from before my eyes;
> cease to do evil, learn to do good,
> seek justice, correct oppression,
> defend the fatherless, dispute for the widow. (1:16–17, AT)

Torah, which for Isaiah is synonymous with the word of YHWH (1:10), does not make victims in cult offerings or in any sort of violence. Rather, it draws all the peoples to it in peace:

> They shall beat their swords into plowshares,
> and their spears into pruning hooks;
> nation shall not lift up sword against nation,
> neither shall they learn war anymore. (2:4)

This vision of the new age mentions "the house of the God of Jacob" (2:3), undoubtedly a reference to the Temple, but quite strikingly there is no mention at all of a reconstituted sacrificial cult.

In general, Micah's prophetic message (ca. 730–700 B.C.E.) is very similar to that of these other prophets, particularly his fellow Judeans Amos and Isaiah.

---

20 von Rad, *Old Testament Theology*, 1: 174–175.

·

He cries out against those who force the old free peasantry off the land and acquire enormous land holdings (Mic 2:1–4), much like Amos and Isaiah. A key passage in Micah is 6:6–8, often considered an addition to the Micah scroll stemming from the sort of postexilic piety that is expressed also in Psalm 51. A case made for this position would support the nonsacrificial reading of the Scriptures as evidence of part of a postexilic, antisacrificial perspective that stems in great part from the prophetic tradition. The second half of this passage reads:

> Shall I give my firstborn for my transgression,
> the fruit of my body for the sin of my soul?
> He has told you, O mortal, what is good;
> and what does the LORD require of you
> but to do justice, and to love kindness,
> and to walk humbly with your God? (6:7b-8)

It is quite striking that in this advanced perspective on the divine-human relationship and morality there is nonetheless a recollection of the archaic connection of the offering of the firstborn and transgression. Right relationship with God and reestablishment of order does not depend on eliminating the ills of the human community by killing the firstborn son for the sake of the family or community. It depends on the ancient covenant virtues of *mishpat* or justice and right judgment and *chesed* or steadfast love, the kindness one does for others who belong to the same community or family.

Jeremiah prophesied ca. 626–586 B.C.E. according to the editorial introduction of the Book of Jeremiah (1:1–3), although chapters 42 and 43 suggest his prophetic activity may have continued somewhat longer. He belonged to a family of priests in Anathoth (1:1), and many of the oracles in chapters 2–6 reflect the sort of priestly concern with pollution and cleanness that we find also in Ezekiel (see below). However, the evidence of the text indicates that Jeremiah's message became decidedly anticultic and antimonarchic. The composition of the book represents more than one tradition, including a redaction of the scroll by those whose point of view was determined by Deuteronomy and the Deuteronomic view of history evident in the final form of Judges through II Kings. In spite of the composite character of the book certain things about the prophet's life´ and message come through quite clearly.

Jeremiah is pictured as a prophet who attacked king and Temple. Jerusalemites believed the Temple would save them, but Jeremiah asserts it will not (Jer 7:3–4). Like Amos, Jeremiah holds that God did not require burnt offerings and sacrifice when he led the ancestors out of Egypt (7:22). The kingship, which Jeremiah evidently accepts as a historical given, does figure in some of his visions of a new age (23:5–6; 30:9), and it has to remain an open question as to whether the prophet finally reached the point where he could not see the kingship as part of God's intention for the future. In any event, the ethical imperative for Israelite kings is quite clear. At one point he compares Jehoiakim unfavorably to his father Josiah, and he asks,

> Did not your father eat and drink
> and do justice and righteousness?
> Then it was well with him.
> He judged the cause of the poor and needy;
>   then it was well.
> Is not this to know me?
>   says the LORD. (22:15–16)

"Is this not to know me?" in a very basic sense could be taken as the watchword of these great prophets. To know the God of Israel is to practice justice and righteousness, which means to help the poor and needy. *To know God is to know the cause of the victim.*

In the new age the Temple will not exist, the ark of the covenant will be no more (3:16). There will be a new covenant that is *different* from the one made with the fathers.

> I will put my law within them, and I will write it on their hearts; and I will be their God, and they shall be my people. No longer shall they teach one another, or say to each other, "Know the LORD," for they shall all know me, from the least of them to the greatest, says the LORD; for I will fogive their iniquity, and re-member their sin no more. (31:33b-34)

This is a remarkable vision of the dissolution of the sacrificial mechanism and the liberation from violence. In a new era that God will bring about, an era without sacrificial cult, mimetic rivalry will be broken once and for all. The nations of Israel and Judah, so long in conflict (one that would continue after the Exile in the political and religious battle between Samaria and Jerusalem), will be reunited (31:31). The great Torah, the divine law, which prohibits individual and clan vengeance, ascribing authority and the right to punish to God, whose power and authority is mediated through the leaders who ad-minister the legal structure of justice—this law will no longer be in the form of the divine command imposed by God.

The Torah of the Sinai covenant was unique, an attempt to abrogate the mythology of the god-victims who are placated and summoned in the sacri-ficial cult to restore the community. A system of law involves a qualitative leap from the primitive stage of the sacrificial cult, which maintains a certain control over individual violence by channelling the all against one of col-lective violence into a ritual that normally allows social relations to continue and cohere. However, even though law is a rationalization that weakens and distantiates the sacrificial mechanism, it does not eliminate it entirely. It presupposes that an external authority must hold desire in check, and although it controls individual and arbitrary violence, it rests on the principle that retribution is right and vengeance must be exacted. So it is that mimetic desire and rivalry are presupposed as the very basis of law, even though the sacrificial cult loses, in principle, its primitive power.

In the new covenant, however, this problem with the law is overcome, because it is no longer one that is given through the mediation of the prophet Moses within the context of a sacrificial cult that perpetuated many archaic elements of religion and culture. Rather, the law in the new covenant would be immediate, written on the heart. To use Paul Tillich's terms, it would be neither *heteronomous* in the sense of a "strange," externally imposed law, nor *autonomous* in the sense of a law of human origin, but *theonomous*: the law of God perfectly implanted and realized as the law of the people of God.[21] All mimetic rivalry would cease. One of the signs of the heteronomous character of law is the necessity not only of imposing and enforcing it but of having some people exhort others to obey it and to remember the authority behind the law. But now it will no longer be necessary for people to say to each other, "'Know the LORD,' for they shall all know me."

The only decisive step beyond Jeremiah among the great ancient Israelite prophets is Second Isaiah's vision of the Servant of YHWH. Before turning to that, however, let us take into account the noteworthy work of Ezekiel, a prophet whose thinking was, paradoxically, both reactionary and advanced among the great prophets.

Ezekiel, prophesying ca. 592 to 570 B.C.E. during the Babylonian exile, makes a statement about sacrifice which is simultaneously full of insight and permeated with a sense of dread concerning Israel's history. Ezekiel depicts the periods in Egypt and the wilderness as a sin-history, not a salvation-history. The dark side of this story reaches its fullest extent in the oracle that says,

> I gave them statutes that were not good and ordinances by which they could not live. I defiled them through their very gifts, in their offering up all their firstborn, in order that I might horrify them. (Ezek 20:25–26)

In the very beginnings of Israel, of which Ezekiel gives his own revised account as a history of rebellion, the sacrificial cult and the law were not good. That usually nonconscious and concealed aspect of the statutes and ordinances, which is connected to the ever-present threat of violence in the sacrificial mechanism, is here ascribed to the doing of the God of Israel. Ezekiel was a prophet who maintained and expressed a strong sense of cleanness and uncleanness and, in a priestly sense, the sacred and the profane. The book itself identifies him as a priest (1:3). As such, he attributes the ambiguity

---

21 Tillich, *Systematic Theology*, 1: 183–186. "Theonomy does not mean the acceptance of a divine law imposed on reason by a highest authority; it means autonomous reason united with its own depth" (185).

of the sacrificial mechanism to the God of Israel. Even the oracle promising a "new heart" and a "new spirit" (36:26), in some respects very reminiscent of Jeremiah, is permeated with the ambiguity of Ezekiel's cultic concerns. Israel in its present state of uncleanness, like "the uncleanness of a woman in her menstrual period" (36:17), will be restored to a state of cleanness (36:29). The people will then remember their deeds "that were not good"—a phrase reminiscent of the laws given by God in the wilderness that were "not good"; they will loathe themselves (36:31), and God will cleanse them.

Ezekiel's imagery of sexual lust and rivalry (chs. 16 and 23) reflects an intuition of mimetic desire and mimetic rivalry and his understanding of the original sacrificial cult reflects an intuition of the victimage required by sacrifice. In struggling with this he has little choice, given the priestly influence on his thinking, but to attribute the originating events to God. Nevertheless, he cannot accept the idea of divine approval of the sacrificial mechanism. He therefore conceives the cult as a necessary stage in a process of revelation, and as such its object is both punishment and instruction: " . . . that I might horrify them, so that they might know that I am the LORD" (20:26). In sum, as a prophet Ezekiel stands very close to the Priestly perspective of Leviticus that views human victimization as calamitous and does not try to conceal or mythologize Israel's failures, even if it cannot see its way clear to liberation from mimetic rivalry and the sacrificial mechanism.

The great prophet whose oracles, sayings, and poems are found in chapters 40–55 of the Book of Isaiah, and perhaps elsewhere in the book (e.g., ch. 61), is usually called Second Isaiah because of his place in the Isaiah scroll. He may well have been influenced by Isaiah, or was understood as a latter day follower of Isaiah. He clearly addressed himself to the exiles in Babylon, perhaps shortly before Cyrus' conquest of the city in 539 B.C.E. (Isa 44:28; 45:1), so his period of prophecy is usually given as ca. 545–540 B.C.E..

This prophet's message claims that Judah's exile was proclaimed in the past by YHWH's prophets (41:21–29; 44:6–8; passim). There will be a new exodus back to the homeland and a new world order. Babylonian Isaiah's utterances about God and his prophets form a kind of implied syllogism:[22] (1) The one true God can announce beforehand what he will bring about. (2) YHWH has done this through the prophets. (3) Therefore, YHWH is God.

> Who is like me? Let them proclaim it,
>   let them declare and set it forth before me
>   since I appointed an ancient people.
> And signs of things to come let them declare.
> Fear not, be not afraid;
>   have I not told you in past times and declared it?
> And you are my witnesses.

---

22   Blank, *Prophetic Faith in Isaiah*, 53–59.

> Is there a God besides me?
> There is no Rock; I know not any. (44:7–8, AT)

One of the most noted aspects of Second Isaiah's prophecies is his theme of the Servant of YHWH. Whatever his own understanding of the identity of this servant, in four poems or songs he is depicted as an individual (42:1–4; 49:1–6; 50:4–9; 52:13–53:12) who is a prophet. He is called to prophesy (42:1), YHWH's spirit is upon him (42:1), and his ear is "opened" by YHWH (50:5). His calling entails speaking God's word to Israel (49:1–3). He encounters great difficulty and persecution, but God will help him and vindicate him (50:6–9; 53). This picture of the prophet is replete with allusions to the prophetic tradition (Jeremiah, Moses, Isaiah, and Ezekiel).[23]

The most remarkable passage is the fourth Servant song, 52:13–53:12. This song or poem is a kind of antiphonal dialogue between the God of Israel and the people. God speaks in 52:13–15 and 53:11–12 and the people speak in 53:1–10. It is important to recognize this formal organization of the passage, as we shall see. The divine voice begins with an "I-they" statement: "my servant shall prosper" in the end in spite of "their" astonishment, for the servant bears the signs of the victim: "so marred was his appearance, beyond human semblance." The third person form in this opening stanza refers apparently to the foreign peoples and their leaders. It is possible that these foreigners are those speaking in 53:1–3 rather than Israel. However, this is uncertain, and since the collective voice of 53:4–6 is so obviously Israel's, I will assume that the same holds for vv. 1–3. I think 53:7–10 is also Israel speaking, but this will be taken up below.

The collective voice, which speaks in the grammatical form of "we-him," describes the servant as ugly from his youth and thus undesirable (v. 2). All were against him. "He was despised and rejected by others, a man of suffering and acquainted with infirmity," who was *persona non grata* because people "hide their faces" from him (v. 3). Verses 4–10 recount the servant's fate. First is the collective realization that he has borne the sins of the community (vv. 4–6), very much like the Greek *pharmakos*, as Girard has pointed out.[24] The *pharmakos* was a victim who was singled out, expelled from the community, and lynched. Oedipus in *Oedipus Rex* is a good classical example of the *pharmakos*.

Girard goes on to contend that a "spontaneous historical event" is being described, an event that has both a collective and legal character, which he discerns in the further reflections of the collective voice (verses 7–10).

> By a perversion of justice he was taken away.
> Who could imagine his future?

23 Williams, *Gospel Against Parable*, 151–152.
24 Girard, *Things Hidden*, 156.

> For he was cut off from the land of the living,
>   stricken for the transgression of my people.
>   They made his grave with the wicked
>   and tomb with the rich, his
>   although he had done no violence,
>   and there was no deceit in his mouth. (53:8–9)

It is not so clear to me that this is the spontaneous scapegoating of an individual that the poem relates, although it is possible. However, what we *do* know with certainty as historical facts are these: that thousands of Judeans had been taken into exile and that the earlier prophets of the exilic period, Jeremiah and Ezekiel, are presented as seeing themselves as suffering on behalf of their prophetic mission (Jer 11:18–23; 12:1–6; 16:1–13; 20:4–8; Ezek 3:24–4:17). Many biblical scholars and Jewish readers are inclined to hold that Second Isaiah here presents an image of Israel in the form of the Servant of the LORD and draws on the prophetic tradition for many specifics of this image. Girard is therefore right about the insight into the sacrificial mechanism that the poem expresses, but not necessarily correct in ascribing it to one specific event. Girard's comments about this in *Things Hidden* do not explicitly indicate that this spontaneous event was either contemporaneous with Second Isaiah or part of ancient Israel's history. Either would fit his theory, of course, but as a Christian reader he understands it as a prophecy, a prophetic vision or intimation of the future Christ-event. There is no reason, of course, why the Servant may not be construed both as an image of ideal Israel and as an anticipation of the Christ of the Gospels.

The mention of "my people" in v. 8 raises the question whether God's voice enters here or whether, perhaps, God is the speaker in all of vv. 7–10. The latter is possible, and would make a considerable difference in my interpretation of the passage. The objections to God as speaker are two. (1) The divine voice would be referring to himself in the third person in v. 10a ("it was the will of YHWH to crush him with pain"). (2) And in 10b the Hebrew text reads a second person singular: "when you make his life an offering for sin." Most translations follow the third person singular of the Vulgate, "when he offers his life." But if we stay with the Hebrew text, it appears to be the people persona speaking to the God persona.

In fact, inconsistency of pronoun usage and reference is quite in evidence in the Hebrew Bible, so one cannot use an occasional inconsistency as a warrant by itself. What I prefer to see in vv. 7–10 is the further statement by the people persona, which takes on a reflective, interpretive tone, particularly in vv. 9b-10 ("he had done no violence. . . . it was YHWH's will to afflict him"). The "my people" v. 8 could be a slip where the narrator allows his voice to come in. It is well known that one voice can allow, usually unintentionally, another voice to slip in, for example, the "Kohelet says" that interrupts the first person voice of

Kohelet in Eccl 7:27.[25] Moreover, "my people" was a common epithet not only in oracles presenting divine speech but in the repertory of phrases ascribed to the prophets themselves.

I would therefore read vv. 7–10 as the continuation of the collective voice, although in a different mode from vv. 4–6 (descriptive-reflective rather than primarily confessional). The importance of this for interpretation is that the inconsistency concerning divine agency in the Servant's suffering is not ascribed to the divine voice. In v. 4 the people avow, "We thought him stricken, smitten by God, and afflicted," and v. 10 says,

> "Yet it was the will of YHWH to bruise him;
>   he has made him sick.
> When you appoint him as an offering for sin,
>   he shall see his offspring, he shall prolong his
>   days. . . . (AT)

If v. 10 belongs to the people persona then there is an inconsistency in the *people's* apprehension of the sacrificial mechanism, an inconsistency of which the prophetic composer may be well aware. Just as the Yahwist cult tradition shows a certain awareness of victimage which it tries to mitigate while remaining rooted in cultic presuppositions; and just as Ezekiel uncovers the horror of sacrifice while feeling compelled to ascribe it somehow to God—so also the people's statement in Isaiah 53:1–10 reflects the tradition of ambiguous preservation of the sacrificial mechanism and perspective.

But it is a different matter with vv. 11 and 12:

> Out of his anguish he shall see light;
> he shall find satisfaction through his knowledge.
> The righteous one, my servant,
>   shall make many righteous,
>   and he shall bear their iniquities.
> Therefore I will allot him a portion with the great,
>   and he shall divide the spoil with the strong;
>   because he poured out himself to death,
>   and was numbered with the transgressors;
> Yet he bore the sin of many,
>   and made intercession for the transgressors.

"Because he poured out himself (his life—*nefesh*) to death": this is the key, as I construe the passage. The Servant willingly gave himself for his people. It was not God who caused his suffering, it was oppressors. As the divine voice says in an oracle found in ch. 54:

---

25 Fox, "Frame-Narrative," 83–84. "Ecclesiastes" is the standard English translation of "Kohelet" or "Qohelet" in Hebrew; it is based on the Greek and Latin title of the book.

> If any one stirs up strife,
> it is not from me;
> whoever stirs up strife with you
> shall fall because of you. (54:15)

"Strife"—the conflict of mimetic rivalry which results in violence—does not come from God. The two lines seem to indicate strife within the Israelite community (15a) and strife in the form of attacks upon Israel (15b). In my reading I see the Servant as the object of oppression resulting from this strife. He does not intend to become a "sacrifice," and God does not subject him to suffering, although the narrator perceives that the people continue in the ambiguity of the monotheistic tradition as rooted in the sacrificial cult.

This sense would fit Israel, ideally conceived as the covenant community producing the prophets and suffering for the sake of a new Israel and a new world of the future. The poem could also be a dramatic way of talking about Second Isaiah, some other contemporary figure, or someone in the future (the latter thus corresponding, at least in part, to the Christian tradition of interpretation).

In any case, if this reading is plausible it offers a further step in the disclosure and dismantling of the scapegoat mechanism. Jeremiah envisioned a new covenant and a new Torah that would be present and real in Israel apart from the sacrificial cult and the operation of retribution. Second Isaiah's fourth Servant Song, which is a dramatic representation of the Servant's healing suffering, discloses the power of the sacrificial mechanism in the scapegoat ritual; its foundation in contempt for the victim; its operation through oppression; the human predicament of those who have benefitted from the suffering of the scapegoat; and God's approval of the one who is not simply an arbitrarily chosen victim but who offers himself when necessary as part of his calling in order to overcome the strife and violence stemming from rivalry.

As for a nonsacrificial reading of the New Testament (see Mabee's essay in this volume), it would view the Christ as very much like the Suffering Servant of Second Isaiah. The early church, of course, began to construe the ministry, suffering, death, and resurrection of Jesus of Nazareth as a fulfillment of the Servant passages in Isaiah and references to a righteous sufferer in the Psalms, so of course the figures would be similar. Beyond that, the New Testament has extended narratives devoted to this central figure, who was given various titles besides prophet and servant of the LORD.

3. Sacrificial and Nonsacrificial Readings: A Brief Comparison

This essay does not pretend to encompass all types and variations of sacrificial and nonsacrificial approaches to Scripture, but I hope I have been generally fair and accurate in offering a sacrificial reading, even though it is quite clear that my sympathies lie with a nonsacrificial reading of Scripture. Perhaps the overlapping points of agreement in this brief comparison could become part of the basis of dialogue for biblical interpreters and theologians whose convictions and interpretive methods otherwise sharply differ. Note the following points of agreement:

3.1. The importance of sacrifice

Both readings largely agree on the importance of sacrifice—sacrificial institutions and rituals—in the biblical traditions. This agreement would also lead to a convergence of views on the importance of religion (however evaluated), not only in the biblical texts and history, but generally in human history up to the present in the Western world.

3.2. The importance of prophecy and apocalyptic in biblical interpretation and theology

I have not dealt with apocalyptic in this essay, and in some respects it is quite different from ancient Israelite prophecy, but the two share in general a dramatic vision of divine judgment and transformation of the world. The depth of the human predicament without God, the crisis occasioned by this predicament or sin, and the visionary as a reflecter of bad mimesis (the mimesis of mimetic desire and rivalry) and communicator of good mimesis (the mimesis of transformation as intended by God) are unquestionably shared in both genres of text and religious orientation. Those tendencies in modern intellectual history which ignore the importance of religion result in neglect of, and sometimes contempt for, prophecy and apocalyptic. However, both sacrifical and nonsacrificial readings of the Bible will agree on their importance.

3.3. The inevitability of violence

The two approaches do not have a meeting of the minds concerning the dynamics of sin (how it is generated; see below), but they are in accord on this much: human beings are caught up in a grave predicament for which the traditional religious word "sin" is as accurate as any to use. This sin generates violence; thus within the conditions of human history as we presently know it violence is inevitable.

3.4. For Christians, Christ as the center of life and salvation-history

This essay has focused on the Hebrew Scriptures, so my remarks here will be minimal. It is obvious that there may be a Jewish nonsacrificial reading of the Jewish Scriptures or Hebrew Bible, of which we have one in this volume (Lasine on Levite violence in the Torah). I would simply note that the respective Christian views on the importance of sacrifice, religion, prophecy and apocalyptic, and the inevitability of violence due to human sin find their point of departure and return in the Christ of the New Testament Gospels.

And what are the points of disagreement?

3.5. The ultimate value of sacrifice

Whatever the ubiquity of sacrifice in world religions and its crucial role in biblical texts, the question remains: Is it ordained by God? Is it a God-given institution? The sacrificial approach says yes, there is obviously nothing wrong with it or God would have condemned Abel's sacrifice in Genesis 4. On the other hand, the nonsacrificial approach says no—a no qualified in the following sense. Sacrificial institutions appear from the beginning of human history, and sacrifice itself goes back to paleolithic times. The people Israel were continually involved in cultures in which sacrifice was at the center of life. However, we can see, as developed in the nonsacrificial reading of the Hebrew Scriptures, that the texts relate the revelation of a God who sides with victims and who summons people to become disengaged from sacrifice and its origin in rivalry and collective violence. The pull of this revelation is gradual, but nonetheless constant and potent. Even though the full illumination of this revelation is still clouded by a certain ambiguity in most of the Torah and the Prophets, it does reach a height of articulation in the last Servant Song of Second Isaiah.

3.6. In prophecy and apocalyptic: who or what is the source of violence?

The sacrificial reading has no problem with God as the source of violence, which is, after all, divine judgment on human sin. The nonsacrificial reading agrees that many texts in the prophets and in apocalyptic material read as though God is the ultimate agent of violence, but it offers two qualifying considerations: (a) Many of the prophets condemn violence and sacrifice and utilize good mimesis in enacting a transformed Israel. (b) Prophecy and apocalyptic, like all other expressions of a point of view *sub specie Dei*, must use language conventions available in given historical situations. The upshot of this is that, just as in the case of sacrifice, a phenomenon or practice may be presented as though God intends it (in keeping with traditional language), but in fact it is human beings that perpetuate violence and bring it on themselves. In other words, it is difficult to disengage completely from traditional thought forms which ascribe everything to God, including violence, just as it is difficult to disengage from sacrificial institutions, which were the mainstays of older cultures.

3.7. May violence be ameliorated within history itself?

The sacrificial reading says no, human sin and and thus human violence will continue until history is brought to an end by God. And this divinely appointed end will unfortunately have to be violent because there is no other way to divide between the redeemed and the unredeemed. The nonsacrificial reading holds that although it is unrealistic to expect any kind of utopia within the present conditions of history, nonetheless violence may be ameliorated or overcome in specific circumstances through good mimesis. The revelation attested in Scripture, which demystifies and demythologizes scapegoating and reveals the God of victims, is working itself out in the world through those who reenact it. It has effect in history, like leaven in the dough.

3.8. What, precisely, generates the human predicament?

For a sacrificial reading it is the violation of God's commands, including the original prohibition of Genesis 2. For a nonsacrificial reading the predicament may be viewed as a violation of God's love, which takes the form of structure including prohibitions. However, the primal transgression is the all-against-one of collective violence which leads to sacrifice. Sacrifice is not *originally* God's command but the ritual transgression thereof. It, like all the pillars of culture, becomes God's command in the sense that it, like the divorce Moses permitted because of the people's "hardness of heart" (Matt 19:8; see Mabee's essay in this volume), is a proximate solution to problems of rivalry and conflict for want of something better. In short, the nonsacrificial reading is based on a theological affirmation which coexists with and supports a social scientific hypothesis: (1) The social scientific hypothesis is that culture has its origin in collective violence, which is rooted in a nonconscious process that begins with mimetic desire; this desire, in turn, realizes itself in mimetic rivalry and conflict. Sacrifice and scapegoating are the universal human means of attaining social order. That is, order is brought about through the victimage mechanism, which is concealed in prohibition, ritual, and myth. (2) God is loving and just and does not intend the structures of violence (or sin) that human beings perpetuate. God thus reveals that he sides with victims and intends a final reestablishment of the rule of love.

In short, the sacrificial reading confirms the necessity of *atonement* in the sacrificial sense, and so it confirms the necessity of *God's violent action*. It is interesting that although sacrificial readings of Scripture are generally poles apart from modern critical theory, they are fundamentally similar, in a metaphysical and theological sense, to readings of texts and the world by thinkers like Nietzsche and Heidegger who observed not only the fact of violence, but also affirmed its value as part of being itself, a value that the authentic humans of the future would appropriate and use for their own ends. A nonsacrificial approach, however, sees sacrificial atonement as part of the human predicament. Since the structures that generate that predicament are unconscious and concealed in myth and cultural forms, they must be illuminated so that the nonviolent nature of God and ultimate reality will be revealed.[31]

---

31 For a sustained nonsacrificial reading of the Hebrew Scriptures and the Gospels that includes a critique of Freud, Heidegger, and Jung in particular, see Williams, *The Bible, Violence, and the Sacred.*

V

Un/rivaling
the Old Testament

BEFORE THE LAW

Charles Mabee

Abstract

It is similarity, not difference, that engenders rivalry, conflict, and violence, according to the theory of violence developed by René Girard. This essay proceeds to "un/rival" the Jewish and Christian scriptures by unraveling some of the conventional representations of their similarity. This task is accomplished by dissociating the Christian meaning and significance of the life and death of Jesus from traditional Jewish expectations of a messiah. It is the similarity of Christian claims about Jesus (on the one hand), with Jewish expectations of a messiah (on the other), that has generated centuries of vicious and lethal rivalry between the two traditions. Yet closer examination of the New Testament, as we will see, justifies relinquishing the term "messiah" with reference to Jesus altogether.

In a related discussion this essay examines the treatment of Torah and law in Matthew's gospel. Matthew's Christian perspective constitutes a shift from the Jewish perspective; a shift from the categories of prohibition and observance status *after Mosaic* law, to the prescriptive categories of faith and promise established under the Abrahamic covenant *before* the advent of the law. In this regard the Matthean Jesus himself deconstructs or unravels the "Old Testament": he fulfills the law by retrieving its precursor in Jewish covenental tradition—the faith of Abraham and God's promises to Abraham and his descendents. Thus with regard to law also, Matthew is not concerned with establishing a "new" testament in rivalry with an "old." It is the difference rather than the similarity between the testaments that concerns him and, with regard to our contemporary hermeneutic interests, it is that difference that un/rivals them.

The Girardian Symbiosis of Violence and Religion

In the thought of René Girard violence and victimization are no strangers to religious experience.[1] The intimate connection between them is most fully

---

1 The reader will find an exposition of the crucial role of mimesis in this process elsewhere in this book.

exposed in Girard's *Violence and the Sacred* and *Things Hidden Since the Foundation of the World*.[2] He returns to this theme again and again throughout the former work. For example, he writes: "Religion in its broadest sense must be another term for that obscurity that surrounds man's efforts to defend himself by curative or preventative means against his own violence."[3] Subsequently he refines this point by noting:

> Religion manifests little curiosity about the origins of those terrible forces that visit their fury on mankind but seems to concentrate its attention on determining a regular sequential pattern that will enable man to anticipate these onslaughts and take measures against them.[4]

At a later point he observes, "the sole purpose of religion is to prevent the recurrence of reciprocal violence."[5] Midway through his study he reaches the conclusion that "violence is the signifier of the cherished being, the signifier of divinity."[6] In summary form, near the conclusion of his book he observes:

> All religious rituals spring from the surrogate victim, and all the great institutions of mankind, both secular and religious, spring from ritual. Such is the case with political power, legal institutions, medicine, the theater, philosophy and anthropology itself. It could hardly be otherwise, for the working basis of human thought, the process of 'symbolization,' is rooted in the surrogate victim.[7]

Religion sanctifies rituals by symbolically transforming the sacrificial victims that stand at its genesis into gods. Thus, the mechanism of surrogate victimage is viewed as the linchpin of ritual, which Girard views as the dawn of all those cultural institutions whose purpose is to mollify and control the perpetual threat of violence in human community.[8]

Girard contends that we have a bird's eye view of this process of the sacralization of violence in the book of Job.[9] This is summarized in Girard's simple statement in *Double Business*: "The mechanism of the scapegoat victim can always be recognized behind all religious operations."[10] Sandor Goodhart has summarized Girard's view of the interconnectedness of religion and violence in this way: "The sacred is violence efficaciously removed from human

---

2 Here Girard notes: "Religion is nothing other than this immense effort to keep the peace" (*Things Hidden* , 32).
3 Girard, *Violence*, 23.
4 *Violence*, 32.
5 *Violence*, 55.
6 *Violence*, 151.
7 *Violence*, 306; see also *Job*, 72.
8 *Double Business*, 206. As unambiguously as possible, he writes: "Religion is really the generative force behind human culture."
9 Cf. esp. the description in *Job*, 27–28.
10 *Double Business*, 104.

communities, and violence is the sacred deviated from its divine position and creating havoc in the city."[11] More than intimately related, in the Girardian universe, violence and religion are two sides of the same coin—religion embodying violence in socially acceptable amounts of intensity.

By establishing this essential symbiosis between violence and religion, Girard restores our understanding of religion as the center of human experience. Who would deny that violence as such is integral to human history? As a result, Girard is able to conclude "that only an investigation of the founding of religion will yield the secret of man."[12] The result is that "religion is thus more primary than philosophy,"[13] because philosophy is ultimately the product of religion. In this play between religion and violence, religion itself is double-edged in that it both conceals and reveals the violent origins of society that are grounded in mimetic desire. In order to lessen violence, religion must pay the price of covering up the truth of innocent victimage. After the innocent victim, truth itself becomes the second victim. But truth is the enduring victim of religion, a sacrifice repeated by symbolic words (myths) and acts (rituals). This concealing aspect of religion and the culture that it generates results in its *idolatrous* nature, that is, its propensity for creating false gods out of society's victims.[14] Girard describes the existential reason for this idolatry as follows:

> Men who cannot look freedom in the face are exposed to anguish. To escape the feeling of particularity they imitate another's desire; they choose substitute gods because they are not able to give up infinity.[15]

Hence the primacy of mimetic desire stands behind all religious expression.

Without doubt, historically religion has substantiated the most wanton acts of human violence by appeal to the holy. The great Western religious traditions have hardly escaped complicity in this phenomenon. The promise of Girard's thought is to lay bear the dynamics of this violence in the most unambiguous terms possible, beginning at the level of textual analysis of religious texts themselves. From the standpoint of content, the Bible has functioned both as the means of masking violence, as well as a revealer of it. Everything, it seems, is dependent upon *how* one reads it; and, at times, understanding how biblical authors interpret previous texts.[16] If a masking of

---

11 "*I am Joseph*," 54–55.
12 *Things Hidden*, 3.
13 *Things Hidden*, 15.
14 See *Double Business*, 219.
15 *Deceit*, 65.
16 The clearest example that Girard gives of the Bible reading "against itself" occurs in his work on the book of Job. In discussing the additions to the dialogues found in the book he writes: "All the additions to the Dialogues do violence to the original text; they are

violence is operative in a text, hermeneutically we cannot allow it solely to speak for itself. In this regard, Girard writes:

> We reject without question the meaning the author gives his text. We declare that he does not know what he is saying. From our several centuries distance we know better than he and can correct what he has written.[17]

More to the point in the Girardian approach is his statement: "All interpretations that do not attempt to demystify persecution are in fact regressive despite their noisy avant-garde posture."[18] At another point Girard notes: "One must either do violence to the text or let the text forever do violence to innocent victims."[19] Hermeneutical and theological problems begin in earnest when one takes seriously the perspective that the revelation happens to those who are initially predisposed toward the same mimetic and violent tendencies that are common to all experience.

Throughout the era of historical and social-scientific criticism of the Bible, theologians have wrestled with the problem of its conceptual center. To date, no absolutely satisfying theology has emerged which persuades the academy. It is evident that Girard, professor of French language, literature, and civilization at Stanford University, approaches biblical texts from a very different viewpoint. The approach that he has proposed does suggest a new way to map out a coherent biblical theology. The purpose of this essay is to develop a step further the way to the unity of the Bible that Girard suggests. As such, I will attempt to build upon his insights and develop his thought in a more explicitly theological way than he has himself until now. The result is an argument that is suggested to me by Girard's insights, but one that he has not explicitly proposed.

Again, Girard reads the entire Bible from the standpoint of a single unifying theme: God's revelation of the victimage mechanism which stands at the origins of culture, its continual operation in society, and the way which leads to its dissolution. In his theology, the New Testament is more revelatory than the Old because the revelation of this victimage mechanism emanates most

---

victorious acts of persecution in that they have succeeded, until now, in neutralizing the revelation of the scapegoat. Everything that is not Job in the Book of Job, with the powerful support of the exegeses forming a vengeful circle around the Dialogues, endeavours to conceal the essential message: to falsify it or, better still, to bury it again, suppressing it entirely" (*Job*, 143). Girard subsequently makes clear that he is reading the book of Job from the vantage point of the gospels (*Job*, 164). Thus, while it may seem inappropriate to speak of a Girardian method of interpretation in the strict sense, nonetheless, his scapegoat theory certainly gives rises to a certain "way" of reading the Bible: a "non-sacrificial" reading (cf. *Things Hidden*, Book II, ch. 2).

17 *Scapegoat*, 4.
18 *Scapegoat*, 52.
19 *Scapegoat*, 8.

explicitly from the death of Jesus. He conceives of the New Testament as the revealed word of God that ultimately rejects the rabbinical reading of the Hebrew Scriptures that is centered around the concept of Torah. For him the Hebrew Bible really is the "Old" Testament in the sense that it exists in a half-world between religious texts in general and the New Testament. For example, following Max Weber's view of the Hebrew Scriptures, Girard notes that "at several stages the biblical writers have an undeniable *tendency* to take the side of the victim on moral grounds, and to spring to the victim's defense" (my emphasis).[20] I mean by *half-world* Girard's view of the Old Testament as having merely a *tendency* to side with the victim. More to the point, Girard states: "In the Old Testament we never arrive at a conception of the deity that is entirely foreign to violence."[21] At another point Girard terms the Old Testament a "text in travail; it is not a chronologically progressive process, but a struggle that advances and retreats."[22]

The theological problem remains, therefore, to determine ways to both distinguish and appropriate the Hebrew Bible—to define further this half-world—without entering into mimetic rivalry with the Jewish religious community that both generated it and continues to interpret it differently. I propose that the best way to achieve this is through a hermeneutic of the cross.[23] I believe, furthermore, that a key element to the solution of this problem in the New Testament itself is suggested in the gospel of Matthew, the text with which I will begin the process of theologizing Girard's thought.

Un/rivaling the Old Testament

The relationship between the Old and New Testaments is a problematical issue that dates to the historical environment of primitive Christianity. The problem which New Testament writers faced was the rejection of their claims about Jesus by the already existing Judaic tradition. At the birth of New Testament faith, the Hebrew tradition was *already present*. It was also the defining element in Jesus' life and teachings. Clearly, the absolute exceptionality of Christian claims about the life and death of Jesus was not evident to the majority of those in the Hebrew tradition. The result was a highly conflictual form of rivalry for the conceptual center of Yahwistic religion between rabbinic Judaism and the emergent Christian community. Tragically, the

---

20 *Things Hidden*, 147.
21 *Things Hidden*, 157. And, again, "only the texts of the Gospels manage to achieve what the Old Testament leaves incomplete" (*Things Hidden*, 158).
22 *Violent Origins*, 141. He continues, "I see the Gospels as the climactic achievement of that trend, and therefore as the essential text in the cultural upheaval of the modern world."
23 The fullest explication of a "theology of the cross" based on Girard's thought is provided in Robert Hamerton-Kelly's recent *Sacred Violence: Paul's Hermeneutic of the Cross*.

revelatory character of events associated with Jesus claimed by Christian believers, and the denial of them on the part of mainstream Judaism, has continued to fuel an anti-Semitism that has been to one degree or another an integral part of Western cultural history from that day until our own.

At a deep and relatively unconscious level, the continued historical existence of Judaism has represented a protracted threat to the very existence of Christianity. Indeed, Judaism and Christianity each represents a critique of its counterpart. For if Jesus is indeed the final one sent from God, then Judaism, which has failed to acknowledge this fact even as it functioned historically as the matrix of Christianity, must be *fundamentally* misguided or incomplete.[24] If Jesus penetrated to the core of his own religious Scriptures and experience, and that religion failed to capture the significance of what he had to say and how he lived his life, then how could Judaism be accepted on equal terms by the Christian tradition?[25] In this sense, for the writers of the New Testament, the existence of the Hebrew Scriptures prior to the Jesus event was as much of a handicap as it was a resource. In fact, it was the primary task of the writers of the New Testament to transform the Old Testament into a noncompeting resource, to domesticate it. In Giradian terms this means the removal of it as *rival*. In other words, the task the New Testament writers faced was one of decontextualizing the Hebrew Scriptures from the historic Jewish experience which somehow failed to perceive the meaning of Jesus: to strip it to the absolute terms of its message which transcended this experience.

In one of his most penetrating insights, Girard informs us that conflict is born in similarity, and not difference. It is the ability of a culture to codify differentiation that enables it to survive.[26] It is because Christianity and Judaism contend for the same thing, that conflict has characterized so much of

---

24 Christians have historically been traditionally better disposed toward the Hebrew prophets in the Judaic tradition than the Torah. Girard, for example, notes that while the Old Testament's prophets wished to renounce all forms of sacrifice, "this is only carried out in the Gospels" (*Things Hidden*, 240).

25 In fact, Girard understands the books of the Old Testament as "rooted in sacrificial crises, each distinct from the other and separated by long intervals of time, but analogous in at least some respects. The earlier crises are reinterpreted in the light of the later ones" (*Violence*, 66). In Girardian terms, the partial nature of the resolution of the sacrificial crises in the Old Testament is the chief feature which distinquishes it from the New.

26 It is the loss of differentiation that causes violence to threaten the existence of society. In *Double Business*, 117, Girard writes: "If there is a trait common to all cultures, from primitive religions to the contemporary counterculture, it is indeed the primacy of difference in the sense of a negation of reciprocities." Also see *Violence*, 57. This, for example, is a major reason that the plague was so feared and generated the scapegoat mechanism in ancient society: "The distinctiveness of the plague is that it ultimately destroys all forms of distinctiveness" (*Double Business*, 137). The threat of totalitarianism in the modern world is also rooted in the same principle: "Every human force is braced in a struggle that is as relentless as it is senseless, since no concrete difference or positive value is involved. Totalitarianism is preceisely this" (*Deceit*, 137).

their common existence. What is that same thing? Is it Jesus? The answer is surely no, because, as already noted Judaism *as such* is relatively unconcerned with Jesus and claims nothing about him remotely comparable to orthodox Christianity. The Jewish views of Jesus are *derived* views and perspectives, derived from the Christian claims which come before them. What, then, is the one thing for which the Jew and the Christian strive? It seems to me that the answer lies in the correct interpretation of the events which generated the Hebrew scriptural tradition and accompanied the Israelite historical experience with its God. The contention, in other words, was over the handling of the "root metaphor" which would give shape and meaning to Israel's life experience, a metaphor (I will argue) that is one and the same with the Girardian perspective—the victimage mechanism. The contention arises over the contextualization and recontextualization of the metaphor of the victimage mechanism that took place throughout Israel's history. The Jesus of the New Testament characterizes an Israel that had exchanged commentary—the stuff that builds community—for the events themselves. For him, this commentary upon the Torah is the stuff of culture, and is bound to the double business of concealing as well as revealing that which lies before the Torah. Jesus appears to urge a life that existed prior to or before the law, rather than a life that contextualized it or applied it to ever-changing historical situations. Contextualization always resides in the half-world of concealing as well as revealing, an approach to the Torah that appears amazingly foreign in New Testament texts.

In fact, Jesus apparently challenged the fundamental chronological foundation upon which mainstream Judaism rested. The Torah in Judaic tradition tended to be cumulative and absorbent, grounded in the ancient events associated with the Exodus and Mt. Sinai. The way of Jesus, on the other hand, pointed to the peeling back of layers of legal interpretation and uncovering the stark reality of what lay *before* it—the fullness of which was embodied in his death. If this interpretation is correct, the fundamental contention before Judaism and emerging Christianity was a chronological one: the Jew contending for the ever-increasing weight of the historical tradition which tended to absorb those who encountered it, and Jesus contending for a counter-hermeneutics that moved against the stream of time, uncovering the events that preceded the tradition. In this sense, the Jesus of the New Testament is one who decontextualizes or deconstructs the Mosaic tradition.[27]

At the heart of the Torah tradition stood Moses. He had arisen in conjunction with the Egyptian experience, discovering the commandments and prohibitions in the context of release from slavery in Egypt. This Torah is the

---

27 To this point Girard writes: "In a good many respects, the mission of Jesus is opposed to that of Moses, who is concerned with arbitration and legislation (Luke 12, 13–14)" (*Things Hidden*, 204).

ultimate gift of the Egyptian experience and unfolds contextually out of it. For the Christian, following the way of Jesus, emphasis is directed back *before* Egypt to Abraham. In Girardian terms we might say that the problem with the exodus tradition is that it does not forgive the victimizer, and thereby, never absolutely supersedes the categories of victimizer/victim which the Jesus of the New Testament does.[28] Even this all too human response to oppression is shunned by Jesus. The New Testament looked to the presence of God *before* Abraham as the event which undergirded and made possible the entire Egyptian experience of liberation. This event was pre-Torah in the sense that it predated the process of narrowing of Torah into law which was underway in the Judaism of Jesus' day.

We may say that for Christianity, the point is this: the story of Moses is fundamentally contextualization of Abrahamic faith. That Moses is the towering figure of the written Torah means simply that the written Torah itself is basically commentary in character. For Judaism, Moses is central because he is the one who gave the initial body of instruction. From this standpoint, Moses is primary and Abraham is proleptic. In this regard, Christian exegesis runs counter to the mainstream of Judaic tradition, thereby establishing a framework of otherness. Within this otherness stands the possibility of "unrivaling" the communities that stand as heirs of the Old and New Testaments.[29]

The Dialectics of Matthew

It is standard in New Testament studies to acknowledge the creative way in which Mark portrayed the life and death of Jesus in the creative literary form he termed "gospel" (Mk 1:1). Once scholars determined the chronological priority of Mark, the dependence of Matthew's gospel upon it was clear. Matthew accepts the basic premise of Mark that the fundamental significance of Jesus lay in his death. This, as Paul had already established, became the benchmark of orthodox Christian thought, and has remained so throughout Christian history.[30] And, yet, that very benchmark was clearly problematic to the writer of Matthew because of its stark and ill-defined nature. It was an event that begged for and finally demanded interpretation. What did the violent death of Jesus mean?[31] What was its significance for everyday life in the

---

28 Matt 5:44.

29 Of course, within the Old Testament itself, this dynamic is not an absolutely new thing. It carries on the spirit which is found perhaps most clearly in the books of Job and Jonah—books that never achieved the status of the Mosaic Torah.

30 Fundamental to Mark, and to subsequent Christian thought is the fact that the violent death of the innocent Jesus actually happened. Girard acknowledges his own endebtedness to Freud for understanding the symbiotic relationship between actual murder and myth (*Violence*, 201).

31 A clear statement of the meaning of Jesus' death is given by Girard in *Job*, 161: "Jesus is

faith? How, in short, could one contextualize it? It was Matthew and Luke among the canonical gospels that began the process of contextualization of the death of Jesus so enigmatically set forth by Mark.

In Matthew, this process paradoxically began with the decontextualization of the Mosaic law. Matthew wishes to show that if the death of Jesus meant anything beyond the tragedy of violence to a single innocent man, it meant the end of the absoluteness of the law given to Moses at Mt. Sinai. It meant the downgrading of this law from ultimacy to penultimacy. The gospel of Matthew solidifies this argument by firmly linking the life of Christ to Abraham rather than Moses in the opening genealogy. The intention is to give voice to all those innocent victims against whom the use of violence had been legitimated by the law. This issue provides an excellent jumping off point for a brief discussion of Matthew's gospel that is more specifically Girardian in orientation.

The literary structure of the gospel of Matthew is contested by New Testament scholars. The theological structure is perhaps easier to decipher. The huge block of material in chapters 5–25 seems to have the general theological purpose of shedding much of the commentary or contextual skin of the Mosaic law and uncovering the absoluteness of the will of God which stands behind it. In this way we may say that the gospel of Matthew has two fundamental theological parts:

1. Chapters 1–4 and 26–28 represent a theological frame that harkens back to the Markan narrative of the life and death of Jesus. This section affirms and reinforces the centrality of the life and death of Jesus as established in Mark's gospel. Everything that happens in this gospel takes place in the circumstances afforded by the life and death of Jesus; nothing Christian exists apart from this life, and especially this death.

2. Chapters 5–25 consist of a theological block that seeks to unfold the meaning of the life and death of Jesus through his teachings by penetrating to the central core of the Mosaic law. Just as the entire gospel is framed by chapters 1–4 and 26–28, so is this huge middle section (which

---

the perfect victim, because he has always spoken and behaved in accordance with the Logos of the god of victims. He provides the only perfect image of the event which is at the root of all our myths and religions." In another text he notes: "Jesus provides the scapegoat *par excellence*—he is the most arbitrary of victims because he is also the least violent." This "always makes Jesus the victim *par excellence*, in whom the previous history of mankind is summed up, concluded and transcended" (*Things Hidden*, 209). The important thing is to establish the non-sacrificial character of the death of Jesus: "There is nothing in the Gospels to suggest that the death of Jesus is a sacrifice, whatever definition (expiation, substitution, etc.) we may give for that sacrifice" (*Things Hidden*, 180). Nevertheless, this non-sacrificial character of the death of Jesus must not obscure its centrality in Girard's work. Note Aidan Carl Mathews's statement: "The Cross itself now stands at the center of Girard's project" ("Knowledge of Good and Evil: The Work of René Girard," in *To Honor René Girard*, 19).

is certainly the heart of the gospel) framed by the Sermon on the Mount (chapters 5–7; hereafter, Sermon) and the Last Judgment (chapter 25). The Sermon and the Last Judgment form the theological axis points of the gospel around which revolve the Markan Jesus who dies uniquely, and the teacher Jesus who penetrates to the core of the Mosaic law and makes significant strides toward its decontextualization.

Thus we see that the gospel of Matthew is fundamentally dialectical. First, it stands in dialectical relationship to the gospel of Mark (to which presumably the author had access while composing the gospel). The insights of Mark are not abandoned. The death of Jesus, and the life of an innocent man which preceded it and gave it significance, remains the cornerstone of the faith. Yet Mark is also held to be an inadequate and incomplete interpretation of Jesus. The teachings of Jesus in Matthew, above all exemplified in the Sermon and the Last Judgment, play off against the Markan Jesus and explore rich new ground that lies unexplored in the earlier gospel. The issue that Matthew faces is the incarnation—the incarnation of the death of Jesus in the realities of everyday life. He uses it as a hermeneutical tool to unmask the tyrannical side of the Mosaic law. This point may be summarized in this way: because of the looming significance of his death in Matthew's gospel, the teachings of Jesus take on a whole new level of significance. Conversely, without the teachings, the death remains shrouded in the fragmentary nature of Mark's gospel.

As the centerpiece of dialectical thinking in the gospel of Matthew, the Sermon also exhibits a dynamic internal dialectics.[32] Legal thinking has a tendency not to be dialectical, but to be formal and apodictic. The problem faced in Matthew is that of maintaining a nonlegal, dialectical discourse in the process of penetrating to the core of the law itself: the problem is how to bring the death of Jesus into the sphere of the law and not be caught up in the kinetic force of new law making which will continue the process of concealing as well as revealing. Matthew achieves this by counterbalancing the various commands operative in the Sermon. Donaldson writes:

> There are in the sermon a whole range of imperatives which make equally unqualified claims upon us. And these commands are not mutually compatible. This is hermeneutically important. . . . It is, in my opinion, true that without the larger context of the Sermon on the Mount and *without the balance of other imperatives, the command not to resist evil is both impossible and itself evil.*[33]

What Donaldson terms "balance," I prefer to call dialectic; but his conclusion and mine are much the same. We agree that the entire Sermon is not

---

32 I am indebted to Lewis R. Donaldson for this point. See "'Do Not Resist Evil' and the Question of Biblical Authority." Donaldson builds his own discussion out of the earlier work of Hans Windisch, *The Meaning of the Sermon on the Mount.*

33 Donaldson, 35 (emphasis added).

composed of religious law to be obeyed literally at all times and places. In fact, it is not law at all. It is a kaleidoscope of communal relationship seen from the standpoint of the victim, a view that exists *before* the implementation of orderly societal justice. It is the view of the one for whom even the framework of the liberating Mosaic law is still oppressive and concealing. The Sermon is, in short, pre-law or pre-justice. Whereas Moses contextualized, Jesus decontextualized: "Because you are obstinate Moses permitted you. . . . Now I say to you" (Matt 19:8–9a). Whereas the Mosaic law tended to be orderly and structured, the words of Jesus were imprudent and uncategorical. Why? Because Matthew portrays Jesus primarily as interested in peeling back the law to the unstructured province of unfettered reality. Thus, the interior meaning of the concept of the "hardness of heart" of the "Jews" in Matthew's gospel is bound up with the way that they had traditionally refined and applied the Mosaic law, rather than conjuring up the unfashioned religious experience that existed before it (i.e., the faith of Abraham).

Finally, the gospel of Matthew stands in dialectical relationship to the Hebrew writings that immediately precede it in the Christian canon. The significance of the canonical position of this most dialectical of gospels could hardly have been arbitrary for the framers of the Christian Bible. By its position as first in the "new" canon, the gospel of Matthew not only is placed in dialectical relationship to the Hebrew Scriptures, but it facilitates the same dialectical dynamic for the entire New Testament. This dialectic is generated by the engagement with the central feature of the Hebrew writings, namely the Mosaic law. In effect, the gospel of Matthew brings the Mosaic law into dialectical relationship with the death of Jesus, and Matthew understands this engagement to be one which disarms the law. The law is now seen to be what it really is, not only a revealer of life, but also a concealer of hidden violence against innocent victims. Understood in this way, the Sermon and the Last Judgment should be viewed as the end product of this dialectical process. The overall intention in both cases is not to comment upon or to unpack the Mosaic law, but to reveal its concealed underbelly. This is what is meant in Matt 5:17–20:

> Think not that I have come to abolish the law and the prophets; I have come not to abolish them but to *fulfill* them. For truly, I say to you, till heaven and earth pass away, not an iota, not a dot, will pass from the law until all is accomplished. Whoever then relaxes one of the least of these commandments and teaches men so, shall be called least in the kingdom of heaven; but he who does them and teaches them shall be called great in the kingdom of heaven. For I tell you, unless your righteousness exceeds that of the scribes and Pharisees, you will never enter the kingdom of heaven.

The key terms in this passage take on a new meaning when read from a Girardian perspective, in particular a reversal of the common interpretation of the fulfillment of the law. The Girardian thrust to the question of the origin of culture implies that Jesus intends to do what the law could not intrinsically do itself, that is, to reveal the innocent blood that was spilt *prior to* its own implementation. The fulfillment of the law, in other words, is more profoundly understood as the uncovering of that which exists *before* the law, rather than *after* it. This is a reversal of the way that traditional Christian exegesis has understood this concept. For it, a kind of chronological scheme is devised which puts Christianity at the end of a historical process in a posture of innate superiority. The New Testament term for this is "fulfillment." This view postulates a higher spirituality evolving out of the law. Such a view does violence to both Judaism and itself and ought to be abandoned.

Matthew Before the Law

René Girard's proposal for the reading of religious and mythological texts is a recent variation of Paul Riceour's widely noted category of "hermeneutics of suspicion." For Nietzsche, Freud, Marx, and now Girard, things are not what they appear to be on the surface of the text. Rather than straightforwardly revealing anything of the divine or human realms, a religious text is viewed as part of a community's covert manipulation of historical data.[34] Mythological and religious texts are written by the persecutors of innocent victims. They have the intention of legitimizing the rituals put in place by a priesthood for the purpose of regulating the orderly recurrence of a lesser form of the originating violence. Myths and religious texts do not tell the awful truth in the stories that they tell because they legitimize violence—albeit a lesser form of violence—and they are written from the standpoint of victimizers, rather than victims. However, according to Girard, the Bible is a unique text among those typically classified as religious, in that it struggles to tell the truth of the victim—that his death will not serve to bring permanent peace and tranquillity to the community. In this sense, by Girard's reasoning, the Bible in its dynamic of dialectical reasoning is not essentially a mythological or religious text at all, but one which succeeds in revealing the true nature of all the others. For him, mythological stories should not be read to understand better the Bible, but the Bible should be read to understand better mythological stories.

In our discussion above, we have argued for the centrality of the gospel of Matthew in the Christian Bible because it secures the Hebrew Scriptures for the dialectical understanding of Christian existence. We may add to this the notion that the gospel serves as an introduction to the remaining corpus of

---

34 Concerning religious texts in general, Girard writes: "In reality the religious text is a first violent recoil from crude forms of violence; it is also a complex economy in which this same violence is in part assuaged by sacrifice, in part camouflaged, ignored, and transfigured" (*Double Business*, 169).

New Testament books. The gospel of Matthew, in other words, provides a Christian hermeneutic for reading the Hebrew writings, as well as embodying a comprehensive hermeneutic of Christian life. It does this first and foremost by utilizing the cross of Jesus as a hermeneutical tool by which violent human realities existing *before* the Mosaic law might be uncovered and brought to light. Because the discernment of human violence is more sweeping in the Christian perspective (existing as it does in the shadow of the death of Jesus) than in the Torah, the demands are greater as well: "You, therefore, must be perfect, as your heavenly Father is perfect" (Matt 5:48).[35] Only the death of Jesus makes perfection a possibility, because perfection is only thinkable in the absolute identification with the victim that the law still is unable to eventuate.

The gospel of Matthew plummets beneath the Mosaic law in two especially imaginative ways: morally, in the series of antitheses to the law in the Sermon (Matt 5:21–48), and religiously, in the Last Judgment. The antitheses to the Mosaic law clearly portray the Matthean Jesus in a contrary light to the law. Here the law is not denied, but it is intensified. The law is viewed as inadequate because it is unable to penetrate the depth of human suffering brought about by innocent victimage:

> You have heard that it was said. . . .
> But I say to you. . . .

Here Jesus points out that the law is based on reflection and commentary upon that which has preceded it. It is, in other words, reflective of the wisdom of the past. The problem from a Girardian perspective is that such wisdom already reflects partiality. The Matthean Jesus cuts against the grain of this way of thinking and runs counter to it. Here the wisdom of Jesus is not understood to culminate from the traditions of the past, but it is portrayed as that which confronts those traditions in an effort to make them fully impartial. The intent is not, as in later Christian spirituality, to write the morality of God on the human heart. The intent is to reveal the dynamics of victimage *previous* to any particular conception of morality. The crucial point is that the human behaviors that Jesus excludes from the life of God in the antitheses are not illegal. It is not illegal to lust after a woman, to divorce one's wife, to perform acts which one has sworn to God, to seek retaliation through the legal system, to hate one's enemy. The realm of such activities is hidden from the law, and thereby conceals the ravages of human victimization.

The Last Judgment brings the reader into contact with the religious realities at play prior to any system of ethics and morality. We recall the terms given for the judgment:

---

35 Girard notes the difficulty in following out the prescription for perfection: "We are not healthy pagans. We are not Jews, either, since we have no Law. But we are not real Christians, since we keep judging" (*Double Business*, 34).

Lord, when did we see you hungry and feed you, or thirsty and give you a drink?
. . . And the king will answer them, "Truly, I say to you, as you did it to one of the
least of these my brethren, you did it to me." (Matt 25:37, 40)

From a Girardian perspective, this statement represents the wedding of
authentic human behavior with true religion. It is the end of false religion. It is
false religion that is concerned with the interior issues of the psychology of
guilt and innocence. From the religious *and* legal perspective it is important to
determine *why* someone is hungry, thirsty, a stranger, naked, sick, or in prison.
In all likelihood it is imagined that one deserves such predicaments because of
sin. Such is the religiosity of Job's friends, and these friends are the archetypes
of the religious personality. In the Matthean passage, Jesus effectively removes
all religious consideration when dealing with the disadvantaged and the
unprivileged. For him, the issue is not *why*, but *whither*. Religion asks for
divine motivation for the human affliction, while Jesus simply proclaims
solidarity with the marginalized victim. For him, the religious cause for
human suffering is an obsolete issue because suffering has no religious
meaning; it has "merely" human meaning based on the consequences of free
choice. Thus, while human suffering is frequently understandable, it is not
justifiable. Such considerations belong to the political, legal, and religious
realms that already stand subsequent to the suffering of innocent victimage.
A reading of these texts from Matthew informed by a Girardian perspective
highlights the way in which they run counter to the accumulated wisdom of
human religion and ethics. It is instructive to note that whereas religion and
ethics conventionally lead to life, the pericope following the Last Judgment
indicates that the words of Jesus lead to death: "When Jesus had finished all
these sayings, he said to his disciples, 'You know that after two days the
Passover is coming, and the Son of man will be delivered up to be crucified'"
(Matt 26:1–2). It would perhaps be more accurate to say that the words of Jesus
are death, that is, the full and complete embodiment of the deaths of innocent
victims that stand at the foundation of culture. Jesus must die, in Matthew's
gospel, because he has revealed these awful truths in his teachings—truths
that had been covered up by the leaders of the religious and moral realms,
namely the priests and elders. It is no accident that they are the ones who
immediately plan his arrest and eventual crucifixion (Matt 26:3). Seen in this
light, one senses just how revolutionary the teachings of the Jesus of the New
Testament are: they are not simply a full frontal attack upon human culture,
but the foundation of violence that stands *before* culture. It remains for Christian theologians to work out the full implications of the teachings of Jesus (or
at least, the Matthean Jesus), in this area of the contention centered on the
category of the messiah. It is here that the residue of "salvation by law" still
remains lurking beneath the surface in the Christian community. It is the
deepest outpost of violence that lies within the Christian bosom.

From Law to Messiah

The Hebrew term "messiah" is deeply rooted in legal, political, and religious spheres, and unfolds directly out of them. Sigmund Mowinckel, in his classic study of the concept, writes:

> Among all the persons and objects which may be anointed there is one who is 'Yahweh's Anointed' in a special sense, one who is '*the* Anointed,' namely the king. It was primarily as a priest-king that a king was anointed, that is, as a sacral king who represented his people before the deity, and thus also took a leading and active part in the cult. Anointing made him a 'holy' person, similar to the priest in character and function.[36]

The messiah was the major figure in Judaic thought that most fully integrated the full vista of ancient Israel's culture. In addition, the office became the embodiment of this culture's hopes and aspirations during the post-exilic period. In the absence of an earthly king, great hopes were placed on a future, eschatological king who would "restore Israel as a people, free her from her enemies, rule over her as king, and bring other nations under her political and religious sway."[37] Therefore, the term "messiah" is inextricably a political one. I define the political arena as the one in which the powers, aspirations, and desires of a social unit are adjudicated or negotiated by relatively non-violent means. The term "messiah" is political in this sense because it both elicits a particular set of internal cultural aspirations over against other potential ones, and it places the entirety of ancient Israelite culture and emerging Judaism in fundamental dissymmetry to other peoples in the sense that the expectant messiah specifically comes out of Israel, the chosen of Yahweh. In all of this the term never completely escapes the taint of vengeance, or the threat of vengeance. As the term enters the mainstream of Judaism, the office of messiah maintains its political base, even as it is fused more and more with eschatological vitality. It is this religious, legal, and political base of the office that is challenged by Jesus and the New Testament.

It is by now widely accepted among historical-critical scholars that Jesus laid no personal claim to the Judaic office of messiah. Neither, in an absolute sense, does the New Testament make this claim on his behalf. It is crucial for confronting anti-Semitism that Christianity clarify its historical claim about the messiahship of Jesus and come to terms with the rivalry with Judaism that

---

36 Mowinckel, *He That Cometh*, 5.
37 Mowinckel, 7. He goes on to say: "This conception of the future king as a this-worldly political figure is clearly and explicitly present in most if not all of the passages in the Old Testament which refer to him. According to the express testimony of the evangelists it was against this political conception of the Messiah, present in the minds and thoughts of the disciples and of the multitude, that Jesus had to contend. Just as the word 'Messiah' has an eschatological character wherever it has become a clearly defined term, so too it has a political sense from the beginning."

this claim has engendered. A position informed by Girardian perspectives would suggest the wisdom of Christians relinquishing the term altogether. Better to relinquish the term than to co-opt it. Better to acknowledge the metamorphosis into something inherently different, with a new structural foundation, than to attempt to maintain the artificial historic ties to the past. It is certainly true that the Hebrew term *messiah* is not precisely translatable into the Greek *christos*. The New Testament itself is clear on this point. In fact, the New Testament makes it abundantly clear that the *christos* can only be understood as the *messiah* in a highly restricted sense. Rather than any sort of identification with the legal and political order, the *christos* is distinguished in the gospels as the one who must die because of his identification with the victims of religion, law, and politics. In this sense the New Testament decontextualizes the Hebrew conceptuality of messiahship from its wider social sense and sets it solidly on new footing. It is in that sense that the death of Jesus to one degree or another permeates every passage of the gospels.

It is particularly fruitful to examine the issue of differentiation between *messiah* and *christos* against the backdrop of kingship. Kingship is operative in both terms, and that is the point of connection between them. But what has been too little emphasized in theology has been the disparate conception of kingship that is embedded in each. One ought primarily to distinguish the two terms on that basis. I am tempted to say that each term holds a particular hermeneutic of kingship. The key perspective here predates Girard. Freud writes:

> "The idea," writes Frazer, "that early kingdoms are despotisms in which the people exist only for the sovereign, is wholly inapplicable to the monarchies we are considering. On the contrary, the sovereign in them exists only for his subjects; his life is only valuable so long as he discharges the duties of his position by ordering the course of nature for his people's benefit. So soon as he fails to do so, the care, the devotion, the religious homage which they had hitherto lavished on him cease and are changed into hatred and contempt; he is dismissed ig-nominiously, and may be thankful if he escapes with his life. Worshipped as a god one day, he is killed as criminal the next."[38]

The embryonic religious, legal, and political dimensions of the concept of messiahship are rooted in the violence indicated in this description. In fact, this description clearly shows that the very idea of kingship is moored in violence.[39] Jesus is killed because his life and teachings represented an intrinsic challenge to the violent nature of the office of kingship itself. He revealed its violent nature by utter identification with the victimage dimension

---

38 Sigmund Freud, *Totem and Taboo*, 44.
39 For insightful descriptions of the sacrificial nature of kingship in Girard's writings, see *Things Hidden*, 51–57, 66–67, and *Job*, 91–94.

of it in his teachings and in his life. This identity of Jesus with kingship is in reality only identification with the underbelly of kingship, the king as victim of his people. Freud and Girard are in common agreement that the king is nothing less than a victim with a suspended sentence.

Jewish hopes connected with messiahship evolve out of the context of Jewish apocalypticism, itself only possible on the basis of Mosaic law which preceded it. Apocalypticism is a particular chronological scheme that presupposes a situation in which dominant political power lies in the hands of one's enemies. As a result, it frequently expresses the hope that the present tables will be turned in a future age in which God's justice will be established for all to see. It is frequently explicit in the way that it encounters the enemy with a vindictive spirit. As such, it was built on the same hermeneutical scheme as that of the rabbinic discussions of the law: it developed upon generations of speculation and discussion, concealing its origins in the mechanism of innocent victimage. And just as was the case with the law itself, the hermeneutics of the Jesus of the New Testament and the gospel writers ran chronologically counter to it. They attempted to unmask the king as innocent victim, as a figure of misplaced central cultural identity. Had Christianity remained true to its origins, it would have become a staunchly non-messianic religion, rather than the quasi-messianic religion that it became. For here, as with the law, the intention of the *christos* was to unmask, to deconstruct the entire idea of messiahship. The entire problem was bound culturally to the specifics of the Hebrew people from the beginning. Had Judaism not invested so heavily in messianic hope, the entire issue may well have been bypassed by Jesus.

Conclusion

If Christianity is to play its self-conscious role as the unmasker of violence in society at large, it can only do so if its theologians remove the violence embedded within its own soul. At the most fundamental internal level this violence is directed toward the religious community that produced the texts upon which the faith is built, the so-called Old Testament. Whether concealed or revealed, Judaism and Christianity have functioned as rival religions from the inception of Christianity. The way out of this conundrum is suggested by the Girardian project brought into the context of the Matthew's gospel. I have tried to do that in an imaginative way in this essay, since Girard himself has not explicitly addressed this topic. Crucial in the Girardian perspective is the insight that similarity, not difference, engenders violence. Thus, in order to minimize the conflict between them, it is essential to establish theologically that the Judaic conceptual blocks of Torah and messiah are essentially not the way of Jesus.[40] The Jesus of Matthew accomplished this in the context of the primitive church in terms of the understanding of Torah prevalent at the time. Following this courageous model that journeys into untested territory, Christianity must more clearly disassociate the meaning of the life and death of Jesus from expectations in the Jewish community associated with the messiah. This work remains to be accomplished in a thorough and convincing way.

40 While contesting some individual perspectives, I am very much in sympathy with the central point of a recent article by Jacob Neusner wherein he argues the essential otherness of Christianity from Judaism. He writes that Christianity "is not a kind of Judaism. It is wholly other" (Neusner, "The Absoluteness of Christianity and the Uniqueness of Judaism," 19). He continues with the insight that "to the Gospels Judaism in all forms is simply not much to the point" (19). This is precisely the posture that is needed to eliminate the centuries long uneasy alliance between the two religions.

PART THREE:
Contemporary Issues

vi

Colonial Violence
and Inca Analogies
to Christianity

Tod Swanson

Abstract

In a move reminiscent of Karl Barth, René Girard makes the religions a disease for which Jesus Christ is the cure. My purpose in this chapter is to reformulate certain aspects of Girard's theory in a way that divorces them from what I think are Christian overclaims. My thesis is that if Girard's scapegoating process is reconceived as a thoroughly post-cultural phenomenon that occurs between societies (rather than as a pre-cultural phenomenon that founds single societies), then the polarity he sets up between Christ and the religions will break down. By tracing the mimetic play of European Christian and native South American cultures in the sixteenth and seventeenth centuries, I will argue, first, that Christianity conceals its own foundational violence toward other ethoi, and, secondly, that the religious response of native South American traditions works to expose and mitigate Christian violence.

René Girard is one of those rare scholars who, like Freud, or Ernst Becker, is remarkably good at explaining the whole of human culture in terms of a single principle. The very fact that he does so may be a clue that his argument is over determined. But any theory that can be made to explain so much warrants serious consideration. An important barrier to wider consideration of Girard's work is the unabashedly Christian use to which he puts theory. In a move reminiscent of Karl Barth, Girard makes the religions a disease for which Jesus Christ is the cure.[1] To this many thoughtful people respond in disbelief; he can't be serious! After the unprecedented destruction of indigenous cultures by Christian colonialism, after the holocaust, it seems too late in history to make claims that sound suspiciosly like Christian imperialism. Nevertheless, Girard's basic insights stand on their own quite apart from his claims about Christianity.

My purpose in this chapter is to try to reformulate Girard's theory in a way

---

1 Girard says quite explicitly that the gospels are "the only text that can bring an end to all of mythology," by which he means all religions (*Scapegoat*, 101).

that divorces it from what I think are Christian overclaims. My thesis is that if Girard's scapegoating process is reconceived as a thoroughly post-cultural phenomenon that occurs between societies (rather than as a pre-cultural phenomenon that founds single societies), the polarity between Christ and the religions will break down. By tracing the mimetic play of European Christian and native South American cultures during the Conquest in the sixteenth and seventeenth centuries, I will argue first, that Christianity conceals its own foundational violence toward other ethoi, and secondly that the South American religions, which colonial Europeans considered particularly barbaric, can actually work to expose and mitigate Christian violence.

1. Girardian Overview of the Problem

To set the stage for my argument, it is necessary to examine Girard's reasons for claiming that, apart from Christ, cultural resources for unmasking foundational violence are generally nonexistent. Because Girard wants to get to the origin of culture itself, he begins with precultural primates who imitate each other. Their increasing imitation erodes the boundaries between selves until the imitators attack each other to reestablish their own distinctiveness. Mimetic violence then escalates until it is transferred to a marginal third party too weak to retaliate. The violence stops and a society is forged out of the union of former rivals.

It is easy to see why, in Girard's view of things, there can be no cultural or religious resources for uncovering the innocence of this victim. The ruse of transference will only work if the victim can be credibly blamed for all of the violence without any substantial segment of the population remembering his or her innocence. Therefore, Girard focuses on the selection of a marginal individual, such as an orphan or a cripple, who can leave behind no culture of the victims that might testify to his or her innocence.[2] On the one hand the entire blame for violence has been shifted onto this individual by the real perpetrators, and on the other, he or she manifests the power to stop violence. Because this combination is at once terrifying, mysterious, fascinating and salvific, the scapegoat becomes uncanny and is transformed into deity. And it is this mystification that is the origin of all religious culture. Since by definition all religions are systems for mystifying the foundational sacrifice of arbitrary individuals, no amount of ecumenical conversation could uncover the violence they conspire to conceal.

The question then becomes, if this is the nature of violence, how can it best be mitigated? Since Girard defines violence as a permanent part of human biology, the goal is not to end violence altogether but to limit it justly. The

---

2 Girard claims that "the persecutors always convince themselves that *a small number of people, or even a single individual*, despite his relative weakness, is extremely harmful to the whole of society" (*Scapegoat*, 15).

religious solution of scapegoating and sacrifice is a relatively adequate way of achieving that goal but it is unjust because irrational. Those who are guilty of violence escape punishment, while the innocent are needlessly sacrificed. To achieve a more rational approach the scapegoat must be demystified by exposing its innocent and accidental character. But how?

Girard's answer is the gospel narrative of Jesus' death and resurrection. By narrating the scapegoating of a man whose innocence they firmly maintained, the gospels expose the secret of scapegoating concealed in every religion since its foundation. This desacralizes the old methods for controlling violence and creates a climate in which the legal system, a more rational way of limiting violence, can be developed. Since no culture could discover the secret of its own violence, the story of Jesus takes on the Barthian character of a revelation that brings an end to religion.

The reasons judged to be behind scapegoating will determine how this cure is assessed. For Girard, scapegoating is not simply an error, but neither is it a distortion necessary to human perception or identity formation. Culture is evidently not necessary to human nature but only a deeply repressed illusion developed to prevent the human race from destroying itself. What is needed is that the repressed memory be brought to light and that a more adequate alternative for the social function of religion be put in place. If repression and the need to limit violence are the only factors behind scapegoating, then Girard's solution works. The fact that Christians continue to scapegoat does not present an insurmountable obstacle. As the Christian message becomes more widely accepted and rational legal systems take hold, scapegoating can be expected gradually to diminish.

If the problem of violence is reformulated as cross-cultural from the beginning, however, Girard's proposed cure seems less effective. In so far as we are able to investigate it human identity is always already corporately formed by a variety of languages, cultures and religions. If we begin with this presupposition, what Girard calls a "sacrificial crisis" would have to be reformulated as a breakdown of existing relations between cultures, or at least between individuals with distinguishable corporate identities. The status quo ante is then not that two or more individuals have arrived at a truce by sacrificing a third, but that two or more cultures have entered into an alliance by sacrificing a third culture. For example, Jews and white Christians make peace by scapegoating Islamic fundamentalists; black Christians and Islamic fundamentalists make peace by scapegoating Jews, etc. The "sacrificial crisis" would then refer to a blurring of the ethnic map to the extent that established patterns of scapegoating break down. For example, Russians begin to imitate western democracies or Jews begin to imitate the tactics of Islamic fundamentalists.

If ethnic scapegoating is primary and even constituitive of all human religious identity, then two of Girard's major theses about the concealing and revealing of violence become questionable. First, if individuals are scapegoated as bearers of a corporate ethnic identity, then the minority culture that survives them will have symbolic resources for unmasking their innocence. It may be the case that "plague bearers" have no separate culture, but if the marginal person is sacrificed as a "nigger" or a "Jew" then whole cultures are left for whom the innocence of the victim is the most obvious thing imaginable. If a black man is lynched, black churches will sing negro spirituals that compare him to the innocently persecuted Hebrew slaves. If individuals are scapegoated as Jews, there are survivors like Elie Wiesel who will memorialize their innocence. Although I have used familiar examples, this is true all over the world wherever individuals are scapegoated as members of a despised minority culture, who either cannot or choose not to retaliate violently.

Secondly, if the story of Jesus' crucifixion and resurrection is reinterpreted as a foundation narrative that creates and sustains one ethos at the expense of others, then it cannot unambiguously unmask violence. Like all foundation narratives, it conceals its own scapegoating of Jews and other stereotyped contrasts to Christian identity. In my judgement the synoptic narratives belong to a cross-cultural genre of literature that one might call the testimony of scapegoated cultures. Although Nietzsche in *The Genealogy of Morals* argued persuasively that such literature conceals resentment, Girard has now shown that the narratives of the strong conceal their own resentment and their own violence. What I will argue in the following pages is that despite their concealment of some forms of violence, the testimony of traditions scapegoated by dominant Christian cultures can play a positive role in unmasking and overcoming Christian violence. To develop my argument, I will make use of an extended example: the scapegoating that occurred in the wake of that greatest of modern sacrificial crises, "the age of discovery" or "the age of conquest." What makes this such an interesting case for understanding the correlation between scapegoating language and violence is that Spain, the dominant imperial power of the age, carried out its conquest of the Americas with more concern for both rational legality and Christian ethics than has ever occurred in imperial ventures before or since. While they did not have the benefit of modern texts on violence in religion, they did make strenuous efforts to limit their violence by the two things that Girard considers to be the cure for violence: the gospels and the legal system. Yet, something clearly went wrong. Catholic missionaries and princes who intended to evangelize without violence ended up arguing that Christian love itself required the overthrow of native governments and the destruction of their cultures. Our question, then, is what happened? What role did the Christian symbols and the legal system play in instigating or disguising this violence?

2. José de Acosta and the Indian Conversions

On the eve of the Conquest, the ethnic map of the world was secure. The Europeans, who considered themselves descendants of Japheth, had forged a relatively common identity by contrasting themselves, on the one hand, to the African descendants of the "cursed sexual deviant Ham," as they put it in their racist theologies; and they contrasted themselves, on the other hand, to the so-called Asian descendants of Shem, most clearly represented by "the Christ-killing Jews and the Moslem heretics." In 1492, the year America was conquered/discovered, Spain had unified its sacred spaces by expelling the Jews and the Moors. Their patron, St. James, had acquired the title "mata-moros," Killer of the Moors. In short, the boundaries of the map were sealed by what Girard would recognize as established patterns of scapegoating. Then suddenly a vast continent was discovered with its millions of people who could not be placed. The map of ethnic identity was unsettled. For complex reasons which could be interpreted in a Girardean manner, Christians who intended to extend their faith to the New World peacefully ended up scrambling to realign their identity, contracting truces with some Indian cultures by ex-terminating others. To see how the language of ethnic scapegoating actually worked in the application of New Testament and legal precedents to the case of New World peoples, I will examine the writing of Father José de Acosta.

I choose Acosta, the sixteenth–century Jesuit provincial of Peru, because of the public and representative character of his writing. Acosta was a thoughtful moderate, somewhere between Ginez de Sepúlveda, the canon lawyer who justified enslavement of the Indians, and the radical Bartolomé de las Casas. His work formulates mainstream Jesuit thought on how to Christianize the Indians in an ethical and legal fashion. It lays the theoretical groundwork for the Jesuit "reductions," those influential institutions recognized by the Spa-nish crown and popularized by Hollywood in the film *The Mission* as humane solutions to the Indian problem. Acosta is therefore a good example of how theologically and legally educated Christians responded to the age of dis-covery and to the new mimetic crisis it provoked.

As Father Acosta studied Inca culture, he was clearly unnerved by the uncanny resemblances to Christianity—particularly by striking likenesses to the Trinity, baptism, communion, and confession—in the ideas and rituals supposedly taught by native culture heroes. One might think that the recog-nition of such similarities would have allowed Acosta to ascribe some value to native symbols within the continuum of nature and grace. But as Girard would have predicted, the similarities made Acosta more nervous than did the differences. For one thing, the similarities he recognized blurred the dis-tinction between "nature" and "grace;" that is, they resembled too closely the very Christian mysteries that Catholics attributed to supernatural grace alone.[3] And it was these particular mysteries that served as cultural boundaries, dis-tinguishing the Christian ethos from Moslem philosophy, from Judaism, etc. Since the Incas were not Christians, it seemed to Acosta that the native

3 See Pierre Duviols, *La destruccion de las religiones andinas*, 80.

analogues had to have been derived from a demonic mimesis of Christian revelation.

Perhaps what made the theory of demonic imitation so persuasive was the frightening juxtaposition of symbols that resembled those of Christian revelation with foreign practices that seemed violent and unnatural. In native convents, for example, young women lived chaste lives, but only so that they could later be sacrificed. Acosta reasoned that therefore "we ought not assume the devil loves chastity, but only that he is trying to rob God of his glory by copying Christian convents."[4] The more he studied native religion, the more convinced he became that "there is scarcely anything instituted by Jesus Christ . . . which the devil has not counterfeited . . . and carried off to his gentiles."[5] Because, for Father Acosta, the Father of Lies is the master mimetic, the more uncanny the likeness between Inca religion and Christianity, the greater the evidence of demonic presence in Inca religion.

The question that occurs to a reader of Girard is whether these similarities were heightened after the first contact through some kind of mimetic process or whether they were there in Inca religion all along. One answer to the question comes from Garcilasso de la Vega, the son of a conquistador and a woman of the Inca royal family, who wrote around 1610. In an attempt to defuse violence toward Indians, Garcilasso wrote a veiled apology of Inca religion in which he denied the existence of any genuine similarities to Christian revelation. According to Garcilasso the alleged demonic imitations were actually the imaginative creations of Spaniards who "interpreted [Aztec and Inca religion] according to their pleasure or prejudices, and wrote things down as truths which the Indians never heard of."[6] It is important to note that Garcilasso particularly denies any likenesses to the Trinity or the Gospel story, those symbols which had long distinguished Christian culture from Judaism and other ethnic rivals:

> . . . the assertion that *Icona* is their word for God the Father, and Bacab for God the Son, and Estruac for God the Holy Ghost; and that Chiripia is the most Holy Virgin Mary, and Ischen the blessed St. Anne, and that Bacab killed by Eopuco represents Christ our Lord crucified by Pilate: all these and similar things are inventions and fictions of Spaniards, and the natives are entirely ignorant of them.[7]

Despite his pro-native bias Garcilasso is also forced to account for the mimetic behavior of Indians:

> When the Indians said that their God was one in three and three in one, it must

---

4 José de Acosta, *Historia natural y moral*, 240–42.
5 José de Acosta, *Historia natural y moral*, 235.
6 Garcilasso de la Vega, *Royal Commentaries of the Incas*, 123.
7 Garcilasso de la Vega, *Royal Commentaries of the Incas* 1, 124.

have been a new invention of theirs, made after they had heard of the trinity and unity of our Lord God, to curry favor with the Spaniards, by saying that they had some things resembling our holy religion. . . . All these things were invented by the Indians in the expectation that they might gain something by the resemblance. I affirm this as an Indian, and as knowing the nature of Indians.[8]

Three interesting conclusions can be drawn from Garcilasso's claims. First, that for whatever reason, both Spaniards and Indians evidently heightened the analogical similarities between their respective corporate identities. Secondly, that an acute observer of the late sixteenth–century political scene could recognize this process as provocative of violence. And thirdly, that a native observer like Garcilasso could see that to prevent the imminent outbreak of violence against his people, the escalation of similarities had to be reversed.

It seems likely then that what Acosta describes are not simply chance likenesses but what Girard would call a "sacrificial crisis" of escalating mimesis. It was in this environment, when generalized violence against the Indians was imminent, and indeed already occurring, that numerous Christian lawyers and theologians sought to redraw the map of ethnic differences. Significantly the stated purpose of these maps is to control violence. For the purposes of this essay Acosta's map will suffice as an example.

To establish legal and moral limits on the use of violence in evangelism, Acosta ranked the non-Christian peoples of the world according to their degree of contrast from the Spanish Christian ethos. Directly beneath European Catholics in Acosta's scheme is the highest class of barbarians, "who do not diverge greatly from right reason." He distinguished this group by what he called the "the notable use of letters," and he added, "wherever literary traditions and books exist, people are more human and especially politic." By this he means that they have a legal system based on natural law, so that between Europeans and the literate peoples of the Indies, such as the Chinese and Japanese, there should be a complete truce. Such peoples were to be "brought under the sway of the Gospel mainly by their own reason, [that is, nonviolently]."

Since even the Incas were not literate, Acosta created an intermediate class of cultures whose natures were relatively developed and who therefore could not be construed as stark opposites of Christ. For Christ to fulfill the natures of these people, they required only the benign supervision of literate princes. Such foreign princes were to act with constraint, allowing the Indians to retain those of their "laws and usages which were not contrary to reason or the Gospel." But it was the Europeans themselves, of course, who remained the standard of a human nature completed by Christ.[9]

8 Garcilasso de la Vega, *Royal Commentaries of the Incas* 1, 121.
9 José de Acosta, *De procuranda Indorum salute*, 46–47.

For its time, Acosta's policy of relative nonaggression toward the first two classes seems enlightened. But in light of Girard's work, it is interesting to note that it is precisely those groups with whom the truce is made, the literate Chinese or Japanese and the "civilized" Incas who were most like the Europeans and thus potentially their greatest rivals. In fact neither the powerful Japanese nor the relatively powerful Incas were the real scapegoats, for beneath these few not too unnatural natives, Acosta distinguished a third class in which he located the great bulk of South American cultures. It is toward this vast majority of cultures that he believed violence was appropriate.

Acosta distinguished this third group by its lack of both literacy and settled towns. "It includes savage men . . . having scarcely anything of human feeling . . . changing their places of residency frequently or having fixed ones which more resemble dens of wild animals."[10] Clearly Acosta could not verify empirically that the "vast herds" of Indians had no human feeling, but in his European Christian eyes, the dispersed settlement patterns and seasonal migrations typical of most Indian cultures seemed to indicate that they lacked the enjoyment of human company—that most basic of human feelings on which the commonweal was built. And once this was established, all of the other antisocial vices could simply be projected onto this category of nomadic peoples by association. For example, it included cannibals "who always thirsting for blood, are cruel to strangers," and others "who, while not blood-thirsty like tigers" are "timid and generally given over to the vices of Venus and Adonis."[11]

In short, this third category includes many of the characteristics Girard associates with scapegoat victims, and Acosta explicitly described it as the counter-image of his nature-grace Christology: "on the whole" he writes, they are "barbarous peoples, who being outside the supernatural light, also lacked philosophy and natural doctrine."[12] Like anti-Christs, these entire cultures are the very antithesis of that Hellenic nature graced in the incarnation and embodied in the Spanish nation.

Once he had reestablished their diametrical opposition to Spanish Christian identity, the Indian scapegoats could become the objects of Christian compassion. For Acosta, these barbarian Indians were not animals but souls for whom Christ died—souls that were now trapped in violent demonic imitations of Christianity. In their present state, they did violence to their own natures and therefore charity dictated that they be forced to "leave the forests and gathered into towns" where they could "be taught . . . to be human beings."[13]

10 José de Acosta, *De procuranda Indorum salute*, 47.
11 José de Acosta, *De procuranda Indorum salute*, 47–48.
12 José de Acosta, *Historia natural y moral*, 216.
13 José de Acosta, *Historia natural y moral*, 47.

In carrying out this policy, their European guardians were to be "guided by that charity that suffers all things and does not seek its own interest."[14]

Acosta admitted that since freedom belongs to the very nature of faith it seemed both unchristian and illegal to harvest Indian conversions by violence. Yet he also conceded that "to reconcile two such opposites as violence and liberty in a way that charity can render coherent" was beyond his capacities.[15] Clearly, corralling such people against their will would normally violate human nature, both in the eyes of the law and in the light of the gospels—but after examining the nature of the Indians in relation to Spanish Christian identity, he became convinced that without some use of force these particular peoples would "never come to clothe themselves in the liberty and nature of the children of God."[16] Because their dispersed settlement patterns had allowed them to be scapegoated as Christ's unnatural opposites, these people hardly seemed to have a social nature to violate. The whole point, as Acosta saw it, was to give them one so that it could later be completed by Christ without coercion.

The policies I have just described were implemented in the Jesuit reductions and in other alternative solutions. They were designed as a Christian attempt to rescue the Indians from the unnatural violence that was both Christ's opposite and his uncanny double. Yet within a few decades these policies led to the extinction of entire peoples, cultures and languages. Others survived but their populations were decimated by slavery, disease, and torture. What I find unnerving is the humane language of Christian ethics and love with which these policies were formulated and carried out. Because the Indians had been scapegoated as Christ's opposites, Christians had no difficulty believing that they were actually rescuing the Indians from violence. Spanish Christianity did not, however, have the last word. Ironically, it was after the survivors of the scapegoated rural Indians had been detained in camps that the mimetic process began in earnest. I will suggest that in this Indian copying of Christianity lies a resource for uncovering Christian violence in the Americas.

In order to facilitate conversions, Spanish missionaries systematically superimposed the symbols from the life of Jesus onto the culture heroes, deities and creators of the peoples they resettled in pueblos. The idea was to force the copy-cat demons to "testify against their will," by juxtaposing the genuine to the mimetic revelations. Christian feast days were therefore introduced on the major native festivals, churches were built on sacred ruins, and the second council of Lima required crosses to be raised on all pagan sites.[17] Soon it

---

14 José de Acosta, *Historia natural y moral*, 138.
15 José de Acosta, *De procuranda Indorum salute*, 137.
16 José de Acosta, *De procuranda Indorum salute*, 137.
17 See Duviols, *La destruccion de las religiones andinas*, 128. The quote is from Acosta, *Historia natural y moral*, 376.

became difficult to venerate any native place or time without simultaneously venerating the Christian double forcibly installed in its place. As a result, native symbols became trapped in a web of overlapping and imitative meanings from which they could never again be completely untangled.

With this accomplished, Acosta believed Jesus Christ had won out over the copy-cat demons who had previously held the Indians captive. Writing in 1589, he rejoiced that everywhere "the Cross of Christ has been planted." By imitating the demonic imitator, Christians had caught the devil "in his own noose," and defeated him "with his own weapons." Readers were assured that if there is "any accursed minister" of the devil's still practicing, "it is out in the caves or mountaintops," in "very hidden places . . . far removed from the name and practice of Christians."[18]

Some thirty years later, however, it was discovered that instead of creating one-way bridges to Christianity the superimposing of Christian symbols on native analogues had created a systematic ambiguity. It was, after all, the native web of sacred geography that had dictated the placement of the crosses, and this allowed native worship to continue underground, concealed in ironic reversals of Christian meanings. The shamans and native culture heroes had not been banished to "very hidden places far from the name and practice of Christians," but were in fact flourishing under the cover of Christian signs.

When the missionaries systematically planted the cross on local deities, native peoples across South America simply identified their cultural heroes with Jesus. And when this happened, in their minds at least, the entire native ethos gained the status of Christian revelation. By the same logic, everything that contrasted to the native ethos (namely white European culture) became a counter-image of Christ. This allowed for the reversal of white Christian scapegoating: Whites and not Indians were now portrayed by native peoples as the demonic enemies of Christ.

3. The Rhetoric of Reversal in Yekuana Religion

One classic example of such a reversal is found in the *Watunna*, a Yekuana creation cycle from the Orinoco area in Venezuela.[19] In this narrative a creator named Wanadi flees across the jungle pursued and imitated by his demonic twin, Odosha. As he flees, Wanadi creates the various ethnic groups including "good white people called Fañuru" (a corruption of "españoles"). Reversing the Spanish charges that Indians were unnatural because they lacked settled towns, the *Watunna* says that Wanadi created towns for the Indian people, Yekuana. He is said to have wanted to make a town for the whites, as he had for

18 José de Acosta, *Historia natural y moral*, 376.
19 Marc de Civrieux, *Watunna*.

the Indian groups, but he was forced to leave the Fañuru early because the demonic Odosha was right behind him.[20]

When Wanadi's demonic twin, Odosha, arrived at the place of the Fañuru people, he incited them to envy what Wanadi had given to the Indians and to go to war with the Yekuana on that account. According to the story, "he deceived the Fañuru" because he told those white men "who were sad and abandoned" without a town that Wanadi was evil: "he made you poor, he didn't leave you anything," while up ahead "he made a beautiful town for other people" (the Yekuana). "That is not good," Odosha told them, "you ought to march against them, take their houses . . . kill [Wanadi]." When they arrived in the lands of the Indians, the story says, the whites were very poor, naked, "they had no bows, arrows, nothing."[21]

Significantly, Wanadi promised to give the whites all they needed, but by this time the whites were so full of "hatred and envy because of what Odosha had told them" that they wanted only to rob the Indians. In Girardian language, the Fañuru wanted to steal the objects of Indian desire. And that, according to the Yekuana, "is how evil came" because that "is how war, injustice, and robbery began."[22] The whites then became the primary antagonists of creation. Out of envy they pursued the native culture hero across the forests until eventually they captured him, and crucified him under the direction of missionary priests. What follows is the Yekuana passion narrative:

> Then some other men came out who were hidden, called Fadre [Padres]. "Who are you?" they asked [the creator]. . . . "I'm Wanadi," he answered. . . . The Fadre didn't like how he answered: "You're an imposter. You're not Wanadi, you're Odosha," they said . . . and for that lie we are going to kill you." Then they beat him with whips . . . asking "Who owns this town, these houses? Who owns this earth?" "It is all mine said Wanadi, I made it all, I made you too." "Deceiver! [said the priests], "Everything is ours, nothing is yours, and for that [deception] we are going to punish you.
>
> ". . . Kahiuru [the Spanish captain] sent for a post to hang him on. It was shaped like a cross. . . . When they brought the [cross], they nailed him there with iron points. "It's done," they said, "Now let's leave him in the road to die."[23]

The debate here is over who is really Wanadi, the original creator, and who is the demonic double, Odosha. Who are the true Christians and who are the demonic imitators? The missionaries, of course, preached Christ's claim to deity against that of the arch-mimetic devil Wanadi. According to them, the killing of the mimetic pagan culture Wanadi represented founded a new

---

20 Marc de Civrieux, *Watunna*, 77–79.
21 Marc de Civrieux, *Watunna*, 77–79.
22 Marc de Civrieux, *Watunna*, 77–79.
23 Marc de Civrieux, *Watunna*, 81–82.

alliance between white and Indian Christians. Indeed it is Wanadi's defeat by the cross that transformed the violent savages into cultured human beings. One colonial missionary to the Orinoco area, Father Matías Ruíz Blanco, wrote with confidence that Christ, "the divine Laborer who began to sow the pure seed of his Gospel in those uncultured hearts, has not ceased to send workers who . . . have penetrated those jungles, planting the holy Cross where it had never been . . . worshipped, reducing those savage beasts to the tameness of lambs."[24]

In their version of the events, however, the Yekuana reversed the charges. What had looked like the death of paganism is reinterpreted as an envious murder of the innocent Yekuana creator. Since Wanadi set the pattern for the Indian way of life, if he is the demonic impostor, then Yekuana culture is a stolen imitation of white Christianity. But if he is the creator, as this narrative affirms, then missionary attempts to eradicate or steal the Indian way of life reflect the envious actions of Odosha.

Like Acosta, the missionaries who killed Wanadi were confident that the victory of the cross was final. But if we return to that scene, we will find they were mistaken:

> [The] commanding officer called Wamedi, the rooster. He sent him to the moun-tain to watch [the cross] and tell them when Wanadi died. . . . When the sun rose, Wamedi sang. . . . "Wanadi's gone!" . . . [H]e didn't sing the death song . . . [T]he Fadre and the soldiers came to see what happened. They looked at [the cross]. Wanadi was hanging there. . . . He was dead. . . .[But] it was a trick. . . .Wanadi was just hanging there like an empty shell. . . . He had gone back to Kushamakari.[25]

The scene then ends when the Yekuana "people came from all over to celebrate" and shouted: "Wanadi isn't dead."

Because Wanadi is the one who originally taught the customs stereotyped by missionaries as demonic, his escape sets a precedent for ethnic rebirth. But the culture that is reborn out of Christian persecution is not the same as that which existed prior to conquest. In the pre-contact period Wanadi may have been somewhat more like Girard's portrait of the scapegoat—that is, a more ambiguous figure sacrificed for destructive acts and deified. But what we have in the *Watunna* is the resurrection, not of a scapegoated individual, but of an entire culture whose understanding of violence has been forged by the process of being scapegoated—of a remnant whose transformed myths now testify to the innocence of an unjustly sacrificed cultural hero. And this resurrection of the innocent reveals the secret of violence that sustains the dominant Chris-tian culture.

We are now in a position to examine the dialectic of concealment and

24 Matías Ruíz Blanco, *Conversion de Piritu*, 57.
25 Matías Ruíz Blanco, *Conversion de Piritu*, 57.

revelation in the cross-ethnic play of religious rhetoric. For our purposes the cross can be taken as an example of what occurs with any religious symbol. For the early missionaries in the Orinoco area, the cross is proof of the holiness and justice of their own religion's victory over the demonic and violent religion of the Indians. No doubt part of the missionaries' confidence lies in the crosses and other visible symbols of Christian identity which the converts wear. But that confidence also blinds them to the double meaning the cross has gained in the course of its battle with Yekuana religion. Hidden in the sign of missionary victory is the wily vitality of Wanadi.

> The [Spanish] stopped looking [for Wanadi's life-signs]: "We killed him ," the priests said. . . . They kept [the cross] as proof, as a sign. That's their reminder. Later, they made lots of crosses to show people. They say: "On this post he died." They didn't know. . . . They say they killed him. It's not true. They couldn't. He tricked them and got away.[26]

Native culture may appear to have died, yet concealed in the very proof of its passing is the promise of its resurrection. And whatever else they may conceal, the myths of this resurrected culture reveal the innocence of Christianity's victims.

4. Conclusions

In contrast to Girard I have started from the assumption that cultural-linguistic diversity is a permanent and inherent part of human nature. Because sacrifice is constituitive of ethnic identity, including Christian identity, sacrificial violence cannot be exposed once and for all, and it cannot be simply replaced by a legal system. All cultures have some form of legal system and all legal systems conceal and continue the scapegoating of their respective cultures.

The Gospel story of the innocently crucified Messiah seems unique only if one compares the literature of dominant cultures such as the Greeks with the literature of a scapegoated minority such as that of the early Christians. But if one compares the synoptic gospels with the Yekuana *Watunna* or with the Inca "Lament on the Death of Atahualpa," the *Watunna*, or the literature of other colonized peoples, one finds numerous parallels. My thesis is that the gospels' power to uncover scapegoating is not a universal revelation but a relational one. That is, it does not expose Christian scapegoating of Jews or Romans, but Jewish or Roman scapegoating of Christians. As such it can be used analogically by victims of Christian scapegoating to turn the tables.

In this paper I have chronicled a process of scapegoating and counter-scapegoating. The writings of José de Acosta and the myths of the Yekuana

26 Matías Ruíz Blanco, *Conversion de Piritu*, 57.

each attempt to unmask demonic violence concealed in the other's religious symbols. In doing so, the white and Indian sources also mutually scapegoat each other. While Acosta portrays the Indians as illiterate antisocial dupes of demonic mimesis, the native sources portray the missionaries as Wanadi killers, demons, and antisocial homeless people who envy Indian towns. Furthermore, the scapegoating on both sides is connected with real violence: Acosta, for example, was trying to conquer the Indians, and from time to time native groups have fought back.

But even if both groups of texts conceal scapegoating, it is nevertheless true that the native myths reveal the violence that white Christianity conceals, and furthermore they reveal this violence as infidelity to Christ in the form of the crucified Wanadi. Perhaps this is not a freak coincidence but a by–product of the way Girard's scapegoating process works. In order to transfer the object, escalating violence to a third party, the scapegoat's similarity to the belligerents' core identity is first heightened and then distanced. In the Yakuana case, for example, this would mean that the cultural hero Wanadi's similarity to Christ is first heightened through the process of missionization, and then distanced, rendering him uncanny for non-Indian Christians. I would now like to argue that the tradition of the *hidden messiah* makes such reversals potentially significant for Christians.

The very meaning of "Christ" has roots in Christian interpretations of Isaiah 53, where the suffering of a despised people at first appears to reveal their enmity with the God of author and reader. But as the reader discerns the true identity of this suffering people, his or her own estrangement from God is disclosed: they turn out to be the servants of God suffering for the reader's sins. This theme is continued in Matthew 25 where people fail to recognize Christ in the sick and the prisoners, and in Acts where Paul on his way to persecute heretics hears a voice crying "Saul, Saul, why are you persecuting me?" Because of passages like these, Christians half expect the Messiah to be hidden in the victims of their own actions, and conversion to be a reconciliation with God through a recognition of these victims.

The South American situation fits the pattern. White Christians at first attribute Indian suffering to lostness or estrangement from God. But when the death of the native cultural hero like Wanadi is recast as crucifixion, the paschal identity of white Christians is evoked. Caught off guard, they find Wanadi where they expected Jesus and their penitential empathy is transferred to the Indians. The effect is uncanny. Suddenly, the suffering of Christ is linked to the resistance of those who bear the hidden effects of white culture and missions. In these mirrors behind Christ's back the scapegoating and violence Christ conceals can be clearly seen, and Christian motives are thrown into question.

This may at first seem to be nothing more than Girard's solution adjusted to compensate for the concealing function of ethnic symbols. That is, even though he is now refracted through a mirroring culture, it is still Christ who reveals the scapegoating mechanism so that it can be replaced by a legal system. But there are other ways in which the solution I propose differs from Girard's. One is the problem of motivation. In the solution I suggest here corporate self-love for the cultural hero Christ is transferred back along the analogical lines of similarity to Wanadi, and from him to the scapegoated culture. It might seem that this would simply co-opt the Yekuana symbol, Wanadi, something like turning the holocaust into a mere type of Christian crucifixion. But because cultural heroes like Wanadi are the historical products not only of heightened similarity but also of distanciation, they cannot be easily assimilated to the repentant scapegoater's own identity. What is created is a sense of empathy or love for the analogically different.

This empathy gives one an uncanny window into the systematic scapegoating hidden in Christianity. It would be naive, of course, to suppose that such empathy alone could persuade a dominant Christian culture to give up power or to correct systemic biases in its legal system. If there is a change in the power structure, no doubt it will be through the more material resistance of the scapegoated culture. Yet the empathy created through the ironic reversal of a culture's historic scapegoats creates a new cultural space for change. Through the empathy created by liminal figures like Wanadi, the culture of white Christians now might come to include a more conscious suspicion that systematic violence may be hidden in its own legal system and in its religious symbols. This new empathy could make them fear that the violence concealed in their culture might be destroying something very like what they themselves hold sacred. All of this makes the dominant culture less resistant to the legal changes being pressed by the scapegoated culture. And it may give white Christians reason to hope that any Indian limitation of their power is not a limitation of God's power, but is rather a part of God's lessening of violence in the world. Thus it may motivate assent and even cooperation.

In short it is my thesis that the limitation of violence and the increase of love toward God and neighbor is indeed at the heart of the gospel message. Yet to unmask Christian violence and to widen the scope of Christian love, Christians need to read their foundation narratives indirectly by analogically linking Christ to his historical doubles—those gods and heroes of neighboring cultures who have been scapegoated as Christ's opposites. This would entail a move beyond religious self-sufficiency to a time in which, for Christians, the new redeemers are the historic victims of Christian violence resurrected from their invisibility.

A new age in which Christ's crucified Indian doubles return from their underground concealment is also imagined by various South American Indian groups. Most of these sources merely hope that the present order will be stood on its head, so that white Christians will become the servants of the Indians. Some, however, imagine an age of nonviolent reciprocity between white and

Indian worlds under the governance of an Indian Messiah. According to one Peruvian Quechua narrator, "When the world turns over, Inkarri [the mythic cultural hero killed by Christ or the "priest," Pizarro,[27] is going to return, and he is going to walk as he did in ancient times. Then all people, Christian and gentile, are going to find each other."[28] On that day "even the black bitter heart of the *misti wiraqocha* [white Christians] will have become sweet; then we will all be of one pure heart as in the days of our Inca grandfathers."[29]

Certainly, René Girard has done much to clarify the role of violence in human culture and religion. If violence is indeed an integral part of human nature, as he claims, it is no doubt utopian to hope that the presently warring ethoi "will all be of one pure heart," as the Quechua millenialist imagines. But certainly history has also shown that the gospel narratives and the legal systems of dominant Christian majorities do not simply end violence either, as Girard hopes. In this chapter, I tried to argue that there are grounds for a more moderate hope. This hope is that Christian scapegoating can be partially unmasked and violent passions partially transformed through the resisting and witnessing presence of indigenous Indian victims like the Yakuana.

27 Gregorio Condori Mamani, *De nosotros, los runas*, 23.
28 Alejandro Ortiz Rescaniere, *De Adaneva a Inkarri*, 130–32.
29 Ricardo Valderrama and Carmen Escalante, "El Apu Ausangate en la narrativa popular," 177.

"Provoked Suicide" and the Victim's Behavior

Charles D. Orzech

Abstract

René Girard's theory has yet to be considered in light of non-western materials. In this article I show how Girard's theory of mimetic desire and victimage helps us to distinguish a violent and sacrificial strand of the Buddhist tradition from the nonviolent core teachings of Buddhism with which it is often confused. I argue that examples of Buddhist nonviolence provide powerful arguments in favor of extending Girard's theory to include a "transformative mimesis" which effects an identification of oppressors with victims and which breaks the cycle of sacrificial violence. After having examined a variety of material from throughout the Buddhist tradition, I examine the self-immolation of the Vietnamese monk Thich Quang-Duc in 1963, as it exemplifies the violent and sacrificial strand of Buddhism. The article concludes with reflections on nonviolent Buddhist tradition, on Martin Luther King Jr., and on Gandhi. While Girard's theory is usefully applied to the Buddhist tradition, its application to the nonviolent aspects of Buddhism calls into question the privileged place Girard accords to the Gospels in world religions.

1. Girard's Theory and the History of Religions

René Girard's theory of religion and its relationship to violence has stirred considerable controversy in some quarters of the academy, though it has largely been overlooked by historians of religions specializing in non-Western traditions. This is particularly unfortunate since virtually all discussions of Girard's theory have focused on Western religious traditions. One hopes the situation will soon be remedied; this article is a gesture in the direction of bringing Asian materials into the debate. Surveying Buddhist notions concerning desire, self-sacrifice, and violence, I will argue first that Girard's theory is useful beyond the limits of Christian culture, and second, that evidence from Buddhism and other traditions justify some extensions and revisions of Girard's view of mimesis. Third, the same evidence leads me to

137

view Girard's insistence on the extra-human source of the Gospel revelation as a dismemberment of human experience and of ethical responsibility. I will further argue that this dismemberment—one might call it a displacement involving "others" or "the other"—accounts for some of the attractiveness and apparent explanatory power of the theory while constituting its primary difficulty. It is this displacement coupled with Girard's great talent as a myth-maker that deserve careful evaluation. By moving outside the perspective of Jewish and Christian traditions, we can extend, refine, and supplement Girard's work.

Although Girard's theory is explicated elsewhere in this volume, it is appropriate to review several key points before we consider it in the context of Buddhism. According to Girard, all forms of religion, mythology, and ritual, indeed, the creation of human culture itself, are founded on the murder of an individual by a group. The mechanism which necessitates this murder is mimesis, or, as Girard puts it, "mimetic desire." Two individuals compete for the same object and as "rivalry becomes acute, the rivals are more apt to forget whatever objects are the cause of the rivalry and instead become more fascinated with one another. . . . Each rival becomes for his counterpart the worshipped and despised model and obstacle, the one who must be at once beaten and assimilated."[1] The rivals become doubles. As the rivalry escalates the combatants become indistinguishable. This "undifferentiation" is often represented in myth and literature as a plague of reciprocal violence which threatens the continued existence of social and cosmic order.[2] At some point the group polarizes against this threat by selecting a scapegoat, an individual who, while actually innocent, is seen as the cause of the imminent breakdown of order.[3] The "scapegoat" is sacrificed, and the sacrifice not only "prevents the spread of violence by keeping vengeance in check" but is the source of new order or reestablished order.[4] Thus, the victim is often divinized and both the breakdown of order and its reestablishment are attributed to divine plan. "It [the scapegoat] is even believed to have brought about its own death."[5] Indeed, in situations where oppression has been internalized this is precisely what happens.

This series of hypotheses has adjunct to it two further axioms which are at the heart of both the theory's power and its problems: First, sacrificial violence conceals its own origins while giving rise to religious and cultural forms. "The structuring power of victimage remains hidden."[6] Second, until the middle

1 Girard, *Things Hidden*, 26.
2 Girard, *Double Business*, 139.
3 Girard, *Scapegoat*, 18–22.
4 Girard, *Violence and the Sacred*, 18.
5 Girard, *Things Hidden*, 27.
6 Girard, *Double Business*, 165.

ages, such victims were not seen as innocent, but as guilty or divine. Gradually people have become sensitized and able to recognize the really arbitrary persecution and violence behind such "lynchings," and this new-found skepticism is a direct result of the influence of the Gospel texts, texts which reveal the arbitrary nature of religious violence and the innocence of the victim. "The Judaeo-Christian texts have produced a disintegration [of sacrificial religion], whose effect has, however, been slowed down and moderated by the churches' sacrifical reading [of those texts]."[7] Thus, all the world's religion and mythology are founded on violence. Only the Gospels are true revelation.

As a historian of religions and a specialist in Buddhism and Chinese religions, I have mixed feelings toward the work of René Girard. On the one hand it is refreshing to find such bold, comprehensive, and yet nuanced theoretical work after so long a period in which such undertakings were out of fashion. Indeed, Girard's work presents the most comprehensive overview of religion and culture since the works of Durkheim, Freud, and Marx, those giants whom he emulates and opposes.[8] Girard, like Freud, is a master reteller of myths, a master storyteller. Nevertheless, this boldness must impel us to examine his theories very carefully. In Girard's advocacy of mimetic desire and consequent universal victimage as the engine of all culture, the historian of religions cannot help but be reminded of the totalizing theories of an earlier generation—of Sir James G. Frazer or Edward Max Muller. Even before the sophisticated theories of Durkheim, Freud, and Marx were challenged by "postmodern" movements, historians of religion recoiled from Casauban-like theorists who sought the "key to all mythologies."[9] Indeed, in the present postmodern climate where all totalizing narratives are associated with the extreme intellectual and political hubris of modernism, Girard's theory may strike many as atavistic.[10] The privileged place Girard accords the Gospels (if not to most of historical Christianity) seems a throwback to imperialistic Christian theological apologetics, to a time before the days of Ernst Troeltsch or Friedrich Schleiermacher.

While Girard has by no means answered all criticisms, he has acquitted himself well on some of these points, arguing, for instance, that to exclude certain hypotheses on an *a priori* basis is antiscientific.[11] Indeed, Girard argues that his is a scientific hypothesis and that like all scientific hypotheses it

7 Girard, *Things Hidden*, 288.
8 For Girard's analysis of contemporary academic culture and his discussion of it in terms of mimetic desire and universal victimage see *Double Business*, 199–229.
9 George Elliot, *Middlemarch*, 15, 57.
10 David Harvey, *The Condition of Postmodernity*, presents an excellent overview.
11 Robert G. Hammerton-Kelly, *Violent Origins*, 112–115, and Girard, *Things Hidden*, 35–40. The criticism of Girard's definition of "scientific" is one of the few interesting points raised in an otherwise remarkably obtuse review of *Violence and the Sacred* by the normally perceptive Hayden White. See "Ethnological 'Lie' and Mythical 'Truth.'"

is in some sense both a "meta-narrative" and reductive.[12] Yet, Girard argues, it is through the proposing and questioning of such totalistic hypotheses that the scientific advances which characterize our world have been achieved. Girard claims that his hypothesis accounts for more of the data of human culture than other theories, and it goes without saying that the method of science, the testing of hypotheses, is for Girard, the only way to proceed. Girard's hypothesis is also easily misundertood as "thematic." Rather than pursuing a grab bag of themes Girard proposes a hypothesis which seeks to account for the shape of our world by positing mimetic desire and victimage as structuring principles which, having done their work, disappear from view.[13] To some this may seem very hard to swallow, but there are numerous quite obvious analogies in the sciences. To mention only one example, the "big bang" theory of cosmic origination presents an explanation for the observed features of the universe by appealing to events that cannot be directly observed.[14]

In terms of heuristic value there is much to be said for this theory. Therefore I will proceed, in a spirit both sympathetic and critical, to make use of Girard's hypotheses and to test them against material which has remained largely outside of his purview. This material is from South, Southeast, and East Asian Buddhism. I will adhere to Girard's methodological style by proceeding morphologically and structurally, for the most part slighting contextual and historical issues and examining material which obviously resonates with Girard's theory: Buddhist Self-Immolation.[15] As I will show, Girard's theory is helpful in distinguishing between two important Buddhist attitudes toward violence that are usually conflated. But if we really wish to contribute to a cure for violence then we must refine Girard's theory concerning mimetic desire along lines suggested by Thee Smith in his "King and the Black Religious Quest to Cure Racism" (in this volume) and in my own analysis below.

I will begin my examination of Buddhism with the core tenants of nonviolence (ahimsā) and the destructive nature of desire (tṛṣṇā, "craving"). I will then turn to the ancient roots of an alternative violent Buddhist tradition of self-sacrifice which competes with and is often confused with the nonviolent strand of the tradition, and I will follow this dual trail through stories and myths to the self-immolation of the Vietnamese monk Thich Quang-Duc in 1963.

---

12 Girard, *Things Hidden*, 39.
13 Hammerton-Kelly, *Violent Origins*, 111–115.
14 Recent research results are putting strain on the "Big Bang" theory. See John Noble Wilford, "The Big Bang Survives an Onslaught of New Cosmology."
15 Careful reconstruction of historical contexts beyond what I have attempted here should be the next step in the assessment of these hypotheses.

2. Mimetic Desire and Nonviolence: The Buddhist Perspective

As presented in the West from the time of Edwin Arnold's *The Light of Asia*, Buddhism has been the rationalistic and nonviolent world religion, the religion which might succeed Christianity as more in harmony with Enlightenment scientific views. While differences have not gone unremarked, Buddhism has been dubbed "the religion of analysis" and compared with the philosophies of David Hume and Friedrich Nietzsche.[16] Its pacifistic elements were powerfully attractive from the late nineteenth century right up through the Vietnam war, and Buddhism is among the fastest growing religions in America and Europe. Perplexingly, Buddhist self-immolations were couched in pacifistic rhetoric, particularly among Buddhists.[17] As I will demonstrate below nonviolent sentiments may with justification be seen as the core of the Buddhist message, and such sentiments (the doctrine of *ahimsā*) are found throughout the tradition. Nonetheless, nonviolent elements are easily and often purposely confused with a thread in Buddhism which promotes violent self-sacrifice with the aim of restoring order, and we can recognize in these self-sacrifices the violent sacred so well described by Girard.

Nonviolence or "noninjury" is the first of the Five Precepts incumbent upon all Buddhists, lay and monastic alike: "I undertake to observe the rule / to abstain from taking life."[18] The *Sutta Nipata* admonishes us to "Put by the rod for all that lives, / Nor harm thou any one thereof," and violence is excoriated in the *Rules of the Discipline* as one of the four most serious types of offenses.[19] Along with sexual misconduct, theft, and false claims to magical attainments or insight, violence is punishable in the most severe manner sanctioned by the tradition: expulsion from the community.[20]

The basis of the Buddhist rejection of violence can be traced to the pan-Indian doctrine of karma which teaches that "The iron itself createth the rust, / which slowly is bound to consume it. / The evil-doer by his own deeds / Is led to a life full of suffering."[21] Violence is by nature reciprocal and the doer of evil deeds is consumed by and comes to embody those very deeds. So too, those who oppose evil with force come to resemble those who are evil. "There is only one eternal law: hate never destroys hate, only love does."[22] Com-

---

16 Jacobson, *Buddhism: The Religion of Analysis*, 162; Welbon, *The Buddhist Nirvana and Its Western Interpreters*, 184–193.
17 Prebish, *American Buddhism*, 21, 28.
18 Conze, *Buddhist Scriptures*, 70.
19 Conze, *Buddhist Scriptures*, 79.
20 Conze, *Buddhist Scriptures*, 74.
21 Conze, *Buddhist Scriptures*, 84, quoting *Dhammapada*.
22 Lal, *Dhammapada*, 39.

petitive action or retaliation for evil deeds only leads to a further spread of evil. This is because karma is fundamentally mimetic.[23]

Buddhist theology locates the root of karmic mimesis in a doctrine of the destructiveness of desire and as such, the Buddhist analysis of desire has much in common with Girard's analysis of desire. Thus of the Four Noble Truths that are the foundational insights of the Buddhist tradition the first truth, that all existence is characterized by "suffering," is rooted in the second truth, that of "craving" (*tṛṣṇā*), or desire.[24] Blind desire is ultimately inseparable from the delusion of individual and unique selfhood (*ātman*), a selfhood that is only an illusory reflection of another's socially constructed desires. Buddhism therefore sees the destruction of selfish desire and egoism as its chief aim and preaches that there is no real abiding self (*an-ātman*). Since selfhood is constructed upon the desires of others the elimination of the notion of an independent self which results in a stance of selfless service cuts through the cycle of mimetic desire.

In an early biography of the Buddha, the *Buddhacarita*, we find an analysis of desire and its consequences as the lynchpin of the story of the Buddha's enlightenment. This story encapsulates Buddhist doctrine and the key formula of Co-dependent Origination (*pratītyasamuttpāda*), the social construction of the world through acts of desire based on ignorant selfishness. In this story the Buddha seeks the answer to the cause of "suffering, old age, and death." He finds his answer in human obliviousness, in ignorance of the reality of a changing world. The root of this ignorance is karma and desire:

> [He] saw beings appear & pass away according to their deeds
>   & grew in compassion: for surely those of evil deeds
>   go to evil destiny (& those of virtuous deeds
>   set forth for heaven). . . .
> nowhere do creatures find peace or stability . . .
> surely the vision of the world is covered over with lust & delusion
>   for they cannot see how to set out on the true path
>   because of their suffering. . . .
> desire joined with craving
>   roars through the forest of deeds.[25]

Desire only breeds more desire, while enlightened selflessness transforms the situation through nonreciprocal behavior. The classic Buddhist answer to the destructive fires of desire is nowhere put more beautifully than in the devotional poem *Sátapañcāśatka* by the second century Mātṛceṭa:

---

23 Indeed, in a Buddhist anticipation of Freudian analysis, habitual patterns (and this is what karma amounts to) are usually based on a desire to imitate.
24 See Eliade's analysis in *A History of Religious Ideas*, 93–95.
25 Beyer, *Buddhist Experience*, 192–95. Spacing in the original.

men are not so kind to those who love them
as you are to those who do you harm
    to an enemy bent on evil
        you are a friend bent on good. . . .
with patience you conquer those who revile you
    with blessings those who harm you
    with truth those who slander you
    with love those who injure you.[26]

The only way out of "the forest of deeds" is decidedly nonviolent and the destructiveness of competitive desire and victimage, indeed, of the 'doubling effect' of competitive rivalry so incisively discussed in Girard's "*To Double Business Bound*" is visible throughout the Buddhist tradition. This doubling is perhaps exemplified by the contrasting behaviors of the Buddha and his self-appointed rival and cousin Devadatta, who, according to Buddhist lore, challenged the Buddha for leadership of the community.[27] So too, Māra, the lord of death who challenges the Buddha's attainment of enlightenment can be seen as a double. Indeed, in the *Aśokāvadāna* Māra is defeated once again by the monk Upagupta who then requests as his reward that Māra magically assume the appearance of the Buddha, for while Upagupta has seen the "teaching" of the Buddha he longs to see the dead teacher's physical form. Māra complies with Upagupta's wish and Upagupta then worships the "image." In an interesting twist Māra himself protests Upagupta's apparent idolatry. But Upagupta explains that "Just as men bow down / to clay images of the gods, / knowing that what they worship / is the god and not the clay, / so I, seeing you here, / wearing the form of the Lord of the World, / bowed down to you, / conscious of the Sugata, / but not conscious of Māra."[28]

Even more pointed is the story of the Anger-Eating Demon found in the *Samutta-Nikaya*. There, an anger-eating demon assumes the throne of Sákya, king of the gods. The more the gods angrily protest this usurpation, the more magnificent the demon grows until he is Sákya's double. Finally Sákya himself bows down to his demon double and humbles himself, refusing to be angered, with the resulting defeat of the demon.[29] Similar doubling found throughout

26 Beyer, *Buddhist Experience*, 4–5.
27 Conze, *Buddhist Scriptures*, 58, citing *Buddhacarita*.
28 Strong, *Legend of King Aśoka*, 195–96. Girard has put his finger on an interesting connection between mimesis and magic, in a way that goes beyond the observations of Frazer on the topic. Buddhist discipline ranks unsubstantiated claims to magical attainment as among the most serious breeches of the discipline and the Buddhist tradition, and like the Christian tradition, has maintained an uncomfortable and ambivalent stand toward "wonders." I would suggest that the heart of this ambivalence involves the "magical" mimetic capabilities of persons and images and perhaps, as Girard suggests, a fear of being unable to distinguish image from actuality, or Buddha from disciple. Jean Baudrillard discusses this problem in his *Simulations*, 5–13.
29 Warren, *Buddhism in Translations*, 426–27 citing *Samutta-Nikaya* xi. 3.21.

Indian mythology has been entertainingly explored by Wendy Donniger O'Flaherty.[30]

As is quite apparent from these stories and others like them, Buddhism's analysis and rejection of what Girard terms "mimetic desire" has been a central pillar of the Buddhist tradition. As an antidote to mimetic desire Buddhism encourages an alternative mimesis based on humble and selfless behavior.[31] The use of this mimesis results in a transformation of violent competition and victimage into positive emulation and identification with the victim. Yet, as in the case of Christianity, the picture is more complex than this, and much of the violence linked to Buddhism as a total historical phenomena has been overlooked. As I will demonstrate below, the injunction to eliminate the "fiction" of the continuing, real self (*ātman*) as construct of desire has engendered two distinct models of behavior in Buddhist mythology and practice: one that valorizes violent self-sacrifice and one that valorizes adherence to a nonviolent course. These two models are too easily conflated in a notion of religious self-sacrifice or "provoked suicide" both by Buddhists and non-Buddhists alike.[32] The sacrifical and violent model of Buddhist behavior predates Buddhism, originating in the Vedic tradition of fire sacrifice which Buddhism, to some extent, emerged to protest.

3. Agni's Robe: The Vedic Sacrifice and Buddhist Self-Immolation

The sacrificial model of Buddhist behavior is directly traceable to pre-Buddhist Vedic sacrifices. The chief Vedic sacrifice was performed on a fire altar of 10,800 bricks and celebrated the rebirth of the creator god Prajāpati.[33] Prajāpati created the world but in the effort became 'unstrug' or exhausted to the point of death. It is not hard to recognize here what Girard calls "the sacrificial crisis." The world/deity is literally falling to pieces. The fire, Agni, offered Prajāpati immortality if he would sacrifice himself to Agni. By his sacrifice Prajāpati is reborn and the world he created is reborn with him. Also

---

30 O'Flaherty, "Sexual Doubles and Sexual Masquerades." Also see her *Other People's Myths.*
31 Some Buddhist theologians reject even this kind of mimesis, but most Buddhist teaching relies directly upon it.
32 Only recently have studies (Clifford) acknowledged the darker side of the Buddhist tradition. The events in Śri-Lanka, the archetypal place of "tolerance" for three generations of Buddhologists, have heightened awareness of the possibilities for Buddhist oppression. Nonetheless, little clear analysis has been done and the Vietnamese Buddhist self-immolations of the 1960s cry out for such an analysis, both because they are depicted as exemplary of Buddhist nonviolent protest and because of intimate though largely unnoticed connections with the civil rights movement and the American protests going on at the same time half a world away.
33 For the myth of Prajāpati see O'Flaherty, *Hindu Myths*, 27–28. For the Vedic sacrifice see Frits Staal, *The Vedic Ritual.*

by his sacrifice, Prajāpati realizes his identity with Agni. In the ritual performance of this myth the building of a brick altar symbolises the rebuilding of Agni-Prajāpati and of the sponsor of the sacrifice who is identified with a substitute offering. Also in the performance of the rite each brick of the altar, and thus of the sacrificer, is identified with a verse from Vedic scripture. The final oblations are poured into the fire on behalf of the sacrificer while the community watches from the perimeter of the sacred enclosure. The results of the sacrifice are said to be health, wealth, sons, and immortality in the next world, i.e. the creation of a properly ordered ideal world here and in the hereafter. According to Paul Mus, the sacrifice acts as a template: Destruction in this imperfect world leads to reconstruction here and beyond in a perfect real world.[34]

Buddhist and Jain doctrines of nonviolence must be understood in the context of the Vedic sacrificial ideology. It is a commonplace that the rise of Buddhism and Jainism in the sixth century B.C.E. in North India was intimately connected with a new model of behavior, *ahimsā* (noninjury or nonviolence), and opposition to the animal sacrifices which were central to the predominant Vedic tradition. This is nonetheless not the whole story, and a deep ambiguity concerning ascetic practices and other forms of self-violence emerges when we look at Buddhist stories, particularly those designed to illustrate exemplary behavior. Indeed, sacrifice, particularly self-sacrifice, is a rite that Buddhism seems at once to have rejected and accepted. This has gone largely unnoticed, in part because of a naive acceptance of Buddhist polemics against Vedic sacrifice. While Buddhism rejected the practice of Vedic sacrifice employing animal substitutes, it nonetheless adopted the underlying logic of the sacrifice. Moreover, both in myth and, in some cases, in practice, Buddhism adopted sacrifice without animal substitites. As a result Buddhism, like Christianity, presents the believer with two contrasting models of behavior. The first model operates according to the laws of the "violent sacred," while the other model invites emulation of a nonviolent and anti-sacred kind. It is to the stories that exemplify these contrasting models that I will now turn.

4. Mimetic Violence and Mimetic Nonviolence

Self-immolation by Buddhists during the Vietnam War was widely reported in the popular press, and became perhaps the most riveting image of Buddhism in the modern era.[35] One of the questions asked repeatedly of the Vietnamese Buddhists was whether "religious suicide" was not a violation of Buddhist precepts condemning violence. Buddhist teaching is split on this

---

34 See Mus, *Barabudur*, and particularly David Gordon White's analysis in his *"Dakkhiṇa and Agnicayana."*

35 A brief bibliography of popular press sources is included in the "Works Consulted" section.

issue. The Buddhist *Vinaya* or *Rules of the Discipline* according to which monks and laymen are to live states unequivocally that "He who shall deprive a human being of life, or by uttering praises of death shall incite to suicide, is guilty of *pārājikas*," the gravest of crimes, and is to be expelled from the community.[36] This rejection of self-sacrifice and suicide notwithstanding, we yet find that Buddhism preserves numerous stories, myths, and sayings, some attributed to the Buddha himself, which praise self-sacrifice as the highest virtue and as proof of the enlightened state of the self-sacrificer. Thus, in the case of self-sacrifice the Buddhist seeks to imitate the Buddha but is paradoxically forbidden to do so. Indeed, to use Girard's terminology, the image of self-sacrifice in Buddhism presents the believer with a "double-bind."[37] The reason for this double-bind is that the tradition contains both violent and non-violent models of behavior.

In Vietnam, as in other Buddhist countries, the para-canonical *Jataka* or "Stories of the Buddha's Previous Births" are widely told to children as tales that exemplify the moral ideals of Buddhism. Many of these stories portray the Buddha in previous incarnations practicing self-sacrifice. Among the best known of these tales are "The Bodhisattva and the Hungry Tigress" and the "Hare Mark in the Moon."[38]

According to legend, the Buddha related the tale of the Hare Mark in the Moon after having received alms every day for a week from a rich layman. He then told the layman, "The wise of old times surrendered their own lives to chance suppliants, and gave their own flesh to be eaten," and he related the following story, which I have condensed here.

> Once upon a time when Bramadatta was ruling at Benares, the future Buddha was born as a hare and dwelt in a wood. Three other animals were his companions, a monkey, a jackel, and an otter. And the wise hare would exhort the other three, and teach them the doctrine, saying, "give alms and keep the precepts, and observe fast days." One day the future Buddha looked at the moon and noted that the next day was a fast-day. He then said to his friends, "Do you three keep the precepts and observe the day; and as alms given while keeping the precepts bring great reward, if any suppliants present themselves, give them to eat of your own food."

Each of the three companions finds some food, but saves it to eat later, after the fast day has past. But the hare remains all day in his thicket, thinking,

---

36 Prebish, *Buddhist Monastic Discipline*, 51.

37 Girard, *Things Hidden*, 290–94. Likewise, the Buddha performs miracles such as the famous "miracle of pairs" at Sarasvatī, yet he prohibits others (Piṇḍola, for example) from displaying such supernormal powers. See Thomas, *The Life of the Buddha*, 98–99; LaMotte, *Histoire du Bouddhisme*, 56, 352; and Strong, "The Legend of the Lion-Roarer."

38 For the tale of "The Bodhisattva and the Hungry Tigress," see Conze, *Buddhist Scriptures*, 24–26.

at the proper time I will go out and eat *dabba*-grass (used in Vedic sacrifices). If anyone asks for food, I have none. I will give my own flesh. Such fireiness in keeping the precepts made the throne of the king of the gods hot and he decided to test the hare. Disguised as a Brahmin asking for alms the king of the gods went to the hare, and the hare said, "You have done well in coming to me for food. Today I will give alms as I never gave before; and you will not have broken the precepts by destroying life. Go, my friend, and gather wood, and when you have made a bed of coals, come tell me. I will sacrifice my life by jumping into the bed of live coals." The king of the gods made a fire, and the Hare jumped in, but only felt cold. The king of the gods then admitted his deception, and the hare said, "Your efforts are useless; for if all beings who dwell in the world were to try me in respect to my liberality, they would not discover in me any unwillingness to give." The King of the gods then said, "Let your virtue be proclaimed till the end of the world cycle." And taking a mountain he squeezed it, and with the juice drew the outline of a hare in the disc of the moon. Then in that wood . . . he placed the future Buddha on some tender *dabba*-grass and departed . . . to his own celestial abode. That hare was reborn later as the Buddha.[39]

In this myth the hare adheres rigidly to the fast precisely because it is the morally perfect and "selfless" way to behave, and his moral perfection must be demonstrated through the only "real" sacrifice—self-sacrifice. In an effort to deny the illusory self socially constructed on the basis of mimetic desire the hare eschews even the desire to covet food or life based on it. The hare's behavior is metaphorically "hot"—he gives the king of the gods a "hot seat"— yet the fire feels cool in comparison with his internal fervor. Thus, the Buddhist Dharma or "Law" is more important than life itself, for it is the basis of true life and realization which transcends selfish concerns. The act results not in the expected death of the hare but in his miraculous public demonstration of the Dharma and serves as a basis for his future birth as the Buddha—the one who has awakened to supreme truth and reality. The connection between sacrifice and the establishment of order is clear. The "Hare Mark" is visible to all each month at the time of the recitation of the rules of the discipline, a recitation which is keyed to the lunar cycle. The hare is a willing victim, a sacrifice to the Dharmic order, and while he is "innocent" it is his fervor, *not* his innocence, which is exemplary. In Girard's analysis such an act reflects the oppressive internalization of the process of victimage.

The same collection of *Jātakas* contains another widely known tale that bears some surface similarities to the story of the Hare but carries a different message. "The Preacher of Forbearance" (*Ksantivādijātaka*) is one of the most famous of *Jātaka* tales, one widely known in India, China, and Southeast Asia.[40] In this tale a previous incarnation of the Buddha is practicing as-

---

39 Summarized from Warren, *Buddhism in Translations*, 274–79.
40 For this tale see Francis and Cowell, *The Jataka*, 3:26–29. For a study of this *Jātaka* see MacQueen, "External and Internal Mastery." For the tale in China see Chavannes, *Cinq cents contes*, 4:113–14. My account follows that of MacQueen.

ceticism in a forest. Nearby the King of Kashi is being entertained by his harem and, after considerable drinking, the king falls asleep. Bored with this situation, the women of the harem wander off to explore the forest and they come upon the ascetic. The king awakes and, angered at being abandoned, searches and finds his harem attentively listening to the preacher. The jealous king has his general beat the ascetic, and he asks, "What do you, monk, profess?" "I profess forbearance, Sire, but you think my forbearance is only skin-deep. My forbearance is not skin-deep, but it could not be seen by you for my forbearance, Sire, is firmly rooted within my heart." This only further enrages the king who has his guard systematically chop off the ascetic's limbs, pausing after each to ask "What do you profess?" The king leaves in disgust after giving the ascetic a final kick, while the king's general proceeds to bandage the ascetic's wounds, pleading that:

> He who has cut off your hands and feet,
> your nose and ears:
> Toward him grow angry, Great Hero [Mahavira].
> but do not destroy this kingdom!

And the ascetic replies:

> He who has cut off my hands and feet, my
> nose and ears:
> Long live that king! One such as I does not
> grow angry.[41]

The king's recompense while "offstage" is immediate and miraculous:

> As the king was leaving the pleasure-grove and had passed just beyond the Bodhisattva's range of vision, this mighty earth, which is two hundred and forty thousand leagues in thickness, split like a strong stout cloth and a flame, issuing forth from Avīci (Hell), seized upon the king as though wrapping him about with a red woolen blanket that had been the gift of his family. Sinking into the earth at the very gate of the pleasure-grove, he was established in Avīi, the Great Niraya Hell.[42]

The King of Kashi, often said to incarnate the lord Síva, king of the universe, is portrayed as afflicted by the three key faults that are found at the center of the Buddhist "wheel of life": lust, delusion, and anger. All are merely alternative forms of "clinging" or "thirst" and embody the modalities of desire. The object of desire, the women of the harem, has been stolen away by an apparent competitor, the ascetic. We must not miss the unmentioned but obvious stereotypes here: the tension/identity between the world conqueror and the world renouncer that permeates the Buddhist tradition from its ear-

41 MacQueen, "External and Internal Mastery," 245–46.
42 MacQueen, "External and Internal Mastery," 247.

liest documents, and the widespread suspicion of ascetics for wayward sexuality.[43] Indeed, we have here all the earmarks of a mimetic competition, and even of a persecution text.[44] We have a competition for a desired object, and a circle (the king's guard, his harem) formed around a victim. But what is striking is the stance of the preacher ("Long live that king! One such as I does not grow angry") and the immolation of the king, wrapped in robes of flame. Indeed, the king succeeds in making himself a sacrifice—his unreciprocated desire and hate rebounds upon him.

The difference between the two stories of the hare and the Preacher of Forbearance is a small one and easily overlooked. The story of the hare emphasizes self-sacrifice or self-denial, which itself bears a heavy freight of mimetic desire. The hare makes himself a victim. In contrast, the story of the Preacher of Forbearance emphasizes a total lack of the desire to reciprocate in kind. The preacher *is a victim*, but the example of his victimage transforms all but the most stubborn who see him. Both stories use the theological motif of "selflessness," but the difference in emphasis is significant.

I will return to these two *Jātakas*, but for the moment we need only note the two types of victimage here: one which fuels the process of reciprocal violence and one which stops it.

5. The Lotus Sūtra:
The Behavior of the Victim and the Victim's Behavior

Contrasting immolation stories are not limited to the traditions which characterize themselves as the vehicle of the hearers [of the Dharma] (*śrāvakayāna*). Such tales are found in every branch of Buddhism and are nowhere more graphically juxtaposed than in the *Lotus Sūtra*. One of the most popular scriptures of the Mahayana, the *Lotus Sūtra* served as the primary vehicle of self-immolation paradigms in East and Southeast Asia. I would like to examine two stories from the *Lotus*: that of Bhaiṣajyarāja and that of Sadāparibhūta.[45]

In the Bhaiṣajyarāja Chapter of the *Lotus Sūtra* the Buddha tells of events a long time ago in a world far away, in the perfect world of the Buddha Beflowered by the King of Constellations. The world is flat like the palm of one's hand, has no illness or suffering, and no women. A disciple of this Buddha asked about the great deeds of the Bodhisattva Sarvasattvapriyadarśana (Seen With Joy by All Living Beings). The disciple was told that by cultivating

---

43 For the world conquerer, world renouncer motif see Tambiah, *World Conquerer, World Renouncer*. For the conjunction of eroticism and asceticism and for the motif of the horny monk see O'Flaherty, *Asceticism and Eroticism*, and Eliade, *Yoga: Immortality and Freedom*.

44 Girard lists three persecution stereotypes: of persecution, accusation, and choice of victim. See *Scapegoat*, 15–21.

45 Hurvitz, *Scripture of the Lotus Blossom*, chaps. 23 and 20, Kern, *Saddharma-Puṇḍarika*, chaps. 23 and 19.

painful practices, Sarvasattvapriyadarśana obtained the trance through which he could magically manifest all forms.

Sarvasattvapriyadarśana was overjoyed and vowed that because this accomplishment was due to the teaching of the *Lotus Sūtra* he would make a magical offering of flowers to the Buddha. But then, having made the offering he thought, "Though by resort to supernatural power I have made an offering to the Buddha, it is not as if I made an offering of my own body."

For twelve hundred years he drank oils and fragrent ungents, and then dressed in jeweled garments, and, with the force of his vow ignited his own anointed body. The glow gave light all around to world-spheres equal in number to the sands of eighty millions of Ganges rivers. Within them the Buddhas all at once praised him, saying "Excellent! Excellent! Good man, this is true perserverence in vigor! This is called a true Dharma offering to the Thus Come One [the Buddha]. . . . This is called the prime gift. Among the various gifts it is the most honorable, the supreme. For it constitutes an offering of Dharma to the Thus Come Ones."

His body burnt for twelve hundred years and was consumed. Because of this offering, when he died he was instantly reborn in the same place fully conscious. He went before the Buddha once again, who told Sarvasattvapriyadarśana that he was leaving the world and passing on leadership to Sarvasattvapriyadarśana.

The Buddha said, "After my passage into extinction, whatever [relics] there may be I entrust to you also. You are to spread them about and broadly arrange for offerings to them."

When the Buddha passed away, Sarvasattvapriyadarśana collected firewood and performed the cremation of the Buddha's body. When the fire had gone out he collected the relics, constructed *stūpas*, and made offerings. But he thought, "Though I have made this offering, at heart I am still not satisfied. I will now make further offerings to the [relics]."

Having spoken these words, straightaway, before the eighty-four thousand *stūpas*, he burned his forearm, making this his offering for seventy-two thousand years, thus enabling countless beings to reach total enlightenment. His disciples wept and mourned his loss, saying that he was "lacking something."

At that time, Sarvasattvapriyadarśana took an oath, saying, "I have thrown away both arms. May I now without fail gain the Buddha's golden colored body! If this oath is reality and not vanity may both arms be restored as before!" When he had taken the oath, they were restored.[46]

The scripture then goes on to recommend action based on this example.

"If there is a person who wishes to obtain total enlightenment, if he can burn a finger, or even a toe as an offering to a Buddha-*stūpa*, the results would exceed that of any offering. Even if a man offered a world full of jewels the

46 Summarized from Hurvitz, *Scripture of the Lotus Blossom*, 293–98.

merit gained by him shall not match that of one who adheres to this scripture of the *Dharma Blossom* [i.e. the *Lotus Sūtra*]. . . . If anyone can accept and adhere to this scripture, he too shall be first among all living beings. This scripture can enable all living beings to separate themselves from pain and torment."[47]

This prescription is the basis for common initiatory practices in East Asian Buddhism during which incense cones are allowed to burn down to the skin or in which fingers are burned.

The basis of this story is that all the offerings in the world do not match the merit of offering of the body, because such an offering signifies total "selflessness" and thus, from the Buddhist perspective, the ability to see truth or reality. The offering is characterized as an offering of Dharma, as an act of truth and reality, made either to a living Buddha or to his enshrined relics—the remains of his body contained in a *stūpa* or a pagoda. The offering may be of the whole body or a part of it and the resulting fire illuminates all reality—the ideal world—so that beings who see this act see reality and gain enlightenment. Such enlightenment supposedly results in the total replacement of all ills, the replacement of a faulted world with a pristine and perfect world. Once again we meet with the theme of internal heat, the heat of truth and devotion. Sarvasattvapriyadarsana spontaneously combusts through the force of his vow and he seems undisturbed by the resulting conflagration. Like the hare in the moon—perhaps deliberately so—Sarvasattvapriyadarsana is literally "Seen With Joy by All Living Beings." His self-immolation is a spectacle: he is surrounded by all the Buddhas of the myriad cosmoses in a tableau meant to be used as a blueprint for action. The mimetic dimension is the fundamental one. The joy is that of the witnesses and is generated by the violent sacrifice and the reestablishment of order and community.

The less well-known story of Sadāparibhūta stands in striking contrast to that of Sarvasattvapriyadarsana. Sadāparibhūta's practice and his name are of particular interest:

> At that time there was a bodhisattva-bhikṣu named Never Disparaging (Sadā-paribhūta). O Gainer of Great Strength! For what reason was he named Never Disparaging? Whomever this bhikṣu [monk] saw, be it bhikṣu, bhikṣunī [nun], upāsaka [male devotee] or upāsikā [female devotee], he would do obeisance to them all and utter praise saying: "I profoundly revere you all! I dare not hold you in contempt. What is the reason? You are all treading the bodhisattva-path, and shall succeed in becoming Buddhas!"

As a result, some

> gave way to anger, whose thoughts were impure, who reviled him with a foul mouth saying: "This know-nothing bhikṣu! Whence does he come? He himself

---

47 Hurvitz, *Scripture of the Lotus Blossom*, 298–99.

says 'I do not hold you in contempt,' yet he presumes to prophesy to us that we will succeed in becoming Buddhas! We have no need of such idle prophecies!" In this way, thoughout the passage of many years, he was constantly subjected to abuse; yet he did not give way to anger, but constantly said, "You shall become Buddhas!"[48]

Often beaten for this practice, Sadāparibhūta miraculously heard the *Lotus Sūtra* being preached as he lay dying, and he straightaway attained myriad benefits.[49]

Like the Preacher of Forbearance, Sadāparibhūta refuses to engage in reciprocal anger and, as in the story of the Preacher of Forbearance, his oppressors and accusers suffer for eons in the hells, only later to become the very disciples being preached to in the *Lotus Sūtra* itself. Sadāparibhūta is surrounded by persecutors and finally dies at their hands, yet the tale makes it clear that he is a *scapegoat*, an innocent victim. Where the story of Sarvasatt-vapriyadarśana encourages imitative behavior in exchange for acquiring various merits and benefits, that of Sadāparibhūta emphasizes his "not giving way to anger." As was the case with the hare, the self-sacrifice of Sarvasattvapri-yadarśana is in the service of mimetic desire and his example may be said to represent an internalization of the process of victimage. In contrast, the stories of the Preacher of Forbearance and of Sadāparibhūta champion a selflessness born of a total lack of anger and desire. Yet these stories too are meant to encourage mimetic behavior, a mimetic behavior which in the stories results in the eventual enlightenment of most (but not all) onlookers. The stories of the Preacher of Forbearance and of Sadāparibhūta are good examples of what Thee Smith has called "transformative mimesis" and they invite us to identify with and to emulate the behavior of the victims as a way of stopping victimage.

But there is yet a further twist to the anti-violent saga of Sadāparibhūta, one which underscores the contrasting forms of mimesis at work in human emotions. As Kern points out in a footnote to his translation of the *Lotus Sūtra*, the name Sadāparibhūta can be parsed in two ways: Sadā/aparibhūta and Sadā/paribhūta, the first giving us the reading "Never Disparaging," the second producing the name "Constantly Disparaging."[50] In this pun on the hero's name are embedded the two alternative courses open to humans, the violent course of the sacred victim and the nonviolent transformative course of the exemplary victim. Depending on one's outlook, then, Sadāparibhūta's behavior may be seen as a reproach or as a model.

---

48 Hurvitz, *Scripture of the Lotus Blossom*, 280.
49 Hurvitz, *Scripture of the Lotus Blossom*, 280–85.
50 Kern, *Saddharma-puṇḍarika*, 357, n. 1.

6. Chinese Buddhist Practice and the Vietnamese Self-Immolators

The stories in the *Jātaka* and in the *Lotus Sūtra* served as charters for historical monks and nuns. The first recorded instances of Buddhist self-immolations occur in Chinese chronicles.[51]

The Buddhism of Vietnam and much of Vietnamese culture was strongly influenced by that of China. In Vietnam Buddhist scriptures are read in Chinese translation and, in contrast to the rest of Southeast Asia but like China and Japan, the Buddhism of Vietnam is of the Mahāyāna variety. Thus, Vietnamese Buddhists are familiar both with the *Lotus Sūtra* and with the heroic deeds of Chinese monks. Chinese histories contain the accounts and praises of numerous monks who followed the example of Sarvasattvapriyadarśana. Some of the monks seemed simply to wish to carry out the prescriptions of the scripture. Some loathed their bodies and their world as imperfect. Others immolated themselves in protest against the persecution of Buddhism. All follow the sacrificial paradigm set out in the *Lotus Sūtra*.[52]

Among the first recorded instances of Buddhist self-immolation is that of Fa-yü (d. 397?) who "often desired [to follow] the path of Bhaiṣajyarāja (Sarvasattvapriyadarśana) to burn his body as a performance of worship." On receiving permission from the military governor he, "immediately ate incense powder, wrapped his body with clothes, chanted the *She-shen p'in* chapter (i.e., the *Yueh-wang pen-shih p'in* of the *Lotus Sūtra*), lit a fire and burned himself" to death.[53]

Another monk named Hui-t'ung was reading the *Lotus Sūtra* and he began "loathing his body and prepared to abandon it. . . . He heaped firewood in a shrine in a forest at night, read the [*Lotus*] *Sūtra* up to the Bhaiṣajyarāja chapter, and ordered the firewood to be lighted." As the fire blazed up he chanted the Bhaiṣajyarāja chapter in his normal voice. "By the time dawn had come his body was destroyed by the fire. His bones were collected and a pagoda (*stūpa*) was erected in his memory."[54]

Others burned fingers and arms in like manner in a practice that continues to this day. Yet others, including one monk named Ta-chih, (605–17) hoping to counter persecution of Buddhism, vowed to "exert myself to the utmost in order to explain the correct teachings clearly." He subsequently went to the capital where he submitted a memorial to the Throne praying "I wish your

---

51 For instances of self-immolation in south and southeast Asia see Lingat, "Les suicides," and Thakur, "Self-Immolation."

52 I have summarized this information from Jan Yün-hua's excellent article, "Buddhist Self-immolation in Medieval China." Much of the same material is covered in Gernet's "Les suicides par le feu."

53 Jan, "Buddhist Self-immolation," 246. The chapter mentioned is that discussed above in which Sarvasattvapriyadarśana "throws away" (*she-shen*) his body.

54 Jan, "Buddhist Self-immolation," 247.

Majesty would make the effort to nourish Buddhism. [If you agree to this] I will burn one of my arms at Mt. Sung to show my gratitude." The Emperor gave his consent and made arrangements for a great assembly. "Ta-chih fasted for three days, and then ascended a high canopied platform, where, using a bar of red-hot iron, he burned his arm till it turned black. . . . Thereafter he wrapped the injured arm with clothes, poured wax over it and lit it. The light from his arm shone brightly over the cliffs and peaks."[55]

These Chinese monks, who were well known to the Vietnamese, took the mythic prescriptions seriously. Though they stress different motives for their acts of self-destruction, most Chinese monks performed this act according to the Bhaiṣajyarāja chapter of the *Lotus Sūtra* in a public place before a Buddhist shrine or pagoda. Many of the monks then had their bones or other remains enshrined in pagodas alongside the relics of the Buddha or those of other Buddhist saints. Although little contextual information is available to us, it is clear that in each case the sacrifice is performed as a remedy for an intolerable situation and that the self-immolation is self-initiated. Further, the power of truth which is thought to blaze forth with the light of the fire may be equated with the power of sacrificial violence to remedy spreading disorder. "Selfless" action in these cases amounts to a renunciation of personal desires in order to champion social desires. These self-immolations stand in contrast to the examples of the Preacher of Forbearance or Sadāparibhūta, where reciprocal violence is completely renounced and where the example of nonviolence acts to transform those who observe it.

7. Thich Quang-Duc: The Divinized Victim and the Sacred Order

At the same time that civil rights demonstrations were taking place in the U.S., Buddhists in Vietnam were protesting the Catholic persecution of Buddhists by the Diem regime. The politics are complex, and I will not comment on them now. In any case, government troops opened fire on women and children at a Buddhist protest meeting in Hue, on 8 May, 1963. As a direct response the senior monk Thich Quang-Duc resolved to follow the ancient paradigms of the hare, of Sarvasattvapriyadarśana, and of the Chinese self-immolators. In the account of Frances FitzGerald, "The self-immolation of Thich Quang-Duc in June was the central event of the Buddhist protest movement. It shocked the Americans as much as the Vietnamese; it had an important effect on American policy. And yet it remained mysterious." According to FitzGerald,

It seemed a barbarous, primitive act, an expression of some atavistic memory, yet it had, so far as anyone knew, no precedent in Vietnamese history. Then too, the

---

55 Jan, "Buddhist Self-immolation," 253.

publicity the Buddhists gave to it was most incongruously modern. During those endless minutes when the flames leaped up the robes of Quang-Duc, obscuring his face, and during the slow fall of the charred body from its upright position, a young monk with a microphone called out over and over again in Vietnamese and English, "A Buddhist priest burns himself to death, A Buddhist priest becomes a martyr." The monks called the American reporters to witness the scene. They would later display the heart of Quang-Duc in a glass case and insure television coverage of some of the six other self-immolations. Even those reporters who favored the Buddhist cause could not help feeling that the performance was somehow crass and sacrilegious. But the mystery remained.[56]

This account, by one of the best informed and most perceptive of American observers, demonstrates the difficulty in comprehending such an event, a difficulty compounded by a huge cultural gulf that separated the observer from those involved as well as a stereotyped perception of Buddhism as exclusively nonviolent. Fitzgerald's account, influenced by the indigenous Buddhist framework mediated through the works of Buddhologist Paul Mus, represents an attempt to grasp the event from a Buddhist perspective, a perspective that has commonly obscured the role of violence in Buddhism.

Other, less informed and sympathetic writers suspected coercion and charged that the self-immolators were forced into the act or drugged. Certainly Girardian theory alerts us to the possible presence here of persecution stereotypes. As in the myths and performances of the Vedic Sacrifice or in the practice of Suttee, we see a community form a circle in the process of immolating an individual, an individual who then is "divinized" as a savior of community.[57] The fact that the act might be voluntary in Girard's view only underscores the powerful cultural logic of sacrifice and the ability to conceal its true persecutory nature.[58]

As we have seen in the examples above, the performer of a particular type of Buddhist self-immolation (hare, Sarvasattvapriyadarśana, or Ta-chih) is analogous to the Vedic sacrificer with the one key difference: in the Vedic sacrifice substitutes are used while in these Buddhist sacrifices there is no substitution. The sacrifices of hare, Sarvasattvapriyadarśana, or the Chinese monks, like the Vedic prototype, are performed by fire (Agni) before an assembled community (the Gods, Buddha or assembled Buddhas, the populous) and before a shrine (altar, *stūpa* or pagoda) which symbolically represents the hoped for order and the body of the divinity (Agni/Prajāpati or the Buddha). In the Buddhist case the identity between the *stūpa* and the body is underscored by the Buddha relics it enshrines. The *stūpa* is the equivalent of the Vedic fire altar, and like the Vedic altar, the Buddhist *stūpa* is considered to be a model of the universe.

---

56 FitzGerald, *Fire in the Lake*, 133.
57 I am indebted to Paul Courtright of Emory University for numerous discussions of Suttee and I look forward to his forthcoming work, *The Goddess and the Dreadful Practice*.
58 Girard, *Things Hidden*, 235–36.

Finally, just as in the Vedic sacrifice the Buddhist actualizes "truth" or order in the spoken teaching of the Buddha (a scripture is often read or a sermon is preached) and in the performance of Buddha-like acts of self-sacrifice (Dharma). He thus seeks to realize truth and demonstrate truth, and with this demonstration of truth to recreate himself and the universe. The sacrificial violence is thought to act as a template to reshape reality and to restore order.

Thus, the self-immolations in Vietnam reenacted earlier Buddhist models, which in turn were based on a reworking of the Vedic Indian sacrifice. The sacrificial mythic and ritual structure have persisted for 3000 years. If we now reexamine the events of the sacrifice of the Vietnamese monk Thich Quang-Duc a number of things stand out. First, there had been plenty of precedent for these actions and they were sanctioned by myth and example in Buddhist history. Second, the notion that this was a political protest was in some senses correct, and in others quite wrong. It is correct because it presents this sort of self-sacrifice as *a form of protest*, one directly linked to Vedic and Buddhist sacrificial attempts to restore order. Indeed, Bhikkhu Sobhita, a Vietnamese monk commenting on Quang-Duc's suicide explains:

> Now there exists in China and in Vietnam another form of suicide that is not known in Ceylon. . . . One might call this "suicide through combat" or "provoked suicide." *To safeguard the equilibrium of the country where you practice your religion*, you may give yourself death . . . if some oppression takes place, the oppressed will commit suicide at his [the oppressor's] desk: this is a means of attracting the attention of the authorities.[59]

Bhikkhu Sobita clearly connects "provoked suicide" with the desired reestablishment of order. Whether we consider it dharmic order or not, it is clearly a sacrifice in which one person willingly serves as victim in an effort to "safeguard the equilibrium of the country," a country in which a plague of reciprocal violence has threatened to spread out of control.

But it is incorrect to say, as Mus and others have, that these self-immolations are an *admissible* form of protest.[60] As we have seen, a good deal of the Buddhist tradition condemns such action undertaken for such ends since it does not end the cycle of what Buddhists call karma and what Girard calls violent reciprocity. Third, the setting and the publicity were anything but crass, modern innovations. The rite was performed in front of the Xa Loi Pagoda in the main intersection of the city of Saigon in front of the relics of Buddhist saints and the symbolic presence of true Dharmic order. Publicity—the widest possible audience in Vietnam and in America—was precisely the point. Thich Quang Duc was seeking to preach the Dharma to enlighten both Diem and his followers and John Kennedy and the American people. By

59 Lacoutre, *Vietnam*, 78 (emphasis added).
60 Quoted in FitzGerald, *Fire in the Lake*, 133.

stubbornly affirming what he considered to be truth in the most emphatic way possible, Quang-Duc sought to remake the world. Vietnamese and Westerners, including the throng of reporters, became part of a human sacrifice, part of the crowd polarized around a scapegoat. To some small degree Thich Quang-Duc's sacrificial violence succeded. Finally, in death Quang-Duc followed the pattern set in the *Lotus Sūtra*. He entered meditation and chanted scripture while performing the self-sacrifice. After death he was virtually divinized, and his relics were enshrined in the Pagoda.[61] His charred heart was placed on display along with pictures of him, relics to which other monks and nuns would give the sacrifice. Sadly, the cruel taunts of Madame Nhu, Diem's wife, that she "would clap her hands at another monk barbecue," and that "all the Buddhists have done for this country is to barbecue a monk" seem prophetic.[62] Although the Diem government fell, each further sacrifice had diminished effect. A martyr's cult in the Xa Loi pagoda including the charred heart of Quang-Duc and a painting of the monk wreathed in flames exists to this day but its power to reestablish order is gone.[63]

Buddhists, like Christians, have historically been uncomfortable with sacrificial paradigms and techniques, recognizing that violence is somehow in tension with the fundamental principles of the tradition. Nevertheless, the power of sacrificial violence has insured that violence has a place—perhaps the dominant place—alongside nonviolent ideology. Indeed, the blatant nonviolent statements embodied in many Christian and Buddhist texts have more often than not been held hostage to the practice of sacrificial violence. Even the best educated and trained members of Christian and Buddhist communities find special justification for certain categories of violent acts, especially when a long history of traditional sanction for ritualized acts of violence can serve as a buttress for a tottering institutional order.

Two years after the self-immolations of 1963 and during the civil rights activities in Birmingham, Thich Nhat-Han wrote to Martin Luther King explaining his view of the self-immolations:

> The self-burning of Vietnamese Buddhist monks in 1963 is somehow difficult for the Western Christian conscience to understand. The press spoke then of suicide, but, in the essence, it is not. It is not even a protest. . . . To express will by burning oneself, therefore, is not to commit an act of destruction but to perform an act of construction, that is, to suffer and die for the sake of one's people. This is

---

61 Buddhist theology recognizes no ontological difference between gods, people, animals, and Bodhisattvas. In popular Buddhist works, powerful beings and charismatic individuals are indeed regarded in ways that are covered by the term "divine" in Christian and other traditions.

62 Lacouture, *Vietnam*, p. 80.

63 Information and slides concerning the cult in the Xa Loi Pagoda as of December, 1988 were obtained in personal communication with Professor Phil Brown of the History Department, University of North Carolina, Charlotte.

not suicide. . . . Like the Buddha in one of his former lives—as told in the story of Jātaka—who gave himself to a hungry lioness which was about to devour her own cubs, the monk believes he is practicing the doctrine of highest compassion by sacrificing himself in order to call the attention of, and to seek help from, the people of the world.[64]

Another monk, Thich Thien-An, explained in a 1975 interview that he was among the twenty thousand monks jailed at the time and that "I was released from jail by those monks who died. . . . It is like the Christian martyrs."

> But in Vietnam it is more meaningful, because only seven monks dying released and saved almost twenty thousand people from jail. In Vietnam we consider the first monk to do that a bodhisattva because he died for his religion and to help us. . . . In Buddhism the first important precept is not killing, not killing oneself and not killing others. But in such an emergency there was no other way to help. They were using their bodies like a lamp for help . . . that is a bodhisattva. But in regular conditions it should not be done.[65]

For these monks the self-immolation of Thich Quang-Duc and others in Vietnam was more than just a bizzare form of protest, though from a Girardian point of view it was precisely an atavistic and a primitive act. As an actualization of mythic patterns of sacrifice it was meant as a creative, constructive and salvific act, an act which intended to remake the world for the better of everyone in it. Yet this "good intention" cannot disguise its sacred violence, and Girard's analysis of desire resonates with Buddhist analyses in condemning it.

8. Curing Violence: Girard's Theory and the Transformative Behavior of Victims

It should now be clear that in the Buddhist tradition as in the Christian tradition violent and nonviolent paradigms are often confused and that Girard's work can be of use in distinguishing between them, particularly if we expand the theory to include a good, transformative, and nonviolent mimesis, as the examples of the Preacher of Forbearance and Sadāparibhūta suggest. But Girard's analysis of the Christian case posits a divine revelation which cuts through sacrificial religion, a revelation which in turn is obscured by the Church's sacrificial reading of the Gospels. Girard argues that the revelation of the Gospels must be divine since he has assumed that the structuring power of sacrifice is by nature unobservable. Would it not be simpler to modify the hypothesis, to say that the structuring power of sacrificial violence is *usually* unobservable. Evidence of nonviolent ideology which forms the heart of the

---

64 Thich-Nhat-Han, *Vietnam: Lotus in a Sea of Fire*, 106–107. I owe this reference to my research assistant John Lowther.
65 "An Interview with Thich Thien-An," *Loka*, 1975:137–38.

Buddhist tradition and examples from other traditions could then be accounted for without having to argue that they are not systematic enough or that they too are the product of revelation.

But Girard's petitio principii is also problematic because it leads to a dismemberment and displacement of ethical responsibility. Girard's story is the story of the Fall and the Apocalypse, of sin and salvation and it can lead to a division between us (evil and sacrificial) and It (good and non-sacrificial). Here religion and society are portrayed as completely violent by nature until the totally other, totally good intervenes. Thus, to use a Buddhist parallel cited above, when Thich Thien-An says that Thich Quang-Duc was a bodhisattva he is drawing a line between the Good and the Human. The responsibility for evil is thus, by implication, lifted and the possibility of good is undermined by the attribution of all good to the other. What is more, for Girard only a certain moment in Christianity partakes of revelation. The rest of Christianity and all other traditions wallow in sacrificial violence. This dismemberment is, in my view, a form of violence and goes to the heart of the tension between sacrificial and nonviolent paradigms in Buddhism and Christianity. Ironically it is on this point that Girard's analysis of mimetic desire is precisely on the mark, for if anyone can stop the cycle of reciprocal violence which he so well describes, it must be us, not some "divinity."

The integral nature of human ethical responsibilty in the face of reciprocal violence is the point of parts of the Gospels, of the Buddhist analysis of desire and noninjury, and of its modern day heirs, Gandhi and Martin Luther King.

Thus, it seems fitting that earlier versions of this essay were presented as public lectures given on the first two national holidays devoted to Martin Luther King. Between King and the Buddhist tradition of nonviolence there is an indirect yet real connection. While violent self-sacrifice is an attempt at renovating a form of order ultimately based on violence, the acts of nonviolent resistance in the civil rights movement and the insistance on nonviolence found in Buddhism and typified by the Preacher of Forbearance, attempt to bring into being an entirely new nonviolent world. King's use and understanding of the power of nonviolence and its connection with Christianity is discussed by Thee Smith in Chapter Eleven of this volume. But there is also a connection between King and the Buddhists, a connection found in the writings of Gandhi.

Basing his thought on pan-Indian and Buddhist notions of nonviolence (*ahimsā*) and an insistance on and a witnessing to truth, Gandhi championed a doctrine of *Satyagraha* "truth-force" or "holding fast to the truth" in the face of adversity. Gandhi described Satyagraha as "Truth" (*Satya*), which also implies Love, and "Firmness" (*Agraha*), which engenders and therefore serves as a synonym for force, the force that is born of Truth and Love or Nonviolence.[66]

66 See Gandhi, *The Story of My Experiments with Truth*, 318–19, Chatterjee, *Gandhi's*

It was this notion of standing up for what was true and thereby transforming the oppressors which inspired Gandhi and his followers to acts of nonviolent civil disobedience. By putting forward their bodies and their lives in a *non-sacrificial* manner they exchanged British India for a new world, an Independent India.[67] King had read Gandhi and adopted his stance. According to King, nonviolent resistance is "a means to awaken a sense of moral shame in the opponent," and he quotes Gandhi: "Rivers of blood may have to flow before we gain our freedom, but it must be our blood."[68] It is important that we observe that King does not advocate self-violence or any form of "provoked suicide." Rather, King focuses on holding fast to and acting in accord with what is right so that the vicious cycle of racial violence and the apartheid system which it supports might be broken, and the oppressors might be transformed.

Through the heuristic use and extension of Girard's theory we can appreciate the connection between the nonviolent stance of King and Gandhi and the Buddhist paradigms of nonviolence illustrated in the story of the Preacher of Forbearance. At the same time we can recognize that the sacrificial paradigm in Buddhism, the paradigm found in the story of the hare and of Sarvasattvapriyadarśana and actualized by Chinese and Vietnamese self-immolators, has come too often to the fore. The limits of the violent sacred were as apparent to Madame Nhu as they were to King and are to Girard. Yet, while numerous Buddhists and Christians sought to transform the world through following the nonviolent exemplars, others have confused nonviolence with self-sacrifice, usually in the name of divinity. Simply put, "force is not Dharma, He who uses it is not righteous. Nonviolence is Dharma, Who uses it is righteous."[69]

Religious Thought, 88, as well as the material brought together by Brown, *Gandhi and Civil Disobedience*. For a full discussion of the influences of Buddhism, Jainism, and Christianity on the development of *Satyagraha* see Chatterjee, *Gandhi's Religious Thought*.

67 Gandhi also seems to mix violence and nonviolence. His famous hunger strikes have been the source of considerable controversy both during and after his life as they may be considered a form of self-immolation.

68 King, *Stride Toward Freedom*, 103, and also in "An Experiment in Love," found in *A Testament of Hope*, 18.

69 Lal, *Dhammapada*, 127. I have used the Sanskrit spelling "Dharma" here for consistancy.

"You Will Reap Just What You Sow"

Robert W. Hough

Abstract

The Vietnam War poetry of Donald G. Kemp is examined in light of the theories of the relationship between violence and the sacred put forward by René Girard, Walter Burkert, Paul Ricoeur and Northrop Frye. The poetry is seen to record a confrontation with evil that is not susceptible to the kind of absolution usually offered by religious institutions. The violence of the Vietnam War is seen to be grounded in a false motivation, which makes the violence particularly dangerous for the participants in the war who are not shielded from its effects by an effective military ritual. The notion of the sacred that emerges is based upon the poet's sense of the violation of infinite obligations. Thus the only "curing" of violence suggested here is the unflinching telling of a tale of confrontation with evil found not entirely outside of the poet himself.

1. The Vietnam War as Sacrificial Crisis

The Vietnam War, like all other wars, had its own singular features which made it seem both uniquely horrible and uniquely significant. It is always difficult, of course, to deduce general theories about "violence and the sacred" from cases based upon such unique particulars. Conversely, it is also difficult to start from a general theory, like that of René Girard's, and work toward the elucidation of particular reports of a specific, recent war by means of the application of the theory. However, in working with the poetry of one Vietnam veteran poet, Donald G. Kemp, the theoretical framework for interpreting the relationship between violence and the sacred suggested by Girard seemed, at certain points, to be startlingly applicable. Girard's work, along with that of Walter Burkert, Paul Ricoeur and Northrop Frye, helps to provide sorely needed analytical tools for making use of the most compelling but disturbing poetry produced by American soldiers from their experiences of the War in Vietnam. No single theory is sufficient in itself to open up this poetry, but each one helps a little and Girard's is particularly useful.

A successful war poem has an odd way of crystalizing a poet's personal way of putting the war together so that others see something familiar in that highly individual account of an event or emotion that would otherwise seem only personal. Kemp's poetry is also successful in this manner but, in addition, it really brings the war home—figuratively if not literally. In this regard, Girard's observations concerning the nature of the returning veteran are particularly apt.

> A special sort of impurity clings to the warrior returning to his homeland, still tainted with the slaughter of war. . . . The returning warrior risks carrying the seeds of violence into the very heart of his city.[1]

For Girard, this would likely be true for any warrior returning from any war. But there are some special characteristics of the War in Vietnam which make the poetry produced by these returning warriors particularly worthy of note in this regard and which, incidentally, make Girard's analysis unusually penetrating.

The published poetry of the Vietnam War is now becoming a substantial legacy, and in that legacy some common perspectives of the combatants are revealed. The English poetry of World War I stands similarly as a stark reminder of the horror and carnage of that era. That poetry permanently undercut any facile, patriotic interpretation of the war as an English triumph. The *Great War and Modern Memory*, by Paul Fussell, shows clearly how World War I came to be remembered through the poetry produced by the soldiers. The soldier poets, perhaps more than the historians and political scientists, succeeded in capturing an enduring image of the war and communicating the horror of that image to future generations. The poetry of the Vietnam War may comparably perform the service of providing a necessary leavening for American consideration of its defeat in that war.

It is also possible that the uniqueness of the Vietnam War poetry may reveal something previously unglimpsed about the relationship between religion and violence in general. As the poetry of Donald G. Kemp clearly demonstrates, the war in Vietnam did have what must be called a truly demonic side. Perhaps there was something other than the evil that is an element in all wars. In addition, Kemp's themes are similar to the themes of other Vietnam War poets, though there are some unusual features that cause it to stand apart. Kemp seldom uses simple allegories to make his points, as several other Vietnam War poets do. Instead he makes simple and brutal, but multifaceted statements that are rich in provoking sustained reflection on the war. For this reason, Kemp's poetry is a good place to start in the examination of the "meaning" of the Vietnam War for American society and beyond.

Kemp tells his story of Vietnam in the parabolic language of a poetry

1 Girard, *Violence and the Sacred*, 41.

freighted with a heavy sense of defilement, sin and guilt. Each poem contains a vivid, visual image which seems to haunt the poet, and he may well be attempting to expel or banish demons by exorcising them through poetry. Some of his readers are thus understandably led to attempt a kind of psychologizing about the poet's state of mind while writing. But the purpose here will be to examine the poetry for what it says about the war, not for what it may reveal about the poet's psychological stability. After Vietnam, Kemp does not see the world in the same way, and through his poetry he attempts to communicate, almost by contagion, the same experience to others. The poetry also features what could be called a moral center, or an integrity, based upon Kemp's complex response to a direct confrontation with evil—an evil that he does not locate entirely outside himself.

W. B. Yeats claims that "we make poetry out of the argument with ourselves,"[2] and Kemp certainly records fierce internal debates. His language is rarely unclear, and his poems show a very careful ordering process at work. His primary themes are: the suffering caused by the American soldiers and experienced by them, the defilement-sin-guilt caused by a descent into evil, the ineffectiveness of traditional modes of religious absolution, and the impossibility of completing the ritual of return or reincorporation back into the "real" world. In Kemp's work an element of something like compassion is clear throughout, and that element helps to elevate his poetry to a level of ambiguity rare in the poetry of the Vietnam War. It is ambiguous because the compassion is mixed with a kind of cold horror, since Kemp shows himself acutely aware of causing the suffering that he describes while simultaneously demonstrating an intense identification with the victim. In the following poem, Kemp describes the senseless, indiscriminate slaughter of the Vietnamese, who are dehumanized by racial slurs.

> Ack-47 gun
> aratatatat
> I'm going to waste someone
> aratatat
> There ain't no sense in it
> aratatat
> I'm going to off you, zip
> aratatat
> ratatatat
> ratatat
> And then I killed some more
> aratatatat
> Me and my Ack

---

2 William B. Yeats, quoted in Jon Silkin's introduction to *The Penguin Book of First World War Poetry*, 24.

Civilian or vc
aratatatat
You're all the same to me
aratatatat
There ain't no sense in this
aratatatat
You're dead, you slant-eyed bitch
aratatatat
ratatatat
ratatatat
And then I died some more
aratatatat
Me and my Ack.[3]

Here Kemp, in this parody of "The Little Drummer Boy," sounds like a berserker caught up in the delight of destruction—the kind of delight described so well by Glenn Gray in *The Warriors*. Amid the gunfire, however, there are two separate voices. The first three lines show the hatred clearly, but the fourth line is reflective when paired with its parallel later in the text: "And then I killed some more" pairs with "And then I died some more." The external event of killing is matched by the internal experience reported by Kemp. The effect of the poem is intensified when he refers to the Vietnamese by a familiar racial epithet and describes the killing of a woman, who should not be an acceptable image of the targeted enemy. Through a process of poetic recollection, Kemp recreates an ironic paradigm for the experience of both causing and feeling suffering at the same time. There is no "sense" in this creation of dual suffering, no socially constructive "meaning" to justify the violence; hence it is devoid of the sacrality or the mystery that ought to accompany an effective sacrificial ritual.

In another poem Kemp recalls the phenomenon of the "body count", which Robert Lifton has suggested "epitomizes the war's absurdity and evil."[4]

a statistic on the ground
his blood running from my brain
his closed eyes look thru me
his silence screams in my ears
his lifeless heart
trembling the earth
falling into fissures
bottomless

3 The AK-47 is a Soviet made automatic rifle. For purposes of deception, LURPS (LRRPS-Long Range Reconnaissance Platoon) members like Kemp often carried weapons of a foreign manufacture. All poems are taken, with Kemp's written permission, from the files of First Casualty Press at the University of Connecticut at Storrs. As none of the poems have previously been published, there will be no further notation of sources.
4 Lifton, *Home From the War*, 59.

falling never stopping
blood screaming from my throat
echoes ripping my mind
statistics

Kemp does not approach the dead body with a feeling of compassion for the suffering of others. He shows a direct sense of pure, raw identity, not marred by sympathy. Kemp and the body are on opposite sides of the violent act but they share a single nature, for the screaming, trembling, and endlessly falling seem to happen to both. The horror of the scene has a nightmare quality, as though the poet would never stop seeing the scene with himself inside the dead body. This poem shows, as clearly as any of Kemp's work, that the outward scenes of battle may be mirrored by interior scenes or, as F. R. Leavis calls it, an "inner theatre" in which the exterior event is registered, committed to memory, then replayed later.[5] In Kemp's poetry the inner theatre is the prime reality, for the battlefield and its interpretation are now inside.

As much as Kemp is concerned with his own inner theatre based on ground combat, his poems often concentrate on the effect of the aerial bombing on the civilian population. He does not wring his hands at the horror of it all, but rather describes, in the language of an evil fairytale, the process of destruction he witnessed and now imagines.

bird flies majestically
as a bird of paradise
a red white and blue
turkey
releasing its eggs
embryos of destruction
emerges from the egg
a monster
to create many monsters
the merciless offspring
of the devil bird
it eats women
children
it destroys ancient
philosophies
it attacks humanity
with its talons
bloody talons
its shadow
covers
the earth

5 Leavis, quoted in Silkin, 52.

the parasitic bird
it will kill us all

Here the American eagle is parodied as a turkey and the bomb itself becomes an evil egg. That egg produces the monstrous explosion, but the effect of that evil action spreads beyond the initial explosion to produce an unknown number of further evil repercussions. In succession, the bomb kills innocent noncombatants, then the philosophy that underlies the society under attack (since the bomb attempts to destroy the structure of the society as a whole), and finally humanity itself. Since the Vietnamese are attacked indiscriminately, all humanity is being attacked. Finally, the bomber, seen as a parasite, threatens even those who launch it. The evil action, done in bad faith, ultimately rebounds on the perpetrators.

In examining the language of this poem, it is valuable to employ the categories of Northrop Frye on the nature of archetypal demonic imagery. For Frye the world of the demonic is "the world of nightmare and the scapegoat, of bondage and pain and confusion . . . the world also of perverted or wasted work, ruins and catacombs, instruments of torture and monuments of folly."[6] The appropriate mode of communication for this demonic imagery is parody, and human society is seen as a mob "looking for a *pharmakos*" (sacrificial victim), while that mob is "often identified with some sinister animal image" such as "monsters or beasts of prey."[7] The red, white, and blue parasitic bird is a crude but recognizable representation of Frye's description of the demonic. As Frye notes, at the climax of the demonic image the *pharmakos* and the tyrant share a common fate, an idea at the center of much of Kemp's poetry. For Kemp at issue here is not simply a political disagreement with American policy but rather the realization that a boundary has been crossed that marks the war in terms of a negative religious absolute. The war has become demonic. Girard's notion of the sacrality of the sacrificial victim adds support to Frye's discussion of the *pharmakos*. But it is a further development of this idea that marks Girard's most useful contribution.

When the religious framework of a society starts to totter, it is not exclusively or immediately the physical security of the society that is threatened; rather, the whole cultural foundation of the society is put in jeopardy. The institutions lose their vitality; the protective facade of the society gives way; social values are rapidly eroded, and the whole cultural structure seems on the verge of collapse.[8]

This is the level of religious and cultural collapse to which Kemp's poems point. The sacrificial crisis, thus unresolved, does not serve to validate the society's most cherished values, but fundamentally undermines them.

6 Frye, *The Anatomy of Criticism*, 147.
7 Frye, *The Anatomy of Criticism*, 149.
8 Girard, *Violence and the Sacred*, 49.

2. From "Violence and the Sacred" to Violation and the Demonic

Turning from the air war to the ground war, this next poem reinforces the same stages of awareness regarding the effects of evil action. False motivation eventually destroys those who act upon it.

> One man can pin down
> a whole fucking platoon
> one power machine
> can wipe out
> an entire race
> one false motivation
> destroys forever
> an entire culture
> an entire philosophy
> with each ideal we destroy
> we destroy also some part
> of the future of
> our own existence
> pin down
> a whole fucking existence

The same process is taking place on the ground that is occurring in the air. Kemp starts with the ironic insight that a single sniper can keep a platoon hunting for cover, immobilized. Presumably, a single Viet Cong might thus hold an American platoon at bay. From that insight, Kemp moves from a sense of helplessness and frustration to a reversal of the image: the American power machine is attempting to destroy the "entire race" of the Vietnamese. It is a race war. It is not only the action that is questionable, it is the motivation itself that is at fault. It is a false motivation generated from a core of bad faith. That motivation attempts to destroy a culture and race, a philosophy of life, and ultimately results in the destruction of those driven by such a motivation. Thus there are spiritual consequences for putting into operation this false motivation. Kemp is describing the process of reaping what has been sown.

In the following poem the image is savage and the basic issue is the same, but here Kemp merely implies the final reaping.

> goddamn gunship shaking out my guts
> should have taken 10 years in Leavenworth
> shaking out my guts
> fuck these prisoners
> okay you little punk
> where were you when you did it
> won't talk eh
> out you go shrimp hey farout

a 6 1/2 reverse flip
that was better than disintegrating that Lambretta
gimme another one
don't scream you little bastard
just say geronimo on your way out
its the amerikan way[9]

The execution of prisoners by throwing them out of helicopters is an image that disturbed many Vietnam veterans—an image that has recurred with some regularity in the psychiatric literature.[10] In this poem the racism is stated directly and is combined with a nihilistic delight in destruction, but at several points the tone of the poem changes its apparent savage meaning. For Kemp it is indeed ironic to suggest that he would have preferred "10 years in Leavenworth" to participating in this kind of crime, given the fact that he later received a life sentence for crimes committed during Vietnam flashbacks. Saying "Geronimo" in the last two lines, like American paratroopers do when jumping from planes, is a particularly sardonic idea, while the use of the "k" in spelling Amerika is a familiar shorthand for identifying U.S. atrocities with those usually associated with the Nazis. The savage, despairing irony present in this poem is not unique with Kemp. Other American poets of the Vietnam War used such irony, though seldom with such devastating effect.

In the following poem Kemp implies that the central issue of the war was the intentional evil created by the Americans. The poetry does not support the currently fashionable explanation that the war was a series of ill-fated tactical and strategic blunders that could or should have been avoided. The irreversible and permanent production of evil consequences from evil motives is here seen as the real nature of the war.

people lying face down in the dirt
rivers running red
into the earth which inherits the meek
the faces rise
in sky-bound smoke columns
fires burn
where their fires
have been extinguished
embers reflecting pseudo-light
into 24 hour darkness
the bush still screaming
in the silence of the dead
in the sky
an amerikan woman

9 A Lambretta is a three wheeled motorcycle with a passenger seat attached. Its use in this poem adds to other references to World War II and Nazi Germany specifically.
10 Hendin and Haas, *Wounds of War*, chap. 3.

with a camera between her thighs
taking pictures home to Mother

This may well be one of Kemp's most arresting poems. The phrase "rivers running red / into the earth which inherits the meek" is a startling application of the passage from Matthew 5. Here the meek Vietnamese quite literally are inheriting the earth. The flesh of their faces rises in the smoke from their burning villages. The phrase "fires burn / where their fires have been extinguished" suggests that the burning wreckage replaces the individual, personal "fire" of the people who lived there. Destructive fire replaces anything that might previously have been a creative fire. The fires of destruction are burning, giving off a false light built on the false motivation, and that causes a kind of spiritual darkness to descend which lasts all day and all night, a virtual "24 hours darkness." The photographic recording of the scene for American home media consumption is the obscene final act.

Through many of his poems Kemp records a sense of the violation of infinite obligations. Not only does the war violate human laws, such as the discrimination and proportion standards of the Just war principles, it violates divine law through acts of disobedience of and profanity before the sacred. In this war humanity itself is under attack, and Kemp sees that attack as an infinite transgression. Kemp's awareness of sin arises from his recognition that the war violated the transcendent worth of its victims' lives. Indeed, he approaches a religious sensitivity from the position of a violator. It is not that his religious sensitivity heightens his sense of sin, but the other way around; the surprising realization that he is involved in infinite violation leads to the identification of that violation as sin, the evidence of a dawning religious sensibility.

Paul Ricoeur suggests that the primitive sense of defilement could be summarized as "if you suffer, if you fall ill, if you fail, if you die, it is because you have sinned." Here suffering appears as concrete internal evidence of violation. Suffering is confirmation of that violation and is its measure. "In fearing defilement," says Ricoeur, "man fears the negativity of the transcendent," and this aspect of the sacred manifests itself in the specter of punishment which "darkens the experience of the sacred."[11] The punishment suggested in Kemp's poetry is the loss of human feeling and connection, the loss of centered selfhood. The inner suffering seems to parallel the external violation.

A central problem emerges, however, at this point for Ricoeur. The problem is the "belief that all suffering is the actual realization of this retribution. Thus the demand for a just punishment finds itself confused with the explanation of actual suffering."[12] The interpretation offered here, that Kemp

11 Ricoeur, *The Symbolism of Evil*, 41.
12 Ricoeur, *The Symbolism of Evil*, 42.

records a personal suffering somehow equal to the suffering which he causes, is complicated by the fact that much of the poetry records, quite clearly and in great detail, the suffering of the innocent. No internal suffering can neatly balance that caused to the innocent. Perhaps for this reason, Kemp's poetry records what seems to be a boundless, endless suffering. There is no possible expiation available. Kemp does not shirk personal responsibility, but he does identify others, ultimately the society as a whole, who must share in that responsibility. As Ricoeur says, "because it cannot be reduced to its subjective measure, neither can sin be reduced to its individual dimension; it is at once and primordially personal and communal."[13] This accounts, perhaps, for the consistent double focus of Kemp's awareness of sin as both intensely personal and as the result of a broadly based false motivation that initiated the war.

Kemp wrote several poems directly concerned with the search for religious atonement. The following two poems are similar in the lack of connection between the poet and the Madonna viewed as intercessor. But there are differences in tone that deserve careful attention. In the first poem Kemp introduces one of his central themes, the "one last hope."

> always one last hope
> a cold lonelie walk
> to some church
> an empty church
> silence
> except for a radiator
> in some distant corner
> heels clicking
> past miles of church benches
> i knelt at the foot
> of a statue of
> saint mary
> i said st mary
> she said
> not tonight
> i have a headache

With this touch of rueful humor, Kemp suggests that the "one last hope" is lost since he is dismissed by Mary because she is, perhaps, menstruating. This irony is heightened by the physical character of Mary's refusal; it is not a spiritual dismissal. There is, of course, an oblique hint that some form of sexual contact with her might have been the poet's only way to hope for absolution.

In a very different mood, this next poem shows Mary weeping for the poet, who is in despair. This time, he brushes away her entreaties with the sug-

13 Ricoeur, *The Symbolism of Evil*, 83.

gestion that, since no one can offer him a second chance, her mourning is ineffectual. He has crossed a barrier which is beyond the pale of any absolution.

> weep not madonna
> ive brought it all
> down on myself
> no sense to mourne
> your pity cannot
> help me
> your tears cannot
> quench the fires
> of my hell
> no sense to mourne
> when its too late
> the sorrow in your
> face
> cannot turn back
> the time
> no second chance
> no sense to mourne
> let me suffer
> for myself

This time Mary responds, but he rejects the offer. It does not heal since it does not and can not undo the deeds for which he suffers. The traditional acknowledgment of guilt and the appropriate absolution do not work. They should work, almost magically, but the nature of the violation is too severe for the confession to be effective or for divine aid to heal the wounds.

Since the traditional mode of reconciliation gave no help, Kemp records a search for other methods to ease the suffering. His poems often discuss his use of drugs and alcohol in his search for a fantasy to soothe the pain of reality. Drugs might help to mask the defilement briefly or to kill the memory for a while, but the creation in fantasy of an alternative interior universe dependent on drugs and alcohol does not solve the dilemma.

> i reach a point
> where even my
> fantasies
> are marked with conflict
> the fantasies on which'
> i have so
> strongly depended
> the realitie
> of the bush
> has invaded my protective

false world
i start out
balling some goddess
end up firing
a 60 into some
bastards guts
with realitie
and fantasie both
shot to hell i
guess there is no
place
left to go
the games have ended
the score was
alice cooper 69–bicardi 151.[14]

Both reality and fantasy are impossible places for Kemp to find relief, and there is literally no place left to turn. The war intrudes in such a way as to turn sexuality into its demonic opposite, machine gunning the enemy.[15] Kemp's poetry speaks for other Vietnam veterans who reported no hope in religious absolution, fantasy escape, or any other form of healing available. The sacrificial crisis referred to by Girard has come full circle and has returned to the perpetrator in full force.

What was left for Kemp was simply the process of "telling the tale," as Robert Lifton called the process of carefully naming the nature of the war. Kemp can be relentless in doing this, and can be especially effective, if nearly demonic, in describing the attitude of the soldiers engaged in the fighting. He often uses a form of savage parody to make his point, as in this poem.

Streaking thru the blue
In my bad ass 52
We'll hit the North today
And blow those zips away
Altho we know we won't
all make it back to base
Ohh, such kicks to fly and scream
our slaying song this day
OHHH
Fuck you zips

14 The "60" is the M 60 machine gun. Alice Cooper is a transvestite rock star. Bacardi 151 is a rum with over 75% pure alcohol content.
15 The psychological literature on the war is filled with similar examples of sexual dysfunction, the confusion of sexuality with violence, the abuse of drugs and alcohol, and the despair of the soldiers who can find no solutions. By 1984 it was reported by the Public Health Service Center for Suicide Statistics that more Vietvets had committed suicide than were killed in the war. *The Detroit Free Press*, March 26, 1984.

Fuck you zips
We're going to cut you down
Oh what fun
To pop these bombs
On some poor peasant town
OHHHH
Fuck you zips
Jam it zips
We're going to rip you down
Oh what fun
To ram these bombs
On all un-Christian towns

The sardonic pleasure in destruction is simultaneously stated and parodied. Essential to the satire's effect is identification of the villages as "un-Christian towns" worthy of destruction. The use of the "Jingle Bells" tune for the parody comes, most likely, from the Christmas bombing of Hanoi in 1972. Like much of Kemp's work, the poem is designed to make the reader uncomfortable since it is written in the voice of one who apparently enjoys killing.[16] Parody, as Frye suggests, is an appropriate mode for demonic imagery, and it is clear that for Kemp the war was indeed demonic, and that it is the central focus of his telling the tale.

3. The Rites/Rights of Veterans

The poems presented thus far describe events or states of mind directly connected with Vietnam itself. Kemp wrote many poems concerned with his state of mind while back in the States, and these poems demonstrate the long lasting and pervasive effects of the war. He also realizes that his experiences are not unique. This poem addresses other returning veterans or Vietvets.

WELCOME HOME, BROTHER!!!
YOU RISKED YOUR LIFE, IN THE BUSH.
AND NOW YOU ARE TIRED AND WORN.
AND YOU THINK THAT YOU HAVE EARNED YOURSELF A REST.
BUT DESTRUCTION WILL HAUNT YOU
IT WON'T LET YOU FORGET
AND A BROKEN LIFE, IS ALL THAT YOU'LL HAVE LEFT.

YOU THINK THAT IT'S ALL OVER
ALL THE FIRE, ALL THE DEATH
BECAUSE YOU'RE BACK WITH YOUR WOMAN AND YOUR
FRIENDS

---

16 Kemp seems to have written this piece early in 1973 according to the manuscript notations.

THO, NOW YOU'RE HOME TO STAY
YOU ARE STILL BACK IN THE NAM.

WELCOME, BROTHER, TO THE WAR THAT NEVER ENDS
TO THE WAR THAT NEVER ENDS.

This chilling poem recalls a condition familiar to many Vietvets. It illustrates one of the central aspects of the war for Kemp: something unusual happened that makes the war last forever. In anthropological terms, borrowed from Van Gennep and Turner, the Vietvets remain in a liminal state caught between two realities. They are in a constant state of transition. Permanently altered as they were by their experiences in the war, they are unable to reenter the American society that they left. Kemp was one of thousands of Vietvets who became incarcerated within a short time of their return; a 1973 study by the Federal Bureau of Prisons determined that nearly one-third of prisoners at that time were veterans.[17]

The very strange, even ghostly, event of a major parade in New York City for returning veterans held in 1985 shows how strongly many Vietvets needed a public ritual of return to America. It was hoped that the parade would be an official ritual of welcome and reincorporation for these veterans, all of whom had been back more than a decade, and that it would mark an official end to the war. Frequent statements by veterans that they were called "baby killers" and had been "spat upon" suggest that they believed they alone were blamed for the war in which they served. They were simply the instruments of a national policy, yet they saw themselves being blamed for that policy and its failures. The veterans yearned for a completed ritual process and for removal of their scapegoat status, even if that ritual had to occur a dozen years after the end of the American direct involvement in the war.

A careful consideration of ritual, especially military ritual, and the accompanying centrality of sacrifice, is a useful method for interpreting the situation of the Vietvets. The lives of enemy soldiers could, presumably, be sacrificed for a war's higher mission, but the false motivation produced no such higher mission. The American soldiers, as an intentionally sequestered community, should have been shielded from the severe problems over the killings, since they were not individual moral agents but representatives of the collective national will. Killing in war should not be murder in the eyes of the soldiers, who should be innocent instruments of national political policy. The soldiers' own suffering should be capable of being interpreted as their necessary though regretable sacrifice—an interpretation for right sacrifice for which the services of religion are traditionally enlisted.

17 *The Detroit Free Press*, March 26, 1984.

3.1 War Conditions

The war was supposed to be a war against communism for the defense of a beleagured, fledgling democracy invaded by an external communist threat. However, many commentators, Kemp among them, considered the war to be a war against the Vietnamese as a people, as a race and culture, and as practitioners of a specific philosophy of life. As far as the South Vietnamese government was concerned, most soldiers found the Army of the Republic of Vietnam (ARVN) to be untrustworthy and the government itself to be corrupt, unrepresentative of its people. Thus, for the individual soldier the war was fought for no meaningful ideals but simply for his individual survival.

Fighting simply for personal survival may well be a fact of life for most combat soldiers in most wars, but in Vietnam the lack of any believable overriding purpose made the fight for survival particularly stark. As Colonel H. G. Summers, an apologist for the Army's role, sees it:

> The student deferments, along with the decision not to ask for a declaration of war and not to mobilize our reserve forces, were part of a deliberate Presidential policy not to arouse the passions of the American people. The effect of this was that we fought the Vietnam war in cold blood.[18]

Fighting "in cold blood" means, in part, that the traditional methods for giving meaning to fighting and for killing the enemy and justifying American losses were noticeably absent. The "communists" killed ought to have been acceptable sacrificial victims, but for a number of reasons they were not. First, the killing of civilians, especially women and children, clouded and confused the image of the enemy as appropriate sacrificial victims. Second, the North Vietnamese and Viet Cong who fought so hard seemed to have a sense of purpose and will that made the Americans feel like an invading rather than a liberating army—more like the "redcoats" in another country's revolutionary war, as W.D. Ehrhart pointed out in the PBS series on the Vietnam War. Finally, it became clear to many American soldiers, especially on their return to "the world," that they themselves, most ironically, had become the *pharmakoi* or sacrificial victims to salve the national conscience.

The idea that there is an intimate relationship between war, ritual and sacrifice is not of course unique to the war in Vietnam. Walter Burkert, in *Homo Necans*, draws the parallel clearly: "War is a ritual, a self–portrayal and self–affirmation of male society. Male society finds stability in confronting death, in defying it through a display of readiness to die, and in the ecstasy of survival." He suggests, further, that "for the ancient world, hunting, sacrifice and war were symbolically interchangeable."[19] Vietnam, despite the vast tech-

---

18 Summers, *On Strategy: A Critical Analysis of the Vietnam War*, 62.
19 Burkert, *Homo Necans*, 47.

nological superiority of the Americans, was, in many ways, a war which incorporated many characteristics of that ancient world, since it involved hunting in "Indian country," as the phrase went, in a frontier wasteland filled with malevolent and presumably sub-human inhabitants prone to sudden violence. The search and destroy mission was, at its heart, a hunting expedition. It was a ritualized environment where the will of the divine might well be expected suddenly to reveal itself as it is seldom revealed in the ordinary, non-ritually-charged society. The gods might well be expected to bless such a hunt with success.

One of the crucial elements is the role of the sacrificial victim. For Girard, the process of distinguishing between suitable and unsuitable sacrificial victims is essential for an effective sacrifice. He notes that "between these (suitable) victims and the community a crucial social link is missing, so that they can be exposed to violence without fear of reprisal. Their death does not automatically entail an act of vengeance."[20] The Vietnamese enemy were initially marked as lacking an essential social link because they were communist and atheist; hence they could be seen as standing against both social and divine order. The "fact" that they stand against God is a crucial element in their suitability for violent death (as Kemp parodies in the bombing of "all un-Christian towns"). As Girard sees it, at bottom there is a theological problem.

> The sacrificial process requires a certain degree of *misunderstanding*. The celebrants do not and must not comprehend the true nature of the sacrificial act. The theological basis of the sacrifice has a crucial role in fostering this misunderstanding. It is the god who supposedly demands the victims; he alone, in principle, who savors the smoke from the altars and requisitions the slaughtered flesh. It is to appease his anger that the killing goes on.[21]

When Girard mentions the "true nature of the sacrificial act," he means that the victim is "a substitute for all members of the community." Because "the sacrifice serves to protect the entire community from *its own* violence, it prompts the entire community to choose victims outside itself."[22] In Vietnam, for example, the racial antagonism of American society was briefly overcome during actual combat operations when all participants were united through equal vulnerability in deadly common tasks. Only in rear areas did the racial tension present in American society become amplified and erupt into open violence.[23] It is possible to see in the Vietnam War an attempt to "cure" the racial division between black and white in American society, by scapegoating the Vietnamese as a race that could be a common enemy for both black and white Americans.

20 Girard, *Violence and the Sacred*, 13.
21 Girard, *Violence and the Sacred*, 7. Italics in original.
22 Girard, *Violence and the Sacred*, 8.
23 Attested in numerous sources, including Lifton.

Girard's idea that "it is the god who supposedly demands the victims" finds its resonance in Vietnam as well. To "kill a Commie for Christ" may well be seen as something more than a sarcastic and ironic statement. The American dead could presumably be seen to have died in a sacred cause, since Americans have often seen themselves as a "blessed or chosen people,"[24] whose enemies may be killed to preserve the nation's "divinely ordained" purpose. As Girard notes, "men can dispose of their violence more efficiently if they regard the process not as something emanating from within themselves, but as a necessity imposed from without, a divine decree whose least infraction calls down a terrible punishment."[25] Thus for Girard violence and the sacred are finally inseparable, and they are united through the means of sacrificial ritual. As Burkert sees it, "the power to kill and respect for life illuminate each other" because only in "the experience of killing [does] one perceive the sacredness of life."[26] Thus the process of sacrifice should transform the participants by revealing a sacred mystery of the connection between life and death, and the participants should then receive a new appreciation for the ordinary after transgressing the bounds of the social conventions against the use of violence.

The cognitive content of such sacralized military ritual might look something like this:

1. Our soldiers are innocent representatives of the collective will.
2. The enemy is possessed (infected) and thus of a different order of being.
3. The enemy initiates the violence by attempting to spread the disease.
4. The enemy is then sacrificed in obedience to divine and human commands.
5. Our soldiers show courage in not fearing their own deaths, for as representatives of the collective will their personal fates lose significance.
6. Our soldiers show that the sacralizing shield is working by not fearing the deaths of the enemy, since they can be killed without guilt.
7. Successful sacrifice proves our original innocence and demonstrates our obedience to the divine, thereby resacralizing the society.

For this process to be effective it must be accomplished in the service of a transcendent cause and it must be capable of being repeated. Such a process ought to alter and elevate the status of those who return from the conflict. The irreversible event of killing is done in a primal setting in which, ideally, the participants are shielded from pollution by the rhythm of the sacrificial ritual itself.

3.2 An American Ritual Dilemma

But in Vietnam, a war fought "in cold blood," the killing is not a sacrifice, the victims are not suitable, and the power of the ritual is reversed. In terms of

24 Lifton, *Home from the War*, 150.
25 Girard, *Violence and the Sacred*, 14.
26 Burkert, *Homo Necans*, 21, 38.

the mythic patterns evoked, America becomes Goliath; in Nixon's words, "a pitiful, helpless giant" with a huge but ineffective military superiority. The American soldiers become "redcoats," paid invaders taking the place of the French imperialists and even like the Nazis (Amerikans) in their genocidal assault on the people and culture of Vietnam. The American soldiers become pawns in the triumphant story of their enemies, rather than heroes in their own drama.[27] Finally, the war in Vietnam becomes an inverted kaleidoscope of American "sacred" history, with biblical reference reversed, and the symbols of the civil religion ironically parodied.

When killing does not have the shield typically provided by the sacralizing military ritual, it becomes murder and the soldiers become criminal executioners. Not only are the ethical codes broken, but the religious support system for the national self-understanding is effectively undermined. This is indeed the kind of result suggested by Girard when he wrote that "when the religious framework of a society starts to totter . . . the whole cultural foundation of the society is put in jeopardy."[28]

Perhaps the American soldiers expected to go off on a crusade to thwart the atheistic millenium of communism, but what resulted was an irredeemable catastrophe for both Vietnam and America. In Kemp's poetry one sees his horror at the double catastrophe. What he sees is like an evil *darsan*, a vision of a sacred power usually contained within an image of a deity, but this time it is a vision of the demonic. As Lifton says, the evil in Vietnam was *surd* evil, that is, having no place, not even a negative place, in the previous American universe of religious symbols. *Surd* evil is "evil closely related to chaos . . . in which there is no principle of improvement; its only function is to be endured, rejected, conquered or passed by."[29] Kemp makes his statement of this theme in the following selection from a long poem entitled, "Nine Dragons and One Dragon."

> dead and living dead
> brother betrayed by brother
> oriental humanity betrayed by western power-trips . . .
> . . . you can't reach into the dirt without pulling up a
>   handful of blood.
> how can they live when they have lost all but their
> lives they are dead.
> how can they look at you and try to find what little
>   humanness you may have left
> a woman no older than 18 looks at me with a babie in
>   her arms and
> says with her eyes if you kill us you will have

27 Titiano Terzani, *Giai Phong!*, 218.
28 Girard, *Violence and the Sacred*, 49.
29 Lifton, *Home from the War*, 125.

destroyed your last hope
my last hope
watch those tracers the one you don't see is the one
you feel tearing into your guts
fire and blood and screaming and dying . . .
. . . to take part in the destruction and re-programming
of an entire human culture
to take part in the destruction of oneself
no names no identities just bodies just sorrow
bitterness
and there is no 'one last hope' it all goes at one time

There is a horror that is perhaps even greater than the natural horror of physical destruction on the battlefield. Kemp records the destruction of hope as well as of humanity. He records a notion of violation, of sin, that does not respond to any absolution, religious or otherwise. His vision is of the demonic, a negative absolute, which is revealed during violations that transgress both human and divine barriers. Kemp arrives at a place outside his inherited religious conventions, yet he manages to survive by attempting accurately to describe the nature of the war that he continues to experience. This painful accuracy makes of each poem a kind of confession, very nearly a prayer. Yet if each one is prayer-like, it is not clear to what kind of deity it is addressed. There is, however, a certain value in communicating accurately, if only to himself, the absolute horror show that is repeated every night.

conflicts in my mind
i never thought it
would happen to me
i always knew i
would get it
how can such pain exist
screams for a medic
become
inhuman gurgling sounds
thru a mouth
full of blood
choking inside my lungs
choking out precious air
strangling on my own
insanitie
the sun is turning black
it is all over
i have seen it
so many times before
everie nite
i have died everie nite

At the center of Kemp's work there is always a consciousness of infinite transgression, of a descent into evil. This sense of transgression, and the accompanying descent, may well be seen as the marks of a sense of radical disobedience, a sense of contact with some dimension of the sacred. Kemp's poems are often so ugly that it would be convenient to ignore them or explain them away as expressions of psychological abberations. Yet, if his poems do have a claim to a central moral integrity, it is because they present the war as a tragedy of the spirit. For Kemp the Vietnam War was a war against a race, a culture, a philosophy of life, and the way it was fought dehumanized the American soldiers who fought it. The American military ritual failed to shield the soldiers from the effects of their actions, which continue to haunt them. Glenn Gray says, "what protrudes and does not fit in our pasts rises up to haunt us and make us spiritually unwell in the present,"[30] and this is what Kemp's poems record.

Donald Kemp tells of a violation of moral and religious sanctions that must be seen as an integral part of the story of what happened, and still is happening, to the American soldiers who fought in Vietnam and to the society that sent them to that war. Kemp's poetry points to the urgency of addressing the problem of "curing violence." The advances in understanding the problem put forward by Girard, Burkert, Ricoeur and others may well be useful tools in this endeavor. The difficulties run deep, however, and at least in Kemp's work there is no trace of a final resolution and no certain path to such an end. The only glimmer of hope is in the telling of the tale.

4. Postcript

This essay analyzes the poetry produced by Donald G. Kemp between 1971 and 1973 while he was imprisoned at Waupun, Wisconsin. John A. Lundquist, an organizer for the National Clearing House on Post Vietnam Syndrome, a branch of Vietnam Veterans Against the War, summarizes, in an attached memo in the files, the circumstances surrounding Kemp's incarceration:

Don Kemp came home from Vietnam in 1967, a spaced out veteran of the Army's Long Range Reconnaissance Platoon (LRRP), attached to the Rangers. A man ordered to kill civilians, go on suicide missions, fire on the "friendlies" and upon the opposition just to keep it all going in the name of freedom. When Don arrived home, he quickly developed heavy paranoid symptoms: carrying guns, guns in his car, guns in his house, knives in his boots, GI first aid pouches, and a hand gun under the pillow where he slept. Psychiatric Compensation along with the semblance of medical help was being administered through the Veteran's Administration. The fact that Don's psychiatrist would be leaving the VA as of July 1, 1971, and that he had noted some

---

30 Gray, *The Warriors*, 24.

improvement in Don's condition, were two of the major considerations which, (according to the doctor's testimony), led to the recommendation that Don be discharged from all VA treatment.

Don then went home, and, that night, upon being awakened from one of his terrifying nightmares by his wife—shot her dead with the gun he kept under his pillow. The same gun he slept with to protect himself from the enemy he sees in his dreams.

The trial and conviction of Don G. Kemp, resulting in a Natural Life sentence for the first degree murder of his wife, with the act having taken place during a "Vietnam Flashback" while dreaming, should bring to the forefront of our community's attention the need to investigate and recognize certain symptoms which, to varying degrees, constitute the Post Vietnam Syndrome (PVS). Kemp disputed this account of the murder of his wife. He insisted that he had not killed her and had, in fact, been framed by the police who broke into his house in the night.

This brief background may help the reader understand something of the origin of Kemp's poetry. It is presented as a postscript in order to allow an interpretive or hermeneutic distance (Ricoeur) between our prejucides (Gadamer) or stereotypes (Girard) of Vietvets on the one hand, and our reading and exegesis of the poems on the other hand.

Violence–Religion–Law

A GIRARDIAN ANALYSIS

Edward McMahon

Abstract

René Girard's analysis of the generative role of violence in human culture and religion has highlighted the importance of the epiphany of the "primitive sacred" and the appearance of myth, ritual, and law to channel violence. This analysis is presented and tested particularly with respect to the role of law in classical Roman society on the accounts of Romulus and Remus.

Girard has further claimed in *Things Hidden* that the biblical revelation has definitively uncovered the truth about the relationship of generative violence and religion. This claim is tested with respect to the Sodom and Gomorrah account (Genesis), the oracles of the prophets Jeremiah and Ezekiel, and in II Isaiah and Job. The focus of the New Testament investigation is the gospel of Jesus—the gospel accounts about Jesus and the message of Jesus itself. Girard's analysis is found to have disclosed the deconstructive power of the biblical revelation. He has also shown how the law functions in the Bible's alternative perspective on religion and violence.

The concluding section examines two violent societies—Lebanon and the United States—and shows the place of law (in connection with myth and ritual) in overcoming this violence.

0. Introduction

That prophet of the postmodern world, Friedrich Nietzsche, published in 1878 a collection of aphorisms called *Human, All Too Human*, which presented to its readers his thoughts on religion and government.

> For religion quietens the heart of the individual in times of loss, deprivation, fear, distrust, in those instances, that is to say, in which the government feels unable to do anything towards alleviating the psychical sufferings of the private person: even in the case of universal, unavoidable and in the immediate prospect inevitable evils (famines, financial crises, wars), indeed, religion guarantees a calm, patient, trusting disposition among the masses.

182

The power [of the government] that lies in unity of popular sentiment, in the fact that everyone holds the same opinions and has the same objectives, is sealed and protected by religion. . . .[1]

Nietzsche was too good a classics scholar and too keen an observer of his turbulent times to think that these statements quoted above were the whole truth about religion and government and violence. In the same aphorism he analyzed state decay as the loss of religious legitimation for the state which leads to competition, disregard of law, and violence until the state is abolished and distinctions of public versus private disappear. Both religion and violence, and political authority and violence, go hand in hand. What is given dimly and disjointedly in his "Book for Free Spirits" is seen clearly and in its intrinsic interconnectedness in the thought of René Girard.[2]

In his writings Girard has been developing a theory of what he calls interdividual psychology. This has led him to articulate a view of religion in traditional and ethnological societies which emphasizes the primacy of violence in them and the interconnectedness of the scapegoat mechanism, the appearance of the "primitive sacred," and the origin and development of myths, rituals, prohibitions, and governments to restrain and redirect this violence.

His work since 1975 has given increasing attention to the way in which the Judaeo-Christian revelation has made it possible to see this religious complex at work. Moreover, at key moments in the societies based on this tradition there have been instances of life lived on a new basis of non-sacrificial, nonviolent religion.

Nevertheless the unholy fusion of sacrificial religion and the Judaeo-Christian tradition has occurred and has continued to exert its influence in the twentieth century, though with less force and more public awareness. As a culture critic Girard has noted some instances of the decline of sacrificial Judaism and Christianity but also some frightening upsurges of this phenomenon.[3]

In this essay we will consider Girard's analysis of traditional and ethnological societies, the world as impacted by the Judaeo-Christian tradition, and the modern world. While it is necessary in each case to see the whole "re-

1 This quotation appears in aphorism 472 on pp. 170–71 in Hollingdale's translation. On the relationship of *Human, All Too Human* to Nietzsche's other works see the introduction by Erich Heller in Nietzsche, *Human*, vii-xix.
2 I claim here not some genetic connection between Nietzsche and Girard but a perspectival affinity: both thinkers have seen something important that most other culture critics have missed. For Girard's own mildly appreciative but often critical responses to the Nietzschean project see *Violence and the Sacred*, 292; "Strategies of Madness—Nietzsche, Wagner, and Dostoevski," in *"Double Business,"* 61–83; "Dionysus" and "The Founding Murder in the Philosophy of Nietzsche," in Dumouchel, *Violence and Truth*, 227–46.
3 See his remarks on nuclear weapons in *Things Hidden*, 255–57.

ligious" complex at work, we will try to give more attention to prohibition/law as a constituent element that has received less thematic attention. It is the law and the judicial society based upon it that Girard sees as ultimately giving hope for a curing of violence.[4]

1. Violence-Religion-Law in Traditional and Ethnological Societies

As with the origins of most social phenomena, the appearance of violence, religion, and law among human beings is no longer directly ascertainable. We have to examine both traditional and ethnological societies to develop a working hypothesis to explain how things "must" have been in the beginning. These hypotheses or social scenarios then are evaluated pragmatically in terms of how well they explain other texts and meaningful actions in these societies and how well they explain later developments.

Girard's scenario is based on texts from classical Greece and Rome and tribal societies in Africa, North America, and Oceania. In highlighting certain features of Girard's more comprehensive hypothesis, we will take as an example the lives of Romulus and Remus as told by Livy, Dionysius Halicarnassus, and Plutarch.[5] The significance of this story for the origin and later history of Rome has been described by Horace:

> What drives us: blind madness, some inhuman power, perhaps guilt? Give me an answer! They say nothing, and their faces turn sick and pale, and their battered feelings are numb. This is the answer: a harsh fate haunts the Romans, and the evil of fratricide, since the innocent blood of Remus stained the earth, a curse on all his descendents.[6]

The twins Romulus and Remus were well remembered by both Greek and Latin writers. Their mother had been raped—by the god Mars? by their uncle King Amulius? or perhaps by a "strange phantom?" In any case after their birth the boys were cast adrift in a basket on the Tiber to die. They were saved from drowning and were nourished by a wolf until they were found by Faustulus and taken to his home for upbringing. This blend of legendary and plausible historical details about their infancy was continued by the writers with stories of their coming to manhood. When the brothers learned that they were really

---

4 For a more comprehensive and detailed analysis of Girard's method see Hamerton-Kelly, "Religion and the Thought of Rene Girard" (Chap. 1). For the curative role of ritual see the studies by Orzech (Chap. 7), Hough (Chap. 8), and Smith (Chap. 11) in part 3 "Contemporary Issues."

5 For examples taken from other cultures see Girard, *Violence and the Sacred*; Girard, *Things Hidden*, 7–126; Girard, *Scapegoat* 24–95; Girard, "Generative Scapegoating" in *Violent Origins*, 73–105. The present example develops further the account given by Girard in "The Crimes of the Gods," *Scapegoat*, 89–94.

6 Horace *Epode* 7.

the long-lost grandsons of the man who should have been king, they acted together to overthrow the usurper; in the course of the revolt, Romulus killed the king.

Romulus and Remus then determined to go out and establish their own city. The object which they sought (the right to establish the new city and become its king) sparked an intense rivalry. As Dionysius put it so clearly, "For each group [around Romulus and Remus], exalting its own leaders, extolled him as the proper person to command them all; and the youths, themselves, being no longer one in mind or feeling it necessary to entertain brotherly sentiments toward each other, since each expected to command the other, scorned equality and craved superiority."[7]

The dynamics of the relationship between Romulus and Remus are no surprise to us. We know how it is with twins or for that matter siblings close in age to each other. What we also know, but even less like to admit, is that this relationship of rivalry easily occurs between any two individuals in society. And the frequency of accounts from all types of societies suggests that this is a human universal.

The starting point is the play of desire that begins when any two individuals become aware of each other. In the ongoing interaction between the two individuals one person becomes a subject and the second becomes a model for the other. The subject increasingly seeks to be like its model, imitating first its choice of objects (object-desire) and increasingly imitating the model's desires as such to the extent that the subject wishes to become the model (metaphysical desire). The model participates in this play of desire by conveying to the subject a mimetic message—"Imitate me." As the subject becomes more like the model, the latter increasingly finds itself turned into a rival. Now it conveys the different message—"Don't imitate me," i.e., do not seek to possess my objects or try to become like me. This prohibition arising within the model/obstacle situation serves both to restrain desire but also to stimulate it.

The mechanism which controls the interaction seems to pre-date the situation of encounter of any two individuals, and even the birth of the twins, and be already in place as subject and model-rival move into competition with each other.[8]

As acquisitive mimesis becomes conflictual mimesis, signs of the impending crisis appear. The rivals increasingly become the doubles of each other. The erasure of differences between individuals, families, and groups in society is paralleled by an erasure of differences in the world of nature: there are winds, storms, and plagues which overcome individuals and whole groups.

---

7 Dionysisus *Roman Antiquities* I.85.5
8 Girard's understanding of human mimeticism was expounded in *Deceit* in relationship to several predominantly 19th–century authors. The theory received more theoretical elaboration in Girard, *Things Hidden* (Book I: Fundamental Anthropology and Book III: Interdividual Psychology).

How may one restore order to the society? Small-scale societies with their underdeveloped political institutions lack societal braking mechanisms to bring the crisis to a halt. Experience has shown people in these societies, however, that the crisis can be halted at least for a time by the "removal" (expulsion or death) of the one who "caused" the problem. The next time a social crisis develops something new must be tried (and retried). A surrogate victim must be found and sacrificed., and now the mechanism has been created which will make possible ever new resolutions of the conflict. This is the scapegoat mechanism.

The conflict between Romulus and Remus was also a social conflict between groups of their supporters ("they [Romulus and Remus] divided the whole multitude into two parts").[9] According to one account, Faustulus, marked earlier as a herdsman,[10] tried "to put an end to the strife of the brothers and being unable to do so, threw himself unarmed into the midst of the combatants, seeking the speediest death, . . . "[11] The (self-)sacrifice of Faustulus failed to resolve the conflict, and the death of Remus himself was required. Dionysius twice reports the death of Remus. According to I.87.3 Remus died in battle, but the story in I.87.4 is more revealing, because here Romulus built a wall around what was to be the new city. Remus lept over it saying, "As for this wall, one of your enemies could as easily cross it as I do." At that, Celer, an overseer struck him saying, "Well, as for this enemy, one of us could easily punish him." Remus' attempt to violate the boundaries of the society results in his death, albeit not by Romulus' hands.

For this scapegoat mechanism to operate certain requirements must be fulfilled. Since there is not really a cause for the new trouble, a "true cause" (a "guilty" party) must be designated among the possible causes for the problem. Even if a real (by our standards) cause could be determined, the true offender is not often suitable as a sacrifice. His or her removal would adversely affect the existing network of social relationships, and reprisals and vengeance would ensue, which might well make the situation worse. Thus a marginal individual or group must be found.

Proper scapegoats seem to have "marks" that single them out for persecution: they may be members of an ethnic or religious minority; they may have some physical abnormality (bodily deformity, sickness, madness), or as marginal individuals have the physical characteristics of their age group (women, children, old men); they may have some social abnormality (they are very poor or very rich or simply don't "fit" into the larger group). They may even be twins![12]

In time there developed in Rome a new social crisis. Romulus, the founder

9 Dionysisus *Roman Antiquities* I.85.4.
10 Dionysisus *Roman Antiquities* I.79.10.
11 Dionysius *Roman Antiquities* I.87.2.
12 Girard, *Scapegoat*, 18–23.

of the city, became the scapegoat. According to Livy, "the king had been rent in pieces by the hands of the senators. . . ."[13] The account of Dionysius (II.56.4) describes the banding together of a group of patricians against Romulus. After they murdered him they divided the body; the word used here in Greek has the sense of "tearing apart." Finally each one is given a piece of the body to smuggle out of the senate house to bury.

Plutarch's account in his life of Romulus contains more details of the murder-sacrifice of Romulus. The words used to describe Romulus' death (they "slew" him and "dismembered" him) are words used elsewhere in Greek as sacrificial terminology. The *sparagmos*, dismemberment, of the victim is described as unanimous and done by hand, without weapons. It thus recalls the sparagmos of Dionsysiac practice in Euripides, *The Bacchae*. Significantly, events in Plutarch's narrative take place in the temple of Vulcan. In Roman mythology Vulcan (Greek Hephaistos) was the lord of fire and the divine smith. Although he had been born deformed (his feet were turned backward), as lord of the fire he directed fire in its destructive capacities, particularly volcanoes and conflagrations. In his temple live animals were thrown into the fire and later on in his cult little fish, taken to represent human lives, were sacrificed. But as a dual god he could call a halt to his fury and use his control over fire for the production of useful and artistic things.

Of course even properly sacrificed human beings cannot objectively stop the "accompanying" flood, drought, plague, or epidemic. Yet as frightful as these natural disasters are, what is often more damaging is the long-term social and psychic disturbances which they cause. The post-traumatic shock needs to be confronted.

In traditional and ethnological societies the conflict of desire, the social crisis, and the resolution of it through the scapegoat mechanism leads to the birth of religion. Myths told or written by the persecutors serve to justify or explain what had happened between the individuals in the society and how the crisis was resolved. As mythology develops over time there is a tendency to eliminate any representations of violence, replacing first the collective violence of all against one by reports of individual violence. With further time the texts become utopian, harmless accounts serving as models of morality.[14] This evolution has happened in the surviving materials about Romulus.

The central function of the earliest myths was to describe the appearance of the "primitive sacred." Looking through the myth one can see how the chosen victim was first transformed into the scapegoat: the innocent one became the monster. The scapegoat whose death brought tranquility and life to the community is later seen through a second transference to transcend the very limits of life and death. It is the personification and reification of the group's col-

---

13 Dionysius *Roman Antiquities* I.16.4.
14 On the evolution of mythology see "What is a Myth?" and "The Crimes of the Gods" in Girard, *Scapegoat*, 25–44 and 76–94.

lective violence: this one must be a divinity, a god! The myths first commemorate the god's epiphany and then begin to fill in the blanks of its life-story by giving accounts of the god's "origin" and "career," the other divinities that had come to be, and the relationships that exist among this network of gods and goddesses.

The accounts of Livy and Plutarch make Romulus into a god (daimon) after his death. Late accounts connect this transformation not with the murder of Romulus but with his sudden disappearance and with the testimony of one Proculus Julius, who reported an appearance from heaven of Romulus and a message that he is now a deity named Quirinus.[15]

This epiphany of the primitive sacred is not a mere manifestation of pure, terrible presence. The divinity, formerly victim, becomes the physician and the law-giver for the community, which may be readily seen in the sacrificial politics of a sacred king.[16] More generally it may be seen in the way in which the sacred becomes a model for the forbidden. Prohibitions try to prevent any reoccurrence of the crisis or any act of vengeance by the god by trying to shortcircuit any new mimetic rivalry. Such prohibitions further establish and maintain processes of exchange in society (relations between husbands and wives are specified in marriage rules; food or other objects in economic rules; location in space through housing/hunting/farming rules, etc.).[17] In time, laws as prohibitions are supplemented by positive rules.

For Livy and Dionysius, Romulus had an important role to play as the law-giver of Rome, but here two themes are struck which may seem odd to us. The first is that the law produces social unity—"since nothing else but law could unite them into a single body politic."[18] The second is the importance of social distinctions codified by law for establishing the public peace. Dionysius says that Romulus divided the society into groups and placed leaders over them; on the basis of "kindly services" and "merit" they were further divided into classes, from plebians to patricians.

The scapegoat become sacred is also a model for ritual. The first prohibition distinguishes the victim and the victimizers, the sacred and the profane. Secondarily the prohibited sacred place (the source of a terrible power and pollution) becomes the place of ritual activity. Dionysius expansively attributes to Romulus the establishment of temples, festivals, and sacrifices. He also is made responsible for setting up the ideological system of the religion: he "determined the representations and symbols of the gods, and declared their powers. . . ."[19]

---

15 Dionysius *Roman Antiquities* I.15.6 and Plutarch *Romulus* 28.
16 See here Girard, *Violence*, 104–16, 300–304 and Hamerton-Kelly, "Religion," 25–27.
17 Girard, *Violence and the Sacred*, 223–49.
18 Dionysius *Roman Antiquities* I.8.1.
19 Dionysius *Roman Antiquities* II.18.2.

The repetition of elements of the social crisis in sacrificial ritual is thought to be prophylactic or even curative of further violence. Religions contain both festivals and antifestivals: in the former type we find deliberate violations of normally accepted prohibitions where the social world of distinctions and practices is once a year turned upside down; in antifestivals, on the other hand, the cultural prohibitions are strongly reinforced to prevent the recurrence of the originating crisis through the breaking of any rules. Thus rules are strongly maintained regarding sexual activity, violence, or any other activity that could give rise to disagreements, contests, jealousy, and imitation.

Girard's interpretation of ritual helps us to understand the April 21 festival described by Plutarch that celebrated the birthday of the country. He notes that "at first, as it is said, they sacrificed no living creature at that festival, but thought they ought to keep it pure and without stain of blood, since it commemorated the birth of their country."[20]

The logic of ritual development required that no blood be shed as a way not to provoke once again the whole society into a dangerous upheaval through the blood of the victim, calling to mind the death of Remus. In later times sacrifices were offered at festivals but with the use of a substitute victim for the original victim.

2. Violence, Religion, and Law in the Light of the Biblical Revelation

When we examine the development of Girard's thought on violence, religion, and law, we expect him to turn his attention from world mythology and institutions in largely traditional societies directly to an analysis of our modern world situation. Yet in *Things Hidden* Girard turns from "Fundamental Anthropology" (Book I) not directly to "Interdividual Psychology" but rather to the Judaeo-Christian scriptures (Book II).

For Girard the biblical texts are privileged resources. In the writings of the Pentateuch as well as in the prophets and wisdom literature (Job and certain Psalms) one can find a diagnosis/uncovering of the violence mechanism and the beginnings of a therapy to treat this life threatening illness.[21] There emerges a new perspective, one which will finally reveal the truth about those other resolutions of the crisis—the appearance of the primitive sacred and the reconstitution of communal life and institutions through prohibitions and rituals.

---

20 Plutarch *Romulus* 20.1.
21 For other examples of a Girardian approach to Old Testament texts, see the papers in this volume by Williams (Chap. 4) and Lasine (Chap. 10).

2.1. "I (the Lord) have given you as . . . a light to the Nations."
The Old Testament Revelation

Within the Pentateuch are several narratives that trace once again the "moments" of the sacrificial crisis.

Societal dissolution, collective violence, and the appearance of the all-against-one motif are important structuring elements in the account of Sodom and Gomorrah (Genesis 18–19). Two strangers (angels in disguise) are welcomed by Lot into his home. The law of oriental hospitality required him to provide food, shelter, and protection to them, but suddenly they are the intended victims of the populace—"the men of Sodom, both young and old, *all the people to the last man*, surrounded the house" (19:4). They want Lot himself to cooperate with them and bring the strangers out for them to be raped. Lot offers his two virgin daughters to the crowd as surrogate victims (19:8). They are not socially acceptable substitutes, however, to bring about the unity of the people, for their ties of kinship are too close and reprisals from Lot and his extended family would ensue. Furthermore the crowd wants (at least as much as the intended victims) Lot's own participation in the act of collective violence, and when he refuses to do that, the crowd turns on him (19:9).

The intervention of the angels allows Lot, his wife, and his two daughters to escape. The text notes the extent of the destruction inflicted by "the Lord" on Sodom and Gomorrah (19:24–25), but there is once again, though, a shift in judgment. There is no endorsement of the action of the citizens of Sodom and Gomorrah, no attempt to protect their reputations, no attempt to make them the real founders of a people. Instead, the future of the Moabites and Ammonites belongs to Lot and his two daughters, not to the people of the two cities (19:30–38).

The role of the law in the overcoming of violence in the primal period of humanity is shown in the story of Noah and the Flood (Genesis 6–9). Earlier according to Gen 3:19–20, Adam had instituted the first classification system when he named "every beast of the field and every bird of the air." Then after the flood all kinds of creatures are released from the Ark to repopulate the world. Immediately Noah acts to reestablish the classification system of the world so that these creatures were divided into male and female (7:15) as well as clean and unclean (7:8) categories.

The blessings upon Noah and his sons by God in chapter 9 command them to be fruitful and multiply (9:1, 7), but they are not to "eat flesh with its life, that is, its blood" (9:4). The prohibiton of bloodshed is extended to any bloodshed (animal or human) and is made universal with the explicit threat of new reciprocal violence —"Whoever sheds the blood of a human, by a human shall that person's blood be shed" (9:6). It was on the basis of these blessings/commands that later Jewish thinkers elaborated the seven so-called Noahide laws. These laws were thought to be binding on all human beings, Jew or Gentile.[22]

In the writings of the Hebrew prophets Girard finds a continued subversion of the hitherto accepted mythology with its connection to the sacrificial cult and law. More positively there are disclosed the necessary elements for a cure.

The prophetic corpus contains oracles which show the prominent place of violence within the human realm. Hos 4:1–2, for example, describes only the people of Israel: "Swearing, lying, and murder, and stealing and adultery break out; bloodshed follows bloodshed."[23] The series of five offenses are crimes against the neighbor, all of which make healthy social life impossible.

Ezek 22:1–16 apostrophizes Jerusalem as "the bloody city" (v.2). Yet unlike in chapter 20 where Israel's historical traditions are used to give depth to the accusations, here it is the (universal) divine law which provides the norms by which Jerusalem *and all others* are to be judged.[24] The double accusation of 22:3–4 sets in parallel the shedding of blood with the making of idols (the primitive sacred): crimes of blood also lead to ritual disorders and violations of the law, as we read that people have "despised my holy things and profaned my sabbaths" (22:8). See further the accusations against the priests in 22:26—they have "done violence to my teaching and have profaned my holy things; they have made no distinction between the holy and the common, neither have they taught the difference between the unclean and the clean, and they have disregarded my sabbaths, so that I am profaned among them." The signs of crisis are also evident in the family sphere. Ezek 22:9b–11 lists some transgressions of the sexual taboos that make the integrity and healthy state of the family impossible.

The resolution promised by the prophets is a pure work of God, a new covenant with God and the new gathering of God's people. Jeremiah, perhaps at the festival of booths in 587 B.C.E., recited the oracle recounted in Jer 31:31–34 which foresaw a new initiative by Yahweh. "The days are surely coming, says the Lord, when I will make a new covenant with the house of Israel and the house of Judah"(v. 31). This linking of the "two houses" may suggest the rejoining of north and south into a new total unity (see the "house of Israel" motif in 31:33).[25]

---

22 See Novak, *Image of the Non-Jew*, Chap. 1, for a discussion of the origin of the laws. Of these seven laws two are directed towards one's relationship with the divine (the Law of Blasphemy and the Law of Idolatry, 2 and 3), three involve issues of bloodshed (the Law of Homicide, the Law of Robbery, the Law of the Torn Limb, 4, 6, and 7), and one (5) forbids certain sexual acts (including incest, homosexuality, and bestiality). It is also interesting from a Girardian perspective that the first law commands the setting up of law courts.

23 Wolff, *Hosea*, 65, translates the last offense as "and there is one deed of blood after another."

24 On the universal application of the accusations made here see Zimmerli, *Ezekiel*, 455.

25 Holladay, *Jeremiah*, 198.

Hope for a new gathering of the people by God increased during the exile. Ezekiel speaks of the new gathering of the people: "Thus says the Lord God: I will gather you from the peoples and assemble you out of the countries where you have been scattered, and I will give you the land of Israel" (11:17). The relationship between God and the reunited northern and southern kingdoms is to be marked by a "covenant of peace" and "an everlasting covenant with them" (37:26). On their side "they shall follow my ordinances and be careful to observe my statutes" (37:24) with the result: "My dwelling place shall be with them, and I will be their God, and they shall be my people" (37:27). Restored also will be the Davidic kingship (37:24) and the sanctuary (Temple, 37:28).

The promises of a new people, a new covenant, and a return to the land with a new king and a new sanctuary could have been conceived as a "starting over" on the old path with the possibility or even probability of new rivalries, dissolutions, etc. In this scenario, the scapegoat cycle would be restarted and allowed to continue as always. But both Jeremiah and Ezekiel saw that God was going to make a fundamental change in humanity. According to Jer 31:33–34: "I (the Lord) will put my law within them, and I will write it on their hearts; . . . No longer shall they teach one another, or say to each other, 'Know the Lord,' for they shall all know me, . . ." The polemical counter-point being made here can be seen in contrast to the earlier 9:4–9. There it was said that the Deuteronomic law has not been followed. There was a lack of "trust in any of your kin;" "every neighbor goes around as a slanderer;" furthermore, "they all speak friendly words to their neighbors, but inwardly are planning to lay an ambush" (9:8). Raymund Schwager well notes Jeremiah's positive point: As long as human beings have to be taught by other humans, they need models. But imitation (mimesis) of teachers and masters inevitably leads to rivalries. The tendency toward violence can be overcome at its very roots only when, at least as regards the most profound personal issues, no human needs to instruct another human. In this way and only in this way can the cycle of mimesis be broken from within.[26]

Ezekiel transforms the language of new covenant into speech about a new heart, but with a further nuance. Now God will put his spirit into human beings: "A new heart I will give you, and a new spirit I will put within you; and I will remove from your body the heart of stone and give you a heart of flesh. I will put my spirit within you, and make you follow my statutes and be careful to observe my ordinances" (36:26–27). This takes up the earlier language of Ezek 11:19 where Yahweh promised to give them "one heart," an expression of the new unity at the center of their lives.[27] Now they have a chance to take hold of this new gift (see 18:31) and to keep the commandments.

Ezekiel envisages this change in human beings in ritual terms. According to 36:25 "I will sprinkle clean water upon you, and you shall be clean from all

26 Schwager, *Scapegoats*, 125.
27 On the text-critical problems here see Zimmerli, *Ezekiel*, 230.

your uncleannesses, and from all your idols I will cleanse you." The water of purification replaces the sprinkling with blood (Exod 24:8) which occurred in connection with the earlier ratifications of the covenant in the time of Moses.[28] The water serves to wash away the uncleanness of the body which contaminated people from their contact wtih the idols.[29]

It is with the "Suffering Servant" in 2 Isaiah and Job that we find a remarkably explicit unveiling of the founding mechanism and the proposal of an alternative to all sacrificial forms of Judaism. The four songs of the Servant of Yahweh (Isa 42:1–4; 49:1–6; 50:4–11; 52:13–53:12) portray a human scapegoat. Both the description of 53:2–3 marks him as a ready victim by virtue of his ordinariness ("he had no form or majesty that we should look at him, and nothing in his appearance that we should desire him") as does the readiness of others to reckon him a scapegoat ("He was despised and rejected by others; a man of suffering, and acquainted with infirmity; and as one from whom others hid their faces he was despised, and we held him of no account"). He was further designated by God for that task (Isa 42:1; 49:1–3).

From the perspective of the persecutors what should happen next was clear. He should be condemned to death for the sins of the people ("he was cut off from the land of the living, stricken for the transgression of my [the] people" [Isa 53:8]).[30] From his death should come reconciliation ("my salvation may reach to the end of the earth" [Isa 49:6]). This would lead inevitably to the transfiguration of the victim into an agent of the sacred (if not the sacred itself in a monotheistic society) and the appearance of rituals (50:10–11) and prohibitions involving him.

The Servant Songs, however, take the perspective of the victim and declare him innocent. He is innocent in his own sight ("surely my cause is with the Lord" [Isa 49:4]) and in the sight of God ("It is the Lord God who helps me; who will declare me guilty?" [Isa 50:9; cf. 53:9]). The reversal of his fates lifts up the servant without deifying him (52:13, 15; 53:10–12). He cannot become the object of myth and cult and prohibitons are not his to inaugurate. Still, however, he is the agent of God in respect to law. According to Isa 42:4, "He will not grow faint or be crushed until he has established justice in the earth; and the coastlands wait for his teaching" (Hebrew *Torah*). Furthermore, "I will give you as a light to the nations,. . . ." (Isa 49:6), and in Isa 51:4 the same things are said of God: "for a teaching will go out from me, and my justice for a light to the peoples."[31]

In the Old Testament wisdom literature the book of Job holds a prominent place. When Girard reads the dialogues of the book (3:1–42:6) he finds a new

---

28 Zimmerli, *Ezekiel*, 249.
29 See further Ezek 20:7 and the allegory of the two sisters in chap. 23.
30 According to Westermann, *Isaiah*, 265, Isa 53:8 speaks "of violent action by others aginst the Servant within the context of a court of law."
31 See further Westermann, *Isaiah*, 96, on this parallelism.

revelation of the scapegoat mechanism.[32] In the eyes of the four friends Job is guilty of manifest crimes against justice (22:4–9) and is no better than those who have already followed "the old way that the wicked have trod" (22:15). Job is responsible for offenses against the cult: you are "hindering meditation before God" (15:4) he is told, and his sins make him badly in need of the Torah of God (22:22).

Again, what is striking in Job as in 2 Isaiah is that the scapegoat refuses to acknowledge his guilt (26:1–27:12). Job recognizes that presenting a case in court before Yahweh is difficult (chap. 9), yet he is willing to defend himself and make his own charges against God (chap. 10).[33] Of these countercharges one is that God himself is the "Primitive Sacred," the disruptor of creation (12:15) and civil order (12:17–25). Thus Job's self-defense includes a denial of his crimes: sexual impurity (31:7–12), social crimes (31:13–23), and idolatry (31:24–28). The highpoint of the dialogues is the whirlwind speeches of chapters 38–40 which show once again the prophetic god of violence. Yet the text as a whole in the narrative frame (1–2; 42:7–17) ends with Job as sacrificer (42:8) and the scapegoat transfigured into the man of wealth (42:10–11).

The revelatory power of the Old Testament does not completely break once and for all the power of the scapegoat mechanism. Sacrificial Judaism continued to exist and exert its power. This is seen at its most fundamental point in the continued assimilation of Yahweh to the "Primitive Sacred" in the continued mythological connection of Yahweh with wrath and vengeance. In the prophetic corpus, Joel 3 announces the coming wrath of God against the nations, while Nahum declares God's vengeance against Nineveh. Against this background the prophets have to defend Yahweh against even such charges as that he advocated the slaughter of children to Molech (Jer 7:31; 19:5; 32:35)!

Thus the power of the myths, sacrifices, and laws has been broken with the unveiling of their "true" source and the condemnations of sacrifice are growing. Nonetheless the forms of these continue in existence and operation, yet now they increasingly fail to do their assigned tasks.

2.2 "Go therefore . . . teaching them to obey everything that I have commanded you." The Gospel of Jesus

For Girard the generating power of the scapegoat mechanism is definitively disclosed and broken in the fourfold gospel of the New Testament. Now there exists the possibility of doing away with mythology and the primitive sacred with its sacrifices and prohibitions.

Admittedly, here too the writers of the gospel narratives use the same motifs as persecutors everywhere.[34] In the account of John 11:47–53, for example,

32 Cf. Girard, Job.
33 On this literary device see Habel, Job, 54–57.
34 Girard's own analyses of the gospel narratives are to be found in Scapegoat, 100–212, and

the author describes a meeting of the chief priests and Pharisees to discuss the "signs" of Jesus of Nazareth. Caiaphas, the high priest, counsels the group that "it is better for you to have one man die for the people than to have the whole nation destroyed" (John 11:50). The accounts of the passion of Jesus in the four gospels show many of the motifs we have come to expect in the accounts of the actual sacrifice of a victim. The opponents of Jesus all unite against him: the Jewish political/religious establishment (Mark 15:1); the Roman political authority in Israel, Pilate (Mark 15:15); the people of Jerusalem (Mark 15:29; Luke 23:18); even two criminals who were crucified beside him (Mark 15:32). Jesus is accused of crimes which set him apart from all the people: "We found this man perverting our nation, forbidding us to pay taxes to the emperor, and saying that he himself is the Messiah, a king" (Luke 23:2).

What is different in the perspective of the gospels is that the texts are narrated from the standpoint of the victim. Indeed, Jesus is portrayed as innocent (Matt 27:18–19; Mark 15:14; Luke 23:39–43, 47; John 18:38; 19:4). Even before the passion narratives the gospels reveal the transformation that Jesus has made in the situation of humanity. The account of the demons of Gerasa (Mark 5:1–17) and the exorcism narratives (Matt 12:23–28) show the changed situation which the gospel authors see in the human condition.

The gospels' portrayal of the teaching of Jesus is also revelatory. The so-called "Parable of the Vineyard" (Mark 12:1–12; Matt 21:33–46; Luke 20:9–19) with its continuation reveals *in nuce* the whole scapegoat mechanism and prophetically declares its overthrow. A man rented a piece of property to some tenants, who then attacked the men sent by the landowner to collect the rents. Finally they even killed the "beloved son" of the owner, and now the owner, in anger it is said, will come and destroy the tenants and give the land to others. Jesus' listeners understand the owner as God and the son as Jesus. The Matthean version of this text, however, clearly states that human beings are responsible for this violence—that they are still trapped, as it were, in the sacrificial system and its violence.

The immediate juxtaposition of Ps 118:22–23—"The very stone that the builders rejected has become the cornerstone; this was the Lord's doing, and it is amazing in our eyes"—with this parable turns aside the sacrificial mis-interpretation. By submitting to violence Jesus reveals and upsets the structural matrix of all religion.[35]

Let me suggest five ways in which the message of Jesus as it can be reconstructed from the gospel accounts deconstructs the scapegoat mechanism and offers a positive alternative.[36]

Things Hidden, 180–235. In a forthcoming study *The Gospel and the Sacred*, Robert G. Hamerton-Kelly has done a more technical N. T. analysis of Girard's thesis with respect to the Markan gospel.

35 Girard, *Things Hidden*, 178, 187–89.
36 My reading of Jesus' teaching differs from that of Charles Mabee's essay in this volume.

2.2.1. The Kingdom of God. The teaching of Jesus has as its foundation and horizon the proclamation of the Kingdom of God. It is summarized by Mark thus: "The time is fulfilled, and the kingdom of God has come near; repent, and believe in the good news" (Mark 1:15). The meaning of this language is articulated in part in Mark's parable chapter (chap. 4) and in particular in the parable of the seed growing secretly [Seed and Harvest] (Mark 4:26–29), which emphasizes the certain and imperceptible coming of the Kingdom that is brought about by God alone.[37] Girard rightly distinguishes this Kingdom of God from the Old Testament "Day of the Lord" or the retaliatory coming of a violent God as in some apocalyptic texts. He may well go too far, however, in his portrayal of the teaching of Jesus as presenting fundamentally a non-apocalyptic Kingdom.[38]

2.2.2. The God of the Kingdom. It is true that the God of Jesus is a God of love, a God of victims, a God concerned to bring about the elimination of every form of violence and vengeance. This is not done violently but by the action of a God whose love and mercy calls upon us to conform to God's salvation and not to engage in conflictual mimesis with other human beings.

So, for example, the parable of the wicked servant [Unmerciful Servant] (Matt 18:23–34) speaks of a king who wants to settle accounts with his servants. A servant who owed the king 10,000 talents (something like ten million dollars) was forgiven his debt after imploring the king for mercy. The same servant then refused to have mercy on a fellow servant who owed him 100 denarii (about a hundred dollars), by comparison a very small sum of money. The king in anger told the first servant "I forgave you all that debt because you pleaded with me. Should you not have had mercy on your fellow servant, as I had mercy on you?" (18:32–33). This parable of God's love and mercy shows God leading us into a nonviolent state of human relations. The imperative is then for us to take corresponding action (cf. Luke 7:41–43).

2.2.3. Jesus and Mythology. Even when one combines the testimony of the relatively sayings-less gospel of Mark with the authentic teaching in the sayings traditons of Thomas and Q, it is striking how realistic the teaching of Jesus is. Although rhetorically vivid and frequently paradoxical, the teaching of Jesus most frequently comes from nature and shrewd observations on

---

For him Jesus was a decontextualizer who attempted to present his message decontextualized from his Bible, cult, and religious system. The gospel writers then recontextualized Jesus using the Old Testament and midrash to interpret Jesus, thereby making Jesus into a prophetic critic of cult and law. My reading which follows attributes more positive understanding of law and cult to Jesus himself.

37 The alternative titles given to the parables in the analysis to follow are those provided in Funk, et.al., *Parables of Jesus . . .* The parables discussed in this section of the paper are considered genuine by the members of the Jesus Seminar. See further the preparatory studies published in *Forum.*

38 Girard, *Things Hidden,* 196–205; cf. Mack, "Kingdom Sayings," and Williams, "Neither Here Nor There."

common, everyday life.[39] The language of the mythological world view (three-story universe) is used by Jesus where there are references to God and angels, heaven and hell, and Satan.[40] But this is not done in the way of the myths. There are few allusions to primordial times (see, however, if authentic, the use of Gen 1:27 in Mark 10:2–12) or to the intrinsic character of the end-of-time world (depending upon one's evaluation of the "Rich Man and Lazarus," [Luke 16:19–26 and vv. 27–31]).[41] There is a transhistorical spiritual level to Jesus' encounters with Satan and the exorcisms, but there is also a societal-historical level.[42] And note finally the relatively meager content of Jesus' Kingdom of God language: the Kingdom is primarily formally defined—it is where God's power is active—and has an impact on peoples' concrete circumstances. It does not refer to intratrinity relationships, God-mediator interactions, heavenly life, etc.

2.2.4. The Ritual System. The new understanding of God which Jesus proclaims entails a new understanding of the place of ritual in True Religion. Jesus' teaching contains a fundamental critique of Jewish ritual (and by implication pagan ritual). This appears first in the criticism that Jesus makes of the sabbath law, where the works of healing which Jesus does on the Sabbath are justified by the principle that "the sabbath was made for humankind, not humankind for the sabbath" (Mark 2:27). Second, the ritual law of purity, which is based on a distinction between clean/unclean, is fundamentally undercut by Jesus' words: "There is nothing outside a person that by going in can defile; but the things which come out are what defile" (Mark 7:15). The Temple and the whole sacrificial establishment are relativized by the challenge of Jesus to "Go and learn what this means, 'I desire mercy, not sacrifice'" (Matt 9:13 quoting Hos 6:6).

The curative element in the religion of Jesus is not cultic activity of a "sacramental sort." Whether in Paul's own letters or pre-Pauline Jewish Christianity, a sacrificial interpretation has been placed on baptism and the Lord's Supper. Earlier, though, Jesus does not interpret baptism in this way nor does he baptize people, but is himself baptized (Mark 1:9; Matt 3:13–16). The accounts of the "last supper" in Matt 26:17–29, Mark 14:12–25, and Luke 22:7–38 (shorter ending omitting 22:19b-20) do not make even of this rite a prescribed sacrificial ritual for his followers or later Christians.[43]

The only curative ritual of Jesus appears in the fellowship meals where

---

39 See here Scott, *Hear the Parable*, Parts 2–4.
40 On the interpretation of the temporal references of Jesus, see Boring, "Eschatological Language."
41 The temptation narratives of Luke 4:1–13/Matt 4:1–11 are the creation of the evangelists, not accounts of the historical Jesus (with most commentators).
42 Horsley, *Jesus*, 184–90.
43 This is true even if we read with the longer ending in Luke. The "Do this in remembrance of me" is strikingly associated with the eating of bread and not with the wine-blood.

Jesus ate and drank with his followers (Matt 11:18–19//Luke 7:33–34). The continuation of those meals may have involved the use of the miracle stories now contained in Mark 4–8 as part of an interpretive liturgy. Within this context the reports of healing miracles and exorcisms (5:1–20, Gerasene Demoniac; 5:21–43, Jairus' Daughter and the Woman with a Hemorrhage; 6:54–56, healing the sick; 8:22–26, Blind Man of Bethsaida; 7:24–31, Syrophoenician Woman; 7:32–37, the Deaf Mute) would have had again an epiphanic function. As Paul Achtemeier puts it: "The epiphanic nature of the miracles attached to the account of the feeding would indicate that the liturgy was intended to call the participants' attention to the presence of Christ himself at the meal. As he was revealed in his mighty acts as a *deus praesents*, so he is revealed in the meal as present among the participants."[44]

Although our evidence is limited, Jesus himself seems to have been little involved in giving new instructions on such cultic acts as almsgiving, prayer, and fasting.[45] The sayings in the *Gospel of Thomas* 6, 14, 27, 53, 104, which treat cirumcision and diet in addition to the above topics, also appear to be inauthentic.[46] All this material seems to have been produced as part of the community-rule of the early church. As Girard's theory would see it, this material is naturally enough attributed to the scapegoat-become-community founders so that at a somewhat later state of community development in the controversy with the Jews, the sacrificial interpretation was added.

2.2.5. Jesus and the Law. In his teaching and activity Jesus shows that the ethical demands of God are still in some way connected to the Law as proclaimed in the Hebrew Bible.

The curative role of law with respect to societal disorder may be seen in the example story of Mark 10:17–22. Jesus is asked what is necessary to attain eternal life. His answer is first: "You know the commandments: Do not kill, Do not commit adultery, Do not steal, Do not bear false witness, Do not defraud, Honor your father and mother" (10:19). This citation of the second table of the Decalogue is striking in two respects. Less important is the addition of a new commandment "Do not defraud," but fundamental is the shifting in order which moves the traditionally fourth commandment into last place and the new primacy given to "Do not kill! "

Jesus' second answer, "come, follow me" (10:21), shows that the negative/prohibition side of law must be complemented by discipleship.[47] This is described programatically in the so-called "Great Commandment" account of Mark 12:28–34/Matt 22:34–40/Luke 10:25–28.[48] In Mark Jesus is asked by

---

44 Achtemeier, "Origin and Function," 208. See also Achtemeier, "Toward the Isolation."
45 Betz, "A Jewish-Christian Cult Didache in Matt. 6:1–18: Reflections and Questions on the Problem of the Historical Jesus," *Essays*, 55–69.
46 See Sellew, "Rules."
47 On this passage see Fuller, "Decalogue in the New Testament," and Schrage, *Ethics of the New Testament.*
48 On the historicity of this passage, see Achtemeier, *Mark*, 19–20.

one of the scribes "Which commandment is the first of all?" and he answers with the first words of the Shema based on Deut 6:4: "Hear, O Israel, The Lord our God, the Lord is one" (v. 30). The first commandment enjoins love of God as a unitary, undivided person ("with all your heart, and with all your soul, and with all your mind, and with all your strength."), and the second commandment is to "love your neighbor as yourself." The orientation towards God means that any relationship towards others of conflictual mimeticism or violence is ruled out.

The Markan continuation of this account is interesting. The scribe, Jesus' interloctuor, is described as spelling out the implications of these two commandments —"you have truly said that 'he is one, and besides him there is no other' [i.e., the world of multiple mythological gods and goddesses is thus ruled out]; and 'to love him with all the heart, and with all the understanding, and with all the strength,' and 'to love one's neighbor as oneself,' . . ." Interestingly the text continues—"[these/this] is much more important than all whole burnt offerings and sacrifices!" —insofar as the self-repudiation of the sacrificial world is deemed to be "wise" and Jesus endorses this interpretation—"you are not far from the kingdom of God."

Girard further notes that the victim finds himself/herself transfigured into the law-giver after the sacrifice has been performed. Traces of this sacrificial continuation occur in the Matthean picture of Jesus as New Moses but with some twists.[49] According to Matt 5:17 Jesus announces that he has come not "to abolish the law and the prophets . . . but to fulfill them." But as 7:12 and 28:20 indicate it is the words of Jesus which are the criterion of judgment, the new norms to be taught. According to the former passage Jesus declares: "In everything do to others as you would have them do to you; for this is the law and the prophets." Here the Golden Rule, not laws or mimetic behavior, is declared to be the summation or essence of the teaching of God. The negative formulation given in Matt 5:38–42 shows that there is to be a setting aside of the law on retaliation. This is not to be done in the interests of promoting unlimited violence instead of controlled one-on-one violence; rather the alternative is a taking of the violence upon oneself, but not in a masochistic way.

The final antithesis, Matt 5:43–47, places upon people the obligation to "Love your enemies and pray for those who persecute you." The obligation is to practice pure imitation untrammeled by rivalry, in the words of Matt 5:48, to "be perfect, as your heavenly Father is perfect." This is imitation of a transcendent spiritual force who "makes his sun rise on the evil and on the good, and sends rain on the righteous and on the unrighteous" (5:45). This priority of the law of love is positively illustrated by Jesus in the example story/parable of the Good Samaritan (Luke 10:30–37).

---

49 On the Matthean use of Moses language see the review by Allison, "Gnilka on Matthew."

2.3. "The light shines in the darkness, and the darkness has not overcome it." Sacrificial Christianity

Although Girard believes that a fundamental break was achieved with the gospel of Jesus, he does not naively believe in a first-century golden age when the world was forever transformed. Pools of darkness persisted even at the time, but since then historical Christianity has not extinguished the light even if it has partly obscured it.

A sacrificial reading of the teaching and life of Jesus by later Christians made Jesus into a scapegoat like other scapegoats. The readings of "sacrificial Christianity" in the later New Testament books (Hebrews) and the early Church fathers replaced the radically nonsacrificial understanding with a sacrificial model that makes God like the gods of primitive mythology. The sacrificial reading of the gospel produced an anti-Jewish understanding now to be found in the gospel narratives themselves. This can be seen in the specific motifs of identification of the Jews with the Devil (John 8:42–43) and the assumption of collective responsibility by the People—"all the people answered [Pilate], 'His blood be on us and on our children'" (Matt 27:24–25)![50]

The working out of the gospel logic in concrete historical forms has taken a long time. In the medieval period of Western Europe (1200–1400) Girard finds a mixture of sacrificial Christianity and "true Christianity." Scapegoating activities remain: women, Jews, lepers, and heretics, are still killed in order to remove natural disasters and social unrest. Increasingly, though, something new is happening. No longer do we have only or predominantly "persecution texts," accounts told from the perspective of the persecutors, because now we increasingly have texts told from the standpoint of the victim, texts which reject and expose the falsity of the persecutor's designations.[51] The power of the persecutor's perspective still endures. Yet at least now and hopefully in the future we can identify other people's scapegoats as what they really are—

50 This represents a Girardian reading of the New Testament literature even if one not (fully) endorsed by Girard himself. The question is when and where sacrificial Christianity began to exert its influence: with Jesus himself, with Paul, with the gospel writers, in the later New Testament letters, with Revelation, or only with the subapostolic fathers or Justin Martyr. Girard's own answer seems to be with the production of Hebrews (*Things Hidden*, 227–31), though later reflection has made him question this judgment. He does take seriously the possibility that we never really "had" the truth even with Jesus. Peter's denial and the disbelief of the disciples (in Mark) must be taken very seriously! See Girard, *Things Hidden*, 249–53. Hamerton-Kelly finds the beginning of sacrificial Christianity with Justin's *Dialogue with Trypho*. Christianity as the "New Israel" becomes the double of Judaism and we then have "Chrisitianity as a structure of sacred violence," to use his own felicitous phrase (conversations with René Girard at the Temenos Center, Sonoma, CA, March 2, 1990.) My own view is that sacrificial Christianity really begins to exert itself in the interpretative efforts of the gospel writers.

51 On the continuing power of sacrificial readings see Girard, *Things Hidden*, 249–53. Also Girard, "Guillaume de Machaut and the Jews," *Scapegoat*, 1–11, shows the breakdown of the sacrificial readings.

scapegoats—even if we are still mystified by our own acts of persecution: my enemies are real! The Gospel's curative power continues to exert itself although the illness hangs on.

3. Violence, Religion, and Law in the Modern World

When one looks at all the societies of the world from a Girardian perspective one finds a wide variety of relationships to the primitive sacred on the one extreme and to God and "pure religion"[52] on the other.

In this vein I propose the following typology :

> [The "primitive sacred"]
> Societies in the Throes of Revolution (Modern Lebanon)
> Totalitarian Societies (Hitler's Germany; Stalin's Russia)
> Dictatorships and Police States (Peron's Argentina)
> Autocratic States with State "Churches" (Czarist Russia; Saudi Arabia)
> "Corporate" States (Franco's Spain)
> Fundamentalist Religious States (Khomeini's Iran)
> Monarchical States (Elizabeth II's England)
> Judicial Societies (U. S.)
> The Kingdom of God (The Kingdom in the Book or Revelation)
> [God]

For reasons of space I will comment on only two of these societal types in order to test the "real world" applicability of Girard's hypotheses.

3.1 Societies in the Throes of Revolution

Our modern world continues to generate ever-new forms of sacrificial Judaism, Christianity, and Islam. These "new" fundamentalisms reduce the God of their historic faith to the level of the primitive sacred, the god of vengeance of sacrificial religion. Ever new ideological statements give mythic support to the fundamentalists' plans to identify and destroy their opponents (rivals-models). The rituals of these faiths (Passover, Lord's Supper, Ramadan) become once again like the rites of their pagan sacrificial predecessors (sacrifices to Molech). Law and the monopoly of force by the state is replaced by the violence and terrorism of the competing groups and the cycles of reprisals.

The seemingly endless cycle of violence in Lebanon since 1975 shows the present effects of participation in the sacrifical crisis/scapegoat mechanism. The *New York Times* in August 1989 diagnosed the new escalation of violence there in thoroughly Girardian terms.

---

52 The expression is not Girard's. It is pure or unadulterated in that the religion ultimately would have no admixture of sacrificial elements. Human societies in our "post-Fall" world have yet to attain a fusion of "pure religion" and political structure.

The civil war there actually followed certain unwritten rules. . . . The political and military boundaries that no one had dared breach—call them "red lines"— have now been crossed. . . ." [Today, the phrase "red lines" can stand as a metaphor for any boundary in Lebanon long considered inviolable because it prevents conflict from becoming unrestrained.] The Lebanese themselves are no longer intimidated into quick cease-fires when violence rises beyond normal levels, because anything they are threatened with has already been done to them twice. Iraq and Syria are more than eager to feed their proxies in Lebanon with weapons to play out their own blood feud.[53]

In such situations the Judaeo-Christian tradition needs to reestablish its anti-violent revelatory power in order to help the participants see the nondemonic character of their opponents.[54] Not only are the community's opponents (be they Jewish, Christian, Muslim) not demonic but it is also wrong to "scapegoat" members of one's own religious community as a means for resolving the current troubles (e.g., Amal, Shiite Muslims versus Sunni Muslims or General Aoun versus General Geagea, among the Marionite Christians).

Girard's perspective calls into question the negative judgment that is often placed on the almost overwhelming complexity of factional, class, and confessional differences in Lebanon.[55] These differences have surely led to a "withering away of the State" in Lebanon in the 1950–70s.[56] As Girard has noted, the lack of a central government, legal system, and a governmental monopoly of force leads to increased undifferentiation as the contending parties become doubles of each other. This process ultimately leads to a sacrificial crisis and destruction of a scapegoat as the sytem coalesces in opposition to the one party who is "responsible" for the communal strife.

It is suggestive that the periods of relative peace in Lebanon coincided with the time that the religious groups in Lebanon accepted the divisions of power in the National Pact of 1945. It is a matter for debate whether a new order is best worked out under international auspices (United Nations) or through some kind of negotiations among the religious leaders in Lebanon.[57] Yet the choices do seem clear: continued crisis and violence, some kind of confessional government, or partition. The dismemberment of Lebanon, though, is only a variation on the presently existing situation of crisis unless the boundaries around the newly created units and the internal organization of the

---

53 Friedman, "Going for Broke."
54 See here Shipler, *Arab and Jew*, part 2: Images.
55 Khalaf, "Communal Conflict," persuasively chronicles the transition from partisan, feudal, and class rivalry in 19th–century Lebanon to confessional hostility.
56 See here Malcolm Kerr's description of Lebanon's political process in this period, "Political Decision Making," 187: "Lebanese democracy is not the rule of the *demos*, but simply the distribution of guarantees to the recognized factions coexisting in the country of the means to defend their minimum interests."
57 Note the efforts of Musa Sadr in the 1970s to form a council of religious leaders in Lebanon, cf. Diehl, *Holy War*, 161.

"homelands" is such as to reduce the rivalries and prevent further generative violence from occcurring.

3.2 *Juridical Societies*

In some modern societies the social forms are based only indirectly and at a considerable distance from the scapegoating process. The anti-scapegoating power of the Judaeo-Christian tradition has been more than a little successful in this matter. The God of the biblical revelation has at least iconic status, so that "civil religion" in the state prides itself on its constructive group-building national festivals (Thanksgiving/Christmas). Law and the judicial system which interpret it serve the positive function of chanelling rivalry and promoting healthy competition. Because the legal system also is the agency of public vengeance, there is a decrease in acts of uncontrolled vengeance and in efforts at ritually controlled vengeance. Now the judicial system acts rationally: private vengeance ("taking the law into your own hands") is discouraged as it leads to new reprisals from the other side to "even the score" and threatens to inaugurate renewed cycles of violence.[58]

Even in juridicial societies, however, there are many instances of violence. Mimetic desire directed at the "objects" and "being" of others continues and this leads to new acts of violence. There are "violent criminals" who use force to obtain what they want, and there is always the violence of the State, which tries to get people to follow the laws and to coerce people to accept the socio-economic and political structures of society as they are.

Girard's analysis is not falsified by the appearance of these forms of violence in the liberal democratic state. What he does claim is that "generative violence" no longer occurs as it does in traditional and ethnological societies. This does not mean that certain kinds of violence in society cannot ever lead to what might become generative violence:

> Breaking windows and robbing stores—a "Kristallnacht"
> Robbery against persons—plundering of an ethnic or racial minority
> State violence—"police terror"
> Nationalism—military adventurism against a demonized opponent.

Violence can and does lead to new mythologies of the political right and left: fallen heroes as new idols, new slogans and activities, and new legal codes to rationalize and justify the current situation. But the difference is that we know what is happening through an analysis of the scapegoat mechanism. As long as the revelatory power of the gospel continues to shine we can name our myths, idols, rites, and laws for what they really are.

---

58 The importance of the law in modern societies is described in Girard, *Violence and the Sacred*, 14–17, 20–25.

Levite Violence, Fraticide, and Sacrifice in the Bible and Later Revolutionary Rhetoric

Stuart Lasine

Abstract

According to one biblicist, the Levites' continual association with violence "has been a mystery for decades." This paper seeks to determine whether René Girard's understanding of sacrificial violence can help to solve this mystery. It does so by analyzing the biblical reports of Levite violence together with the priestly writer's portrayal of the Levites as substitutes for the first-born redeemed from Yahweh and sacrifices of the Israelites who direct divine wrath from the community to themselves. Viewed in this context, the Levites' slaughter of three thousand brothers and sons after Moses' destruction of the golden calf (Exodus 32) is a sacrifice, not a just punishment of the guilty. Similarly, Yahweh's destruction of Moses' cousin Korah and his rebellious Levite congregation is part of a "sacrificial crisis," a crisis that is generated by Korah's envy of his "model-obstacle" Moses and resolved by the Levites' reinstallation as sacrifices (Numbers 16–18). While Girard himself does not believe that the book of Exodus tends to bring the victim to light, this analysis suggests that even those examples of Levite zeal which most trouble theologians are designed to prompt the audience to side with the victim. In contrast, postbiblical versions of these stories by writers from Philo to modern revolutionaries tend to appropriate the Levites as prototypal righteous victimizers while minimizing or eliminating their identity as sacrifices. In so doing, they tend to incorporate the perspective of the persecutor rather than to side with the victim.

0. Introduction

This paper is designed to test René Girard's theories concerning violence and the sacred in the Hebrew Bible, in order to gain a fresh perspective on some troubling examples of divine "justice" in the Pentateuch. I will focus upon the "mystery" of the biblical Levites' continuing association with violence, including their slaughter of three thousand brothers and sons after the apostasy of the golden calf.[1] Although commentators usually assume that the Levites are acting as agents of divine justice here, proving that allegiance to God takes precedence over loyalty to family, this approach cannot adequately explain the facts reported in Exodus 32 and misconstrues the relationship between divine wrath and justice. To understand this act of mass fratricide, one must take into account the priestly writer's description of the Levites as substitutes for the first-born redeemed from Yahweh and sacrifices of the Israelites. In their role as sacrifices the Levites act as a "lightning rod" to direct divine wrath from the community to themselves alone (Numbers 3, 8, 18).[2] The Levite slaughter of brothers and sons in Exodus 32 is itself a sacrifice, not a just punishment of the guilty.

I will also argue that the reaffirmation of the Levites as sacrifices in Numbers 18 must be viewed together with the preceding account of Korah's rebellion and its aftermath (Numbers 16–17) if its significance is to be understood. Although scholars usually assume that the story of Korah's rebellion is filled with contradictions, a Girardian analysis of Numbers 16–17 reveals an underlying ideological and literary consistency. Korah's envy of his Levite cousin and "model-obstacle" Moses precipitates a rebellion of Levites that becomes a sacrificial crisis. Initially, the people as a whole identify with the deceased Korah against Moses and Aaron. They are then allowed to deny this dangerous identity by adopting Korah's tribe as their sacrifices. The reinstallation of the Levites as sacrifices is therefore prompted by the disintegration of social order brought about by mimetic rivalry. From a Girardian perspective, the divine "wrath" and "plagues" directed against the Levites instead of their tribal brothers are actually disguised metaphors for the collective violence of the community itself. Thus, while many scholars believe that the priestly stratum of Numbers 16 (and Lev 10:1–7) merely "reflect old rivalries between priestly families,"[3] this chapter, taken together with the other accounts of Levite violence, clearly reflects a deeper concern with the basic social problems of group violence and rivalry among leaders.

According to Girard, the books of Genesis and Exodus alone do not make it possible to stress the radical singularity of the Bible. He believes that only other books of the Law and especially the prophets show an increasing tendency for the victim to be brought to light.[4] The present study challenges

---

1 According to Mendenhall, *Tenth Generation*, 163 n. 62, "the original 'secular' and warlike nature of the Levites has been a mystery for decades."
2 Milgrom, *Studies*, 31.
3 Cross, *Canaanite Myth*, 205; cf. Dozeman, *God on the Mountain*, 189.
4 Girard's preference for the prophets over the priestly material is illustrated by his evaluation of the two literatures as primitive religion. Girard believes that while mythic forms have been subverted in the exodus story, the narrative still retains the characteristics of myth. Myth is one of the three "pillars of primitive religion" (*Things Hidden*, 154). The second is the sacrificial cult, which is "explicitly rejected by the

Girard's assessment of violence in pentateuchal narrative, including those examples of Levite zeal which most trouble theologians.[5] In the concluding section of the paper I will examine the often troubling ways in which these narratives have been cited in revolutionary rhetoric in order to legitimate religious and political purges and liquidations. After a preliminary analysis of Philo's interpretations of the Levite slaughter, I will turn to later retellings of this event, as well as new versions of the wilderness wandering. These versions transform Yahweh's wandering punishment of the generation of ex-slaves into a prototypal revolutionary purge. These analyses will reveal that most of the postbiblical versions of these events do not acknowledge the biblical portrayal of the Levites as sacrifices to the same extent as they appropriate the Levites as a model of righteous victimizers. That is, they tend to incorporate the perspective of the persecutor rather than side with the victim. In so doing, they go counter to the thrust of biblical rhetoric itself, especially insofar as the canonical text now addresses readers other than the actual ancient audience.

1. Levite Violence and Sacrifice in Biblical Texts

1.1 The Levite slaughter at Mount Sinai

Beginning with Levi, the son of Jacob, the Levite tribe is consistently associated with violence in the Hebrew Bible. The Levi of early tradition has

---

Prophets before the Exile," while the third is the primitive conception of the law as a refusal of mixed states that looks upon undifferentiation with horror.

Girard's view is problematic for several reasons. First, his characterization of pentateuchal "law," which is based on the theories of the anthropologist Mary Douglas, tends to devalue the Pentateuch in relation to the prophets, in spite of the fact that the *tôrâ* promulgated at Sinai, which represents the distillation of the religious meaning of the wilderness experience from the Hebrew Bible's own perspective, consistently sides with the victim, and seeks to check scapegoating (see below). Second, many biblicists would dispute Girard's claim that the prophets reject the sacrificial cult. As Gaster puts it, "the truth is that the [prophets] were not against sacrifice per se, but simply against the abuse of it" ("Sacrifices," 157). Third, Girard rarely acknowledges legal and narrative texts that resemble prophetic texts in their values and literary styles. In all these ways Girard's predilection for the prophets recalls Wellhausen's enthusiasm for the prophets at the expense of the priests. Wellhausen dismisses the priestly worldview as legalistic, deadened and divorced from life, characteristics which for him define the Jewish element in scripture. See Silberman, "Wellhausen and Judaism," 75–82. Girard does recognize that the Pentateuch sides with the victim in one respect, however. In *Things Hidden*, Girard is asked how his analysis is valid for OT books other than Genesis. He replies by suggesting that Moses himself plays the part of the scapegoat (together with the associated Jewish community), because he himself causes the sacrificial crisis that ravages Egypt (153). However, "to 'function' normally," Exodus would have to be an Egyptian myth, showing us a sacrificial crisis resolved by the expulsion of trouble-makers, Moses and company. Girard then remarks that here the model has been diverted toward the scapegoat, who is not only human but goes on to form a community of a new type (153–54).

5 See n. 32 below for ways in which troubling aspects of the Levite massacre in Exodus 32 have been rationalized. The story of the violent Levite Phineas in Num 25:6–13 is cited by Robert Jewett as a case in which the Bible "takes sides in a Manichean direction with the heroes of zealous violence" (*Violent Origins*, 139).

been called "unusually violent and cruel."[6] The massacre of the Shechemites (Genesis 34) and the Levite killings at Sinai (Exod 32:25–29) have been cited as evidence that the tribe has "a belligerent, trigger-happy record" in the oldest narratives of Genesis and Exodus.[7] Although the first victims are non-Israelites, most of those slain later are kin. In addition to the "brothers" and "sons" killed at Sinai, there are the Levite followers of Moses' first cousin Korah, although in this case the Levite Moses merely choreographs the destruction of Korah and his congregation at Yahweh's direction. Even after the conquest of Canaan, a Levite (probably Moses' own grandson)[8] colludes in the extermination of the peaceful citizenry of Laish (Judges 18), while another precipitates a bloody war between brother tribes after sacrificing his own concubine to save himself (Judges 19–21).[9]

The reports of the Levites' violent acts are difficult to explain as theodicy if one appeals to traditional notions of justice and fairness. While even Jacob curses the violence and cruelty exhibited by his sons Levi and Simeon at Shechem (Gen 49:6–7), the slaughter of the three thousand at Sinai is in response to an order which, according to Moses, carries divine authority. Indeed, the Levites are actually blessed for their deed. Such violence cannot simply be dismissed as an illustration of the principle that obligation to God takes precedence over obligation to brothers.[10]

In the present text of Exodus 32, all the children of Israel are shown as participants in the apostasy of the calf. "All the people" contribute gold for the fabrication of the molten image (32:3). From this point on, the narrator, Yahweh, and Moses all refer to the body of idolatrous Israelites as simply "the people." After Moses descends from the summit of Mount Sinai, he breaks the tablets, makes "the Israelites" drink of the powdered calf (v. 20), and excoriates his brother Aaron. He then declares, "Who is for Yahweh, [come] to me," a call to which "all the sons of Levi"—and no one else—is said to respond (v. 26). It is then that Moses tells his assembled brother-Levites that Yahweh says

6 Hyatt, *Exodus*, 310.

7 Milgrom, *Studies*, 48.

8 The consonantal text of the MT for Judg 18:30 has "*mšh*," or Moses, although a letter "*n*" or *nun* has been suspended between the *m* and the *š*, so that the grandfather of the apostate Levite can be called "Manasseh," apparently as a sign of respect for the great prophet Moses.

9 On Judges 19 see Lasine, "Guest and Host" and chap. 8 of Lasine, *Justice and Human Nature*. From a Girardian perspective, it is significant that the sacrifice of the concubine, which leads to the near annihilation of the tribe of Benjamin, is the catalyst that finally unites all of Benjamin's brother tribes when they gather "as one man" to make Benjamin acknowledge its guilt, and then seek to destroy this enemy brother (Judg 20:1, 8, 11). Girard argues that unanimity is required for a community to succeed in its use of the scapegoat mechanism (*Job*, 111 and *passim*). It is also worth noting that Levite violence is frequently triggered by, or the cause of, some sort of sexual abomination. This is the case in Genesis 34, Exod 32:6, Numbers 25, and Judges 19–21.

10 Representatives of this popular view are Wolff, *Anthropology*, 187 and Ringgren, "'āch," 192.

that they should strap on their swords, go through the camp, and "slay every man his brother (*'āhîw*), and every man his friend (*rē'ēhû*), and every man his neighbor (*qĕrōbô*)" (v. 27). The sons of Levi follow these instructions, felling about three thousand men (v. 28). Moses then tells the Levites to "fill your hand today for Yahweh," for "every man has been against his son and against his brother," that He may bestow a blessing on them that day (v. 29).

When all the violent acts reported in Exodus 32 are regarded as attempts to mete out just punishment to all the guilty, serious problems arise, not only with the fairness of the punishments, but with the consistency and clarity of the story. Is the drinking of the powdered calf part of a trial by ordeal, the conclusion of which goes untold? If all the Israelites contributed toward the making of the idol, why are only three thousand slain by the Levites? If the Levites are targeting only ringleaders, as commentators usually assume,[11] why is that not stated? Even if the Levites are showing their fidelity to Yahweh (and not fellow-Levite Moses) by answering Moses' call, does this give them the knowledge needed to choose those who are deserving of death and the authority to execute those whom they choose? If the Levites are acting primarily as agents of punishment, why does Moses emphasize that they are to commit fratricide and infanticide, rather than to act as executioners of the guilty, whether or not the guilty happen to be kinfolk? Why is the calf-manufacturer Aaron not punished, when his brother Moses holds him totally responsible for allowing the people to break loose (v. 25)? Finally, why does Yahweh send a plague only after these events occur, and why does the narrator not specify how many people died in the plague (if any), as is done in similar cases (Num 17:14; 25:9)?

An explanation based on the idea of the contagion caused by polluting crimes against God[12] is difficult to justify in this case. In many biblical narratives and laws, violations of holiness seem to pollute the community; this is what leads to the deaths of many. In the rare cases in which it is human beings who slay such sinners rather than the Lord, this is to prevent the outbreak of mass plague that would otherwise overwhelm the community at large.[13] In the present instance, however, the mention of a divinely sent plague comes only *after* the Levite slaughter, a slaughter which, according to the contagion theory, should have precluded the need for such a plague. The fact that many readers (including some of the rabbis) have accused Moses of fabricating

---

11 See the commentators cited by Hahn, *Das "Goldene Kalb,"* 77, and Brichto, "Worship," 15 ("unquestionably . . . the ringleaders").

12 See Greenberg, "Postulates," 23–25. In contrast to Greenberg, Milgrom (*Cult,* 34 n. 127) believes that collective responsibility rather than contagion is the principle behind the destruction of Achan's household (Joshua 7), because contagion requires direct contact or being under the same tent (see Num 19:14). Milgrom contends that collective responsibility is operative whenever the deity is involved, although it never functions in human jurisprudence (see Deut 24:16).

13 Milgrom, *Studies,* 21–24, 57; *Cult,* 33 n. 122.

divine authority to legitimate the Levite slaughter,[14] also implies that it is not a case of human beings acting as Yahweh's agents to enforce a "divine prerogative,"[15] unless one wants to assert that Moses is arrogating this prerogative rather than seeking to avoid contagion.

The fact that the Levites are apparently rewarded with the priesthood for this act in Exod 32:29 would seem to ensure that Yahweh approved of their deeds, at least retroactively. However, this admittedly difficult verse may suggest that the Levites themselves are being installed as sacrifices here, long before their status as sacrifices is described in Numbers 3.[16] Exod 32:27, 29 clearly imply that there were Levite brothers and sons among the three thousand slain. Because *all* the Levites are said to have rallied to Moses' side (v. 26), they are all innocent of any guilt associated with refusal to heed Moses' call, if not innocent of complicity in the earlier sin of the calf. Therefore, at least some of the Levites whose innocence was established by their response to Moses' call are sacrificed by their brothers as the price of the latter's ordination. In fact, the text does not exclude the possibility that *only* Levites were slain as sacrifices by their brothers, if the "friends" and "companions" slain throughout the camp were also members of the Levite tribe.[17]

The fact that a consistently literal reading of the present text leads to such unorthodox conclusions will not come as a surprise if one keeps in mind Girard's theories concerning the sacrificial mechanism. Briefly, Girard argues that sacrifice serves to channel and limit social violence which would otherwise escalate beyond control.[18] Girard believes that much social violence stems from one disturbing aspect of human nature, namely, that humans tend to desire what others desire. That is, desire is "mimetic." The more a person imitates his or her model the more the model becomes a rival for the same desired objects. Unrestrained rivalries threaten order by dissolving a culture's

---

14 See, e.g., the oft-cited midrash in *Tanna debei Eliyahu* (also known as *Seder Eliyahu Rabbah*), chap. 4. The passage is quoted and translated in Leibowitz, *Studies in Shemot*, 620–22. Leibowitz calls this a "minority view" (623). Some modern Jewish commentators have expressed a similar view. According to Cassuto (*Commentary*, 421), "Moses feels that such is God's will." Martin Buber refers to the Levite slaughter as a "revolt suppressed by force of arms at the order of Moses, . . . " (*Moses*, 153). Also see n. 75 below.

15 Greenberg, "Postulates," 27. Cf. Milgrom, *Studies*, 32 and 32 n. 118.

16 The Levites' apparent ordination in v. 29 reads literally "fill your hands today for Yahweh!" On the possible meaning of this phrase in this context see Hyatt, *Exodus*, 310 and Hahn, *Das "Goldene Kalb,"* 77–82.

17 Admittedly, commentators like Gressmann (cited in Hahn, *Das "Goldene Kalb,"* 72) contend that "all" the Levites could not have gathered around Moses because Levite brothers, friends, and relatives were among the slain. This argument is without force, because Gressmann is simply assuming that those slain are guilty individuals, who therefore would not have rallied to Moses' side. On Levite complicity in the calf apostasy, note Hyatt (*Exodus*, 310): "There is nothing in [Exodus 32] to indicate that the Levites did not participate in the apostasy, . . . "

18 This summary is based on *Violence and the Sacred*. For a more recent treatment see *Things Hidden* and the other essays in this volume.

system of differentiations. Although judicial systems serve to control cycles of vengeance and violence stemming from mimetic rivalry in many societies, sacrificial religion can also curb violence, especially when everyone's aggression is diverted onto the same sacrificial victim or scapegoat. Rather than being rivals, all members of the society suddenly become unanimous in their hostility toward the scapegoat. This temporary recourse to violence ultimately helps to maintain cultural orders. For this mechanism to work effectively, the true function of the sacral violence must be hidden from the participants. Moreover, the victim must be a marginal individual who can be sacrificed without fear of reprisal. At the same time, the victim cannot be totally alien, for he or she must resemble the others enough for the sacrifice to "serve as a 'good conductor' [of the communities' violent impulses], in the sense that metal is a good conductor of electricity."[19] Perhaps most important, the victim must be innocent of any crime in order to function as a diversion from actual social crimes and violence. Because the victim's sacrifice brings about a new unanimity and cohesion to the society, the accursed victim is often viewed after the fact as being somehow holy or divine.

In the Book of Numbers, the Levites are "literally sacrifices brought by the Israelites,"[20] whose function is in part to "bear the iniquity" of the Israelites and thereby prevent divine wrath from plaguing them (Num 1:53; 18:21–23). In Girard's terms, the laws governing the Levites make them into "exterior or marginal individuals."[21] In one sense, this fulfills the curse of Jacob, who predicted that his sons Levi and Simeon would be divided and scattered in Israel because of their violence against the Shechemites (Gen 49:7). The deuteronomic laws enhance the marginal status of the Levites in a new way. Because of the centralization of the cult, the Levites must be grouped with the poor, the resident alien, the orphan and the widow as *personae miserabiles*.[22] In addition, the Levites are ritual scapegoats and "substitute victims"[23] in the sense that they replace the first born who must themselves be redeemed from sacrifice to Yahweh after the first-born of Egypt are slain (see below).

Interpreting the Levite massacre as a case of mass fratricide accords well with Girard's understanding of "enemy brothers" and his theory that "the surrogate victim is fundamentally a . . . neighbor of those destined to kill him."[24] Pointing to Jeremiah's warning to beware of deceptive brothers, Girard notes that here the fraternal relationship includes the entire community. In this sacrificial crisis, "violence engulfs the whole society, all its members confronting one another as enemy brothers."[25] Earlier in *Violence and the*

---

19 *Violence and the Sacred*, 39.
20 Milgrom, *Studies*, 29. See Num 8:11.
21 *Violence and the Sacred*, 12.
22 Deut 12:12, 18–19; 16:11, 14. See Weinfeld, *Deuteronomy*, 55, 290–91.
23 Girard, *Job*, 78; *Violent Origins*, 129.
24 *Violence and the Sacred*, 278.
25 *Violence and the Sacred*, 66.

Sacred, Girard had noted that the prophets Amos, Isaiah and Micah, who lived almost two centuries before Jeremiah, "denounce in vehement terms the impotence of the sacrifical crisis and ritual in general" (43). When the sacrificial system has eroded, "neighbors . . . turn to sacrificing one another." Although Girard quotes Empedocles' account of people "devouring one another" in this connection, he could just as easily have cited Micah's condemnation of the leaders who "eat the flesh" of their own people (3:3), together with that prophet's graphic description of his society, in which "they hunt each other" and one cannot trust one's friends and confidants (7:2, 5). The curse of cannibalism is an extreme expression of the collective violence that occurs in a society in which basic bonds between brothers, parents, and friends are broken. It is therefore understandable why the mishnaic rabbi Hanina would recommend that one "pray for the peace of the government, since, but for the fear of it, we men would swallow one another's neighbors alive" (*'Abôt* 3.2).[26]

Moses' order to the Levites can be interpreted as a command voluntarily to sacrifice their brothers, friends and neighbors in order to restore stability and eliminate the need for further reciprocal violence among the covenant brothers. The fact that Exodus 32 is extremely vague about who is responsible for the apostasy and who is punished by Moses and Yahweh highlights the fact that in a sacrificial crisis differences and hierarchies are dissolved. If the people's demand for gods to go before them obscures the distinction between Yahweh and other deities, Aaron's call for a feast to Yahweh to celebrate the calf collapses the distinction between legitimate and illegitimate worship of the one God. The Levites distinguish themselves from their idolatrous fellows by responding to Moses' call and then help to reestablish the communities' system of differences through their sacrifice. Although they sacrifice thousands of victims rather than a single scapegoat, this does not necessarily contradict the "*all against one* character of collective violence"[27] and scapegoating. Those slain are not presented as a group of individuals with differing personal identities. They are drawn as vaguely as the guilty idolators. They function as a collective sacrificial person, in the way that the law defines "legal persons" by their specific functions rather than by their personal characters.

From a Girardian standpoint, the innocent would not simply be the victims of such violence; they would be *targeted* as sacrifices by the community.[28] That is, those reported slain in vv. 26–29 would be *anyone but* the "ringleaders." It is as though Moses were exposing this process by calling for volunteers to be sacrificed, not zealous avengers. Moreover, the fact that the

---

26 *'Abôt* 3.2. For more on the social function of cannibalism (both actual cannibalism and cannibalism as metaphor) in the ancient Near East and in modern traditional societies, see Lasine, "Jehoram and the Cannibal Mothers," 29–37.

27 Girard, *Things Hidden*, 142.

28 *Violence and the Sacred*, 26 and *passim*.

text makes no mention of anyone resisting the onslaught of the Levite swords-
men is most understandable if those who are about to die are volunteer
victims. It is also significant that what precedes the call for volunteers (Exod
32:25) is Moses' perception that the people have "broken loose"—that all signs
of distinction and hierarchy have broken down. Such social chaos is characteristic of the first stage of a sacrificial crisis.[29]

Moses' blessing of the Levites in Deut 33:8–11 may also support this
reading of the Levite massacre. In v. 9, Moses refers to Levi as he "who said of
his father, and of his mother: 'I have not seen him'; neither did he acknowledge (*hikkîr*) his brothers, nor did he know his own children; . . . "
Although some scholars believe that these lines refer to a quality or function of
the Levites rather than the event recorded in Exod 32:26–29, it is best to
follow Driver in concluding that the verse describes the Levites' general spirit
of disinterestedness, while at the same time alluding to the events in Exodus
32.[30] The use of terms such as *hikkîr* suggests that this quality has a legal
dimension, even if the massacre of the three thousand was not an example of
legal collective punishment executed by humans. This word is used to refer to
the legal recognition of a person's individual identity, and to those aspects of
an individual's identity which judges should not acknowledge in rendering a
fair judgment.[31] In the case of the sin of the calf, the Levites are lauded for
treating their brothers as others, that is, for not acknowledging their identity as
anything other than a legal person guilty of a capital offense.

At the same time, the three thousand are executed without due process, a
fact that has not escaped the notice of apologists.[32] This element is stressed
most forcefully by commentators who conclude that the killing was without
any plan and arbitrary.[33] The absence of due process for idolatrous family
members is also a feature of the laws governing the punishment of those
within the family who seduce their relatives into idol-worship. Moses tells the
people: "if your brother, son . . . , daughter, wife, or most intimate friend (*rēaʿ*)
secretly entices you" to worship other gods, you shall not pity or conceal them

---

29 See, e.g., Girard, *Things Hidden*, 142.

30 Driver, *Deuteronomy*, 401.

31 See, e.g., Gen 37:33, in which Jacob acknowledges the torn and bloodied coat of his
favorite son as evidence of Joseph's death, and Deut 16:19, in which Moses warns judges
not to "recognize faces" (i.e., respect persons) in judgment.

32 Jewish apologists often respond to the lack of due process by embellishing the account so
that the Levites become appointed judges whose immediate duty is to punish those who
had been seen adoring the calf by witnesses, after the perpetrator had been warned not to
do so. See Ginzberg, *Legends*, 130. Compare Cassuto, who paraphrases and expands
Moses' instructions to the Levites: "put to death all those who, you know of a certainty
sinned, . . . either because you were actually witnesses, or because they were found guilty
by the ordeal of drinking" (*Commentary*, 421). On the idea that the drinking of the
"calfine" water pinpointed those deserving of the Levite's sword, see also Brichto,
"Worship," 16.

33 See the interpreters cited by Hahn, *Das "Goldene Kalb,"* 74–75.

(Deut 13:6–8). Rather, "you shall surely kill them (*hārōg tahargennû*);[34] your own hand shall be first against them to execute them (*lahămîtô*), and afterwards the hand of all the people" (13:9).

It is significant that this procedure stands in tension with the following law which deals with the case of an entire city that has been enticed into idolatry. Here a scrupulous legal investigation is necessary before any execution can take place. The authorities must "search, investigate, and ask diligently" in order to establish that the accusation is true and the facts are certain (Deut 13:14 [13:15 Heb]). The crucial difference between the two situations is that a family member or intimate friend is so well known to the informer that no investigation is needed. Most importantly, the law must assume that no one would inform on a family member or other loved one unless the fact of apostasy were true and certain. That is, the procedure is counting on familial loyalty as the condition of such loyalty being transcended for the sake of the community's religious purity and stability.[35] In this restricted sense, the law recognizes the moral claim of "brotherhood" in order to admit into evidence the witness-accuser's certain knowledge of the brother's apostasy. Only then does it require the accuser "not to acknowledge your brother" in the sense of Deut 33:9, by informing on, and then executing, the brother.

Given this interpretation of Moses' blessing of Levi and its relation to the massacre of the three thousand, the passages appear as the inverse of Jacob's curse of Levi after Levi's slaughter of the Shechemites. While the Levites use violence against their own families and are rewarded, the tribal ancestor Levi and his brother Simeon use violence against non-Israelites and are cursed. Interestingly, the sons of Jacob use guile and violence against outsiders just after many reports of their father Jacob's use of guile and treachery against *his* brother Esau. Considering that Levi and Simeon are "brothers in crime" in Genesis 34, it is worth noting that the Levite Phineas, whose act of zealotry is so similar to that of the Levites in Exodus 32, does not just slay an outsider, the Midianite Cozbi, but Zimri, a member of Levi's brother-tribe of Simeon (Num 25:14). In light of the fact that the fraternal identity of Simeon and Levi is stressed at an unusual degree in Gen 49:5a ("Simeon and Levi are brothers") as well as in Gen 34:25 ("Simeon and Levi are brothers")—even though these

34 Retaining the traditional Hebrew text (v. 10), which scholars (e.g., Weinfeld, *Deuteronomy*, 94) often emend to eliminate the disturbing suggestion of execution without due process.

35 More recent experience with family informers in Stalinist Russia and Hitler's Germany indicates that one cannot simply assume family loyalty or concern for the community's well being as the only motives for turning on one's family. If the "disintegration of family loyalty was conscious Stalinist aim" (Conquest, *Great Terror*, 378), Koestler's *Darkness at Noon* shows the dehumanizing effect of this policy by exposing the selfish motives which lead the porter's daughter to consider informing on her father, who continues to believe in the integrity of his former commander Rubashov. Koestler's novel is discussed further below.

two are not the only brothers whose mother is Leah—Phineas' act appears to be another case of sacrificial fratricide.

1.2 The Levites as sacrifices and the Korah rebellion

In the Book of Numbers, the Levites are identified as substitutes for the first-born who had been dedicated to Yahweh during the exodus from Egypt (Num 3:11–13, 41, 45; 8:16–19). In this capacity they will atone for the Israelites, ensuring that no divine plague or wrath will fall upon the children of Israel. They also substitute for the Israelites who encroach upon the holy, so that Yahweh's wrath will be directed upon themselves alone (see below). In order to understand the implications of the Levites' sacrificial role in Numbers 3 and 8, the reaffirmation of the Levites as sacrifices in Numbers 18 must be viewed in the context of the rebellion of Korah and other Levites who are dissatisfied with their role and envious of Moses (Num 16:5–12), as well as the subsequent murmuring of the people who identify with Korah (Numbers 17). This analysis will show that Numbers 16 displays considerable ideological and literary consistency, in spite of the fact that it is usually believed to be "riddled with inconsistencies and inconcinnities" which reveal that its editorial "stitching" is "inordinately poor" in spots.[36]

According to some biblical scholars, apparent exceptions to the rule that God alone holds groups collectively responsible are explicable in terms of what is necessary for the community's survival.[37] When Girard speaks of "the danger of disintegration a city might risk when deprived of the savage means of collective violence,"[38] he is speaking of another kind of necessity for community survival: the need for a scapegoat. According to Milgrom, "it is no accident that the brotherhood relationship is stressed" in Num 18:1–6, "the locus classicus for Levitic responsibility."[39] Girard would say it is no accident because envy and mimetic rivalry are greatest among brothers, resulting in an increased need for a scapegoat solution. Girard believes that it is the tendency of human beings to imitate each other's desires which makes envy "so extraordinarily powerful in human society."[40] Imitating the Other engenders conflict, because the more the envied person is emulated, the more he or she becomes a rival and obstacle. On the social level, unchecked mimetic desire leads to rampant violence, which can be controlled by sacrificial religions, in

---

36 Milgrom, "Korah's rebellion," 135; Milgrom, "Rebellion of Korah," 570.
37 Thus, Milgrom (*Studies*, 21) argues that sacerdotal guards must slay those who encroach upon the holy so that divine wrath does not engulf the community at large. Other religious crimes calling for death by humans are also "explicable in terms of their disruptive impact upon the society" (57 n. 214). Also note the conditions under which Israelites are empowered to annihilate those in their own cities, if those citizens have been seduced into idolatry, a sin capable of destroying the foundations of Yahweh's nation (Deut 13:13–19).
38 *Job*, 149.
39 Milgrom, *Studies*, 58 n. 216.
40 *Job*, 51.

which individuals identify with one another in unanimously finding a scapegoat.

The rebellion of Moses' first cousin Korah is clearly based on mimetic rivalry. The sacrificial crisis begins when Korah attempts to collapse the distinction between himself and Moses. He and his fellow rebels claim that all the congregation is holy, and that Moses and Aaron have elevated themselves above the Lord's assembly (Num 16:3). The narrator underscores Korah's imitation of Moses and the congregation of Israelites by describing Korah's band of two hundred and fifty followers as a mini-congregation, using the same word (*'ēdâ*) that is regularly employed to denote the Israelite congregation as a united whole. Moreover, Moses and the rebels echo one another's words in a symmetrical pattern, which highlights the element of imitation even further.[41] For his part, Moses claims to be a totally disinterested representative of Yahweh, which he hopes to demonstrate by proposing that Yahweh "create something new" to destroy the rebels in an unprecedented, and therefore unnatural, fashion (Num 16:28–30).

After the divine wrath has consumed the isolated rebels by means of earthquake and fire, the people as a whole still do not acknowledge the self-destructive folly of Korah's envy and the fact that Moses is not interested in self-aggrandizement. Instead they murmur against Moses and Aaron the next day, saying "You have killed the people of Yahweh" (Num 16:41 [17:6 Heb]). Commentators have been astounded by the people's persistence in their rebellion and their continuing failure to heed the graphic lessons Yahweh provides by means of signs and wonders.[42] Yet the content of the people's murmuring suggests that the people's problem is that they continue to identify with Korah; they still believe that he, like themselves, is one of the people of Yahweh. They are still attracted by Korah's attempt to claim that every single member of the assembly is holy, and that only Moses and Aaron differ from all in the group because they exalt themselves. That is, they seek to make Moses and Aaron their scapegoats.

It is the people's continuing identification with Korah and his project which causes Yahweh's behavior toward them in Numbers 17 to mirror the behavior toward Korah in chapter 16. The people's murmuring and assembling against Moses and Aaron precisely echoes the actions of Korah, Dathan and Abiram (cf. 17:6–7 and 16:3, 13). Yahweh's angry words to Moses and Aaron about the

---

41 Thus, after Korah and his congregation tell Moses and Aaron, "You take too much on you" (v. 3), Moses throws these same words back on these Levites (v. 7). In vv. 8–10, Moses asks these Levites if it is "too little" what God has done for them, that they seek the priesthood "as well." In v. 13 Dathan and Abiram sarcastically mimic Moses' words, asking whether it is "too little" that Moses took them out of Egypt, that he wants to play the prince over them "as well." This pattern of echoing implies that all are standing together, because Dathan and Abiram pick up on the words Moses is directing at Korah and his band. This serves to highlight the identity of all the envious rivals, all of whom view their model-obstacle as exalting himself above them (vv. 3, 13).

42 See, e.g., Leibowitz, *Studies in Bamidbar*, 213–16, 230–31.

people and the people's initial response are reported in exactly the same words used to describe Yahweh's response to Korah and Moses' and Aaron's initial reaction to Yahweh's words: "'Get away from this congregation, so that I may consume them in a moment.' And they [Moses and Aaron] fell upon their faces, . . . " (Num 16:21–22, 45 [17:10]).

What happens next, however, differs significantly in the two situations. In chapter 16, Moses and Aaron go on to intercede on behalf of the people. They ask Yahweh, "shall one person sin, and you become angry with the whole congregation?" (16:22). The Lord then orders Moses and Aaron to tell the congregation to get away from the dwellings of Korah, Dathan, and Abiram (v. 24). Moses does so, warning the people not to touch anything belonging to these wicked men, lest they be "swept away for all their sins" (v. 26). In chapter 17, on the other hand, Moses and Aaron make no attempt to intercede on behalf of the people, and the divine wrath and plague break out immediately. The contrast highlights the fact that all the people are now sinners themselves, so there can be no appeal to the principle that the righteous should be separated from the sinners before punishment begins.

The next phase of the crisis in chapter 17 involves one of the righteous going *among* the sinners rather than being separated *from* them. Whereas Yahweh had earlier told Moses and Aaron to get up "from among" (*mittôk*) the congregation because he intended to consume them (16:21, 45 [17:10]), Aaron now carries his fire-pan into the midst of (*'el-tôk*) the assembly even though the plague had begun (16:46–47 [17:11–12]). In so doing, he is following orders from Moses, who is not said to have received a divine mandate. Aaron makes atonement for the people, standing between the dead and the living (16:47–48 [17:12–13]). Because of his actions, "the plague was stopped" (16:48, 50[17:13, 15]). Without using violence himself, Aaron has acted in the way his grandson Phineas will act at Beth Baal Peor. Phineas also goes among sinners after a plague has begun. Because he spears his Simeonite brother Zimri and the pagan Cozbi *in flagrante delicto*, that plague was also "stopped" (25:8). Phineas' act turns away Yahweh's wrath and makes atonement for the Israelites (25:11, 13).

In one sense, chapter 17 concludes in the same manner as chapter 16: in both cases the people who have witnessed Yahweh's wrath are still afraid that they will all perish (16:34; 17:12–13[27–28]), in spite of Yahweh's demonstration of selectivity in punishment and the effectiveness of Moses and Aaron as mediators (and in spite of the fact that Aaron now possesses the budding rod which signals Yahweh's choice of the house of Levi and which was supposed to end the people's murmuring; see 17:1–8 [16–23]). It is at this point that the Levites are again given the duty of remaining perpetually "in-between" the people and the sancta, so that they might prevent Yahweh's wrath (*qeṣep*) from breaking out among the people again by taking it upon themselves (Num 18:5; cf. 1:53; 16:22; 17:11). This allows the people to disengage themselves from their previous identity with Korah by accepting Korah's tribal brothers as their sacrifices. The Levites will "bear the iniquity" of the Israelites, so that no divine wrath or plague will beset the people as a whole (Num 18:5–6, 22–23; cf. 8:19). If Girard compares the sacrificial victim to a "good conductor . . . of electricity,"[43] Milgrom says the Levites function as "a lightning rod to attract God's wrath upon themselves" when an Israelite trespasses upon the sancta, as did Korah; they are "ransom for Israel."[44] They are to be maintained by the state (i.e., tithe supported) like *pharmakoi*, the Athenian scapegoats,[45] so that they may protect all the people by "siphoning off" Yahweh's wrath.[46] Milgrom is therefore correct to conclude that Num 18:1–7, 21–23 gives the "antidote" to the people's fear that they would die for seeking access to the tabernacle (17:28).[47]

While it may seem ironic that the Levites are now targeted to receive divine plagues and wrath instead of the people, in spite of the fact that they had acted as the agents of divine wrath earlier, this too is appropriate from the Girardian perspective. Sacrificial victims of divine wrath like Oedipus are often believed by the community to have been uniquely intimate with the divine at a previous time,[48] and to have carried out divinely willed punishments, before they are convicted of committing the violent crimes that justify their ultimate vic-

---

43 *Violence and the Sacred*, 39.
44 Milgrom, *Studies*, 31. Another passage in which "ransom" (*kōper*) is capable of preventing a divine plague is 2 Samuel 24. In this case, however, a plague (*maggēpāh*; 2 Sam 24:21, 25; cf. Num 17:13, 14, 15; 25:8, 9, 18, 19) does occur. It is finally stopped when David offers burnt- and peace-offerings (v. 25). The crisis begins when Yahweh becomes angry at Israel and "incites" David against them by telling the king to take a census (v. 1). Numbering the people can precede a military draft. Many rules for purity apply to the army of Israel, the breaking of which could cause a plague. The most relevant rule here is given in Exod 30:11–16. They all shall give a ransom for their lives to Yahweh when they are numbered, so that there will be no plague (*negep*) upon them. The procedure resembles the way ransomed Levites prevent a plague falling on encroaching Israelites in Numbers 8. In 2 Samuel 24, however, the occurrence of the plague is not presented as a failure to ransom soldiers. Rather, the account exposes the operation of the scapegoat mechanism. Apologists have long been troubled by the fact that Yahweh leads David into sin in order to have an excuse to destroy seventy thousand Israelites (2 Sam 24:15). Yet, ironically, it is only here in the books of Samuel–after the narrator has acknowledged that David is subjectively innocent–that David freely and passionately confesses guilt and asks that he receive punishment instead of the people. He did not do so after coveting Bathsheba and committing adultery with her, or after murdering her husband. In Girard's terms, David is a successful scapegoat because he accepts the view that he is guilty and therefore responsible for the plague (see Girard, *Job passim*). While God continues to embody the violence of the community, the narrative makes it clear that the violence manifests itself by means of a scapegoat. It is hardly surprising then that the Chronicler later attempts to obscure this fact by reporting that it is "a satan," and not Yahweh, who incites David (1 Chr 21:1).
45 See Girard, *Violence and the Sacred*, 94–98, 294 n. 7.
46 Milgrom, *Studies*, 46.
47 Milgrom, *Studies*, 18.
48 See Sophocles *Oedipus Tyrannus*, 34.

timization.[49] This process is not only illustrated by the Levites as a tribe but by the fate of Aaron's sons Nadab and Abihu. Many scholars believe that the mention of Nadab and Abihu as having experienced a vision of God after the covenant sealing ceremony in Exod 24:8–9 serves no function.[50] None of the others present are named except Moses and Aaron. However, this example of unique intimacy with the divine *does* appear functional from a Girardian standpoint when one notes that these two later become the victims of a divine punishment that appears to be a parody of an ordinary sacrifice. According to Lev 10:1–7, a passage that bears a number of similarities to Numbers 16–17,[51] Nadab and Abihu brought unauthorized, and "strange," fire before Yahweh, and "fire came out from the presence of Yahweh, and consumed them" (v. 2). This is reported immediately after we are told that Yahweh's glory appeared to all the people in front of the tent of meeting, and "fire came out from the presence of Yahweh, and consumed the burnt offering and fat on the altar" (Lev 9:24). Because the same words are used to describe the devouring of the offering and the devouring of Aaron's sons, it is clear that whatever their mysterious transgression may have been, they die as though they were ordinary sacrificial victims.[52]

If Nadab and Abihu die as though they were sacrificial victims, the fact that the Levites are ordained as a collective human "elevation offering"[53] of the *people* in the book of Numbers (8:11, 13, 15, 21) also invites a Girardian interpretation. If the Levites are actually made to serve in this capacity by the crowd, the wrath that would come down on them after encroachment could be viewed as another projection of crowd violence. While the fraternal ethic may be generated by guilt, as Hodges contends, the biblical presentation of the Levites' role does not support his conclusion that the Old Testament's fra-

---

49 Communities may bestow godlike power onto the "destroyers of monsters" and "idols" they seek to transform into criminals and scapegoats (*Violence and the Sacred*, 87; *Job*, 10–13). The "crimes" of the Levite Moses (killing the Egyptian overseer [Exod 2:11–14] and destroying the "monstrous" Pharaoh) could easily lend themselves to a scapegoating process, as could the massacre of the Shechemites by the tribal ancestor Levi and his brother.

50 E.g., Noth. See Dozeman, *God on the Mountain*, 185 n. 24.

51 See, e.g., Coats, *Rebellion*, 257–60.

52 After their death Moses reports to Aaron Yahweh's pronouncement that Yahweh will be sanctified "through those who are near me" and Aaron responds only with silence (v. 3). Some scholars (e.g., Dozeman, *God on the Mountain*, 189) believe that Moses is rebuking Aaron here. Coats (*Rebellion*, 258–59) suggests that Aaron gave his "tacit approval" for his sons' act and therefore may have been partially responsible for it. His silence is said to emphasize his guilt (259). Although the text offers no firm evidence that Moses is actually rebuking Aaron or that Aaron is silently acknowledging any guilt, when interpreted in this fashion the scene is reminiscent of Moses' rebuke of his brother in Exod 32:21. Whereas Moses had rebuked Aaron for bringing about rampant apostasy through the calf-cult, apostasy so serious that the sacrificial slaughter by the Levites was necessary to end the immediate danger, here it is the inappropriate cultic activity of Aaron's sons that prompts their bizarre sacrificial demise as well as Moses' words to Aaron.

53 This translation (adopted by NRSV) is to be preferred over the usual "wave offering." See Milgrom, "Wave Offering," 945.

ternal ethic leads to an "underlying resentment against a social system which sacrifices the neighbor to the general welfare."[54]

Girard believes that the final moment of a sacrificial crisis is the development of "interdictions and sacrifices."[55] The career of the Levites in Exodus and Numbers also illustrates this aspect of the crisis, as well as the fact that the scapegoat double undergoes both a process of expulsion and divinization.[56] The installation of the Levites in Exod 32:29 begins a process of ritual duties and identity for the tribe that culminates in the book of Numbers after Korah's rebellion. The Levites become not only sacrifices, but marginal outsiders who are at the same time neighbors of the holy to a greater extent than their brothers inside the community.

2. Levite Violence and Sacrifice in Postbiblical Revolutionary Thought

The stories of the Levite slaughter, Korah's rebellion, and the death sentence against the entire generation of ex-slaves in the wilderness have all been reinterpreted and restructured since the biblical period. While some of these retellings have an apologetic intent, others are designed to create a paradigm of legitimate political purges capable of justifying similar acts in the present. Most of these versions do not condemn such violence out of hand. Yet even those which assume that these acts are necessary or laudable often hint at their sacrificial character, thereby suggesting that those who are slain may be innocent.

2.1 The Levite Slaughter as a Revolutionary Act and as a Sacrifice

When the first century Jewish philosopher Philo gives his accounts of the Levite massacre in his *Life of Moses*, he employs the metaphor of contagion in reporting that not all Israelites have become "wedded to their pleasant vices."[57] Because this is the case, Moses calls for those on the Lord's side, in order to test who in the crowed is "incurable," and who is repentant. Those who do not respond include both the rebellious and those who fear reprisal either from Moses or from the mob which has surrendered to apostasy. The Levites respond with zeal and keen "inward feelings which urged them to

---

54 Hodges, "Fratricide," 213. Hodges believes that the Old Testament exhibits an intense concern over "fratricidal guilt," which "is the result of mixed feelings of love and hate toward the brother or neighbor" (202). When universalized, such guilt "becomes the guilt of social status" (207), because "repressed hostility toward the brother generates the wish to be a good neighbor, to cease taking advantage of the weak, and to come to the aid of the unfortunate" (204). In a society based on the fraternal ethic "the brother upholds the rights and dignity of all his brothers, without bias or favoritism toward any" (211). This is the source of the resentment against social systems that sacrifice the neighbor to the general welfare.
55 *Things Hidden*, 143.
56 *Things Hidden*, 143.
57 II. 162.

piety."[58] The order to slay one's fellows is presented by Philo as a second test for the Levites alone, to learn whether they are truly loyal in the depths of their minds. Moses tells the Levites that "between the good there is no kinship and friendship but godliness," and they prove their fidelity by committing "wholesale slaughter of those who but now had been their dearest."[59]

In his treatise *The Sacrifices of Abel and Cain*, Philo makes a provocative comparison between the Levites and those who commit unintentional homicide. He asks why the unholy people who have committed involuntary homicide should be allowed to live in the cities of the Levites, side by side with the consecrated. While the basic answer is that "the good are a ransom for the bad," Philo goes on to note specific similarities between the fugitive killers and the Levites:

> . . . as they whom the Levites receive are exiles, so too the Levites themselves are virtually exiles. For as the homicides are expelled from the home of their nativity, so too the Levites have left children, parents, brothers, their nearest and dearest, to win an undying portion in place of that which perishes.[60]

Philo's comparisons highlight the sacrificial character of the Levites' role, as well as the possibility that they may serve as scapegoats. In leaving their "nearest and dearest," they both resemble those who are "expelled" for killing a human being, and act as "ransom" for them. Philo goes on to note that the Levites also resemble the involuntary homicides in that they "were privileged as a reward for slaying in a righteous cause."[61] If the Levites now live in "exile" from their "brothers" and their "nearest and dearest," they acquired that status—and first began to resemble the fugitive homicides—by slaying their brothers, neighbors and companions during the golden calf crisis.

The fact that the Levites show themselves capable of slaying their brothers is the key to their character for the sixteenth–century Christian theologian John Calvin. Calvin told his audience in Geneva

> You shall show yourselves rightly zealous of God's service, in that you kill your own brethren without sparing, so as in this case the order of nature be put underfoot, to show that God is above all. . . .[62]

---

58 II. 170.
59 II. 171–72. Philo gives two distinct accounts of Moses' order in this work. In addition to the one just quoted, he reports that the Levites had not acted to kill the guilty before Moses' return because they were waiting for a leader who had the right to order the killings (II, 273). In this way Philo demonstrates that the Levites are humble and restrained, in spite of their zealousness. Here Moses orders the Levites to rush through the camp and mow down "not only strangers," but "also the very nearest of our friends and kin." In both versions, Moses' order is presented as an illustration that fidelity to God not only supercedes family ties, but eliminates feelings of kinship and pity toward those slain.
60 Philo, *Mose*, IV. 38. 128–29.
61 Philo, *Mose*, IV. 38. 130.
62 From *Sermons on the Fifth Book of Moses*, as quoted in Walzer, *Exodus and Revolution*, 64.

Calvin's formulation is unsurpassed in its emphasis on the fact that the Levites' deed exhibits God's sovereignty precisely because their fratricidal act tramples upon the natural order, including human nature itself.

As Michael Walzer points out, "Moses' call to the Levites is a political act of the first importance, and as such it has figured significantly in Western political thought."[63] According to some modern socialist interpreters, Moses' order was a necessary revolutionary act. In his book *Moses in Red* (1926), Lincoln Steffens calls this "a red terror." It is "red" because a new political system is being born. Such a terror is not good, but it is evidently natural and therefore divine, "as Moses knew or felt."[64] Steffens asserts that God would have given up the Israelites on the spot, "if Moses had not put a few thousand of them to the sword of sacrifice to teach the rest and appease the wrath of the Lord."[65] While the dismissal of so many dead human beings as "a few thousand" is typical of modern revolutionary rhetoric (see below), similar justifications of such violence as a means to a desirable end have also been made by conservative biblical scholars like Cassuto: "It is better that *a few Israelites* lose their lives rather than that the entire people should perish."[66] This is of course the rationale of expediency which Caiaphas is made to utter in reference to Jesus in the gospel of John (11:50). That analogy underscores the sacrificial aspect of the Levite slaughter, an aspect not lost on Steffens, who speaks of the Levites' "sword of sacrifice."[67]

A more recent Communist reading of the Levites' "red terror" is Wilfred Daim's account of the way Moses and "his Levites" crushed this counter-revolutionary cadre. For Daim the lesson is that "the central idea of the Mosaic revolution is so supreme that it may call, if need be, for the sacrifice even of one's own closest kin. . . . Jesus never disagreed with Moses on this point."[68] Daim also discusses Korah's rebellion in these terms. While the faction responsible for the golden calf represented a "counter-revolutionary

---

63 *Exodus and Revolution*, 61.
64 *Moses in Red*, 108.
65 *Moses in Red*, 116.
66 Cassuto, *Commentary*, 421.
67 That Steffens also viewed the deaths as appeasing the wrath of the Lord aligns him with those biblical scholars who interpret human killings of those who sin against God as being necessary to prevent the outbreak of a divine plague. However, as argued above, the sequence of events in Exodus 32 does not indicate that this process is at work here. In her novel, *Moses: Man of the Mountain*, Zora Neale Hurston has Moses offer a variant of this rationale in his order to the Levites: "If this is to be a great nation, it must be purged of such evil-doers [the leaders and the agitators of the calf apostasy], or all Israel must perish. . . . Spare not a soul who is guilty" (292). In Hurston's account, it is one thousand leaders who are slain (293). Here, national survival is the ultimate rationale, the same rationale which many biblical scholars believe is behind biblical laws with capital penalities and those sins which bring forth divine wrath (see above). As discussed earlier, from the Girardian point of view the creation of scapegoats who are viewed as evildoers can also be a matter of communal survival.
68 *Christianity*, 53.

deviation to the right," Korah's is to the left. If the makers of the calf display a "surrender mentality" by espousing a "fascist" regression to the ideology of Egypt, the activism of Korah's faction corresponds to the "theory of quick victory" which Mao called "adventurism."[69] According to Daim, Korah's accusation that Moses is violating the egalitarian thrust of the revolutionary goals is specific and accurate. His mistake is that he wants to achieve these goals at once. He and his men are short-sighted; they cannot see that there is need for a transitional period, devoted to reeducation and war preparation. Moses is merely a transitional leader, who recognizes that he has to "delay democratization."[70]

Daim claims that *Moses* "liquidated" Korah and his men, just as he had liquidated the faction who made the calf. He is aware that the manner of the rebels' death is presented in Numbers 16 as an unequivocal demonstration that Yahweh is directing the Israelites and *not* Moses. However, he interprets "the flames that destroyed Korah and his men . . . [as] a symbol of that fury with which the Jewish nation swept two hundred and fifty men to their death."[71] In this respect, Daim interprets the symbolism of such divine wrath in the manner of Girard, who also makes an analogy between natural cataclysmic phenomena and communal human violence.[72] When this analogy becomes part of the revolutionary rhetoric of modern writers like Daim, Büchner, and Koestler (on whom see below), it tends to legitimate such violence as both natural and inevitable.

Like other socialist readers of the story, Daim omits reference to the role of envy in Korah's rebellion, an element that had already been noted by earlier political theorists like Machiavelli. Without specifically referring to Korah's rebellion, Machiavelli asserts that before Moses could set about making laws, "he had to kill a very great number of men who, out of envy and nothing else, were opposed to his plans."[73] Envy is not only the key motive for the rebellion of Moses' brother Aaron and sister Miriam in Numbers 12, but the rebellion of his first cousin Korah and Dathan and Abiram, as Ps 106:16–17 makes explicit. As Girard and others have demonstrated, envy signals the presence of the kind of mimetic rivalry that is destructive of social order.[74]

---

69 *Christianity*, 52, 59.
70 *Christianity*, 58, 59. In this respect the logic of Daim's Moses resembles that of Cromwell, whose leadership of the Puritan Revolution was heavily influenced by the story of Moses. See Walzer, *Exodus and Revolution*, 112.
71 *Christianity*, 60.
72 *Violence and the Sacred*, 31, 77; cf. *Job*, 22 on Job 20:26–27.
73 *Discourses*, III, 30, 4. See Machiavelli, *Discourses*, 547. Machiavelli's portrait of Moses as a law-maker contradicts the biblical history, which attributes the creation of all laws to God Himself. Moreover, Moses only becomes involved in the deaths of rebellious Israelites *after* the promulgation of God's laws at Sinai (Exodus 19–24).
74 E.g., Foster, "Anatomy," 165: "[envy is] a particularly dangerous and destructive emotion," which implies hostility and violence "capable of destroying societies."

2.2 The Israelites' "Wandering To Death" as a Political Purge

It is perhaps to be expected that modern revolutionaries would focus on the Levite slaughter in Exodus 32, if not Phineas' act in Numbers 25, to find a model for legitimate killings by human agents for the sake of the community or nation. While Moses does indeed claim that the execution order has been issued by Yahweh, the chapter does not quote Yahweh telling this to Moses, as are other divine orders in the book of Exodus. As noted earlier, even pious commentators and modern biblicists have assumed that the idea originated with Moses himself,[75] suggesting that Moses may have fabricated the divine mandate in order to ensure that his order would be carried out.

It should not be surprising then that modern writers have assumed that the divine order which sentenced the entire generation of ex-slaves to die in the wilderness (Numbers 14) was also Moses' idea, an idea which should be copied by those who want to carry out a "Mosaic revolution" of their own. For example, Marx compares his generation to the Jews whom Moses led through the wilderness, for they "must go under to make room for the men who are able to cope with a new world."[76] Even Machiavelli's statement that Moses had to "kill a very great number of men" could be interpreted to include all the wilderness generation. In fact, Lewis Feuer believes that the "Mosaic revolutionary myth," in which the leader "imposes a collective discipline on the people to re-educate them morally for their new life," is repeated by *every* ideology in some fashion.[77]

In Georg Büchner's drama about the French Revolution, *Danton's Death* (1835), St. Just makes a speech about the need for purges which includes a similar reference to Moses. While much of Büchner's play includes actual material from the revolutionary trials, this speech was created by Büchner, who was himself an active revolutionary.[78] St. Just argues that it is just as

---

75 See note 14, above. Among moderns, Voltaire is perhaps the most scathing in his indictment of Moses for issuing this order. Voltaire imagines the Israelites castigating Moses in this manner:

". . . instead of punishing your unworthy brother, you make him our pontiff, and you order your Levites to butcher 23,000 men of your people [Voltaire is following the Vulgate here, which augments the number given in the Hebrew text by 20,000]! Would our fathers have tolerated this? Would they have let themselves be slaughtered like victims by bloodthirsty priests?" (*Philosophical Dictionary*, 321).

This diatribe is noteworthy in several respects. The Levites are viewed here as an extension of Moses, not as disinterested parties who rally to his side solely because of their fidelity to Yahweh. More important, Voltaire interprets the killings in light of the fact that the text says nothing about those attacked putting up any kind of resistance. His hypothetical speakers find it difficult to believe that their fathers would have allowed themselves to be "slaughtered like victims." Yet, as argued above, this is precisely what the text may imply.

76 Marx, *Class Struggles*, 104.

77 Feuer, *Ideology*, 1.

78 See Beacham, "Büchner's Use of Sources," 51.

permissible for "moral nature" or humanity to shed blood in its revolutions as it is for physical nature to destroy countless human beings in floods and other natural cataclysms in obedience to its laws. He asks, "What does it matter if men die from a plague or a revolution?"[79] Because the Revolution has sped up the progress of humanity, so that four years have accomplished what in nature would have taken a hundred years, it should come as no surprise that "the flow of the revolution throws out its corpses at very dip, at every new turn."[80] The prospect of producing a "few hundred corpses" more (including Danton's) should not prevent the revolutionaries from reaching their conclusion now. It is at this point that St. Just cites Moses:

> Moses led his people through the Red Sea and into the desert until the old corrupt generation had destroyed itself, before he founded the new state. Legislators! We have neither a Red Sea nor a desert, but we have the war and the guillotine.[81]

Like Cassuto and Steffens, Büchner's St. Just believes that the loss of a relatively "few" human lives is not too costly a means to the end he plans for the nation. Again, like Steffens, St. Just finds that the deaths brought about by terror are "natural." His biblical example implies that Moses led the "old corrupt generation" into the desert precisely in order for it to "destroy itself." The desert was as efficient a way to purge the old generation as is war and judicial murder by guillotine.

According to one interpretation of the wilderness experience, the wilderness offered the Israelites the opportunity to shed the dust of slavery and reeducate themselves.[82] In Victor Turner's terms, the desert provided the opportunity for a "liminal process" to occur.[83] While some of the revolutionary theorists quoted above also speak of reeducation, they generally restrict that function to the new generation brought up in the wilderness. As Steffens puts it, the children must pass through the "purifying experience of the natural conditions of the desert," but the "grown-ups must die." For him, "the hardest lesson of all is, not that the reactionaries must die, but that, . . . all of an older generation are reactionaries."[84]

Büchner's inclusion of a biblical citation in the speech of St. Just is remarkable precisely because the French revolutionaries referred to Roman—

---

79 Act II. Scene 7. See Büchner, *Complete Works*, 93.
80 *Complete Works*, 94.
81 *Complete Works*, 94.
82 E.g., Maimonides, *Guide*, III, 32. See Leibowitz, *Studies in Shemot*, 555–56, and Walzer, *Exodus and Revolution*, 54–55.
83 That is, separation from the structured society of Egypt allowed the Israelites to experience one another as "human totals," stripped of all hierarchical identities, before they become integrated into a new social structure in Canaan. See Turner, *Ritual Process*, 94–130. For a discussion of Turner's concept, see Lasine, "Indeterminacy," 59–62, 67–68.
84 *Moses in Red*, 124, 133.

and even Greek—religion and history much more often than they cited the Bible. In the paragraphs following the mention of Moses, for example, St. Just compares the Revolution to the daughters of Pelias, because "it cuts humanity in pieces to rejuvenate it."[85] He then summons all secret enemies of tyranny who carry the dagger of Brutus beneath their cloaks to share this sublime hour with himself and his fellows. The first of these classical references carries an ironic message not intended by the speaker. Pelias is not rejuvenated when he is cut up by his daughters. Medea had tricked his daughters into thinking this would occur, but Medea was actually seeking revenge against Jason's uncle Pelias. Thus St. Just is implying that while the revolutionaries might be deluded into thinking they are rejuvenating humanity, they have only suc- ceeded in destroying human beings.

The reference to Brutus is even more significant in the present context. St. Just has in mind the Brutus who was one of the first consuls of Rome (c. 509 B.C.E.). According to a popular tradition, Brutus presided at the trial and beheading of his two sons, who were accused of engaging in a conspiracy to restore the Tarquins Brutus had overthrown. In Virgil's *Aeneid*, Anchises predicts, "though a father, for the sake of splendid liberty he will condemn his sons when they rise in revolt. Unhappy, however his acts may be told, con- quered by love of country and passion for renown."[86] This is the same message that is usually derived from the story of the Levite massacre. In *Danton's Death* three other speakers refer to Brutus. One says that Robespierre "tried to make a face like Brutus sacrificing his sons. He . . . said that concerning liberty . . . he would sacrifice anyone—himself, his brother, his friends."[87] This willngness to sacrifice brother and friends also recalls the Levites' act.

In this play, however, acts of sacrifice for the cause are usually linked with perversions of natural orders: cannibalism, child sacrifice (to Moloch), fratri- cide and the like.[88] Adapting a statement from a speech by the Girondist Vergniaud, Büchner has Danton say that "the Revolution is like Saturn, it devours its own children."[89] Such allusions should be interpreted in light of Girard's discussion of ritual cannibalism as a sacrifical rite.[90] Büchner's play is replete with indications of the kind of mimetic rivalry that causes social "cannibalism" and the need for a scapegoat.

In this century Arthur Koestler has developed a perspective on group psychology that is based in part on his own experiences with the aftermath of the Russian Revolution during the rule of Stalin. Koestler believes that most

85 *Complete Works*, 94.
86 *Aeneid*, 6.820–823.
87 Büchner, *Complete Works*, 73. The speaker is Paris. The remaining two speakers who refer to Brutus are Lacroix (80) and Dumas (112).
88 Cannibalism: *Complete Works*, 64, 65, 81, 121. Sacrifice to Moloch: *Complete Works*, 119. Fratricide: *Complete Works*, 83, 117.
89 *Complete Works*, 74. On the speech by Vergniaud, see Beck, *Forschung*, 347–49.
90 *Violence and the Sacred*, 274–78; *Violent Origins*, 219.

violence and carnage in human history is due to human integrative and self-transcending tendencies, not individual assertiveness. His formula is "the egotism of the group feeds on the altruism of its members."[91] That is, unselfish devotion and self-transcendence reinforce the self-assertive tendencies of the group. This conclusion is echoed by Erich Fromm, who believes that war "encourages deep-seated human impulses, such as altruism and solidarity, to be expressed. . . ."[92]

This view of human altruism and violence is echoed by the Bolsheviks in *Darkness at Noon* (1941), Koestler's extremely influential novel about the Moscow show trials.[93] At one point the interrogator Ivanov remarks that "the temptations of God were always more dangerous for mankind than those of Satan."[94] He is speaking to his former friend and fellow soldier Rubashov, the novel's protagonist, a revolutionary hero who is under arrest for capital offenses against the Party. The ultimate purpose of the interrogation is to make Rubashov accept the role of "voluntary scapegoat,"[95] much in the way Job's friends attempt to make Job accept guilt so that there might be the unanimity necessary for the effective functioning of the scapegoat mechanism. However, while Job refuses to accept this role, as Girard demonstrates so well, Rubashov finally capitulates. After he has served the party by being held up to public scorn at his show trial, Rubashov muses that he and the others who constitute the "best" of the accused have let themselves "be sacrificed as scapegoats." Yet these scapegoats are not totally innocent; they are "all guilty, although not of those deeds of which they accused themselves" in court.[96] Unlike Job, Rubashov ultimately sacrifices his belief in his integrity and his innocence.

In the end, Rubashov views himself as a Moses whose failure is even greater than that of the prophet. Rubashov has viewed his forty years as a leader of the Revolution as an attempt to lead his child-like people to a communist promised land. He has rationalized the purges and liquidations as the price of admission. In his prison journal he writes,

> man is sluggish and has to be led through the desert for forty years before each step in his development. And he has to be driven through the desert with threats and promises, by imaginary terrors and imaginary consolations, so that he should not sit down prematurely to rest and divert himself by worshipping golden calves.[97]

---

91 Koestler, *Janus*, 83.
92 Fromm, *Anatomy*, 242. For Fromm war is a kind of liminal experience in which class differences disappear, so that the warriors act as what Turner calls "human totals" (see n. 83, above).
93 At least one French newspaper claimed that the novel was the most important single factor leading to the defeat of the Communists in the post-war referendum on the French Constitution. See Koestler, *Invisible Writing*, 404.
94 Koestler, *Darkness at Noon*, 124.
95 *Darkness at Noon*, 184.
96 *Darkness at Noon*, 205.
97 *Darkness at Noon*, 79–80.

In Rubashov's version of the biblical story, the "consolations" offered the people are no more real than the terrors or the calf-idol itself. Once again, the purpose of the forty years in the desert is presented as educational (at least for the survivors), while no mention is made of the fact that in Numbers 14 the long wandering is presented as a capital punishment for the adults. Rubashov's version not only glosses over the very real punishments carried out in the biblical account, but the carrying out of "threats" and "terrors" in his own movement.

Rubashov's initial assumptions about the need to drive sluggish humanity into development are akin to those of St. Just in Büchner's *Danton's Death*, a drama which Koestler utilizes in the novel.[98] Whereas St. Just compares the necessity of the revolutionary carnage to the cruelty of Nature, Rubashov appeals to the "inert and unerring" force of History. Where St. Just speaks of Nature leaving "corpses lying in its path," Rubashov says of History that "she leaves the corpses of the drowned."[99]

Like St. Just, both Rubashov and Ivanov have assumed that the goal of their revolution was to speed up the process of human social evolution. St. Just had said that the strides of humanity are slow; Rubashov believes that man is sluggish.[100] During one of the interrogations, Ivanov asks Rubashov whether they "should shrink from sacrificing a few hundred thousand for the most promising experiment in history."[101] While the numbers of victims have become inflated from the "few thousand" slain by the Levites and the "few hundred" Frenchmen St. Just seeks to add to those already killed, Ivanov's logic, like St. Just's, is based on the same principle that "the end justifies the means . . . the only rule of political ethics; . . . "[102]

Later in the novel, Rubashov's begins to reject this means to the desired end, in spite of the arguments of his new interrogator Gletkin, who notes that while other countries had one or two hundred years to industrialize, the Russians had only ten.[103] That is why they had to shoot workers for every trifling error. As Rubashov comes to accept personal guilt for failing to lead the people up to the Promised Land, as did Moses, he becomes more convinced of the dehumanizing effects of such tactics. He can no longer consider the masses to be nothing more than the "the great, silent [algebraic] X of history," a form of mathematical logic that make no allowance for individual identity and decency.[104]

---

98 The epigraph to the novel is a famous dictum by St. Just: "no one can rule guiltlessly." However, when Koestler has Rubashov ponder Danton's experience, he employs Büchner's version of Danton's speeches rather than the French historical records. See Wetzel, "Revolution," 30–31.
99 *Darkness at Noon,* 34.
100 *Darkness at Noon,* 79.
101 *Darkness at Noon,* 131.
102 *Darkness at Noon,* 127.
103 *Darkness at Noon,* 183.
104 *Darkness at Noon,* 68. Rubashov begins to view Gletkin's rationale for Stalin's terror in a

3. Conclusion: The Reader's Relation
to Biblical Personages and Judging Levitical Violence

The conventional approach to the story of the Levite massacre, which takes the narrative as an account of righteous punishment, represents the perspective of the persecutors. For Girard, it is myths which

> incorporate the point of view of the community . . . that is unanimously convinced that [the killing of the victim] was a legitimate and sacred action, desired by God himself, which could not conceivably be repudiated, criticized, or analyzed.[105]

Yet this study indicates that the story does not require readers to share the perspective of this hypothetical community. Present-day readers can choose to reaffirm the alleged "mythical" perspective of the ancient audience, or to adopt a point of view that denies the legitimacy of the reported acts. The text permits both possibilities. Thus if one does *not* begin with the assumption that the killings explicitly reported in Exodus 32 are punishments of the guilty, those killings—committed by the Levites—resemble a fratricidal sacrifice of the innocent. This "non-mythical" reading "sides with the victim" by representing them as such, and by showing that they are no less innocent than those who slay them. Moreover, this approach accounts for all elements of the present text, unlike readings of Exodus 32 that view this deed as just punishment. This perspective is also harmonious with the accounts of the Levites as sacrifices in the book of Numbers, especially the seemingly repetitious account of the Levites being reinstitutionalized in that role in the aftermath of Korah's rebellion and the people's murmuring.

In order to evaluate the biblical stories about the Levites and holy violence in terms of "the ethics of reading," one must keep in mind that the reader addressed by biblical narrators is assumed to be *related* to biblical personages such as the Levites. They are not presented as fictional characters. Readers are led to identify with—and feel responsible for—all its relatives in the text, whether oppressor or victim.[106] In regard to those biblical "relatives" or ancestors who commit violence, this aspect of the rhetoric of biblical narrative acts as an oblique way of leading readers to acknowledge their own potential to act as scapegoaters. In this sense biblical rhetoric transcends the tendency to scapegoat those we regard as scapegoaters.[107]

---

manner similar to that of Conquest (*Great Terror*, 661), who observes that "Stalinism is one way of attaining industrialization, just as cannibalism is one way of attaining a high protein diet. The desirability of the result hardly seems to balance the objections." In light of the fact that metaphors of cannibalism signal a sacrificial crisis (see above), Conquest's analogy is profoundly appropriate.

105 *Things Hidden*, 148.
106 See Lasine, "Fiction, Falsehood, and Reality," 24–40, and *idem*, "Judicial Narratives," 53–58.
107 See *Violent Origins*, 78.

If one is to understand fully this dimension of the biblical text, one must recognize that Hebrew scripture addresses not only an ancient audience beset by its social problems and crises, but a "canonical audience" informed by the biblical narrators that the text has urgent relevance for their lives as well, no matter when or where they now live.[108] While Girard may be correct about the text as a written record which reveals that the scapegoat mechanism was operative in ancient Israel at some indeterminate point in its history, that same text can function in opposition to scapegoating for the contemporary believing community. For example, the wilderness narrative may now serve to explore the problem of complicity in violence in order to reveal its workings, rather than to continue the ideological concealment Girard and other students of myth assume to be necessary for the myth's continued effectiveness.[109] This survey of postbiblical uses of the wilderness narrative indicates that later readers can either appropriate the scapegoat mechanism described in the text, or deny that mechanism by openly acknowledging its sacrificial aspect.

108　For example, in his farewell speeches, the "you" to whom Moses addresses the laws and admonitions "this day" (Deut 30:11, 15, 19) includes ourselves, who always read those laws "today," for the act of reading always takes place "today," in an eternal present. Moses implies as much when he remarks that the covenant is also being made "with him who is not here with us this day" (Deut 29:14; cf. 5:3). Moreover, those addressed are reminded that what they are hearing has as much relevance for themselves as it did for their ancestors: "it is no vain thing for you, because it is your life" (Deut 32:47). For more on the concept of the canonical audience, see Lasine, "Judicial Narratives, 56–58."

109　Anthropologists often assume that only they can see through the falsity of the natives' myths, which are considered to be nothing more than "cultural dreams." See Lasine, "Indeterminacy," 58, 62–66. When one takes into account the hypothetical audience for whom the texts are rhetorically designed, it becomes clear that many more sections of the Hebrew Bible have an antimythical thrust than Girard believes to be the case. For a full discussion of this issue, see Lasine, review of Girard's *Job*, 98–103.

xi

King and the Black Religious Quest to Cure Racism

Theophus H. (Thee) Smith

Abstract

The traditional Christianity of black North Americans offers an instructive case study in nonviolent transformation. This chapter treats black Christianity as the primary source behind the civil rights activism of Martin Luther King, Jr. It explores King's religious heritage for its power simultaneously to overturn ethnic victimization and to transform the victimizer—for its power to realize what he called "the beloved community."[1] That power resides, by hypothesis, in a performative tradition of mimesis in black religion. The mimetic basis of such performances is twofold, consisting in (1) an imitation of Christ—*imitatio Christi*—in which Jesus as "Suffering Servant" (Isaiah 53) provides a preeminent model for the nonviolent transformation of "victimage" (Girard); and in (2) 'homeopathic' (like-cures-like) applications, where diminishing forms of victimization are employed in order to forestall, counter, or cure victimization in its most virulent, racist forms.

0. Introduction

In the following sections I examine the black Christian solution to a millennial problem in Christian praxis. It is the threefold problem of: (1) how to initiate victims in an imitation of Jesus that navigates between the two poles, equally contrary to his persona in the gospels, of docility and enmity; and in conjunction, (2) how to induce victimizers to desire their own imitation of the God who saves victims, overagainst their continued practices of victimization; and finally (3) how to provide, for both prospective victims and incipient victimizers, a nonconflictual model for the resolution of rivalry and acquisitive, "mimetic desire" (Girard). In the quest for a nonviolent praxis, such a model is called upon to terminate and even deter victimization, and thus

---

1 For an exposition of King's concept of the beloved community see Smith and Zepp, *Search for the Beloved Community*. The term itself, "the beloved community," was coined by the American philosopher, Josiah Royce. See Royce, *The Problem of Christianity*, 125–6.

230

regenerate culture on the basis of new and nonviolent forms of imitation and power.

I also examine these issues from the perspective of René Girard's theory of religion and violence. But the nature of such transformations in the King movement poses a question that remains untreated by Girard's theory: what praxis can insure a culture-wide resolution of mimetic conflict, in which scapegoating and sacrificial compulsions are defused or transcended? For black Christians before and after King this is an ongoing problem of praxis and survival, not theory alone. It is the problem of *curing* racist Christianity as a deformed cult; that is, healing Christianity itself of its deformation as a religion of sacralized violence that is contrary to its own gospel origins. This chapter examines the Afro-Christian cure.

1. Suffering-Servant

"When I was a slave my master would sometimes whip me *awful*, specially when he knew I was praying. He was determined to whip the Spirit out of me, but he could never do it, for de more he whip the more the Spirit make me *content* to be whipt. . . ." That contentment, it may be said, stifled outward political resistance, but it may also be argued that it represented a symbolic inward resistance. . . . a victory of the spirit over the force of brutality.[2]

The transformation of encounters with ethnic violence, into ritual occasions for identification with Christ and his suffering or passion, extend from the period of slave religion in the United States to the King movement of the nineteen sixties. A dramatic instance in the early phase of the tradition is found in a fictional work published in 1810 by Daniel Coker entitled, *A Dialogue Between A Virginian and An African Minister*. Coker's work, probably the earliest publication by an Afro-American of his own writing, is also distinguished as one of the first antislavery texts by a black author. As a young man, Coker (1780–1835) escaped slavery and was later manumitted through the efforts of friends and benefactors. Ordained a deacon in the Methodist church around 1800, he is perhaps best known as the co-founder in 1791, along with Richard Allen, of the movement that led to the establishment of the African Methodist Episcopal (A.M.E.) Church. Allen and his colleague Absalom Jones, who was subsequently ordained by the Episcopal church as its first black priest, separated from the Methodist Episcopal church in Philadelphia following the establishment of segregated seating during Sunday worship.

The *Dialogue* is cast as a defense of emancipation by "an African minister," and as a condemnation of those slavemasters who forbid the religious instruction of their slaves. Its story form is narrated by an African minister,

2 Raboteau, *Slave Religion*, 307–8.

Coker's alter ego, who begins by relating the occasion of a visit from a Virginian slaveholder. The slaveholder politely, even graciously, requests to interview the minister. After opening civilities on both sides this "Virginian" confronts the minister with a charge which has been popularly circulated: he is accused of having "imbibed a strange opinion . . . repugnant to reason and justice," and "wrong in the highest degree," that the slaves should be emancipated. Yet by the end of the dialogue the minister has not only succeeded in defending that "strange opinion." He has also, albeit fantastically, persuaded the Virginian to manumit all of his "fifty-five negroes."[3]

1.1 The slave as "suffering servant"

In the course of his biblical argumentation the African minister purports to tell the slavemaster a true story of one of his enslaved kinsmen, "in his own words." Within this framework we hear about a slave who is unjustly stretched and lashed with a whip because, as we learn in due course, his master considers him too devout and fervent in his religious life. In the first person voice of the slave we read the following account:

> First I am chained, and kept back from my public [church] meetings; secondly, I am chained in and out of the house for thirty and some times forty hours together, without the least nourishment, under the sun; thirdly, I am tied and stretched on the ground, as my blessed master was, and suffer the owner of my body to cut my flesh, until pounds of blood, which came from my body, would congeal and cling to the soals [sic] of my shoes, and pave my way for several yards. When he would have satisfied his thirst in spilling my blood, he would turn from me to refresh himself with his bottle.[4]

At this point in the narration the Virginian, evidently offended by the stark brutality in the depiction, interrupts and entreats the minister to stop the story. But the narrator refuses to capitulate to decorum, insisting instead on fidelity to "the experience of one of those sufferers." However, he does not continue to dwell on the atrocities committed by the drunken slaveholder. Rather, he turns to celebrating the irony that the lashing of the slave actually redounds to an increase of the victim's religious zeal. The narrator represents that zeal in the slave's declaration, that "when I looked and saw my blood running so free, my heart could not help praising my Savior, and thanking God that he had given me the privilege, and endowed me with fortitude sufficient to bear it without murmuring."[5]

---

3 Coker, "Dialogue," 4–5, 31.
4 Coker, "Dialogue," pp. 34–35. Note the contrast embedded in the slave's speech between "my blessed master" and his human master, whose power and authority is relativized or diminished by the expression, "the owner of my body." I return to this contrast below in discussing the Virginian slavemaster's cathartic response in the decision to free his slaves.
5 Coker, "Dialogue," 34–35.

Here is one of the first instances in Afro-American literature of the slave as a type of the preeminent figure who endured the lash "without murmuring." The *locus classicus* for this figure is the Suffering Servant passage from Isaiah 53—a passage still celebrated by Christians as a messianic prophecy of the Hebrew scriptures that was fulfilled in the "passion" of Christ:

> He was oppressed, and he was afflicted,
>   yet he opened not his mouth;
>   like a lamb that is led to the slaughter,
> and like a sheep that before its shearers
>   is silent,
> so he opened not his mouth. (Isa 53:7)

Already the narrator has represented the slave in accordance with Christian mimetic tradition as a suffering servant. Yet a deeper dimension of representation subsequently appears. "Finding this [abuse] a great means to make me more fervent in prayer, [the master] bethought himself of another diabolical strategem to put me to shame." The slave is carried to a nearby blacksmith, fitted with an "iron collar," and then dragged away to labor in a field "although scarce able." But this final torment ushers in the climactic moment in the slave's ordeal: the moment of mimesis in which, by becoming a figure or type of Christ, he experiences his suffering as redemptive.

> When I recollected that my dear Lord and Master had commanded me to bear my cross, and take his yoke upon me, my soul, my heart was elevated. I thought I could have flown, and I went to work with more submission, and with more apparent love than I had done heretofore.[6]

The slave's return to work "with more submission, and with more apparent love" than before is the action that he undertakes in imitation of Christ. For most contemporary readers that action and its accompanying sentiment may seem an extreme form of docility; an acquiescence in one's own victimization that amounts to self-abuse and masochism. However, before we dismiss Coker's representation prematurely let us read it in the context of Coker's authorial strategy as the writer of an antislavery tract.

If we are attentive readers we will not fail to penetrate the authorial presence of Coker in the guise of his *alter ego*, the "African minister" who is narrating the slave's story. But it is neither the slave nor the slave's advocate and spokesperson, the minister, who is the central performer. Rather it is Coker himself who is engaged, by hypothesis, in performing a literary-magical feat. The essential and conjurational purpose of his work is to induce the formation of antislavery convictions in his white readers. His strategy for achieving that feat is to simulate (or model or 'mimick') such a transformation in the person

---

6 Coker, "Dialogue," 35–36.

of the Virginia slavemaster in the narrative. Thus the climactic moment of the *Dialogue* is the Virginian's response after hearing this story. Recall that it is the story of a slave who returned to work for an abusive master, while rejoicing in the commandment of his other Master "to bear my cross, and take his yoke upon me." Marvelously, simply by hearing this rendition of a slave's imitation of Christ the Virginian slavemaster is himself induced to perform the gospel commandment. In the words of Jesus, he determines to "deny himself and take up his cross and follow me" (Matt 16:24). He then promises to do so, fantastically and in defiance of all the strictures of realistic expectation, by emancipating his fifty-five slaves. Therein he 'denies himself': by dispossessing himself of other human beings as 'property' he denies himself as master. Moreover, he experiences such dispossession as an act of allegiance or obedience to the commandments of Christ; as his own performance of the imitation of Christ.

In Coker's *Dialogue* the author's magical or conjurational intent is to induce similar transformations among his white American readership. Through his writing Coker summoned white readers to perform their own imitation of Christ by similarly denying themselves; that is, by the dispossession of their property and by the general abolition of slavery. Of course, with respect to historical reality this literary-conjurational strategy was inadequate to the task. The *Dialogue* was ineffectual for inducing such large scale transformations as the abolition of slavery. But this ineffectiveness resulted, I suggest, not so much from a defect of intent or power (the inability to publish and compel affective reading, for example) but more substantively from a deficiency of mimetic application. It was the same deficiency that curtailed the prophetic efficacy and mimetic performances of Sojourner Truth . Indeed, it is a mimetic deficiency that has persisted in black social prophetism and transformational practices until the recent performances of Martin Luther King, Jr. That deficiency consisted in the inability directly to affect and enlist antagonists in the enactment of their own mimetic performances. In the absence of such engagement practitioners of mimetic transformation have had recourse only to the persons and bodies of the victims themselves.

In the absence of a direct application of mimetic performance that engages the embodied persons of antagonists (just as successful performance requires an embodied practitioner), any transformation such as that which Coker portrayed in the character of his Virginian slavemaster lacks reality. The claim of transformation necessarily appears fantastic; lacking adequate cause, it is mysterious and even occult. Did Coker project that transformation out of sheer hope or desparate fancy? What act, process, or power could sufficiently account for such a change? To borrow a problem of causality from an older era in the physical sciences, what theory can explain such 'action at a distance'—in this case, the psychosocial distance between victims and their oppressors? As a matter of literary criticism Coker's text provides no adequate cause. He could not account for the Virginian's transformation but he represented it anyway, beyond any evident basis in reason, as the expected result of confronting a slaveholder with a slave who embodies the Christian gospel and its truth. Thus Coker projected what he could not explain, but what *should* work according to his theological convictions and his literary-shamanic intentions. That is to say, an authentic encounter with Christ in the person of his ministers or (suffering) servants should be converting.

Indeed, in the theological nature of Coker's expectation lies a phenomeno-logical indication of his role as a shamanic performer. Negatively stated, the text is magical-conjurational precisely because Coker projected such a con-version without adequate rationale, and in defiance of commonsensical expec-tation and ordinary experience. (Ordinary experience is represented, for ex-ample, in Stowe's *Uncle Tom's Cabin*, where Tom's purity of soul inspires a former master's piety but does not affect his final master or, in the end, secure Tom's freedom.) Indeed, the evidence against expecting such a transfor-mation is immediately available in Coker's story itself. The master of the abused slave is depicted as a direct witness to his slave's Christ-like per-formance (unlike the Virginian slavemaster who only hears the story told), yet there is no reported change in his intoxicated and abusive state. Positively speaking, however, Coker's text is shamanic because it effects or intends a psychosocial transformation based on embodied symbol production (Porter-field). On this view the slave is an embodied type of Christ (a suffering servant), whose *imitatio Christi* indirectly transforms the Virginian—in his role as Coker's (conjure) 'target' or (shamanic) 'client.' I will return to these role designations in the next section immediately below. But first let us examine the two loci of transformation: that of the victim and that of the victimizer.

(a) *The transformed victim.* Coker represents the slave as the medium of his own transformation: he encounters violence and victimization at the hands of his earthly master, and then counters that violence by treating it as a type of his *heavenly* Master's victimization. The spiritual, or ritual formula for such a transformation is given in Matthew's gospel in the words of Jesus spoken to his followers, and is quoted by the slave himself in his explicitly stated intention "to bear my cross, and take his yoke upon me" (Matt 11:29). As author, Coker plays upon the congruence between 'the crucified God' and the victimized slave, and makes the joy of that identification the basis of the slave's elation. In this manner the brute fact of undeserved suffering is transformed in a Chris-tological mode, based on the slave's Christ-like experience and response. That is, the slave experiences his own suffering as conformity to, or as mimetic participation in, the sufferings of Christ (as "the fellowship of his sufferings," Phil 3:10). He effectively reconfigures his suffering as Christian suffering ("If you suffer, it should not be as a murderer or thief. . . . However, if you suffer as a Christian, do not be ashamed, but praise God that you bear that name," 1 Pet

4:15–16). On that basis he virtually redeems—gets back restored or even exalted—his formerly mangled humanity.

The gospel ethic of reconciliation to enemies finds expression in the slave's return to his master's service, as he says, with "more submission" and with "more apparent love" than before. Although incredible in conventional terms, such reconciliation is normative for Christians in terms of the model or rule of Jesus as stated in the beatitudes, especially the commands, "Do not resist one who is evil" (Matt 5:39), and "Love your enemies, do good to those who hate you, bless those who curse you, pray for those who abuse you" (Luke 6:27–28). The substance of reconciliation here consists in regarding an enemy (not as a friend but) as an intimate participant in the effort to obey those commands. Is reconciliation on that basis merely fantastic, a self-delusion or pretense? On the contrary, I observe in such reconciliation a phenomenon of 'mimetic intimacy,' in which an enemy functions intimately as an accomplice in the process of one's own transformation. Insofar as one's enemy enables such transformation that enemy is an intimate in the process itself (albeit unwitting or alien in relation to its intent). I return to the concept of mimetic intimacy in treating Girard's theory of mimetic desire below. But first we must take up the risk involved in such intimacy: that the practitioner may involuntarily, despite transformative effects and precisely because of the invasive nature of violence, internalize the negation of one's humanity inherent in such an ordeal. In consideration of this risk I turn in the subsequent section to another version of suffering-servanthood in black religion: the slave as Uncle Tom.

(b) *The transformed victimizer.* The Virginian's transformation is indirect because he does not himself experience the slave's victimization. Nonetheless what he does experience, and to great effect (albeit for occult or occluded reasons) within the structure of Coker's narrative, is an oscillating correspondence between himself and two alternative forms of *alter ego.* The Virginian is confronted with a moment of decision, indeed, whether to identify himself with either the drunken, abusive slavemaster on the one hand, or the slave's "Dear Lord and Master" on the other. As potential versions of himself these alternative masters constitute tensions, tendencies or potencies within the Virginian's nexus of desire. The decision that confronts him consists in determining which master to desire as a model of his own actions: the conventional model of domination—the slave's "owner of my body," or instead the narrator's proffered alternative—the slave's "blessed master." We know from the Virginian's earlier protestations while listening to the African minister's story that he finds the former model repugnant; that he is predisposed to identify his own character with that alternative Master. The literary craft of Coker consisted in his ingenious representation of the folk religious (conjurational) strategy: to foster, exploit and augment such a predisposition in white Americans, so that they would be induced to prefer the latter model to the former.

The components of that transformative practice include compelling the intended 'target' of the performance somehow (here, via storytelling and despite resistance) to 'experience' a victimizer as his *alter ego* and therein to prefer a non-victimizing alternative. The effect is catalytic, but not apart from the accompanying element of the slave's imitation of Christ. Indeed, the cumulative effect of all the dynamic elements prompts the following phenomenological schema. The logic of the Virginian's transformation comprises a synergy in which: (1) a portrayal, representation or dramatization of (2) a victimizer's scapegoating behavior, alongside (3) a victim's imitation of Christ (4) induces, catalyzes or augments the observer's ability to identify with the latter and to dissociate himself from the former. Every element of this schema, I venture, is crucial for its transformative effect. Accordingly, for the dramatization to be compelling or efficacious a participant or observer must be confronted with both alternatives; with a clear choice between a victimizing and a non-victimizing role. Further, the dramatization must induce or catalyze the observer's ability to enact in current circumstances the latter role over against the former. I will take up an analytic treatment of this transformative prescription after reviewing Girard's theory of religion and violence in a subsequent section.

1.2 The slave as "Uncle Tom"

The reality of slave existence was brutal; a small assertion of one's humanity might result in death. The phrase, "No, massa, me no want to be free" (despite the risk of believing it oneself and internalizing white values) . . . is both a depravity and . . . can be a good, a means of survival.[7]

Debates about pathology in the Afro-American psyche usually include the stereotype of "Uncle Tom." The Uncle Tom figure emerged in popular culture from the literary-religious craft of Harriet Beecher Stowe, the nineteenth-century author and slavery abolitionist. From a balanced reading of Stowe's celebrated antislavery novel, *Uncle Tom's Cabin* (1852), we can retrieve her original, intended image of Uncle Tom as "the saintly, subservient slave who loved as he suffered; of the dutiful, abused servant who forgave unto seventy times seven, not because of truckling instincts but because he was a true Christian."[8] The Christian integrity of Stowe's character, however, deteriorated under subsequent popularization in the theatrical entertainments of the late nineteenth century. In minstrel shows across the country a caricature of Christian longsuffering emerged, in which "Uncle Toms groaned biblically under the lash. . . . Tom himself became a bobbing, bowing flunkey, a toady, a grotesque saint capable only of drugging his race into genteel apathy."[9] A

7 Cone, *The Spirituals and the Blues*, 28.
8 Fisher, Introduction, vi.
9 Fisher, Introduction, vi.

discrepancy exists therefore, between the servility of this caricature on the one hand and the nobility of character in many Christian slaves on the other. In this connection we do well to recall the character of Stowe's reputed model for Uncle Tom, Josiah Henson, an escaped slave, antislavery activist and author.

Henson was, according to commentator Walter Fisher, "a man many times larger than his fictional counterpart and many times nobler than the mean connotation which his name bears in the American language today."[10] So great a discrepancy between fiction and reality may indicate one form of the victimization of black people during the post-Reconstruction era in the United States. In that period Afro-American communities in the South were regularly subjected to lynchings, ritual immolations and random, unpunished murders. Character distortion in the popular imagination was symptomatic of more lethal forms of socially sanctioned violence. Yet this distortion can also be linked to a deficiency in Stowe's psychological foresight. Her strategy for overcoming ethnic prejudice in the minds of her reading audience was to stake everything on an idealized representation of Tom as the good Christian slave. Slaves were regarded as "good" if they behaved submissively to their masters in accordance with the apostle Paul's injunction in the New Testament: "Slaves, obey your earthly masters with fear and trembling, in singleness of heart, as you obey Christ. . . . Render service with enthusiasm, as to the Lord and not to men and women" (Eph 6:5,7). Inevitably the religious virtue of obedience was exploited by masters, missionaries and the slavery system to reinforce the slaves' docile compliance to their exploitation. Heedless of reinforcing this pernicious use of Christian scripture, Stowe's literary strategy depended on her readers' acclamation of such subservience as exemplary behavior in a slave.

It must also be admitted that slaves themselves were constantly at risk for internalizing this manipulative standard of behavior. A stunning example is provided in Henson's slave narrative, *Father Henson's Story of His Own Life*. In that narrative Henson recalls an incident in his role as overseer of the other slaves on his master's plantation. One night the slavemaster came to Henson's cabin, woke him from sleep and, in a great show of distress, entreated him to oversee the transporting of all the slaves from Maryland to Kentucky. "There were eighteen negroes, besides my wife, two children and myself, to transport nearly a thousand miles, through a country about which I knew nothing, and in mid-winter."[11] Henson knew that his master had mismanaged the estate, that his brother-in-law had initiated proceedings to take over, and that the master's character had deteriorated under the conditions of drunkeness, desperation, and the loss of all other resources. One sign of his extremity appeared in the master's condescending to beg his own slave to save him, as Henson

---

10 Fisher, Introduction, 5.
11 Henson, *Father Henson's Story*, 48.

recounts: "For two or three hours he continued to urge the undertaking, appealing to my pride, my sympathies, and my fears, and at last, appalling as it seemed, I told him I would do my best."[12]

Here Henson acknowledges quite explicitly that it was not his Christian virtue or Christ-like love for his master that prompted his assent. In contrast with Coker's slave as portrayed in the preceding section, Henson's natural passions of self-pride, fellow-feeling and pity, and finally fear for himself and his family's future were the motivating forces of his action. During the prolonged entreaty the master was clever enough to arouse those passions by various devices. He alternately praised Henson as the best of overseers, apologized for former abuses, and threatened that all the slaves might be separated or, worse, sold south to Georgia or Louisiana if Henson did not comply. And throughout this emotional barrage there recurred that unnerving event of solicitation "with urgency and tears, by the man whom I had so zealously served for over thirty years, and who now seemed absolutely dependent upon his slave."[13]

Given this cauldron of influences we are not surprised to learn that Henson was confronted with a dilemma when, during the journey north, the opportunity arose to free himself, his family, and the other slaves. Inadvertently crossing the Ohio river near Cincinnati, they were informed by the black residents that this was free territory and thus they need not return to bondage. Henson, suppressing his own desire for freedom and that of his party, commanded them all to continue: he successfully completed their transferral to Kentucky. Later Henson did indeed carry out his own escape and that of his family, and over a period of years participated in the Underground Railroad and assisted in the escape of numerous other slaves. Additionally he improved his learning and mastered literary expression. It is to that mastery that we owe the eloquence and self-penetration of this confession regarding that infamous day in Ohio:

> Often since that day has my soul been pierced with bitter anguish at the thought of having been thus instrumental in consigning to the infernal bondage of slavery so many of my fellow-beings. I have wrestled in prayer with God for forgiveness. Having experienced myself the sweetness of liberty, and knowing too well the after misery of numbers of many of them, my infatuation has seemed to me the unpardonable sin.[14]

This disavowal of his former deed is precisely the basis for regarding Henson, in the terms of the commentator cited above, as "many times larger than his fictional counterpart and many times nobler." For a person who repudiates former actions in such terms has acquired a capacity that remains unre-

---

12 Henson, *Father Henson's Story*, 47.
13 Henson, *Father Henson's Story*, 46.
14 Henson, *Father Henson's Story*, 53.

presented in Stowe's characterization: the capacity to discern the difference between obedience as a theological virtue and obedience due to psychosocial conditioning.

On the one hand Henson remembered thinking that releasing the slaves would be like stealing, and that ministers and religious speakers had often insisted upon "the duties of the slave to his master as appointed over him in the Lord." Also he recalled that, confronted with the enticements of freedom under such circumstances, "still my notions of right were against it."[15] Later he learned to console himself "with the thought that I acted according to my best light, though the light that was in me was darkness." In the final analysis, however, it appears that Henson came to acknowledge the very real conditioning of his mind under racist domination. That acknowledgment is most striking where, recounting the start of his journey with unusual autobiographical transparency, he revealed that "to all who asked questions I showed my master's pass, authorizing me to conduct his negroes to Kentucky, and often was the encomium of 'smart nigger' bestowed on me, to my immense gratification." Finally, Henson acknowledged the degree to which the anticipated approbation of his master confirmed his decision to be obedient.

> I had undertaken a great thing; my vanity had been flattered all along the road by hearing myself praised; I thought it would be a feather in my cap to carry it through thoroughly; and had often painted the scene in my imagination of the final surrender of my charge to master Amos, and the immense admiration and respect with which he would regard me.[16]

Here Henson has provided us with a self-analysis that confirms contemporary studies of individuals and groups who undergo the rigors of social domination. "They are at one and the same time themselves and the oppressor whose consciousness they have internalized," claims South American philosopher, Paolo Freire, in his *Pedagogy of the Oppressed* (1970). Freire's "consciousness they have internalized" has elsewhere been called "internalized oppression." Internalized oppression is an increasingly familiar psychosocial phenomenon, examined in differing terms by diverse studies that treat: the colonized mentality; the abused child or spouse; the concentration camp victim; the victims of cult conditioning or brainwashing; women and ethnic minorities undergoing social oppression, and so on.[17] Again, such internal-

---

15 Henson, *Father Henson's Story*, 51, 54.
16 Henson, *Father Henson's Story*, 49, 52.
17 Freire, *Pedagogy*, 32–33. On specifically Afro-American varients of this phenomenon see Lipsky, "Internalized Oppression," and Wilson Moses's discussion of the "universality of the experience of submission" in addition to the mimetic aspects of "the myth of Uncle Tom" in *Black Messiahs and Uncle Toms*, 58–60. Cf. the alternative figure of "Sambo" discussed in Elkins, *Slavery*—a discussion that generated controversy over the stereotypical and fictive status of this personality type; see also Elkins's comparison of slavery to concentration camp experience. For related analyses of the phenomenon of internalized

ization appears to be an involuntary or reflex phenomenon of the human psyche, to which a victim inevitably succumbs by assenting, to some degree, to a subordinate identity or role as imposed by an oppressor.

A promising course of inquiry for a future study would correlate the data of internalized behavior with René Girard's theory of mimesis and violence. Particularly fruitful would be Girard's concept of mimetic doubles, in which the desire to imitate each other establishes rivalry between two persons who alternate as models for each other's desires. Such reciprocity of desire more authentically reflects the Afro- and Euro-American relationship, which involves complex alternations of love and hate, imitation and rejection, and cooperation and rivalry (as in Henson's account of his conflicted feelings for his desperate master). A theory of imitation under the conditions of social domination might usefully account for Freire's observation that oppressed classes of people "have a diffuse, magical belief in the invulnerability and power of the oppressor."[18] Probably more familiar is the mimetic behavior of prisoners and captives as noted, for example, in the case of Nazi concentration camp victims: "Survivors are often accused of imitating SS behavior. Bruno Bettelheim has argued that 'old prisoners' developed 'a personality structure willing and able to accept SS values and behavior as its own.'"[19] Once again, however, I would stress the involuntary nature of such imitation.

> Having internalized the norms and values of the dominant group, members of an oppressed group often mistreat each other in an *unconscious* imitation of their own suffering. A dialectical perspective understands that *no oppressed group can remain immune* to the institutionalized and socially empowered untruths which purport to "justify" its oppression.[20]

All of these issues are raised, but then avoided, by Harriet Beecher Stowe in her figural creation of Uncle Tom. However well-intentioned Stowe's portrayal, the relative lack of complexity in her creation is exposed by the actual life story and anguished self-consciousness of Josiah Henson. Remarkably,

---

oppression among colonized subjects see Memmi, *The Colonizer and the Colonized* (Boston: Beacon Press, 1967), p. 187–188, and also Memmi's *Dominated Man*. On internalized oppression among concentration camp victims see Des Pres, *The Survivor* 116–117. Finally, for a definitive statement of the phenomenon and an extensive bibliographic citation see Sherover-Marcuse, *Emancipation and Consciousness*, 134–35, 144–45. See also Sherover-Marcuse's references to Herbert Marcuse's representation of internalized oppression as a "psychic Thermidor," and her reference to Anton Pannekoek's formulation of internalized oppression as a "secret power" or "*geistige* [spiritual] power" of the bourgeoisie within the German proletariat who, following the revolution of 1918, "rebuilt bourgeois domination with their own hands after it had collapsed" (134).

18 Freire, *Pedagogy*, 52–53. Freire's comment suggests an exploration which I am unable to pursue here: correlating the issue of internalized oppression with a discussion of mimesis and magic.

19 Des Pres, *The Survivor*, 116–117.

20 Sherover-Marcuse, *Emancipation and Consciousness*, 4. Emphasis mine.

Henson dared to expose his self-awareness before an often unsympathetic public, but Stowe lacked a corresponding courage in her fiction. To his credit Henson interrogated himself: Did I willingly serve and obey out of love of God, or due to an insidious domination to which I succumbed? It was precisely that complexity of self-interrogation that Stowe omitted in her central character, despite the testimony of Henson's narrative and her reported encounters with the man himself.[21]

Perhaps Stowe's characterization of Uncle Tom, by flattening out or fleeing from the complexity of such testimonies as that of Henson, bears significant responsibility for the false image that we retain today of black Christian virtue. It is the image of the docile slave and, now irrevocably, attaches to all black persons "whose behavior toward whites is regarded as fawning or abjectly servile."[22] Finally, Stowe's literary strategy was flawed in its assumption that a straightforward display of the undeserved suffering of the good and innocent is itself sufficient to counter their violation. For such an assumption does not take into account the pernicious and contagious nature of scapegoating as a principal form of victimization. From a more informed point of view, evidence of the innocence or virtues of a victim are far from constituting a bar to victimization; they can ironically activate and even attract scapegoating attacks. It happens not infrequently that the innocent and virtuous offer more malleable targets for the accusations to be fabricated against them. On this view Stowe's representation of black Christian heroism is inherently ambiguous: both valorizing and an incitement to new abuse. For she did not, and probably could not, anticipate how the appeal to pity can be worse than ineffectual; how the effort to establish a field of human sympathy, based solely on a portrayal of the suffering of the good or innocent, can backfire.

It may be anachronistic to expect that Stowe could foresee the degree to which her representations of pious submissiveness would attract and even augment victimization. But for our part *we* need not remain so naive. At least we should not be surprised that eventually the dominant response to Stowe's pious Tom became contempt, ridicule and further abuse. Indeed, within a few years of the international acclaim of her work the public entertainment tra-

---

21   According to Fisher, Stowe's novel was based on a fragment of Henson's autobiographical narrative, first published in 1849 and thus prior to Stowe's 1852 publication of *Uncle Tom's Cabin*. Fisher also reports that Stowe engaged in two conversations with Henson before writing her novel, in 1849 and again in 1850, and finally supplied a preface to the 1858 edition of *Father Henson's Story of His Own Life*. See Fisher's Introduction the 1962 edition of Henson's *Story*, previously cited. On the other hand, Wilson Moses argues that "it is very doubtful that the historical Josiah Henson really was the model for Uncle Tom," and cites the following sources for his view: Stowe's own publication, *The Key to Uncle Tom's Cabin* 42–45; and Winks, ed., *Autobiography*, xviii-xxii.

22   Fisher, Introduction, v, quoting *Webster's New World Dictionary of the American Language* (1951).

dition of minstrelsy, launched just a decade earlier,[23] seized upon the Tom character and exploited the novel's popularity for profits and comic effect. Ironically, it was precisely because of its popularity and success in aiding the antislavery movement that the novel "perpetuated stereotypical images of the black as surely and effectively as did any minstrel performance." To be sure, this result more directly derived from the songs that accompanied the stage versions of the novel. "Uncle Tom on stage had little in common with his characterization in the novel. The story was twisted to suit the purposes of the adaptors, who in many cases recognized and exploited comic features as commercial windfalls."[24]

But in addition to their profitability, we may surmise, the minstrel shows constituted ritual occasions for unanimity and catharsis through the public ridicule and laughter generated by the "Tom" caricature. That unanimous laughter still resounds the end of the present century, more than a hundred years later. Moreover, we are obliged to suspect a correlation between that laughter and its social context of racist violence. "Perhaps the best measure of Stowe's novel is the violent reaction it produced in her Southern contemporaries. Not only was the book banned throughout the South and anti-Tom literature issued, but on one occasion Mrs. Stowe received a package containing an ear severed from some unfortunate slave."[25] Such vengeful and capricious acts of violence were succeeded by, and consistent with, the nation's paroxysm of lynchings and live-body burnings decades later. The complexity of such violence is indicated by the routine nature of the attacks against black people, attended by their pervasive stereotyping in the comic tradition of minstrelsy—a stereotyping that continues in minstrelsy's successor forms of entertainment in twentieth-century vaudeville, film, and television portrayals. More insistently: the convergence of the nation's socially sanctioned murders, with its socially cathartic laughter, requires a kind of analysis that understands and anticipates such complexity. Such an analysis is readily available in René Girard's theory of ritual violence and scapegoating.

2. *Pharmakeus*

What is not yet available in Girardian theory, however, is an analytics of nonviolent transformation in history and culture. This is most disappointing given that the theory calls for such transformations and implicitly requires such analyses.[26] It provides a brilliant analytics of victimization, and a trans-

---

23 Dennison, *Scandalize My Name*, 88.
24 Dennison, *Scandalize My Name*, 172.
25 Dennison, *Scandalize My Name*, 172.
26 "There can no longer be any question of giving polite lip-service to a vague 'ideal of non-violence.' There can be no question of producing more pious vows and hypocritical formulae. Rather, we will more and more often find ourselves faced with an implacable

formative (nonsacrificial) hermeneutic of the Christian gospels, yet without a complementary treatment of ameliorative social and historical transformations based on those analyses or the gospels. Moreover, as an analytics of social violence Girardian theory does not seem disposed to address pragmatic or 'praxiological' questions. That indisposition, which some regard as an intellectual strength for a theory, on this view indicates the theory's most telling defect. Rather than belabor the matter we must treat deficiency as our own incentive to supply what is lacking: in this case to advance, in terms of a praxis of transformation, the project Girard has begun in terms of an analytics of sacrifice and a repristination of the gospels. With this turn toward praxis I attempt, in effect, to 'stand Girard on his head' in the way that Marx inverted Hegel's philosophy from speculative to praxial priorities.

In the turn to praxis I trust that I advance Girard's under-represented interests. Girard alludes to those interests in various places, yet without elaborating their implicit praxial dimension, as in the following 'prophecy.'

> There will be others, in any case, who will repeat what we are in the process of saying and who will advance matters beyond what we have been able to do. Yet books themselves will have no more than minor importance; the events within which such books emerge will be infinitely more eloquent than whatever we write and will establish truths we have difficulty describing and describe poorly, even in simple and banal instances. They are already very simple, indeed too simple to interest our current Byzantium, but these truths will become simpler still; they will soon be accessible to anyone.[27]

I must say that I detect here a disposition of *laissez-faire* that is at least morally questionable, and at worst jeopardizes the survival of our species by leaving the attainment of nonviolent cultures to chance occurrences. In fact, we need not wait for the future to bring about the immediate accessibility of nonviolent "truths." The present book is one of those written in the context of events of the recent past that make such truths accessible. The King movement of nonviolent civil disobedience, and its Gandhian predecessor movement among others, constitute precisely such events. Are we not obliged to create a literature, as one course among all the others at our disposal, that promotes the understanding and deepens the impact of such events? The present essay, at any rate, enjoins the creation of a literature that treats not only theory and analysis but also practice and application.

---

necessity. The definitive renunciation of violence, without any second thoughts, will become for us the condition *sine qua non* for the survival of humanity itself and for each one of us" (Girard, *Things Hidden*, 136–37). How to reconstitute cultures, for "the definitive renunciation of violence, without any second thoughts," is the issue of praxis that Girardian theory invites but then neglects.

27 Girard, *Things Hidden*, 135.

2.1 The *pharmakeus* as *pharmakos*

Our English cognate forms like pharmacy and pharmaceutic, pharmacology and pharmacopoeia, all derive from the Greek word, *pharmakon*. Most recently the double-valenced use of this word, to mean either medicine or poison or both at once, has been brilliantly expounded by Jacques Derrida in his extensive essay, "Plato's Pharmacy."[28] Indeed, Derrida's essay skillfully elaborates the three variant meanings of the Greek form: not only *pharmakos* (victim or scapegoat) and *pharmakon* (medicine/poison), but also *pharmakeus*, a sorcerer or magician. In this section we see how all three variants are highly significant for understanding African American experience. We have already traced the applicability of the *pharmakos*, or scapegoat variant, to black experience. Now it is illuminating to recall the second meaning, *pharmakon* or medicine/poison, and also to develop a third variant, *pharmakeus*, sorcerer or magician. In the black cultures of North America the *pharmakeus* is most commonly known by the vernacular terms, "conjuror," "conjure doctor" or "hoodoo doctor." Indeed, a consideration of the threefold variation of the Greek root suggests similar variations of the Latinate word, *conjure*. A correlation of *pharmakos*, *pharmakon*, and *pharmakeus*, with parallel aspects of Afro-American conjuration, would be highly advantageous. (Because the English word "conjure" has been appropriated and indigenized in Afro-American culture, it is crucial to retain it here. However, the Greek root and its variant meanings provide a useful threefold schema of conjure phenomena.)

The first variant proposed is (1) the conjure client, that is, a client who may be seeking redress from, or anticipating injury from, someone else (someone else's conjure), and hence a prospective or current victim—a *pharmakos* or where relevant a scapegoat. This formulation retrieves the Latin etymology of the term: the now obsolete meaning of conjuring as conspiring against someone in the sense of the word, *con-jurare*: to swear (conspire) together as does a 'jury' or as a group of witches or sorcerers casting spells against a victim. The second variant in the meaning of "conjure" is double-valenced, precisely like the curative/toxic meanings of the word, *pharmakon*. Just as a *pharmakon* is both medicinal and poisonous, so too are (2) conjure prescriptions, featuring a pharmacopeic repertory that includes both healing and harming substances (herbs and gravedirt, for example) and practices (both benign and malign tricks and spells).

Finally, the third variant follows from the first: in the etymological sense the *con-juror* is a 'juror,' one who swears by uttering an oath or spell for the purpose of sorcery, or who conspires with a client to aid or harm another by sorcerous utterances. Contrary to English conjure or sorcery traditions however, and consistent with the pharmacopeic reference above, (3) the Afro-

28 Derrida, *Dissemination*.

American conjuror is as much a healer or "doctor" as a sorcerer. Even malign conjure involves *materia medica*—natural and artificial materials such as herbs or whiskey—that are treated like medicinal prescriptions but for purposes of harming or poisoning. Rather than solely a system of magic spells, witchcraft, or sorcery, African-American conjure traditions are also healing traditions. Conjure is therefore conjunctive or holistic in the sense of joining together elements of a whole (a *gestalt*) that are conventionally bifurcated and opposed. To summarize: the three pharmaco-conjurational categories are (1) the *pharmakos* or conjure victim or client, (2) the *pharmakon* or conjure prescription, and (3) the *pharmakeus* or conjure practitioner. It is notable, in this regard, that the *pharmakos* (victim) and *pharmakeus* (practitioner) may coincide in the same person in those cases where the practitioner is also a target of malign phenomena requiring conjurational transformation. Notable as well is the coincidence of the *pharmakos* (victim) as an embodied *pharmakon* (tonic/ toxin), discussed in the final section below.

Martin Luther King, Jr., provides just such a case where the practitioner of transformation is also a victim. It must first be acknowledged, however, that according to Girardian theory the scapegoat is already an agent of transformation. This power is reflected in the apotheosis or divinization of figures who were formerly victims and scapegoats. Such an apotheosis is a recurrent pattern in both mythological and historical sources, and is based on the scapegoat's miraculous power to unite individuals and factions formerly at each other's throats. The transition of the same victim from criminal to hero, demigod or god, resides in the transformative power of the scapegoat. Precisely as the most accursed and toxic figure in the community, the scapegoat is able, by dying, to focus and purge the most virulent fears and animosities of the community.

> The effect of the scapegoat is to reverse the relationships between persecutors and their victims, thereby producing the sacred, the founding ancestors and the divinities. The victim, in reality passive, becomes the only effective and omnipotent cause in the face of a group that believes itself to be entirely passive.... If the relationships at the heart of these groups can deteriorate and then be reestablished by means of victims who are unanimously despised, obviously these groups will commemorate these social ills in conformance with the illusory belief that the scapegoat is onmipotent and facilitates the cure. The universal execration of the person who causes the sickness is replaced by universal veneration for the person who cures that same sickness.[29]

Examples of the sacralization of the scapegoat abound (see Girard's *The Scapegoat*). In the context of this chapter I cite only the most relevant case. The celebration of Martin Luther King, Jr., as a black American cultural hero,

---

29 Girard, *Scapegoat*, 44.

conforms to the pattern of the apotheosis of a victim. Admittedly, the aspects of criminality and divinization in the case of King cannot be as extreme or as developed in contemporary societies as they were for ancient or traditional cultures. (Precisely because we are more self-aware of scapegoating as well as sacralizing processes, such processes are less compelling for us.) Nevertheless, our increasing commemoration of King as a civil rights martyr sufficiently confirms the terms of this discussion. Jailed ostensibly for breaking laws as a practice of (nonviolent) civil disobedience, he also endured continuous harassment and investigation by agents of the Federal Bureau of Investigation for supposed communist alliances and treasonous activites. The F.B.I. also charged King with sexual transgressions or misconduct (adulterous and cross-ethnic) unbefitting a married man and a religious leader. In this connection he was similarly accused, years after his death, in the memoir of his former colleague and sometime rival, the Rev. Ralph David Abernathy.[30] Indeed, he was during his lifetime the object of intense intra-ethnic rivalry and public criticism among black church religious and political leaders, particularly in his hometown of Atlanta.

King's experiences therefore conform to that of the typical scapegoat who is accused of crimes most dangerous to the state and to civil society (communist allegiance during the Cold War), and who is the object of sexual suspicions and rumors if not convicted of transgressing the strongest taboos (here not incest or bestiality but Southern proscriptions barring black male and white female erotic relations). Of course we easily forget King's criminal persona as our (black and white) communities' scapegoat, because we are part of the culture that now apotheosizes him as the sacral agent of our social harmony. His eventual assassination culminated an extended sacrificial career (arrests, jailing, harassed marching, bombings, stoning in Chicago, a knifing incident, and so on); a career that enabled his society to consolidate civil rights legislation and egalitarian practices in a democratic culture that valued and espoused them. Even King's Nobel Peace prize served a salvific function for his country: by honoring the 'prophet' himself the prize 'saved the appearances' of the prophet's people, who could now be represented before the world as the sponsors of a national (Afro-*American*) will to fulfill vaunted democratic aspirations. In such terms we have yet to come to the end of our celebration and exaltation of this martyr to the nation's most sacred self-image and ideological commitments.

2.2 The *pharmakos* as nonviolent *pharmakon*

However, King was not only a *pharmakos* (victim) but also a *pharmakeus* (practitioner) and *pharmakon* (tonic/toxin). By the term *pharmakeus* I refer to his shamanistic ability to achieve the nonviolent amelioration of conflicted

---

30 Abernathy, *And the Walls Came Tumbling Down.*

situations for his client communities, specifically black communities under-going legalized discrimination and civil rights violations. The two features of shamanism most prominent in King's vocation are (1) the shaman's self-cure as a condition *sine qua non* of curative ability in relation to clients, and (2) the shaman's use of his or her own body as a site of "symbol production" in the curative process.[31]

As a practitioner of nonviolent religion in the Afro-American tradition, Martin Luther King, Jr., reenacted the gospel story in a salvific rather than a sacrificial mode. More precisely: the King movement induced participants and observers alike to perform their own imitation of a nonviolent model who saves rather than sanctions new victims. The movement achieved this distinction by crafting, on the streets and before the public media of the nation, ritualized reenactments of the gospel story in which a victim secures salvation for co-victims and victimizers alike, without thereby requiring or initiating the creation of new victims. Indeed, civil rights history attests that such performances were catalytic and widely transformative for current and future communities of victims and victimizers.

As we have seen, a crucial aspect of King's black Christian heritage was its mimetic or imitative features—its derivation from a long tradition of Christians practicing the imitation of Christ. In contradistinction to the conflictual mimesis presented in Girard's theory, King's imitation of Christ constituted a "good mimesis" that is nonconflictual and nonsacrificial.[32] On the one hand black participants in the movement faced the difficult problem: How do I overturn my victimization without creating a new class of victims (that is, how to resist nonviolently)? But the freedom movement addressed as well an equally agonizing problem in black religious history: How do I transform victimizers without incurring the internalized effects of abuse? The solution that emerges from this study is a conjure prescription that consists of the embodied person as a tonic/toxic *pharmakon*. The cure prescribed is homeopathic on the basis of a nonviolent model, in which the victim's own body and person serves as *materia medica*—toxic to the victimizer if violation ensues, but tonic if victims are saved. To this end public displays of victimization were devised in which any violation of the victims' bodies would clearly reveal their scapegoat status. In such displays precisely what is toxic for victimizers if abuse

---

31 Porterfield, "Shamanism," 725–26. In Porterfield's view shamanism is personally *embodied* symbol production for the purpose of psychological and social *conflict resolution*. With reference to psychic conflicts it is instructive to note that shamans have often been the subject of their own curative abilities. To repeat Porterfield's emphasis we may say that the shaman personally embodies his or her own therapy. Studies of the shaman as a neurotic, and shamanic insight as analogous to schizophrenia, have stressed the pathological aspect of the shamanic personality. But balanced observers also stress the curative dimension: "As Eliade puts it, the shaman is not merely a sick man [sic] but a sick man who has been cured and has become an agency of curative powers." Hughes, "Shamanism and Christian Faith," 395–96. Cf. Eliade, *Shamanism*.

32 Spariosu, *Mimesis*, ix–x, xv–xvi, 97, 100.

occurs—that is, public recognition of their identity as persecutors and scapegoaters—can become tonic if scapegoating is terminated and prospective victims are saved.

As the preceding sections show, the essential structure of this remedy was imitation of a nonviolent model by both victims and victimizers brought together in 'mimetic intimacy.' Moreover we may infer that the essential practice was bequeathed to King and his generation by slave practitioners and their spiritual heirs during succeeding periods of American social history. But what King and his colleagues discovered, as perhaps the most proficient practitioners of the tradition to date, were ritual performances that reduced the contaminating side-effects of this cure for the victims themselves. The examples of Coker's slave and Stowe's Uncle Tom evince a possible side-effect for victims who practice the *imitatio Christi*. It is possible to make the sacrificial misconstrual that it is the victim's suffering or even destruction that is desired by God or that is efficacious for transformation. On the contrary, King's practices avoided mere martyrdom or provocation leading to the conspicuous abuse or self-sacrifice of victims. Implicitly in the movement was the principle that Girard's theory states explicitly: that what is actually transformative is an exposé of the scapegoating process itself. In this regard proficient ritualists like King have crafted public performances that steer participants between the deficiency of passive displays on the one hand, and the excesses of provoking and internalizing more abuse on the other.[33]

This discussion represents King as a consummate conjurational performer in the African American tradition. Although he showed that he was mindful of excesses to be avoided (and although he was constantly reminded of such excesses by his critics), he nonetheless proceeded to craft social rituals of ecstatic suffering. Such displays were ecstatic because they enabled victims to be transformed from mere sufferers (from their *status quo*) into heroes. Thereby he also countered their internalized self-disesteem. At the same time those public demonstrations enabled observers and even protagonists to become converts and allies rather than persecutors. The freedom movement contrived such demonstrations in the form of agonized (compare the Greek, *agon*) festivals, during which masses of participants and, vicariously, an observant nation were initiated into an 'ecstatics' of self-sacrifice. Television viewing of police brutality against participants 'awoke the conscience of a nation' (King), leading to federal legislation and a new public ethos that has irrevocably ameliorated the victimization of black Americans.

Of course, as with any repertory of practices, King's public performances were not always efficacious. (Such performances are as much a matter of improvisation, trial-and-error, and experiential proficiency as we find in the

---

33 For illuminating discussions of this and other principles of nonviolent activism see especially Bondurant, *Conquest of Violence*, Hanigan, *Martin Luther King, Jr.*, Sharp, *The Politics of Nonviolent Action*.

practice of any discipline, skill or art; hence the need for new and increasingly more proficient practitioners is an ongoing need, more urgent and not less.) But where such performances succeeded they provided alternative rites for a society that has become highly self-conscious of, and scandalized by, its own propensities for scapegoating. Indeed, this heightened state of public consciousness has become increasingly sensitive and pliable in the modern period. This is a fact that Girard acknowledges as both hopeful and problematic; problematic in that, wherever we fail to provide more effective, non-sacrificial means for resolving the conflicts that scapegoating conventionally addressed, populations tend to seek more effective and catastrophic sacrificial means such as totalitarian and reactionary societies employ. In most western societies it is now hypothetically possible, however intractable events may prove in practice, to influence social opinion toward terminating continued assaults on clearly designated victims. Yet precisely this state of affairs also bears its problematic aspects.

Our peculiar contemporary danger is that a reductive use of performative mimesis—the superficial imitation of King's tactics, for example—eviscerates and deforms the tradition of nonviolent religious activism that we have examined. A limited focus on techniques and strategies can become manipulative and self-serving, and hence contrary to the spirituality of Afro-Christian tradition as a source of American social activism generally. Since the black freedom movement of the fifties and sixties we have witnessed an increasingly self-interested and non-transformative employment of ritual activism. I do not mean simply that a loss of religious content, rhetoric or observances has occurred. Indeed, protest marches and other public demonstrations can easily display an explicit religious and moral commitment. The practitioners may nonetheless lack the ability to create mimetic intimacy between the conflicted parties based on their mutual imitation of a nonviolent model. Because they neglect to display for public view a model of transformation like the *imitatio Christi* or a mimesis of comparably efficacy, they inevitably perpetuate rivalry and conflict regardless of other measures of success.

Following the black freedom movement and the anti-Vietnam war activism of King and other religious leaders, the United States has witnessed similar forms of public protest that draw upon predecessor traditions. Activists involved in these successor movements have learned that ritual forms of activism involve performative and symbolic aspects that are highly effective for influencing public opinion. They may nonetheless neglect to give attention to the primal and sometimes volatile mechanisms of ritual as presented in Girardian theory on the one hand, and to the genuinely transformative potential of ritual as displayed in Afro-Christian practice on the other. Such practitioners may, for example, realize and exploit the incantatory power of biblical or religious symbols and representations. They may still lack a more profound grasp of the efficacy of a nonviolent model like the *imitatio Christi*, and of its transformative power for both victims and victimizers in American culture.

The prospect for more proficient performances of such indigenous traditions of 'mimetic alchemy' depends on the continuing emergence of practitioners who understand the kind of pharmacopoeic and conjurational dynamics examined above. Cultures of nonviolence still require leaders who are not only initiates themselves in such practices, but who can initiate and induce others to participate in the transformative processes. But what are the prospects for the large scale amelioration of social patterns of domination that victimize and scapegoat target groups? Here we differ from Girard who maintains a pessimistic view of social change on such a scale. Against that pessimism (otherwise called realism) we may invoke the black religious experience of curing racism which, though not completely successful, involves a centuries-long quest for individual and mass transformations.

No one can deny this tradition its efficacy, neither political radicals nor radical theorists. The tradition still conveys the spirituality that has sustained a people from its experience of chattel slavery in the past, to its present survival under more sophisticated and perhaps more intractable forms of domination and victimization. Rather, on this question of prospective effectiveness it is appropriate to adopt a heuristic disposition, supported by historical and ongoing evidence from all cultures of nonviolence. We can continue the quest for more and more efficacious means of transformation, and use this praxis to review and revise Girardian and other theories of social violence. On this view theory is supplementary to a praxis that poses the consummate human project of our time and all history. It is credible that the cascading impact of multiple communities engaged in that praxis could transform the human prospect in the foreseeable future.

Victims on Violence

"DIFFERENT VOICES" AND GIRARD

Chris Shea

Abstract

René Girard has articulated a theory of violence that directs our attention to its victims with unusual intensity. This emphasis is implicit in titles such as *The Scapegoat* and *Job: The Victim of His People*. In these and other works Girard claims to overturn the accounts of violence as told by perpetrators. He seems engaged in restoring the truth of victims as arbitrarily selected "scapegoats"—selected not essentially because of crimes against society but because they bear certain marks or "stereotypes of persecution." Upon closer scrutiny, however, Girard himself can be seen to advance an arbitrary view of violence, representative of a specific class of persecutors: men. Male views of violence predominate in Girard's theory as elsewhere in Western intellectual history and discourse. Ironically, in his victim-centered theory Girard does not attend to the particular group of victims whose experience and view of violence threatens to overturn his theory: women.

This critique of Girard's work focuses more on gender studies than on religious studies. The implications, of course, are compelling for theories of religion as well. The chapter juxtaposes to Girard's theory the social research of Carol Gilligan in the area of gender and moral development. Gilligan's book, *In a Different Voice*, is presented in order to add the missing voice of women to Girard's one-sided view of social violence. A concluding section connects the discussion to Alice Walker's "womanist" perspective on curing violence in her novel, *The Color Purple*.

1. Introduction

The value for me in an examination of René Girard's work is not that I believe that his theory, in a presentation unalloyed by skepticism, offers a panacea for violence. Nor do I find convincing his claims for the universality of the workings of "mimetic desire," his "scapegoat mechanism," or the "founding murder." What can be instructive about Girard's work, to my mind, is its revelation of the way that certain of society's institutions, particularly religious institutions, *think* about violence.

As a place to begin to think about the mythology of violence, therefore, Girard's work can be invaluable, but only as a beginning. Girard's work is not without its difficulties. In this essay I propose to deal with one of the major problems raised by his thesis.

1.1 On victims

In *The Scapegoat* Girard lays out his "stereotypes of persecution." These are those groups in society most likely to be singled out as victims: (1) children, (2) old people, (3) those with physical abnormalities, (4) women, members of (5) ethnic or (6) racial minorities, (7) the poor, and (8) those whose natural endowments (beauty, intelligence, charm) or status (wealth, position) mark them as exceptional.[1] Girard is content to list these types together, although there would seem to be several significant divisions possible within this group. That is, we might sort out those whose circumstances have made them victims, but who also have or have had the opportunity to be persecutors. For example, boy children may grow up to be persecutors, old men may have been persecutors earlier in their lives, or those who find themselves in a minority may seek out a place where their kind is numerically dominant. We might also identify two more groups: those "born to be" victims (women or those with congenital deformities), and those who may chose to avoid victimage (beauty, intelligence, talent, wealth may be concealed, after all).

Having identified these stereotypes Girard goes on through successive volumes, in *Things Hidden* and in *Job*, to focus in particular on those who have been selected out for scapegoating because of their exceptional gifts or special status in society. Oedipus and Pentheus in Euripides' *The Bacchae* are kings, for example; elsewhere Girard takes great pains to establish Job as the leader of his people; compare the subtitle in *Job: The Victim of His People*. But in the list of stereotypes of persecution these would seem to be special cases: they have apparently come to prominence as the leaders of the persecutors, since it is the persecutors who control the victimage mechanism. Of all those on the list, therefore, they might be thought to be the ones who could most readily avoid victimage. There is also in those cases a plausible explanation for their victimage in addition to Girard's "cycle of mimetic violence:" a "revenge of the victims" motif. Consider, for example, Pentheus and the Bacchae,[2] or the recent execution of President Nicolae Ceausescu in Romania.

1.2 Different voices

Girard seems rather indifferent to the voices of those who, by virtue of finding victimage a permanent and inescapable condition, might be supposed

---

1 Girard, *Scapegoat*, Chapter 2.
2 This may be why Girard chooses rather perversely to regard the Bacchae as "a mythological substitution of women for men in regard to violence" (*Violence and the Sacred*, 139), which keeps the plot firmly in the realm of "mimetic violence." See below, section 2.2.

to have the most experience of persecution—women and "cripples." Although women must comprise the largest constituency of any pool of victims, although their exhaustive experience with persecution in every stage of their lives, in every time, in every place might be imagined to produce insights into the system worthy of note, and although they have produced a considerable body of literature, still Girard devotes a negligible portion of his work to the voice of these victims.[3]

This is an unfortunate omission, since he has by this created a closed system in which literature and myth express either the view of (1) persecutors justifying the actions of persecutors, or (2) persecutors sympathizing with the victims of their fellow persecutors. In discussing either type of literature or myth, Girard has not dealt with questions that are often identified as peculiar to the traditional victims in society, for example: Why me? Have I done something to deserve this? Is it proper for me to do to others what has been done to me?

Elsewhere in this volume my colleagues (Theophus Smith and Cheryl Kirk-Duggan prominent among them) have addressed just such questions. Their sensitivity and gentle humanity go a long way toward rectifying Girard's omissions. I would like to join Cheryl Kirk-Duggan particularly in presenting the views of those perennial victims, women, with the intent of restoring the voice lost to Girard's worldview. I propose to set alongside Girard's construct two works: Harvard Professor of Education Carol Gilligan's *In a Different Voice* and Alice Walker's *The Color Purple*, also discussed in Kirk-Duggan's fine analysis (see ch. 13).

2. Gilligan's Problem

In an already classic piece of analysis, Gilligan presents a problem encountered in administering Lawrence Kohlberg's series of tests designed to measure moral development from childhood to adulthood. The responses of two eleven-year-olds to a dilemma posed by the examiner sparked Gilligan's interest. Her description of the procedure:

A man named Heinz considers whether or not to steal a drug which he cannot afford to buy in order to save the life of his wife. In the standard format of Kohlberg's interviewing procedure, the description of the dilemma itself—Heinz's predicament, the wife's disease, the druggist's refusal to lower his price—is followed by the question, "Should Heinz steal the drug?" The reasons for and

---

3 The only work written by a woman to which he alludes is Mme. de Lafayette's *La princesse de Clèves* (*Deceit*); the relationship of Herodias and Salome (*Scapegoat*) is his only example of mother-daughter interaction (and they are hardly typical); Proust is cited as spokesperson for the feminine point of view (see below, section 2.2). For a complete discussion of this point, see Moi, "The Missing Mother," 23–25.

against stealing are then explored through a series of questions that vary and extend the parameters of the dilemma in a way designed to reveal the underlying structures of moral thought.[4]

Jake's response. Gilligan focused her attention particularly on two of the sixth-grade respondents, Jake and Amy. Jake's response:

> For one thing a human life is worth more than money, and if the druggist only makes $1,000, he's still going to live, but if Heinz doesn't steal the drug, his wife is going to die.[5]

Gilligan reports Jake's elaboration:

> Asked whether Heinz should steal the drug if he does not love his wife, Jake replies that he should, saying that not only is there a "difference between hatred and killing," but also, if Heinz were caught, "the judge would probably think it was the right thing to do . . . the laws have mistakes, and you can't go writing up a law for everything that you can imagine."
>
> Fascinated by the power of logic, this eleven-year-old boy locates truth in math, . . . "the only thing that is totally logical." Considering the moral dilemma to be "sort of like a math problem with humans," he sets it up as an equation and proceeds to work out the solution.[6]

Amy's response. Gilligan suggests that, by Kohlberg's standards, Amy's response presents:

> a very different impression, an image of development stunted by a failure of logic, and inability to think for herself. . . . [S]he replies in a way that seems evasive and unsure.[7]

Amy's response to "Should Heinz steal the drug?":

> Well, I don't think so. I think there might be other ways besides stealing it, like if he could borrow the money or make a loan or something, but he really shouldn't steal the drug—but his wife shouldn't die either. . . . If he stole the drug he might save his wife then, but if he did, he might have to go to jail, and then his wife might get sicker again, and he couldn't get more of the drug, and it might not be good. So, they should really just talk it out and find some other way to make the money.[8]

Pressed by the interviewer, Amy clings to her assertion that Heinz should *both* not steal the drug *and* save his wife, proposing that the druggist should

4 Gilligan, *Different Voice*, 25–26.
5 Gilligan, *Different Voice*, 26.
6 Gilligan, *Different Voice*, 26.
7 Gilligan, *Different Voice*, 27–28.
8 Gilligan, *Different Voice*, 28.

just give it to the wife and then have the husband pay back the money later. . . . If Heinz and the druggist had talked it out long enough, they could reach something besides stealing.[9]

Jake's answer earns him a score of between 3 and 4 in the Kohlberg construct of six stages of moral development (six is the highest score); Amy's response is scored a full stage lower (between 2 and 3).

2.1 Gilligan's analysis

Gilligan noted, in analyzing the pre-teens' interviews in the conventional manner,[10] that Amy had heard a different question from the one posed by the interviewer. Amy responded to "Should Heinz *steal* the drug?" while Jake and the interviewer were united in the assumption that the central question was "*Should* Heinz steal the drug?"[11]

In ferreting out the premises underlying Jake's and the interviewer's (and Kohlberg's and moral philosophy's) understanding of the problem, Gilligan made a series of observations about the question and Jake's response:

1. Jake factors into his solution the law, acknowledging its power to preserve order, while conceding its limitations ("the laws have mistakes");[12]
2. he assumes others are equally in agreement with the proposition that laws may be broken as with the notion that stealing is wrong ("the judge would probably think it was the right thing to do");[13]
3. he equates moral problems with mathematical ones, presuming that such dilemmas have solutions, that they are solved in the manner of equations ("sort of a math problem with humans"), and that the same solution will be derived by all who apply logic to the problem ("the judge will probably think it was the right thing to do"), although, when considering whether there is a right answer to moral problems, he realizes "there can only be right and wrong in judgment";[14]
4. the question takes the mode of action (stealing) for granted, presuming it to be a likely solution to the problem.[15] ,

About Amy's construct of the problem, Gilligan notes:

1. Amy sees the narrative not as a "self-contained problem in moral logic" but as the initial step in a process which has consequences into the future ("he might save his wife then, . . . he might have to go to jail, . . . his wife might get sicker, and he couldn't get more of the drug");[16]

---

9 Gilligan, *Different Voice*, 29.
10 Gilligan and Kohlberg have been collaborators; see their "The Adolescent as a Philosopher: The Discovery of the Self in a Post-Conventional World," *Daedalus* 100 (1971): 1051–86.
11 Gilligan, *Different Voice*, 31.
12 Gilligan, *Different Voice*, 26.
13 Gilligan, *Different Voice*, 26.
14 Gilligan, *Different Voice*, 26–27.
15 Gilligan, *Different Voice*, 31.
16 Gilligan, *Different Voice*, 29.

2. she finds soliciting the cooperation of the druggist (or others) the most reasonable solution and assumes that on consultation others would willingly provide assistance ("if Heinz and the druggist had talked it out long enough, they could reach something besides stealing");[17]
3. she defines morality as "the recognition of responsibility for one another, a perception of the need for response";[18]
4. "she assumes the necessity for action and considers what form it should take."[19]

Gilligan's conclusions deserve extended quotation:

> In resolving Heinz's dilemma, Jake relies on theft to avoid confrontation and turns to the law to mediate the dispute. Transposing a hierarchy of power onto a hierarchy of values, he defuses a potentially explosive conflict between people by casting it as an impersonal conflict of claims. In this way he abstracts the moral problem from the interpersonal situation, finding in the logic of fairness an objective way to decide who will win the dispute. But this hierarchical ordering, with its imagery of winning and losing and the potential for violence which it contains, gives way in Amy's construction of the dilemma to a network of connection, a web of relationships that is sustained by a process of communication. With this shift, the moral problem changes from one of unfair domination, the imposition of property over life, to one of unnecessary exclusion, the failure of the druggist to respond to the wife.[20]

2.2 Gilligan's thesis and Girard

I take the time to cite at length Gilligan's exegesis because I believe her book makes an important point: many theorists of social, psychological, and moral development in the West, while anxious to claim universality, have been faced with the impossibility of molding women's experience to their models. Rather than abandon their theories, however, they have either dismissed women's experience or downgraded it. For a concrete example, Gilligan cites Freud:

> The penchant of developmental theorists to project a masculine image, and one that appears frightening to women, goes back at least to Freud (1905), who built his theory of psychosexual development around the experiences of the male child that culminate in the Oedipus complex. . . . After trying to fit women into his masculine conception, seeing them as envying that which they missed, he came instead to acknowledge, in the strength and persistence of women's pre-Oedipal attachments to their mothers, a developmental difference . . . responsible for what he saw as women's developmental failure. . . . Freud concluded that women "show less sense of justice than men, that they are less ready to submit to the great

17 Gilligan, *Different Voice*, 29.
18 Gilligan, *Different Voice*, 30.
19 Gilligan, *Different Voice*, 31.
20 Gilligan, *Different Voice*, 32.

exigencies of life, that they are more often influenced in their judgements by feelings of affection or hostility."[21]

That Girard's works derive ultimately from the same tradition is indisputable—he refers extensively to Freud's works, for example; his "triangular desire" is an obvious variant of the Oedipal triangle.[22] Like Freud, too, unable to fit women comfortably into his schematization of human desire and loath to retract his assertions of the "truth" of his interpretation, he simply dismisses women from his "community."[23] Thus, *The Bacchae* of Euripides is no longer about the Bacchae, the women followers of Dionysus who tear to pieces the intruder Pentheus, but about some male band who, driven mad by "mimetic rivalry," do the dirty deed.[24]

Moreover, Girard has neglected, in the discussion of the scapegoat and Greek tragedy, his own best example: Euripides' *Medea*.[25] Here is a character who bears more of the marks of persecution (see section 1.1 above) than Oedipus or Pentheus; she is a woman, a stranger, of an ethnic (perhaps racial) minority, distinguished by special gifts (Medea means "the cunning one") and status (as a foreign princess, descendant of the Sun, and possessed of gold beyond the dreams of the Greeks around her). She is being forced into exile by the King of Corinth who fears her (at this point in the tale she is innocent of any wrongdoing). The myth accuses her of murdering the King, his daughter, and her own two sons.

By the rules of Girard's own construct, the drama should conceal the history of a leader scapegoated by her own people. Women, however, are outside the circle of mimetic violence, and Girard dismisses the protagonist with a comment about "Medea's insane behavior." Surely this is persecutors' talk here— why has Medea *really* killed her children, while Oedipus is a holy innocent, slandered by the mob?

However, it is not only that Girard, having classified women as universal victims (since they are born inescapably to their fate), appears uninterested in their plight as the victims of mimetic violence. Having ignored for the most part the literature produced by and about women—he is indifferent to their place within his theory—he is also apparently reluctant to use women's perceptions to test his conclusions. Thus he constructs a faintly ludicrous argu-

21 Gilligan, *Different Voice*, 6–7.
22 Toril Moi ("The Missing Mother," 30–31) suggests that Girard feels Oedipal hostility toward Freud.
23 *Girard, *Violence and the Sacred*, 140. He goes on to justify the exclusion of women, "The role played by women in the religious and cultural structure of a society—or rather the minor importance of that role—is graphically illustrated by the social framework prevailing in certain South American villages. . . . " His point is expressed more forcefully in the 1972 Grasset edition: "leur absence de rôle" has been replaced in the English translation by the more palatable "the minor importance of their role."
24 See above, n. 3.
25 Girard, *Violence and the Sacred*, 9.

ment for permitting Proust—whose women are notoriously males in disguise—to speak for women.[26]

What might he have learned, had he stopped to ask? I have some further observations about Gilligan's theory and examples.

2.3 Heinz's dilemma, revisited

Heinz's dilemma is, from one point of view, a curious problem to pose to sixth-graders. The question is loaded in an attempt to limit the choices of action to two: to steal or not to steal. This is, of course, contrary to what common sense would dictate; the question seems to favor the least viable solution. Consider the response of your neighbors and kin when they discover you chose breaking-and-entering (surely the drug is not an over-the-counter preparation that might be shoplifted) over borrowing the money from them or making some arrangement for repayment with the druggist. Therefore, one might be forgiven for understanding the question as a test of honesty. That is, the correct response is to hold out as long as possible for those solutions which do not involve breaking the law.

Ah, but it isn't a real problem, is it? It's a hypothetical situation from a hypothetical world which both Jake and the interviewer understand. Amy erred in locating Heinz and his wife in the real world.[27] In this hypothetical world, we might argue:

1. everyone acts alone, without parents, neighbors, friends, co-workers, kin (Heinz's wife is apparently helpless);
2. strangers are assumed to be hostile (the druggist refuses to lower his price);
3. breaking the law is not only a reasonable solution to a problem, it's the only solution.

But, we might argue, although this world does not resemble the world we know, still it is an appropriate venue for what may be the true question concealed in Heinz's dilemma: not "How should Heinz solve his problem?" or even "Is it proper to steal?" (the questions Amy may have been answering) but "Are you prepared to break the law when the occasion warrants?" or (deeper still) "Do you know when violence is justified?" In other words, we might put a cynical interpretation on Heinz's dilemma and label it a quiz from the guerilla-leader-in-training school of moral development, saying in effect, "We want

---

26 See above, n. 3.

27 Gilligan hints at this in *Different Voice*, 69: "women's judgments are tied to resolution of real, as opposed to hypothetical dilemmas." She cites in support Norma Haan's 1975 and Constance Holstein's 1976 studies which she summarizes as indicating "moral judgments of women differ from those of men." For a fuller discussion, see also Gilligan, *Different Voice*, 100–101.

    I might argue that Gilligan's insights about moral judgment need not be dichotomized into a gender issue; she might concede that men are under some pressure to express opinions in conformity with the "party line" of society's expectations, just as women are.

you to obey the law, but we also want you to exhibit the initiative, guts, and independence you may need as a leader in the never-ending battle against authoritarian oppression." Since, in general, society is not particularly concerned to enroll women in the Future Freedom Fighters of America, we might perhaps leave room for other interpretations, or at least alternate that question with this one, "Should Heinz ask someone for help?" and brand as morally deficient all those who answer, "No, he should handle it himself, even if it means stealing the drug."

3. Different Worlds

Girard's world. It is a world like the world of Kohlberg's problem, I would contend, which Girard's theory inhabits. In the claustrophobic confines of the cycle of mimetic violence:

1. all desire leads to conflict. The question asked, in Kohlberg's terms, is not "Should you *victimize?*" but "*Should* you victimize?" That is, no other course of action is admitted as viable. Thus, faced with an Other who appears in superior position, in possession of a desired object, an individual is not allowed to feel indifference (and walk away), fear (and run away), admiration (for the Other's superiority), love (for the Other for his superiority), or any other emotions but jealousy to the point of open hostility;

2. no man has friends, neighbors, kin, or allies who might attempt to halt his victimization. Although Girard appeals to tribal societies for examples and gives his "founding murder" the patina of the primitive, and although we are apparently to imagine ourselves in a time and place where strangers, for example, are automatically the object of barbarous cruelties (as in some worst-case Neolithic village), we are at the same time apparently to imagine ourselves in a time and place where ties of kinship have eroded to the point where a family would permit its old, handicapped, or female members to be brutally murdered by neighbors, second-cousins, or schoolmates, that is, in some nightmarish megalopolis;

3. no one ever learns from experience. Although apparently all persecutors were once victims (as children) and will eventually return to that status (as elders), no one learns compassion or empathy or altruism or even an escape hatch from the gruesome system of which all are potentially victims. Trust no one;

4. laws which represent the collective wisdom of centuries of humanity are nonetheless powerless to solve the problem of mimetic violence, and all people are, in any case, eager to violate those laws which do attempt, however futilely, to control violence.

Amy's world. Neither the world of Kohlberg's problem nor the world of

Girard's theory has much in common with Amy's world, as Gilligan describes it (see above, section 2.1):

> a world of relationships and psychological truths where an awareness of the connection between people gives rise to a recognition of responsibility for one another, a perception of the need for response . . . [where Amy's] understanding of morality as arising from the recognition of relationship, her belief in communication as the mode of conflict resolution, and her conviction that the solution to [Heinz's] dilemma will follow from its compelling representation seem far from naive or cognitively immature.[28]

Jake's world. Of course, Heinz, not Jake, inhabits the world of Kohlberg's problem. Presumably Kohlberg, the interviewer, and Jake are all perfectly aware of this; they understand the narrative to represent a hypothetical situation in a hypothetical world, to be, in fact, a story or myth. The respondent is not asked, for example, to imagine himself in that situation, an instruction which would have elicited from Jake a greater variety of solutions to the problem, perhaps, or a more tenacious insistence on the strictures of conventional morality. That Jake at least recognizes that he has been asked to locate Heinz in an alternate reality is obvious when he says later, when asked to "describe the person you are in a way that you yourself would know it was you":

> I'd [say] that I don't believe in crime, except for when your name is Heinz.[29]

We might argue here that Amy has put herself into Heinz's place and responded from the perspective of her own (real) world. That is, she has heard the question as "What would you do if you were Heinz?" Jake, on the other hand, might be thought to have responded from the standpoint of a scriptwriter. That is, he has interpreted the problem as a scenario for an upcoming movie-of-the-week and responded with the choice which would make the most interesting story.

If most male respondents feel free to inject the elements of skilled storytelling (suspense, foreshadowing, innocent heroes and dastardly villains, etc.) into their responses to hypothetical moral situations, then such exercises may be invalid in assessing their personal tolerance of violence, for example.

4. Stories of Violence

Gilligan and Pollack in a 1982 study have done their male students an injustice, for example, when they dwelt on the "seemingly bizarre imagery of violence" which cropped up in their writing. In one exercise in which students

---

28 Gilligan, *Different Voice*, 30.
29 Gilligan, *Different Voice*, 33–34.

were asked to write a "story" about a picture of a couple seated peacefully on a bench alongside a river, more than 21 percent of 88 male respondents wrote stories featuring violence. None of the 50 women did. Gilligan cites this tale as typical:

> Nick saw his life pass before his eyes. He could feel the cold penetrating ever deeper into his body. How long had it been since he had fallen through the ice— thirty seconds, a minute? It wouldn't take long for him to succumb to the chilling grip of the mid-February Charles River. What a fool he had been to accept the challenge of his roommate Sam to cross the frozen river. He knew all along that Sam hated him. Hated him for being rich and especially hated him for being engaged to Mary, Sam's childhood sweetheart. But Nick never realized until now that Mary also hated him and really loved Sam. Yet there they were, the two of them, calmly sitting on a bench in the riverbend, watching Nick drown. They'd probably soon be married, and they'd probably finance it with the life insurance policy for which Mary was the beneficiary.[30]

We do not suppose the student composed his tale from a desire to escape reality by casting himself as Nick who is, after all, dying in a particularly horrible way. We assume the student approached the assignment with no interest other than in making the "story" more intriguing to his audience.

When Gilligan goes on to adduce this piece as evidence of men's "association of danger with intimacy," we may feel that she has perhaps fuzzied the boundary between reality and fiction. After all, if the student had been asked, "when you and your girlfriend last did this, how did you feel?" his response might have been more in line with the women's answers.

Girard too, it seems to me, is guilty of confounding responses to case histories presented as hypothetical (literature, we might say) and responses to case histories presented as real (history or psychology, we might say). That "Put out his eyes" is the response to the moral conundrum, "Oedipus has killed his father and married his mother. What should he do?" is perhaps best read as a reflection of the myth-maker's desire to shock his audience into response. That Girard can identify a large body of literature in which murder plays a prominent part is not surprising. But it is also not surprising that few mystery novels deal with any crime other than murder; it is not because locked-door murders in English country houses are common in life, but because only murder seems important enough for the sleuth's (and story-teller's) attention.

4.1 Gilligan and the scapegoat paradigm

Because Girard has chosen to argue that literature and myth are somehow truer than other descriptions of human behavior, perhaps we should best

---

30 Gilligan, *Different Voice*, 40.

present the point of view of women from a work of literature, rather than from the experiments of a social scientist (although Girard does not hesitate to adduce that kind of evidence in support of his case). However, before we turn from Gilligan's work, I might note that the scapegoat mechanism does surface in the course of Gilligan's analysis.

In Matina Horner's studies of competition, respondents were asked to complete a story from this beginning:

After first term finals, Anne finds herself at the top of her medical school class . . .

Oddly enough, in this situation several of the women gave violent responses, one of them fantasizing

a jubilant Anne, at the top of her medical school class, physically beaten and maimed for life by her jealous classmates.

Horner used such case studies as this in formulating her "fear of success" syndrome, which she particularly identified with women.[31]

In Gilligan's terms, Girard's theory may play on the oldest fears of both the sexes: male-to-male mimetic desire which leads always to mimetic antagonism might reflect the "fear of connection" Gilligan ascribes to her male subjects. Similarly, the scapegoat mechanism may reflect the "fear of success" Gilligan and Horner ascribe to their female subjects.

4.2 *Violence and* The Color Purple

Since Girard evinces a preference for literature and myth as witness to human experience, over data provided by the social sciences for example, let's put Alice Walker's novel, *The Color Purple*, alongside Gilligan's model. I do not mean by this to preempt Cheryl Kirk-Duggan's masterful treatment also in this volume, but only to make additional observations stirred by my reading of Gilligan's work.[32]

First of all, as I have observed above (section 1.1), Girard has consistently avoided first-person narratives by "victims" in his collection of "great" literature. In this way he has tipped the scales in favor of his own theory, since his narratives often display these characteristics:

1. they are about violence—violent problems, violent solutions. No "boy meets girl, boy loses girl, boy gets girl" here;
2. they climax in great, gulping paroxysms of violent action—massacres, blindings, suicides, beheadings, etc.;

---

31 Matina Horner, "Sex Differences in Achievement Motivation and Performance in Competitive and Noncompetitive Situations" (diss. U. Mich. 1968), cited by Gilligan, *Different Voice*, 14–15, 40.

32 I trust the reader will forgive me if I unintentionally repeat some of Kirk-Duggan's points; our lively seminar sessions at the Westar Institute have given me so much material I hardly remember which ideas are my own.

3. these climaxes are in general followed by only brief scenes of reconciliation or merely by epilogues, leaving the impression that the explosion of violence, and not the solution of a problem, was the goal of the
   narrative.

This may represent the type of narrative many men prefer; consider the
story of Nick, above (section 4). The reason Girard has neglected literature by
women may be in part precisely because so much of that literature, when it
does deal with violence, appears to cheat the reader of the ending he has been
taught to prefer. In *The Color Purple*, for example, Celie toys with the idea of
killing Mr.____, only to reject it in the end. In fact, although talk of violence
pervades the novel, the audience is at a double remove from any emotion
stimulated by the description of violence. The epistolary format interferes with
the immediacy of the description, and the victim as first-person narrator
precludes any identification with the violence of the victimizer. Indeed, Walker's format precludes even the kind of identification possible in a third-person
narrative which deplores the use of violence with lengthy descriptions of it.

In some sense then we might say that Walker's novel is about what much
literature and myth only pretend to be about—the transformation of violence.
Walker has rewritten the plot of any number of pretenders. Let's take an
example from the popular culture—the target audience of Greek tragedy,
Shakespeare, and myth in their own day—*Destry Rides Again*. You may recall
that in this classic Western James Stewart plays the sheriff without a gun, who
intends to clean up raffish Bottleneck by peaceful methods, with negotiation,
charity, and sweet reason. Of course the villains prove intractable, and the
whole plot builds to a climactic scene in which Destry fires his gun at last and
kills the outlaw chief. In Walker's version, we may imagine, Destry would
have sworn never to fire a gun and *would never have fired one*. The transformation of community from savagery to civilization would have been accomplished with negotiation, charity, and sweet reason.

But then Walker's novel is not presented as a blueprint for the transformation and redemption of a whole civilization (winning the West) or of a
whole town (even lowly Bottleneck). We might argue that these problems are
too hypothetical, not real enough, to attract the attention of a novelist grappling with the moralities of personal violence. That novelist perhaps might
scorn the vision of violence as some menacing mushroom-cloud of a deity,
present at the beginning and responsible for the end of all. Walker's novel is
about the soul-journey of a single prisoner of violence who changes, transforms, redeems herself and those around her—a manageable task, a real task.

For an analysis of Walker's message, I can do no better than to refer the
reader again to Kirk-Duggan's discussion (ch. 13). For a perceptive, illuminating—and realistic—discourse on the causes and cures of violence, see Theophus Smith's article (ch. 11). I am pleased to leave the reader in the capable
hands of my colleagues in these matters. In conclusion, I would contribute to

our prescriptions for curing violence three lessons to be learned from Celie's soul-journey:

1. Celie learns stubbornly to resist dividing the world into friend and foe, them and us. Thus, she makes room for Shug, the rival, the interloper, in her "web of relationships."[33] This task, of course, is most difficult when faced with the Great Dichotomy: male and female. But, in the end, Celie, who could not bring herself to speak the name of any man, connects with Albert. When Theophus Smith reminds us not to make victims of victimizers, he too is opting for a world in which everyone has a name, a face, and no one can be reduced to an object of society's violence;

2. Celie rejects the use of violence in every situation in which she finds herself, while acknowledging that only Christ has perfect self-control;

3. Celie learns to embrace the multiplicity of life, to see the world as full of options for action, for connection. In Carol Gilligan's terms, we might say that she renounces the security of the on-off, right-wrong, zero-sum game that Kohlberg's question, "*Should* Heinz steal the drug?" typifies. She risks danger to her self-esteem ("I can't prove that I'm right") in exchange for a freedom of action so broad that she can even embrace the author of her miseries. And she, the female hero, brings those around her safe home to a new way of thinking. Thus, Albert, nearly "cured" of violence, says:

I think us here to wonder, myself. To wonder. To ast. And that in wondering bout the big things and asting bout the big things, you learn about the little ones, almost by accident. But you never know nothing more about the big things than you start out with. The more I wonder . . . the more I love.[34]

---

33 Gilligan's term, *Different Voice*, 32. See the concluding quotation in section 2.1 above.
34 Walker, *The Color Purple*, 290.

xiii

Gender, Violence, and Transformation in The Color Purple

Cheryl A. Kirk-Duggan

Abstract

Alice Walker's classic novel, *The Color Purple*, celebrates the transformation of Black women and critiques the violent abuse that characterizes the human condition. The novel focuses on the relationship between Celie and God as it dramatically unfolds within various communities, but most especially, the Black female community. In so far as the text reflects persecution, *The Color Purple* makes an intriguing case study for analyzing René Girard's theories about scapegoats and violence. The context for Celie's personal journey to freedom and wholeness is a primal myth of violence and scapegoating: the patriarchal myth of male domination over women. But unlike Girard, who dismisses first person narrative accounts of victimage, Walker demands that the reader enter the world of the text as the one victimized.

This chapter focuses on Celie as "suffering servant" and scapegoat, as set overagainst violence and the socializing control of domination. Feminist and rhetorical hermeneutics provide the resources for analyzing the myths and rituals that perpetuate violence, and for observing Walker's model for nonviolent transformation. Nonviolent transformation replaces the Girardian mimetic rivalry with agape, actualized as Theophus Smith's concept of mimetic intimacy (see chapter 11). Mimetic intimacy with God frames Celie's existence. Such intimacy grounds her experience of theodicy, and forges her life within a theology of creation where sexuality celebrates the communion of humanity. Rather than a Girardian cure by means of the sacrificial death of a scapegoat, Walker cures violence through self-actualization nurtured by agape. The royal color purple symbolizes transformation: new life for victims and victimizers.

0. Introduction

In *The Color Purple*, Alice Walker explores the relationship between Celie, the protagonist of her fictional biographical novel, and God. From a literary critical perspective, Walker's treatment of Celie engages René Girard's psychosocial scapegoat paradigm. Walker maintains her African-American traditions as she narrates the oppressions, the insanities, the loyalties, and the triumphs of Black women. They are the only people she respects "collectively and with no reservations."[1] While depicting a dysfunctional Black family in a southern community, this novel transcends geography and ethnicity by unfolding a personal history of violent abuse that characterizes the human predicament. Walker gathers remnants of human dilemmas and 'quilts' them into tapestries of functional, terrifying beauty. In her patchwork of purple, she stitches the fabric of daily violence perpetrated against her characters and the violence they each commit upon each other. Walker's characters thus seek a regeneration from that violence—a regeneration that will break the cycles of oppression.[2] Thus the characters of *The Color Purple* encompass the world's populace. Its people experience oppression on the basis of gender, racial, class or social identity. In texts of persecution like *The Color Purple*, we see how the larger society singles out entire groups of human beings for annihilation to create "the perfect city" or environment.[3]

This essay explores Walker's persecution text to reveal the dynamics of scapegoating and victimization framed by violence and domination that ultimately ends in transformation as agape replaces mimetic rivalry. This essay first focuses on Celie, who epitomizes (a) the biblical concept of "suffering servant" in her relationships to herself, other females, and God, and (b) the Girardian concept of "scapegoat" in her relationship with Mr.____ and Shug. God and the female community support her quest for love and survival. Initially, men do not. Secondly we examine violence and the socializing control of domination—a domination that creates tension between genders within the community—as the context for the narrative. Finally, I suggest that Walker's answer for curing violence is the transformation of Celie and her community, symbolized by the color purple. Throughout, the essay uses feminist and rhetorical analysis to display the essence of noble, authentic humanity as presented in *The Color Purple*. The nobility of Celie's faith journey toward authenticity evolves, as her story reflects the normative biblical hope of intimacy with God and mutuality with community. It is a journey towards transformation or curing violence. Aided by God, Celie metamorphoses from a lowly caterpillar into a magnificent moth. Her ultimate understanding of God and life is the essence of human authenticity implicit in the royal color

---

1 Howard, "Alice Walker," 314.
2 Christian, *Black Women Novelists*, 180–81.
3 Girard, *Things Hidden*, 129.

1. Gender Expressed: Celie's Role
as "Suffering Servant" and Scapegoat

The Color Purple is the story of Celie's personal journey to freedom and wholeness, set in a persecution text of male violence and scapegoating. Girardian persecution texts describe accounts of real, collective violence from the perspective of the persecutor.[4] By contrast, Walker writes from the perspective of the victim. Nowhere in his literary theory does Girard deal with narrative written in first person about first person victimage. He focuses both on the pattern and contours of collective violence that cross cultures, and on how one mobilizes violent mobs to act.[5] Yet a reduction of that violence to the individual microcosm can make a general idea more specific. Even the persecution that Celie experiences at the hands of Mr.____ reflects the collective violence that he, in turn, experiences from the larger society. But rather than approach the text through the absurdity of victimizers' justifications of persecution, Walker demands that the reader face pain and injustice through the eyes of the victimized.

As storyteller, Walker also portrays Celie in the biblical role of a "suffering servant" who undergoes an "Exodus of faith." Celie's exodus from the socializing control of domination shapes Walker's narrative. Here we can usefully employ Phyllis Trible's view of storytelling as an act that unites the writer, text, and reader of biblical narrative.[6] Trible's schema creates a forum for discerning the subtle as well as the obvious aspects of Celie's exodus. Through a critical use of feminist hermeneutics, scripture can serve as a resource for liberating women and other victimized peoples. For many biblical scholars, for example, the elements of slavery and liberation found in the Exodus tradition reflect the cohesive interaction between the Bible and the African-American experience. But the Exodus image calls women also—calls them to leave the servitude of patriarchal family and the certitude of patriarchal religion. The spirituality of that same image however requires that patriarchal oppression, no matter how universal or dominating, must not mask the reality that God is always at the center of a struggle for liberation.[7]

The "suffering servant" metaphor portrays Celie's ongoing plight as she grapples with her own liberation toward selfhood and dignity. Walker's portrayal epitomizes a role frequently ascribed to women in biblical narratives, where "women, not men, are suffering servants and Christ figures."[8] Their sacrificial role makes these characters Christ figures. Grossly abused women in the Old Testament include the raped and discarded princess Tamar, the

---

4 Girard, *Scapegoat*, 9.
5 Girard, *Scapegoat*, 18–19.
6 Trible, *God and the Rhetoric*, 1.
7 Fiorenza, *In Memory of Her*, 343, 348; Trible, *Texts of Terror*, 5.
8 Trible, *Texts of Terror*, 2.

violated, dismembered and unnamed concubine of Judges 19, the slain and sacrificed virgin daughter of Jephthah, and the abused, rejected slave Hagar. All of them encounter horrors of violence and victimization in Hebraic patriarchy. In particular, Abraham's female slave Hagar becomes a harbinger of Israel's escape from Egyptian bondage. While Hagar does not request or receive aid from the deity, she claims her own exodus when she escapes from Sarah's oppression.[9] (Coincidentally, the Hagar saga resurfaces in sixteenth-century North America as a biblical justification for slavery; the pro-slavery constituency dubbed blacks "Aunt Hagar's children": the expelled and outcast who suffered gross servitude.)

The "suffering servant" is first celebrated, of course, in the Songs of Isaiah, which depict Israel's "return from exile as a new Exodus in which Yahweh the shepherd will lead the people."[10] The New Testament symbol of suffering servanthood is Christ, the "Good Shepherd." His redemptive, vicarious activity reveals the loving and merciful character of God in an Exodus of hope and reconciliation. Building upon the Exodus motif, the suffering and passion of Jesus becomes the suffering and passion of women. This is Elisabeth Schussler Fiorenza's reading of the gospels. From a sociological and theological perspective it stresses ministerial love and altruistic love, in order to produce a feminist reading of Jesus as the Sophia (wisdom) of God. As wisdom, Jesus is the God of victims and outcasts who suffer injustice. The feminist view of Jesus' teaching on the reign of God calls all women to discipleship or wholeness, self-actualization, and empowering solidarity. On this view the suffering of Jesus is paradigmatic for, and empathetic to, the call to suffering and persecution which prohibits patriarchal, dominant relationships. Jesus, the prototypical suffering servant, is the one who liberates and elevates, while women disciples emerge as exemplars of suffering discipleship and true leadership. Thus the discipleship and apostolic leadership of women are integral to Jesus' option for a praxis of agape and service over submission to patriarchy.[11]

As suffering servant, Celie emerges as a redemptive figure amid the misogynist tendencies in her culture. As scapegoats, Celie and Mr.____ emerge as victims in a persecution text. Differentiating between the biblical, anthropological and psychosocial meanings of scapegoat, Girard develops the psychosocial meaning in his definition of the term. Scapegoats are victims of unjust violence or discrimination. Scapegoating includes the blame or punishment for everything from others' "sins" to all kinds of tensions, conflicts and difficulties based on delusion.[12] In *The Color Purple*, for example, Mr.____ unconsciously scapegoats Celie because society has scapegoated him. Scape-

9 Trible, *Texts of Terror*, 1–13.
10 Trible, *Texts of Terror*, 50.
11 Fiorenza, *In Memory of Her*, 131–35, 138, 153, 315–18, 320–21, 334.
12 Hamerton-Kelly, *Violent Origins*, 74.

goating implies a Freudian displacement that includes all rituals resembling the Levitical, sacrificial atonement. In that ancient ritual, one of the two goats chosen to be sent alive into the wilderness symbolically represented the sins of the people. Similarly, Mr.____ displaces onto Celie all the injustices he has known at the hands of his own father and white society.

Within this scapegoating myth, neither Celie's innocence nor her use as scapegoat is obvious. Although the scapegoat or hero-victim is usually a stranger,[13] Celie is Mr.____'s wife. She could only be considered a stranger in the sense that Mr.____ wanted to marry Celie's sister, Nettie, but circumstances forced him to marry Celie instead. "Mr.____ finally come right out an ast for Nettie hand in marriage. But He [Celie's stepfather] won't let her go."[14] When Mr.____ asks for Nettie's hand in marriage again, Nettie's stepfather claims she is too young, that Mr.____ has too many children, and a reputation riddled with scandal. The answer is the same: "I can't let you have Nettie. She too young. . . . But I can let you have Celie." Three months later an exasperated Mr.____ returns to see Celie again, because the woman helping him has quit and his own mother refuses to help anymore. In that scene Celie's "Pa" makes her parade around like a show horse. The reader learns that Mr.____ requests marriage to Celie not through a proposal. Instead he asks, "That cow [dowry] still coming? He say, Her cow."[15] In that moment and in later instances of verbal and physical abuse, Mr.____ does not realize that he is scapegoating Celie. Nonetheless Celie, the innocent party who polarizes the universal hatred that Mr.____ experiences, is his scapegoat. As Girard indicates, an "infinite play of substitutions, modifications, subtle transfigurations and wily inversions" inherent in the scapegoat system convinces society that scapegoating is nonexistent.[16] Similarly the true role of persecutors and victims remains ambiguous in Walker's narrative. In both cases unjust persecutors do not see themselves as unjust. The innocent or arbitrary selection of the victim cannot be explicit, or the myth will be ineffective. Such myths perpetuate attitudes about inferiority and the seeming necessity of abuse. Stimulated by racism, misogyny and sexism, the myths sanction crimes of sex and violence. The institution of marriage allows Mr.____ to verbally, psychologically, and physically abuse Celie. Even though Celie is now part of the community by marriage, the abuse of Mr.____ at the hands of the larger society makes her an outsider to him. A pernicious unity exists among the insider African-American male infrastructure: men who feel threatened and must vicariously defend themselves as a group through such attacks as

---

13 Hamerton-Kelly, *Violent Origins*, 82.
14 Walker, *The Color Purple*, 7–9. The reader assumes, just as the protagonist does, that the man they call "Pa" is Celie and Nettie's father. Only toward the end of the narrative, at his death, do they learn that their real father was lynched, and that the man they knew as Pa was actually their stepfather.
15 Walker, *The Color Purple*, 7–9, 12.
16 Girard, *Job*, 5, 152.

Mr.____'s abuse against Celie. Celie's victimage mirrors Mr.____'s own quandary.

Mr.____, like any man imprisoned by institutionalized racism and poverty, sees his wife as a trap and blames her for his failure. Since the true culprit of their mutual oppression remains inaccessible, the woman becomes the target upon whom the man can vent his frustration. Society insists on trying to control the psychological and material conditions under which Black people struggle. Realizing that society will not let him be a man, Mr.____ blames and therefore scapegoats women. The resulting frustration ends in the abuse of the wife/child. "Briefly it made him feel good"—that is, feel superior to someone.[17]

Many women accept the blame of men as valid, believing that they have not supported the man's threatened manhood. In this connection, Celie shows how victims in texts come to accept camouflaged persecution myths.[18] The persecuted victim exists behind the myth. Celie lives behind and under the myth that male-female relationships demand abusive dominance. The persecution or abuse becomes the punishment of a crime through the largely unconscious myth-making process. The violence meted against Celie becomes the punishment of her crime of femaleness, through the unconscious myth-making process of necessary abusive dominance in male/female relationships. The crime and the punishment set up an important aspect of human order—an order in which Celie is the scapegoat responsible for two crimes: society denies Mr.____ his manhood, and his father prohibited him from taking Shug as his wife.[19] As the novel progresses, Celie challenges Mr.____'s dominance by her relationship with Shug and her move to Memphis. But male inadequacy fuels abuse toward women when a Black man's lost pride is pitted against a Black woman's mounting strength. When such pressures defeat husbands, they respond by seeking to destroy their women.[20]

Victimizers corrupt life and try to make others think that they are gods.[21] As male abusers destroy life, their female victims become the unfulfilled and discarded objects of machismo. During her pilgrimage Celie suffers negation from others, and self-hatred for her physical appearance and the way she dresses. Though she has given birth twice and been the repository of Mr.____'s semen, Celie does not know love; she remains a moral virgin.[22] As her stepfather pushes Mr.____ to marry Celie, he claims, "She ain't fresh tho. . . . She spoiled. Twice. . . . She ugly He say." Later Celie reflects, "I hate the way I look, I hate the way I'm dress." Celie sees Mr.____ looking at Shug's black, flawless skin in her provocative clothes. Before she knows it, tears meet

17 Christian, *Black Women Novelists*, 188.
18 Williams, "The Innocent Victim," 322.
19 Williams, "The Innocent Victim," 322; Walker, *The Color Purple*, 49, 56-7.
20 Bal, *Lethal Love*, 190-94.
21 Walker, *The Color Purple*, 204.
22 Walker, *The Color Purple*, 81.

under Celie's chin and she becomes confused.[23] Later, after Celie coura-
geously chooses to leave for Memphis, Mr.____ takes yet another opportunity
to sabotage Celie's inner strength through verbal abuse: "You'll be back, He
say. Nothing up North for nobody like you. . . . [W]hat you got? You ugly. You
skinny. You shape funny. You too scared to open your mouth to people. All
you fit to do . . . is . . . take out her [Shug's] slop-jar. . . ."

As Girard asserts, the stranger-scapegoat always appears more powerful than
he or she really is.[24] Notably, in Walker's novel the tension does increase as
the scapegoat's desires or activity counters that of the victimizer.

The selection of a human scapegoat generates anxiety and fear beforehand
and violence afterwards. But when the death of the scapegoat occurs a new
mood of harmony and peace follows. Paradoxically, as Girardian analysis
indicates, the scapegoat can symbolize both supreme benevolence and supreme malevolence. Belief in the scapegoat's benefits will follow its death and
myths celebrate its resurrection.[25] In *The Color Purple*, however, neither
Mr.____ nor society kills Celie. And even when silent, Celie does not ac-
quiesce in her persecution but acts to self-actualize. Indeed, when Celie
cannot find affirmation from relationships with men, she looks to God for
relationship and identity.

In one sense, the lack of male affirmation places Celie outside the community and she becomes an existential stranger. While she stands both within
and outside of the community, does she have an insider or an outsider God?
Using Girard's categories, is her God the "God of persecutors" or the "God of
victims?"[26]

2. Transformation I: Celie's Intimacy
with the Suffering God

Celie's God is not the insider God of the male infrastructure that permeates
The Color Purple. Rather, her God is the biblical God of outsiders and outcasts: a loving Creator, sustainer, reconciler. Celie's concept of God has roots
in a tradition of internal convictions unlike the American majority culture and
class. Her belief system, typically African-American, relies on life-giving af-
firmations of a strong oral tradition. This system of "soul theology" empowers
and gives healing for psychic and spiritual survival. Soul theology posits the
grace, goodness, providence, justice, majesty, omnipotence and omniscience
of God along with the goodness of creation and the equality, uniqueness,
mutuality, perseverance, and communal nature of persons.[27] In opposition to

---

23 Walker, *The Color Purple*, 9, 77.
24 Walker, *The Color Purple*, 212; Hamerton-Kelly, *Violent Origins*, 91.
25 Hamerton-Kelly, *Violent Origins*, 83–92.
26 Girard, *Job*.
27 Cooper-Lewter and Mitchell, *Soul Theology*, vii–xi.

such empowerment, victimizers use scapegoating to control and order the powerless into "godforsaken" exile.

But rather than destroying the victims' experience of God, the insecurity of exile can galvanize one toward religion. Religion in Girard's view refers to the obscurity that frames a peoples' efforts to defend itself, by preventive or curative means, against its own violence.[28] By inference, religion can prepare individuals to cope with violence as well. As "suffering servant," Celie's intimate relationship with God eventually allows her to transcend the battered spouse syndrome (the violence that she participates in by virtue of her silence). That God-human relationship undergirds her transformation. As discussed by Theophus Smith in chapter 11, the christocentric "suffering servant image" provides a model for nonviolent transformation, and shows a correlation between mimetic co-suffering with Jesus and reconciliation with the enemy. Celie's co-suffering with Jesus affords a transformation. Within this process Mr._____ serves as an enabler toward her transformation, thus replacing the mimetic desire (Girard) or rivalry between them with mimetic intimacy (Smith).

Celie shifts from silent invisibility to a robust relationship with herself and with others. Celie's resurrection is a metamorphosis from unknowing child to adult with a new, vibrant, incontrovertible awareness of God that asserts: love nurtures, hate kills. This reading in no way romanticizes the insidiousness of violence in relationships, but shows the prospects for change as opposed to absolute futility. Her heinous predicament affords her a choice for noble authenticity as she comes to experience love and community. With God's help, Celie wants to share the potential for authenticity with others, especially her sister. Celie vows to protect Nettie from their stepfather. She offers herself to be raped instead.[29] Thus Celie as victim of incest becomes her stepfather's scapegoat, taking on violence otherwise directed toward her sister Nettie and their ailing mother. Here we find in Walker's narrative an instance of Girard's concept of victim substitution.

Girard claims that sacrificial substitution leads to confusion, because the life of the sacrificial institution depends upon its ability to conceal the displacement. Once having focused on the sacrificial substitute, the object first singled out for violence fades from view. But some attention must remain on the original object, or the substitution does not remain intact and the sacrifice loses all efficacy.[30] Although Celie availed herself to her stepfather as scapegoat, his relationship with Nettie is ambiguous. The mother's premature death and the numerous childbirths suggest that the mother continued to be the stepfather's victim. Still, as Mr._____'s scapegoat, Celie is the victim of his rage against his suppressive father and the larger community. But her being

28 Girard, *Violence and the Sacred*, 23.
29 Walker, *The Color Purple*, 4, 8.
30 Girard, *Violence and the Sacred*, 4–6.

scapegoat does not protect Shug, because Mr.___ does not see another man as rival for Shug. (Thus Girard's sacrificial substitution theory does not work for Walker's narrative because Celie as victim is not a substitute for everyone in the community.)

Celie appears to help the community, as opposed to protecting the community from their own violence. For example, Celie gives away her own material possessions for others.[31] She becomes the Good Samaritan herself when she takes her husband's trollop, Shug, into Celie's own home and nurses her back to health. While Mr.___ has sex with both of the women during this period, that does not diminish the genuine affection that Celie has for Shug and vice versa. The issue is not Celie's and Shug's acquiescence to this bizarre and unnatural living arrangement. There has never been any marital bonding between Celie and Mr.___. With the male characters deficient, Celie's only meaningful relationships are with women. Shug and Celie fill an empty vacuum in each others lives.

> To Celie, Shug is the woman she would like to be—assertive, beautiful, in control of her life. . . . Shug's first reaction to Celie is [a] jealous retort. . . . But Celie . . . takes care of Shug, Albert's lover, like she's a baby, and Shug in turn introduces Celie to the mysteries of female sexuality. In many ways, Shug becomes the mother Celie never had. . . . And in some ways, Shug's ability to love Celie reconciles the blues singer to her role as mother. . . . In effect, these two women nurture each other.[32]

A Girardian analysis would look for triangular or mimetic desire in the relationship between Celie, Shug, and Mr.___. But first, in sharp contrast with Girardian theory, the desiring subject is not always male. In fact Walker's characterizations present the following scheme: Celie as subject, Shug as object of her desire, and Mr.___ as her rival. To repeat: the Girardian construct maintains that triangular desire can explain all sacrificial rituals and religious beliefs concerning victims and scapegoats. But in this novel such a claim cannot be confirmed and conflicts with Walker's interpretation. In *The Color Purple*, mimetic rivalry between the subject and the model or object does not increase as the difference between them decreases—as in Girard's "crisis of distinctions." Shug (object), does not become Celie's double, and the mimetic violence does not intensify between them. Rather, Celie and Shug become friends!

Girard maintains that a male/male/female model corresponding to subject/rival/object "recurs as an absolute, ahistorical structure."[33] But the passionate, violent, and ambivalent sequence of desire that Girard sees between the subject and rival does not occur between Celie and Mr.___. Girardian

---

31 Walker, *The Color Purple*, 9.
32 Christian, *Black Feminist Criticism*, 194–95.
33 Moi, "The Missing Mother," 21–23.

theory continues to be problematic. Girard claims that a novel which does not contain mimetic desire, as he prescribes, is not a great novel. While he avoids studying women as literary subjects, Girard claims to posit theories with universal implications. When other scholars have placed women in superior positions, Girard argues for assigning women to characterizations of "passive spectators at a masculine tragicomedy." He asserts that women at best only pretend to be self-sufficient in order to woo and conquer men.[34] But the strength and conviction of the women in *The Color Purple* refute Girard's theory of women as insignificant, docile parasites.

To the contrary: Celie helps others, suffers empathetically with them, and cares for their needs.[35] Here the important issue is that men reject Celie, the "suffering servant," as she carries her cross. Her transformation occurs as she transcends that rejection. Celie's experience as "suffering servant" displays the following concepts: (1) her existence in *Imago Dei*, (2) the mutuality of women and men in creation, and (3) the issue of theodicy.

First, Celie's idea of *Imago Dei*—the idea of her own existence in the image of God—informs her choice for a meaningful relationship with God. Mimetic intimacy and the immediacy of those moments with a hidden, yet listening God frame her existence. Her intuitive reliance on God provides assurance of belonging, concern, and innocence in spite of reality. When her mother asks about the first pregnancy, Celie responds, "She ast me about the first one Whose it is? I say God's. I don't know no other man or what else to say. When . . . that little baby come out my pussy chewing on it fist you could have knock me over with a feather."[36] Celie's understanding of her body approximates her undeveloped concept of God. But her naivete does not paralyze her from choosing to relate to God. In effect, her act of choice authenticates her existence in the image of God.

Secondly, *The Color Purple* is also a story about males and females in a good creation. Shug's logic, for example, implies that in spite of evil and human sin every person remains part of God's good creation. Shug answers the question of sin in a confession of her own experience. She argues that one is a sinner by virtue of being born into a world that does not afford any other option. And sinners have good times. Shug contends that, although they worry about God, when sinners feel God's love they do their best to please God by doing what pleases themselves. She believes God loves people unconditionally, even those who refuse to wear the garb of religiosity. One only feels God if you bring God with you, for one ought to "come to church to share God, not find God."[37]

Such a "creation theology" (Matthew Fox) also dictates that Mr.____ should treat Celie with respect, and reject relating to her through subjugation and

---

34 Moi, "The Missing Mother," 23–26; cf. Girard, *Deceit*, 140. See also Kofman, "The Narcissistic Woman," 41–42.
35 Walker, *The Color Purple*, 67, 106.
36 Walker, *The Color Purple*, 3.
37 Walker, *The Color Purple*, 200–201.

violence. In Genesis, for example, the unique, independent woman helps transform the earth creature into a sexual being.[38] Sexuality means the celebration of the communion, not the division, of human bone and flesh. This type of expression reflects mimetic intimacy—an intimacy between human beings in communion with God. On the other hand Girard discounts the power of sexuality to create human order. "There is no reason to view permanent sexuality [in contrast to the periodic excitation of males among other mammals] as a factor of order rather than disorder."[39] Again, Girard ignores the female presence within created order by focusing on the male-dominant interactions. Yet the potential for Celie to transform Mr.____ is part of created order. As her image of God matures she knows the goodness of herself and creation. She knows fulfillment and learns a sense of life that rises above the many abuses toward enhancement of life.

Third, Celie's transition from abuse to transformation underscores the question of theodicy—the question of the goodness of God given the reality of evil. Rape, misogyny, beatings, and being forced to live as invisible property represent evil deeds against innocence. Her faith in God coupled with her painful existence raise the question of theodicy. Celie's role of "suffering servant" equips her to live in silence until she becomes powerful and assertive in her new understanding of herself, and her royal place in life as fulfilled, divinely-imaged woman. Her inner power and strength and her material resources grow as she experiences fulfillment through positive self-identity and within her community. Celie's experience of theodicy is a shift from being a scapegoat toward mimetic intimacy, spiritual and physical transformation.

Rarely does Celie blame God or others for her own suffering. But moments do occur when Celie feels estranged from God. Initially, Celie can tell God alone about her rape. She writes letters to God. Her experience of God moves from that of a stout white male banker, through her painful wilderness experience where she discounts God, to God's becoming "everything that is [good] or ever was or ever will be."[40] Particularly poignant is Celie's discovery that Mr.____, with premeditated cruelty, withheld all of her sister's correspondence for over twenty years. This sister meant everything in the world to Celie. Then she learned of this spiteful meanness. "My daddy lynch. My mama crazy. All my little half-brothers and sisters no kin to me. My children not my sister and brother. Pa not pa."[41] She no longer writes letters to God. While a *deus otiosus*—hidden God—may not cause the evil, a silent, incommunicable God becomes a trifling, lowdown and forgetful man who does not listen to poor Black women. If God listened to poor Black women, the world would be a different place.[42] Yet, from her earliest memory, Celie knows of

38 Trible, *God and the Rhetoric*, 103–4.
39 Girard, *Things Hidden*, 87.
40 Walker, *The Color Purple*, 11, 96, 198–200, 202.
41 Walker, *The Color Purple*, 183.
42 Walker, *The Color Purple*, 199–200.

one person with whom she can share all her troubles. Celie can and does pour out her heart to God. And, as she turns to God, Celie begins to view those particular human beings who abuse her as responsible for her suffering.

Celie and modern abused women experience similar mental, emotional and physical abuse as they stand outside a (biblical) covenant community and wrestle with an absent, silent God. Women stand outside of the covenant when they are abused or victimized in misogynist patriarchy. Victimage alienates the individual from the self and identity with God. That disconnection can make the woman dysfunctional to the point that she cannot achieve self-authentication. As a scapegoat, however, her problem is not that God has ceased to care or speak but that victimage does not allow her to hear. In this connection Celie's relationship with God is dialectical. On the one hand, she relates to God in a special way as an intimate child of a covenant community. On the other hand, her victimage gives the appearance of her standing outside of the covenant.

Celie actively waits for opportunities to grow and transcend her "caged" existence. After learning that her husband withheld her sister's letters over the years as a technique of premeditated cruelty, Celie experiences shock, anger, and rage. Her powerless existence resembles death. Reflecting on another aspect of her crucifixion, Celie asks God why she has been forsaken by God (compare Ps 22:1 and Mark 15:34: "My God, my God, why have you forsaken me?") She wonders how she can go on and not kill. Ironically, Shug reminds her, "Hard to be Christ too." In this connection, Celie exerts a type of Christological power and oneness with God the Father/Mother when she tells Mr.____, "Until you do right by me, everything you touch will crumble."[43] Furthermore, under Shug's tutelage Celie comes to believe that God loves "everything you love—and a mess of stuff you don't. . . . God love admiration. . . . Not vain, just wanting to share a good thing." God wants to please humanity and wants to be loved like everybody else, like the Bible says. As Celie becomes mentally free from that "old white man" God and the role of scapegoat, she experiences a revelation. Her eyes open and she realizes that compared with any minute part of creation, Mr.____'s evil diminishes.[44]

The revelations that heighten Celie's world view frame her transformation, in contradistinction to a Girardian transformation theory that requires a sacrifice or murder. A symbol of Celie's transformation of her vision of God, herself, and life appears the first time Celie ends a letter with the closing signature, "Amen," (an attitude of praise) and more poignantly in a letter with a full closing—a closing which defines her identity in terms of person and place.

> Amen,
> Your Sister, Celie

43 Walker, *The Color Purple*, 150, 213.
44 Walker, *The Color Purple*, 203, 202–4, 204.

Sugar Avery Drive
Memphis, Tennessee[45]

Celie's reaction to abuse and her resurrection induced by love constitutes her experience of *Imago Dei*. Thereafter, Celie can place the responsibility for abuse at the human level. For Girard, however, it is human beings—notably men—and not supernatural intervention that forge the destinies they deserve. Men create their own hell and help one another descend into it. Perdition is an equitable exchange because it results from reciprocal evil desires and evil behavior. The only innocent victims are children on whom scandal is imposed from the outside without any participation on their part. Fortunately, all men were once children.[46]

The preceding section traced Celie's realization that the responsibility for her abuse involved male domination, undergirded by violence, power, and fear. Next, we examine the conflict and suffering caused by misogynist domination and cruelty in personal relationships, in an effort to pinpoint the source from which problems rise.

3. Transformation II: Celie beyond the Socializing Control of Domination

Domination in interpersonal relationships hinges on control and leads to destructive results. We are inevitably called upon to examine such relationships in biblical narratives. Our assessment of the nature of these relationships depends upon whether we give moral, religious, or political authority to the texts, and depends also upon how that authority interprets the balance of power. Often the institutionalized western or Christian reading of those biblical stories, where female characters play key roles, shows either denial of the power issue or simply presents a monolithic, misogynist view. In some biblical texts, indeed, women represent danger or death. As cited earlier, Fiorenza shows that a feminist reading of Jesus' vision and teaching about the reign of God calls for total female empowerment and prohibits patriarchal domination. For her part, Mieke Bal suggests that analyzing any text involving women should focus on the relationship between "dominance" and specific forms of depiction as a way to spotlight the control motif and the resulting dissonance.[47]

In Bal's schematics, femaleness is the catalyst for dominance. This makes any woman in a relationship with any man a potential lethal woman. The term "lethal" refers to a psycho-sociological phenomenon with literary implications. A lethal woman means a female presence that may cause a man to react with abusive or dominant activity. Such violence can occur in a physical, legal,

---

45 Walker, *The Color Purple*, 204, 221.
46 Girard, *Scapegoat*, 134.
47 Bal, *Lethal Love*, 3.

or an unconscious psychosocial manner. Though mere property, the lethal woman causes adultery and deception.[48] Contrary to Girardian theory, male interests in a misogynist culture presume all females are potential lethal women. Women's presence acts like a drug that forces men to act out their frustrations on women: men become addicted to abuse. Conversely, Girard's theory teaches people to avoid seeing female characterization as a catalyst for abuse. Rather, women are passive, and are rarely protagonists. Girard's sacrificial scenario is a "genderless cultural model with sweeping claims to universality,"[49] which fails in treating narrative about vital female characters.

The role of Herodias in Girard's analysis of "The Beheading of Saint John the Baptist" provides such an example. There he argues that the issue is sibling rivalry of the brothers. "Except for the prophet, there are only enemy brothers and mimetic twins in the text: the mother and the daughter, Herod and his brother, Herod and Herodias."[50] Girard does not place Herodias as an equal player but as a mimetic (homosexual or anthropocentric) twin. Since the subject and rival must always be male in triangular or mimetic desire, Herodias must (1) be made an object and must (2) lose direct influence over her husband. Although Herodias cleverly enlists her daughter to gain the death of the prophet, Girard reduces her role in the configuration from that of human being to mimetic prize. For Girard, "mimetic triangular desire transfigures its ostensive object, distorts the mediator, and conceals the origin of the subject's own desiring . . . [accelerating] desire into violence."[51] But this scenario does not work in *The Color Purple*.

Mimetic desire does not transfigure Shug, distort Mr._____, or conceal the origin of Celie's desire. For the violence that almost occurs between Celie (subject) and Mr._____ (mediator) does not proceed from Celie's desire for Shug (object). Rather, the accelerating impulse toward violence in Celie proceeds from her abysmal grief and anger when she realizes the full extent of her abuse at the hands of Mr._____. The turning point occurs when she learns that, over the years, Mr._____ has denied Celie access to letters from her sister—and therefore has denied all access to her sister. If there is a concealed desire in the accelerating impulse to violence that overtakes Celie upon this realization, it is desire for her own thwarted wholeness and nurture in the intimacy of a sister's love. The realization of so great a deprivation provokes Celie overwhelmingly, as the following passages attest.

> Saturday morning Shug put Nettie letter in my lap. . . . He been keeping you letters, say Shug. Naw, I say. Mr._____ mean sometimes, but he not that mean.
> She say, Humpf, he that mean.
> But how come he do it? I ast. He know Nettie mean everything in the world to me.

48 Hamerton-Kelly, *Violent Origins*, 81; Bal, *Lethal Love*, 25–28, 34–35, 95.
49 Schor, *Breaking the Chain*, xiii.
50 Girard, *Scapegoat*, 128–130.
51 Schweiker, "Sacrifice, Interpretation, and the Sacred," 799.

Shug say she don't know, but us gon find out.

Us seal the letter up again and put it back in Mr.____ pocket. He walk round with it in his coat all day. He never mention it. . . .

I watch him so close, I begin to feel a lightening in the head. Fore I know anything I'm standing hind his chair with his razor open. . . .

Mr.____ look behind him. Put that down, he say. Women always need to cut this and shave that, and always gumming up the razor.

Shug got her hand on the razor now. She say, Oh it look dull anyway. She take and sling it back in the shaving box.

All day long I act just like Sofia. I stutter. . . . I stumble bout the house crazy for Mr.____ blood. . . . By time night come, I can't speak. · . . .

Dear God, What with being shock, crying . . . it took a long time to read just the first two or three letters . . . [Then] Mr.____ and Grady come home.

Can you handle it? ast Shug.

How I'm gon keep from killin him, I say.

Don't kill, she say. . . .

But it so hard, I say. . . .

Hard to be Christ too, say Shug. . . . Thou Shalt Not Kill, he said. . . .

But Mr.____ not Christ. I'm not Christ, I say. . . .

Naw, I think I feel better if I kill him, I say. I feels sickish. Numb, now.

Naw you won't. Nobody feel better for killing nothing. They feel *something* is all.[52]

That Mr.____ stooped to the depths of depriving Celie of one of her earliest bonding relationships shows the extent to which male mimetic desire can require female victimage and domination. Indeed, there is distortion here: a distorted concept of love in which the woman is man's property. Moreover adultery, abuse, or any negative result of dominant relationships is blamed on the lethal, deadly woman. In this connection, Bal suggests that one study the text from the perspective of reader response inherent in a particular culture. She argues that such a reading shows the possibility that dominance has a coherence and authority in culture. This type of control and power causes sexism. Perhaps contemporary audiences in the United States have been so repulsed by the portrayal of domination in *The Color Purple* because the novel mirrors the pervasive male dominance in this culture. Not recognizing that the distortions evident in this portrayal are due to the tense, ambivalent relationship between women and men undergoing domination, they accuse the novel or novelist of the effects. On the contrary, it is the socializing control of domination, operating in this culture between a woman and a man, that creates distorted or lethal love.

The following analysis of the tension between love and dominance focuses on how Celie tells her story. Celie chose to record her journey in letter form.

52 Walker, *The Color Purple*, 124–25, 150–51.

Throughout Celie's letters in this epistolary novel, "storytelling" became the vehicle for the message of faith and the quest for identity. Letters sent and received reflect God's faithfulness and Celie's struggle for personhood. In *Deceit, Desire, and the Novel*, Girard contends that novels are written by persecutors for persecution (in third person narrative). But this claim places *The Color Purple* outside of his literary analysis. Notwithstanding that claim, Walker's epistolary form, written from the perspective of the victim, affords the reader intimate access to Celie's victimage and transformation. The beauty of Celie's unfolding God-consciousness results from the deep love that Celie unearths for herself. *The Color Purple* successfully pursues Celie's passage from "suffering servant" to triumphant human.

The final phase of this dominance critique concerns the aim of the novelist and the reception of her work by the audience. Some critics find Walker's portrayal of Celie feigned, since the epistolary novel form makes an unlettered teenage Celie a much more suave character than she can possibly be without the benefit of education or gentility.[53] To the contrary, Celie's character proves convincing. Celie attended school for a short time and beyond that, Nettie helped Celie "with spelling and everything else she think I need to know . . . to teach me what go on in the world." At the same time Celie's letters contain her Black "rural idiomatic language" which allows the reader to "feel Celie's transformation intensely."[54] More pertinently, the matter of how the reader processes the story of *The Color Purple* is a function of how people react to life's struggles, specifically to issues of domination and suffering.

For example, some scholars have severely criticized *The Color Purple* for its one-sided representation of exclusively male brutality. Larger society and particularly African-American men have lambasted Walker and others for denigrating the Black male image. They claim that female novelists like Walker became popular by capitalizing on society's fear and hatred of Black males. One of her loudest critics, author Ishmael Reed, contends that Walker's appeal occurred because "her ideas coincide with this Reaganite attitude that all of the social problems in the United States are caused by black men." In response, "Reed wrote a rebuttal of sorts in his 1986 satirical novel, *Reckless Eyeballing*, about goose-stepping feminist theatrical producers who mentally trample a young male playwright."[55] Black author Charles Johnson claims that the Black male public image is extremely low, so much so that much of society thinks Black men do not have fathers. Literary agent Marie Brown says the problem is not gender, "but a publishing industry that assumes black

---

53 Harris, "On *The Color Purple*," 157.
54 Walker, *The Color Purple*, 10–11, 17; Christian, *Black Feminist Criticism*, 94.
55 Nixon, "Black Male Writers," 25–28. Because Black female writers took center stage and Black men receded during the last decade, some observers began to address the problem by seeking out the cause. Black writer Charles Johnson claims that (1) women purchase most of the fiction, and (2) the industry itself tends to promote Black female writers and neglect their male counterparts, symptomatic of a society that largely despises Black men.

fiction should be about black pathologies, or at least the hard experiences of being black."[56]

For her part, Walker responded to such criticisms while participating in a recent panel of noted African-American female authors and playwrights. In that forum she affirmed not only her creative license as a writer, but also her belief in the self-actualization of Black men and Black women together in community:

> [W]hen I'm writing, I'm not really thinking about, you know, fragile egos. I'm really trying to express my own experience. . . . I'm trying to deal with my own history and my own family often. . . .
>
> One thing that has struck me over the years, listening to the criticism, is how in my novel, *The Color Purple*, the men become transformed. So that by the end of the novel they're doing entirely different things than they're doing in the beginning. I mean, they're sitting together with the women, they're listening to the women, they're sewing with the women. Mister asks Celie to marry him again. You know, they're friends.
>
> And yet these things, this kind of development on the part of men, is never, ever noticed by anyone. Now what does that mean? I think it really does mean that when men stop acting in a macho way, other men cannot even see them. . . . We expect men to continue to be macho actors in the world, destroying the planet as they're doing. When in fact if we could just see them when they become gentle, when they become somebody that women can talk to, we stand a chance of maybe saving the world. . . .
>
> I have so much faith in black men–I think I have more faith in them than they have in themselves . . . because–look, I grew up with Martin Luther King . . . with Malcolm X . . . the man I share my life with refused to go to Vietnam. And that to me is manly.[57]

Moving from analysis to prescription, Walker explores the Black woman as creator and the Black woman's quest for wholeness beyond the limits of racist and misogynist traditions. These ventures toward beauty and fulfillment concern the health of the community and the relationships which must occur if the Black woman and her community are to survive. Walker's commitment to this task operates in her unique language, her process of deepening self-knowledge and self-love, and in her willingness to challenge existing conditions and honestly report what she sees.[58] Her commitment is also evident in the fact that most relationships in *The Color Purple* evolve from dominance and dissonance to symphonic harmony. Abuse and conflict are transcended by

---

56 Nixon, "Black Male Writers," 26.
57 Donahue, "Black Female Authors and Playwrights," 4, 9–10.
58 Christian, *Black Feminist Criticism*, 82–83.

reconciliation and wholeness. Thus Celie's story does not end with abuse, or with her repressed ignorance. Rather, her story closes on notes of love and retributive justice, a fact that was also emphasized in Walker's panel discussion:

> Audience member: When Ms. Walker's book *The Color Purple* came out . . . those two sisters cared about one another. The love kept them alive.

> Audience Member: The movie . . . was wonderful . . . But it omitted several transitions where a black man went from domineering, violent, brutal . . . to [being] non-macho; you know, sensitive.

> Alice Walker: Oh, the movie was very different. But that's because you can't . . . film a book really. . . . Very important things were left out, [for example] the lynching of Celie's father. You know that most of the people in reviewing the book insist that she was raped by her father instead of her stepfather. . . . [But] her real father was the reason that she really had a lot of the courage that she finally had, because he left her, you know, money, and . . . a possibility for a better life.[59]

Some readers, especially male critics who seem to have an obsession with violent retributive action as the necessary response to previously imposed violent acts, have difficulty with Walker's ending. These readers fail to realize that they too, at this point, are victims of interlocking oppressive systems. Often men cannot fathom a woman choosing transformation over retaliation. But such a preference for stereotypic violence exposes "society's fear of women's independence of man . . . [and] call[s] into question society's definition of woman at its deepest level."[60] Such readers do not want relationships restored, but want them annihilated. Annihilation perpetuates violence; transformation transcends.

Everything Celie ever wanted is hers as she pens her final letter: Celie is with Albert and Shug as the reunion between themselves and between Nettie, Samuel, Adam, Tashi, and Olivia takes place. She has learned the truth of her real parents. Celie has inherited property, including a store where she sells her own creations. Moreover Celie accepts herself as a person released from the shackles of bondage to an uncaring, unloving God. Finally, a twist of ironic humor and Godlike retributive justice occurs when the stepfather, who morbidly abused Celie, dies in the sex act while mounted on top of his latest child bride. Retribution and humor add to life's many threads of purple.[61]

59 Donahue, "Black Female Authors and Playwrights," 13.
60 Christian, *Black Feminist Criticism*, 198–99.
61 Walker, *The Color Purple*, 250. Another instance of narrative humor, whether deliberate or coincidental, weaves together Celie's experience with the biblical Exodus story. We have already noted the elements of divine-human liberation that connect the novel to the Exodus tradition. But a comic connection also emerges, based on Celie's perception that male genitalia exist in the same class as frogs. (Walker, *The Color Purple*, 261, 290.)

4. Curing Violence through Transformation:
The Royal Color Purple

"I think it pisses God off if you walk by the color purple in a field somewhere and don't notice it."[62] The leitmotif of *The Color Purple* celebrates creation: purple is a manifestation of the royal, creative principle in life. Purple also signals triumph and a quest for the nobility and dignity of persons. Finally, while a Girardian critique shows the pervasive force of violence and scapegoating in shaping culture, mimetic intimacy transforms without requiring sacrifice. Without violence Celie ends up with everything she ever wanted and more, from atonement with God to learning the truth of her real parents and gaining financial security. Walker's remedy in *The Color Purple*—her 'cure' for violence—is not more red-blooded violence and sacrificiality. Rather, Celie escapes the socializing control of domination because of the support and love she receives from Shug and from Nettie's memory. Her transformation is rooted in a "soul theology" of mimetic intimacy with both God and community.

In place of the theme of transformation, many readers conclude that *The Color Purple* is a story about lesbian love. Yet Walker's novel focuses more broadly on the bonds and love shared in sisterhood. It is indeed a sisterhood that she extends to include "Celie's sexual love for Shug, their initiation into a vision of sensual spirituality, which is nature's essence as symbolized by the color purple."[63] However, Celie experiences a love from Shug that is so tied to a creation theology, that the resulting love Celie comes to have for herself transcends any sexual love experienced between Celie and Shug. *The Color Purple*, on this view, is neither about Black male abuse of Black females nor

---

When Celie returns to Georgia and decorates her bedroom, she places the purple frog carved by Albert on the mantel. In Exodus, chapter 8, God plagues the whole country with frogs–although Rabbi Akiba argued that the writer's use of the singular noun form for "frog" meant that "there was only one frog which [was so immense that it] covered the whole land." (Weingreen, *From Bible to Mishnah*, 20.) Furthermore, the frog was deified in the person of the Egyptian goddess Heqt, who aided women in childbirth. Thus the royal color purple in the frog carving which becomes Celie's mantelpiece can incorporate both women's fertility and male genitalia. Finally, this nexus of associations renders the mantelpiece not simply a phallic symbol, but a blend of the powers of reconciliation and humor in creation.

62 Walker, *The Color Purple*, 200.
63 Walker, *The Color Purple*, 190. In some respects Shug was the woman Celie wanted to be. In others, she was the mother Celie never had. (Shug also reconciled the blues singer to her own role as mother, which then leads her in search of the children whom she had abandoned and claimed she did not miss.) Walker's development of the sexual relationship between Celie and Shug developed out of two aspects of familial love. The natural bonding between women, as sisters and as mother and daughter, is the first. The second familial motif is the "sexism that men direct against women unless women generate relationship among themselves and create their own community. . . . [For example] incest . . . emphasize[s] Walker's point that men, even when they are intimately connected to women may still be dangerous to them." Walker, *The Color Purple*, 193–194.

about lesbian love, but about transformations that create healthy relationships. In particular, Celie's transformation is a process grounded in agape and nurtured through ritual.

Rituals of sharing and support create solidarity, empowerment, and personhood. By celebrating all of nature as sacred, Celie's understanding of power and personhood changes. The love and support she receives help her to place her experience in a larger context of vital, created order. In so doing, she learns that her own potential for self-actualization through divine and human community overrides the pain and grief of the past. New myths help her transcend an existence of living death and give birth to new life. New rituals occur within God's holy temple of extended family. The 'good news' of active love for neighbor demands participation and communication. Such communal sharing creates empowerment, which brings about transformation. For example, during a table scene Shug, Celie and Squeak announce their impending departure to Memphis, and Sofia announces she is now home. All the women gain strength at that moment, as the absurdity and pathos of the years of abuse and the response from the men evokes infectious laughter to the point of tears.[64]

In the end, the women do not symbolize victims but victors. Three women achieve their triumphs in various ways: Nettie goes to and returns from Africa; Celie expands her conscious society to include females and males; and Shug becomes a devastating female intransigent. In this way *The Color Purple* compels recognition of the pain and beauty that coexist in the world. Neither disillusionment nor anger paralyzes the characters. They are victors because each one chooses a lifestyle and so lives, transcending victimage! All the women in *The Color Purple* survive the tragic injustice of their life situations. No delusions of grandeur about changing the sinful structures of male misogyny and white racism exist. And sometimes the tax of rebellion seems too much to bear. But finally their sense of community allows these women to stand together in defeat and triumph without resorting to scapegoating.

5. Conclusion

In weighing the evidence, this court of literary theory finds that a Girardian, one-dimensional critique cannot deal with Alice Walker's characterization of Celie. From a Black feminist perspective Girardian theory lacks the capability for an adequate critique of women as protagonists and victims. As a literary theory that claims universal dimensions, Girard's scapegoat paradigm ends up being reductionist. Any reductionist theory tries to eliminate the differences that Walker celebrates. From a Girardian perspective, Walker's offering does not qualify structurally as a novel, particularly a great novel. Girard claims all great novels reflect mimetic and mediated desire. Has the novel itself become

---

64 Walker, *The Color Purple*, 190.

the scapegoat for critical literary theoretical elitism? Alice Walker tells another story.

Walker's alternative to a scapegoat theory that requires murder is the transformation of victims and victimizers of racial and gender related violence. In this regard *The Color Purple* admittedly does not belong to the literary canon of René Girard—that is, the canon of white males of which Girard is a member. But in order to make a valid universal claim, Girardian scapegoat theory needs to be inclusive of literature where women are protagonists, and where a new mood of harmony occurs not through a heroine's or hero's death, but through transformed myths, rituals, and ethos.

As one of the artifacts of popular culture, this novel provides both a forum and a hermeneutic for discovering how people perceive the world and themselves. *The Color Purple* explores the moral evil, violence and suffering that occurs in dysfunctional families and within larger society. It also releases God from the constraints of stained glass and formal liturgy to pervade all creation. Celie addresses her letters to that God, a loving God. Her anti-mimetic God desires wholeness and beauty as symbolized by the color purple, the antithesis of the dysfunctional families described in this novel. At first sexism, racism, and oppressive sadism circumscribe the broken communities in the novel. Those injustices contrast with the wholeness and beauty which Celie finally achieves. God transfigures her in a Christological pattern, from an object of derisive sadism to a Christlike example of humility, love, and beauty. The resolution of the theodicy dilemma makes this work implicitly theological. The God in all of creation is revealed as the God of victims and persecutors, and of the sacred and profane symbolized by the beauty of the color purple.

Apocalyptic Religion
in Christian Fundamentalism

B. Robert Bater

Abstract

The published works of René Girard interrogate relentlessly the nature and origin of human violence. No theme is more constant in all his oral or written utterance. In one volume of his work however—*Things Hidden since the Foundation of the World*—Girard is drawn to reconsider the biblical intimations of Apocalypse which he, in common with biblical fundamentalists, finds fascinating and remarkable. Girard sees an ironic fulfilment of the gospel Apocalypse in the fact that humanity now faces its first objectively apocalyptic moment. He is well aware, of course, that fundamentalists all along have been predicting this fulfilment in the form of world annihilation. Yet Girard is more afraid of our modern derision of fundamentalist-like prophecies than he is of the possibility that their apocalyptic predictions and activities might either help to precipitate nuclear cataclysm, or induce smugness in the face of an ecological Armageddon.

In this essay fundamentalist and Girardian apocalyptic are juxtaposed, the origins, character and goals of modern fundamentalist apocalyptic noted. The result is that even as the remarkable power of Girard's apocalyptic presentiment is acknowledged, his seeming beguilement by a fundamentalist apocalyptic (which is ultimately diametrically opposed to his own) does raise a serious question of judgment that reaches well beyond the sphere of apocalyptic. In face of the present danger, it is far from clear that apocalyptic fundamentalists present a lesser threat than the legions of postmodern secularists whom Girard is so zealous to refute.

0. Introduction

Under the arresting heading, "Science and Apocalypse," René Girard returns at one point to what is for him a familiar theme—the fascination of modern intellectuals with ancient Greek culture, accompanied by a devaluation if not derision of the Judaeo-Christian heritage. He points to an almost religious respect that has been paid, first to Greek and then to primitive culture. There is a poignant irony in all this for Girard. Let us suppose, he suggests, that intelligent extra-terrestrials were to observe our behavior in the face of a threatened destruction of our planet. Observing the vast number of studies devoted to a certain Oedipus and a Dionysus,

> They should be able to compare all this to a continually decreasing interest in the Judaeo-Christian tradition, whose texts make manifest— in a perfectly explicit form, which should be full of implications for the situation in which we find ourselves— a fully fashioned theory of the destruction of all things. Now these particular texts are not from other peoples' religions, they are from our own religion. For good or ill, until now they have governed, and indeed may still govern, the impulse that is carrying us into the unknown. You might think a society so concerned with observing and understanding itself would be capable of detaching a small battalion of the great army encamped in the shade of the Greek and primitive altars in order to verify if everything is as finally signed, sealed and delivered as it appears to be.[1]

Girard has a way with words that is calculated to leave us with any number of telling phrases ringing in our ears. "The impulse that is carrying us into the unknown" is one such phrase. With similar effect he refers to those texts of the Judaeo-Christian tradition which unambiguously set before us "a fully fashioned theory of the destruction of all things." Girard further leaves no doubt about his conviction regarding the impact of such texts upon our history, and possibly even our future. Far from being merely contributory agents, "until now they have governed, and indeed may still govern the impulse that is carrying us into the unknown." It is hard to imagine a more appropriate point of departure in seeking to grasp René Girard's understanding of the apocalyptic crisis that confronts us.

In this essay I seek to come to terms with Apocalypse as seen by Girard. I do so first by locating the Girardian attempt to address the issue of violence as the ultimate problem of human kind within the company of other major prophets of our era similarly haunted by humanity's seeming passion for annihilation. Secondly, Girard's perception of the enormous irony of the apocalyptic hour now confronting us will be sketched against that backdrop. A third section will juxtapose fundamentalist apocalyptic with Girardian apocalyptic. In this section a sketch of the origins and development of modern fundamentalist apocalyptic will facilitate an examination of key features which stand out in view of Girard's perspective on the present moment.

1. An Age of Violence as Prelude to Ultimate Violence

Arthur Miller once said that all of his plays were written in the gap between things as they ought to be and things as they are. For Girard the name of

---

1 Girard, *Things Hidden*, 261–62.

things as they are is violence. A computer count of the frequency with which the word violence occurs in his writings would reveal a kind of fixation on the term and on all that it conjures up in Girard's comprehension of the human tragedy. Assertions unmistakably confirming a preoccupation with violence in its myriad manifestations stand out on almost every page. Let the following somber warning speak for all the other texts: "Either we are moving ineluctably toward nonviolence, or we are about to disappear completely."[2]

Girard's relentless interrogation of the nature and origins of violence is hardly an occasion for surprise to anyone with even minimal awareness of this century's propensity to genocide. It is a century that had witnessed one hundred million war-associated deaths before its fourth quarter had begun. Such a bare statistic takes no account of the massive recourse to torture as a deliberate instrument of government policy on a worldwide scale or other untold violations of the innocent. In short this is an age of unprecedented violence and stands now under the cloud of what Girard himself refers to as "the ultimate violence."[3]

The human race is set before a choice awesome in its starkness and ultimacy. Girard speaks repeatedly of the way in which the pressure of violence has forced "man" in the present age to choose between violence and truth. "For the first time he is confronted with a perfectly straightforward and even scientifically calculable choice between total destruction and the total renunciation of violence."[4]

At the same time it should be acknowledged that diagnosing violence as the human condition is not the same thing as prescribing its cure. Girard is straightforward in saying that it is not his task to offer solutions, and others have observed that the addressing of concrete incarnations of violence in our midst does not seem of great interest to him. Writing on "Violence and the Bible: The Girard Connection," Robert North points out that while Girard draws attention to the violence that is built into our institutions—our police and prison systems, our international banking and trade—"this particular aspect does not interest him; he refers to institutional violence only as a perpetuation of the unawareness of the scapegoat-system."[5] In a similar vein Charles Davis, in a recent evaluation of Girard's enterprise, confesses that he was drawn to investigate "Girard because of his interpretation of the gospel message as a call to a total renunciation of violence." Yet Davis's conviction that Girard is an apostle of the very Christian exclusiveness that has kindled so many outbreaks of violence in Christian history gives him little ground for satisfaction.[6]

---

2 Girard, *Things Hidden*, 258.
3 Girard, *Things Hidden*, 255.
4 Girard, *Violence and the Sacred*, 240.
5 North, "Violence and the Bible," 25.
6 Davis, *Sacrifice and Violence*, 311–21. For an exposé of the fearful historical con-

To comprehend the energy which seems to drive Girard ever further on this unflagging task, it is instructive to recall how many others in our time have set out on the same quest, however divergent the routes taken. "The works which must be read," says Girard in a footnote, "are those by Hannah Arendt, and Karl Jaspers, and above all Michel Serres."[7] Without attempting to be even remotely comprehensive, we would want to add such diverse studies as those of Konrad Lorenz, *On Aggression*, and Anthony Storr, *Human Aggression*. Authors writing from still other perspectives include Jacques Ellul, Claude Levi-Strauss, Robert Bellah, Alisdair MacIntyre, Robert Jay Lifton, and George Steiner. Their quest might indeed be styled the twentieth-century version of the quest for the holy grail. Merely to list such an assortment of names, chosen in part to dramatize the breadth of the spectrum of ideas they represent (an incongruous company to be sure) may serve to remind us how wide and deep is the conviction that the human race can survive only a little longer, behaving as inhumanly as it has for most of this century.

Although none of those just named can lay any special claim to speak on behalf of the others, the fact that George Steiner like René Girard is both a student of culture and a highly regarded literary critic may warrant my selection of him to voice their commn fears, if not a common solution. Almost any one of Steiner's writings would serve equally well to demonstrate his repeated return to the subject of violence. In the last of a series of radio lectures published under the title, *Nostalgia For The Absolute*, Steiner articulated a suspicion that was later to find more passionate and chilling expression on the lips of a onetime Wehrmacht officer in his novel, *The Portage to San Cristobal of A.H.*

> It does look as if great forces of ennui, of boredom, build up inside complex social systems and strain for a violent release. In that case war would not be a kind of hideous stupidity of the politicians, an accident, which the sane mind could surely have avoided. No, it would be a kind of essential balancing mechanism to keep us in a state of dynamic health. And even as we say this we know that it's an horrendous absurdity, because we are now at a point where, if we pursue this line of thought, we come up against wars from which there is no survival.[8]

The related passage in the novel inverts that just quoted. The former Wehrmacht officer muses over the correctness and flatness of the postwar generation in Germany, and finds his memory flooded by scenes recalling the incredible intensity of his generation's experience under Hitler.

---

sequences, resulting from a pervasive habit of revolutionary ideologies to justify cathartic purges, see the reference to the Levite slaughter of three thousand brothers in Exodus 32 in the chapter by Stuart Lasine in this volume.

7 Girard, *Things Hidden*, 453, n.72.

8 Steiner, *Nostalgia For the Absolute*, 56.

We drank so deep of history that there can't be much left in the bottle. By God we took a mouthful. . . . God how we lived: Each terrible year like a hundred ordinary years, like a thousand. He was true to his word. A thousand year Reich inside each of us, a millennium of remembered life.[9]

One other instance shows that Steiner's wisdom on the subject of violence pushes well beyond this somber suspicion. In his interrogation of what it means to be human, Steiner abhors Hannah Arendt's thesis of Jewish passivity in the face of the onslaught. Devoting one of his essays in *Language and Silence* to holocaust studies of the Warsaw Ghetto uprising and of Treblinka (esays by Chaim Kaplan and Jean-Françoise Steiner respectively), Steiner contends:

The mystery is that even *one* man should have retained sufficient remembrance of normal life to recognize man in his companions and in his own brutalized image.[10]

2. The Ironic Fulfilment of the Gospel Apocalypse: Humanity Faces Its First Objectively Apocalyptic Moment

The fearful irony of our contemporary correspondence with the conditions delineated in the apocalyptic passages of the gospels is set out by Girard in *Things Hidden* under the heading, "Science and Apocalypse." Without (so far as I can see) employing the term "irony," Girard is at the the same time vindicated, tantalized and horrified by the multiple forms of the ironic that he finds pervading our situation. The most obvious irony is also the most horrifying, that betokened by an "objectively apocalyptic situation." Girard seems to accept—but is this also spoken in irony?—the judgment of political scientists such as Raymond Aron, that peace is maintained by nuclear armaments alone. For he affirms that the specialists are absolutely right when they "tell us without a blink that this violence alone can *protect* us."[11] Of course, what constitutes the objectively apocalyptic situation is the fact that the human race is capable of destroying itself. Humanity then is compelled to look for peace "under the shadow of the ultimate violence."[12] Again ironically, President Reagan certified that logic by naming the MX missile "Peacemaker."

One of the consequences is a drastic foreclosing of our options. Had there been any possibility of a retreat from our complex technology, that possibility is now altogether removed. "The machine," says Girard, "is so well set up that it would be more dangerous to stop than to go forward. The place to look for

---

9 Steiner, *The Portage to San Cristobal of A.H.*, 127, 129.
10 Steiner, *Language and Silence*, 167.
11 Girard, *Things Hidden*, 255.
12 Girard, *Things Hidden*, 255.

reassurance is in the very heart of the existing terror."[13] The observation is not Girard's: a sobering confirmation of his assertion emerges from the realization that today's fastest missiles allow no time for human decision making. The decision, like the firing of the missiles, must be programmed.

To recognize our abject obeisance in the face of the terrible new god human hands have created only deepens the irony. Humans have always purchased peace at the hands of their idols, which, in Girard's understanding of the relationship between violence and the sacred, are precisely a sacralized form of violence. But we have arrived now at the apotheosis of that process. Girard seems equally justified in seeing "the bomb" as the object of a new "latreia" (worship), which, like the prince of this world, is enthroned above a host of priests and worshippers who exist only to do it service. And just as the priests of the ancient sacral rites had to beware of contamination from drawing too near to "the power," so too the modern priests must be wary of nuclear contamination, albeit measured with scientific instruments.

Even the names of the most deadly missiles take after the most potent divinities, Titan, Poseidon, and Saturn—the god who actually devoured his own children. The presupposition of all this, as Girard's interlocutor, Jean-Michel Oughourlian, clarifies, is that science and technology could only have invented these doomsday weapons on the basis of the radical desacralization of nature, which itself was consequent upon the gospels. We are thereby brought to what might seem the most arresting irony: the scriptures, most particularly the gospel Apocalypses, are fulfilled. One has only to read the daily news paper to know that the terrors of the Apocalypse are at hand. With respect to violence the whole human race now finds itself in a situation reminiscent of that of primitive society, with the difference that we are now fully aware of it.[14]

Indeed, Girard goes so far as to maintain that this is the first generation in a position to hear the text in the fully radical sense in which it was intended.

> This new-found ability comes to us because the sacrificial reading has ceased to cohere and contemporary history has entered upon a period of unprecedented crisis. We have before us a series of interconnected events that can only bring home to us—now on a world scale—the situation presented to us in the Gospels themselves as the historical precondition for the first announcement of the kingdom.[15]

As Girard himself is well aware, this has the ring of the contemporary apocalyptic preacher about it. Indeed it could almost have been written by someone like Hal Lindsey, whose rather lurid predictions of the end of the

---

13 Girard, *Things Hidden*, 256.
14 Readers of Robert Lifton will correlate this point with his concept of "Nuclearism," an entrapment of the mind and soul which also becomes a chronic state of psychological dependency upon the nuclear stand-off. See, e.g., Lifton and Falk, *Indefensible Weapons*.
15 Girard, *Things Hidden*, 260.

world have been read by more people around the world than the works of any other author in the last two decades. (Perhaps Lindsey's mentor, the dispensational scholar John F. Walvoord, would provide a more serious and plausible comparison.) Girard, of course, stops well short of exact correspondences such as Lindsey discerns for example in Rev 9:18, where the death of a third of mankind in a plague of fire, smoke, and sulphur is regarded as a clear prophecy of thermonuclear Armageddon. Girard would obviously deplore such hermeneutical extravagances. Yet he has also expressed regret that we are so afraid of the fundamentalist preachers' apocalyptic interpretation that we have stopped preaching about it altogether in our churches. Indeed, he goes so far as to suggest that there is something more than coincidental in the fact that the Catholic Church stopped preaching about the Second Coming and the Last Things at the very moment that nuclear holocaust became an actual possibility.

Furthermore, Girard contends that in order to induce the devotees of intellectual modernity into a serious consideration of apocalyptic reality,

> we must be able to offer them some even more striking examples of convergence between Scripture and history, some evidence more spectacular than anything we have offered yet. We need something conspicuous enough to be visible at all times and to all men. The "signs of the times" mentioned in the Gospel—which humankind is reproached for not being able to read—must no longer have the least ambiguity, so that an inability to detect them can only come from an inexpressible desire not to see and not to hear the obvious.[16]

But all this while we have been virtually ignoring what, for René Girard, is the most crucial point. However self-evident it may seem to us that the apocalyptic texts are to be read sacrificially, the gospels intend the Apocalypse to be understood non-sacrificially. That is, the violence of the Apocalypse is neither sent nor administered by God; it is of human design arising out of the intricately woven web of human compromises and cowardices.[17] Curiously, Girard upbraids journalists, atheists, and apocalyptic Christian sects for insisting upon a sacrificial reading whereby the violence of the apocalyptic terrors is sent by God. Atheists do so to obscure the otherwise embarrassing relevance of the texts. Apocalyptic sects seemingly rejoice in man enduring self-induced torment, but persist in clinging to the notion of a violence visited upon us by God.

Eminent New Testament scholars do not fare much better with Girard. None have been more eminent in this century than Rudolph Bultmann, and none have been at greater pains to free the liberating power of the gospel from

16 Girard, *Things Hidden*, 254. But see, among what are now innumerable examples of "intellectual modernity," which are clear exceptions to Girard's perception, the Cornell Colloquium papers on "Nuclear Criticism" published by *Diacritics*, 1984.
17 See Girard, *Things Hidden*, 203 for a particularly clear affirmation of this.

the distortions of ancient mythological worldviews in which they are en-
crusted. It is evident to Girard however that Bultmann, like other biblical
critics, failed to resolve the enigma of the Kingdom and the Apocalypse.[18] Just
as Albert Schweitzer defined the enigma by placarding Jesus as the preacher of
imminent Apocalypse, Bultmann assumed that God was the author of the
apocalyptic vengeance. That is, he took the sacrificial reading to be a given,
but one which could only be viewed as an outmoded Jewish superstition with
no potential to be the bearer of gospel meaning. Over against this hermeneutical failure Girard sees one of the most felicitous gains of his non-sacrificial
reading to be the underlying unity of the Kingdom and the Apocalypse that is
manifested.

3. Girardian and Fundamentalist Apocalypse Juxtaposed

What Girard has been telling us under the heading of "Science and Apocalypse" is both startling and profoundly disturbing. To say that we have
entered upon one of history's recurring periods—even of major upheaval and
crisis—would be fearful enough to send a shiver down the spine. That after all
is the way journalists and sometimes historians employ the word, "apocalyptic." However, to say that "contemporary history has entered upon a
period of unprecedented crisis," or upon an "objectively apocalyptic situation," is something "wholly other." It conjures up pictures such as those
evoked by Perry Miller, who entitled the last chapter of his *Errand into the
Wilderness*, "The End of The World," and recounted therein the anticipations
of seventeenth-century American and British writers of the Day of Doom.[19]

No one can miss the transition into some of the darkest secrets "hidden
since the foundation of the world." We have heard these words and felt these
sensations before. Girard is well aware that he is leading us into new territory
so filled with strangeness and foreboding that no one enters gladly and the
most secular among his readers will turn back at its borders.

> In spite of the remarkable examples of structural convergence that seem to
> suggest that the gospel logic is relevant to anthropology, there is no doubt that our
> readers will have been too schooled in the intellectual methods of modernity—
> accepting its notions of what is possible and what is impossible—for them to
> follow us into the territory where we are now trying to lead them.[20]

It is precisely this realization of the scandal of taking apocalyptic notions
seriously that leads Girard, as we saw earlier, to say that we need to hit the

---

18 One of the best accounts of the struggle of both biblical scholars and systematic
     theologians to come to grips with the enigma to which Girard refers, is still that by Klaus
     Koch, *The Rediscovery of Apocalyptic*, the original German edition of which bore the
     intriguing title, *Ratlos vor der Apokalyptic* (Puzzled by Apocalyptic).
19 Miller, *Errand Into The Wilderness*.
20 Girard, *Things Hidden*, 254.

secular reader between the eyes with unmistakable instances of convergence between Scripture and history: "something conspicuous enough to be visible at all times and to all men." He notes that this is what the gospel means by the phrase "signs of the times," and we might add that the convergence is just one step short of the declaration in Rev 1:7 that "every eye shall see him."

In conversation with the present author and others in this volume, Girard has pointed out how different is the American scene from the European in this respect. Fundamentalism is not a significant part of European culture as it is of the North American. Thus it had played little or no part in Girard's thinking before coming to America. He confesses to being somewhat shocked at the vehemence of the mainstream attack upon it—more so than by what its critics have seen as the violent, militaristic or punitive features in fundamentalism itself. Accordingly he warns against the danger of scapegoating the scapegoaters. To this basic disposition toward the fundamentalist must now be added the perception that the fundamentalist, who has always taken the apocalyptic texts of Scripture more seriously, is more likely to see the "remarkable convergence," to recognize unabashedly that we do now stand in an objectively apocalyptic hour. Finally, we note the embarrassing enthusiasm of a large segment of fundamentalist preachers for the preaching of Armageddon. Such sermons are a strong deterrent to the more liberal preachers who now, more than ever, feel the need to dissociate themselves from any notion of a God who is bent on destroying the earth and the human race in order to fulfill seeming prophecies addressed in utterly different contexts two to three thousand years ago.

Obviously some clarification of what we mean by "fundamentalist apocalyptic" is called for if the attempt to juxtapose it with Girard's view of Apocalypse is to be profitable. Realizing that many volumes have been written in the pursuit of adequate definitions of each term individually, we would be well advised to take a minimalist path by proceeding with two or three definitions that have gained widespread acceptance.

3.1 Towards a definition of fundamentalism

A nice example of the complexity of the task of defining and classifying religious beliefs is offered by Gabriel Fackre's recent article. Fackre attempts to establish a typology of evangelical hermeneutics, placing the diverging schools of thought along a spectrum from right to left. He distinguishes eight different degrees of evangelical hermeneutical conviction, beginning from Oracularity and proceeding through three degrees of Inerrancy, three degrees of Infallibility, and concluding with Catholicity. Among other things Fackre notes that some Evangelicals who have discovered Barth, and therefore sit loose to "propositional truths," could not be accepted even in the Catholicity position.[21] We can be sure that an attempt to encompass the spectrum even of

---

21 Fackre, "Evangelical Hermeneutics."

American Christian fundamentalism with comparable precision would be no less complex. [22]

This reminder of the complexity of theological conviction is salutary but misleading, in that it nevertheless deals with only one dimension of fundamentalism. It is equally imperative to view the phenomena from the social, political and perhaps intellectual perspectives as well. Through most of the present century, in fact, social or political analyses of fundamentalism were widely current. Richard Niebur's *The Social Sources of Denominationalism*, and Richard Hofstadter's *Anti-Intellectualism in American Life* and *The Paranoid Style in American Politics*, cover a span of years from 1929 to 1967 and taught their readers to observe fundamentalism from a broader perspective.[23] It was Ernest Sandeen who then redirected attention to the deeper religious roots, and particularly the apocalyptic roots of fundamentalism. For at least a decade after the appearance of his much cited book, *The Roots of Fundamentalism: British and American Millenarianism, 1800–1930*, there seemed to be a virtual consensus that Sandeen was on the right track in insisting that both the roots and substance of fundamentalism were to be found in millenarianism. "For it is millenarianism which gave life and shape to the Fundamentalist movement."[24] Millenarianism is that particular brand of Christian apocalyptic, pessimistic about any amelioration of the world's misery before the return of Christ, which became the majority adventist view in the nineteenth century, and again now in the last half of the twentieth.[25]

The consensus did not hold beyond the decade of the seventies, however. The link between fundamentalism and the apocalyptic mind-set is indeed close; so close that it is rare to find one without the other. But they are not interchangeable terms. Fundamentalism has many roots, the social, political and intellectual being scarcely less generative than the religious. The effusion of old and new fundamentalisms on a global scale in the past two decades has made that fact painfully obvious. No one has acknowledged Sandeen's unique contribution more readily than George Marsden in his widely acclaimed work, *Fundamentalism and American Culture*,[26] which all the while insists on the complexity and seeming irreconcilability of many of fundamentalism's features. Speaking of the American phenomenon in the past century, Marsden wrote:

> Fundamentalism was a mosaic of divergent and sometimes contradictory traditions and tendencies that could never be totally integrated. Sometimes its

22 Many of the positions toward the right end of Fackre's spectrum obviously overlap with fundamentalism.
23 These are of course but a small cross-section of a quite substantial literature.
24 Sandeen, *The Roots of Fundamentalism*, xiii.
25 Sandeen has accepted these distinctions of terminology as proposed by Ernest Lee Tuveson in another major work in the same field, *Redeemer Nation*, 33–35. For somewhat different terms see McGinn, *Visions of The End*, 28–36.
26 Marsden, *Fundamentalism and American Culture*, 200–201.

advocates were backward looking and reactionary, at other times they were imaginative innovators. On some occasions they appeared militant and divisive; on others they were warm and irenic. At times they seemed ready to forsake the whole world over a point of doctrine; at other times they appeared heedless of tradition in their zeal to win converts. Sometimes they were optimistic patriots; sometimes they were prophets shaking from their feet the dust of a doomed civilization.[27]

It is these very paradoxes of fundamentalism which pose such an intimidating but inescapable challenge for that large body of scholars recently embarked upon "The Fundamentalism Project," a five-year interdisciplinary public policy conducted by the American Academy of Arts and Sciences. The results of the study are slated to appear in five consecutive volumes. In his report which sets out the aims and intentions of the project R. Scott Appleby grapples with the seeming contradictions and seeks to pull them together into a comprehensible picture. First of all, he tells us, "Fundamentalisms arise or come to prominence in times of crisis, actual or perceived."[28] Second, the crisis is one of identity in which the group fears extinction *as a people* or absorption into the immersing syncretistic culture. Third, these fundamentalist fears produce, in the early extremist stages a siege mentality. Fourth, historical consciousness with its relativizing consequences, achieved often by means of the "deadly weapon" hermeneutics, is perceived as the leading enemy. Fifth, "fundamentalism finds its initial expression in reaction." The first target in the line of fire may be the insider who is not sufficiently confrontational. But the real threat in Eastern societies is Westernization, and in Western culture, secularization. Sixth, since they grant no privileged status to history or culture, fundamentalists are not truly traditionalists or conservatives. On the other hand, they often seek to out-modernize the modernists by means of canny adaptations, and a shrewd, future orientation.[29] Seventh, fundamentalists see themselves as actors in an apocalyptic drama, the course and outcome of which is predetermined and prescripted in Scripture. Human agency can be instrumental only, never determinative.

Appleby's analysis is decidedly enlightening but requires qualification on the last two points at least. That Appleby's sixth point is accurate is not in question. The Gush Emunim, the ultra-orthodox sect in modern Israel, is cited as a case in point. Examples abound also in the American religious right wing. Given a perceived crisis threatening to erode community identity, and given highly competitive instincts combined with a shrewd contemporary and

---

27 Marsden, *Fundamentalism and American Culture*, 43.
28 Appleby, "Religious Fundamentalism as a Global Phenomenon," paper presented to the Bible, Narrative, and American Culture meeting in Toronto, October, 1989.
29 Appleby cites as a notable example of this posture the Gush Emunim in Israel who adopt modern strategies and dress in contrast to the Haredim, who are truly conservative. On the complex mosaic of Israeli religious ultra-orthodoxy see Margalit, "Israel: The Rise of the Ultra-Orthodox."

future orientation, resort to a species of tacit and unacknowledged hermeneutics becomes virtually unavoidable. Appleby clearly has this in mind when he refers to fundamentalists "manipulating from inside." He rightly observes that this is not interpreted as manipulation by fundamentalist leaders. What needs to be seen with equal clarity is that fundamentalist apologists characteristically take the whole process one step further. Far from admitting to any adaptation, they maintain that it is their steadfast preservation of the institutions of a former golden (Christian) age heedlessly abandoned by liberals which best explains their attraction and rapid growth.[30]

Finally, in reference to Appleby's seventh point it is once again difficult not to be impressed by the discrepancy between rhetoric and reality. On the one hand, the doctrine that the conclusion of the apocalyptic drama is predetermined by God and that human acts can never be determinative of the outcome is "writ in stone." Yet, to take only the one case, there is also the conviction that the End-Time sequence of events cannot commence until the Third Temple is built on the Dome of the Rock in Jerusalem. In this regard the variety of plans and actions by both Jewish and Christian groups to blow up the mosque on the Dome of the Rock, or raise a million dollars through generous American donors for the Jerusalem Temple Foundation—and thereby to ensure that God gets started without delay—makes for a suspense-laden drama while at the same time preempting the divine agency.

3.2 Towards a definition of fundamentalist apocalyptic

Since it is Christian apocalyptic with which Girard is concerned we need not launch out in search of an all-inclusive definition. At the same time however let us not forget the immense capacity of Jewish apocalyptic perspectives especially, not only to open up deeper understanding of Christian apocalyptic scenarios, but even on occasion to reorient them.[31] Yet merely to narrow the focus to Christian fundamentalist apocalyptic does not dramatically simplify the task; the history of even the past century or two is replete with diverse and often exotic manifestations. Fortunately (as I have already intimated) there is one form or embodiment of Christian apocalyptic that is both an essential component of any adequate definition of fundamentalism and whose origins and history provide indispensable clues to other contemporary apocalyptic movements.

To grasp the nature of this contemporary millenarianism, which nowadays prefers the label premillennialism, some awareness of its nineteenth-century

30 Among numerous authors stressing this point, the chapters by Grant Wacker, Martin Marty, and Richard Pierard in Marsden, *Evangelicalism and Modern America*, merit particular attention.

31 If anything, I have understated this. Several works immediately come to mind as studies from a Jewish perspective that have had a significant impact on Christian apocalyptic conceptions. See, e.g., Tuchman, *Bible and Sword*, Malachy, *American Fundamentalism and Israel*; but see, above all, Walzer, *Exodus and Revolution*.

origins is required. To trace it beyond that point is unnecessary if one recognizes with Sandeen that the year 1800 marks a significant break in the history of millenarian ideas and movements. More precisely, the French Revolution precipitated a seismic disturbance in the realm of religion as well as in every other compartment of life. The millenarian revival which burst forth especially after 1830, and which is still with us, surging no doubt to new heights of excitement as the year 2000 approaches, was a clear instance of this effect.[32]

For all who have thought of the nineteenth century as an age of tranquillity it is something of a shock to discover that on the contrary one of the dominant ways of thinking in the mid-nineteenth century was known as "catastrophism." In the realm of the natural sciences the theory of geological catastrophism held that successive ages of geological history were terminated by dramatic changes or catastrophes. In the realm of history, theories that envisaged successive historical epochs, both initiated and terminated in outbreaks of conflict and violence, enjoyed a great vogue. Without doubt both Darwin and Marx imbibed deeply of the springs—perhaps we should say cataracts—of catastrophism. For both it is conflict and upheaval that provide the catalyst which precipitates change and advance and the energy to drive the world.

Precisely this feature of nineteenth-century thought provides, according to Marsden, an essential key to some of the most distinctive features of the newly emerging dispensationalism—the most successful offspring of the post-1830 millenarian revival.[33] What the geologists did with geological history, dispensationalism did with Biblical history. Each of the seven epochs or dispensations (the name suggests a divinely ordered series of ages in world history) ended in violent upheaval. The first, the age of "Innocence," ended with the Fall. The second, "Conscience," with the Flood. The sixth, "Grace," will end with the Tribulation, and the seventh, "the kingdom," will end with Satan loosed and the battle of Gog and Magog. In that sense dispensationalism was conceived in violence. To become aware that in the terms of this scenario we are living right now in the very twilight of the sixth dispensation gives one pause to think.

It can hardly be coincidence that so many of our familiar millenarian movements emerged out of this same period of apocalyptic shaking. Mormonism (which began as an apocalyptic sect) and dispensationalism originated almost simultaneously in 1830. The Millerites appeared a decade later. Although they did not survive William Miller's third and final dating of the end of the world in 1844, they did metamorphize into the Seventh Day Adventists by 1855. The Bible Student Movement, later renamed Jehovah's Witnesses, originated with the prophecy that 1874 would be the year of Christ's invisible

---

32 Sandeen, *The Roots of Fundamentalism*, 5.
33 Marsden, *Fundamentalism and American Culture*, 200–01.

presence. It has prospered through the disappointments of 1914, 1925, and 1975, in each of which the world was unquestionably to end.

John Nelson Darby, the founder of dispensationalism, made six protracted visits to America and found a remarkable acceptance for his scheme of prophetic interpretation. By 1880 it had become a powerful new force in American religious life. It seemed to strike a reponsive chord in the American soul. Certain decades in particular witnessed a quickening of the premillennialist pulse: the popular prophetic conferences of the 1890s, the reaction to World War I, the decade following the founding of Israel in 1948, but especially the decade following the capture of Jerusalem in 1967. The awesome peril of "Mutual Assured Destruction" (MAD) coupled with the good fortune of having a friend at court in the person of President Ronald Reagan—himself a thinly veiled dispensationalist—brought this particular form of fundamentalist apocalyptic to new heights of popularity and influence during the decade of the eighties.[34]

To understand that appeal it would be essential first of all to take note of two or three of the cardinal tenets of dispensationalism as yet unmentioned. More central even than the sequence of seven dispensations (in sports jargon we might refer to God's seven gameplans for the course of world history) is the insistence that God has two entirely separate plans for Israel and for the Christian Church. A third non-negotiable tenet concerns the separation of the Rapture from the Second Coming of Christ by the seven year interval of the Tribulation. At the Rapture, the next major event in history, Christ comes on the clouds (but not to earth) for his saints; at the Second Coming, to wrap up the battle of Armageddon, Christ returns with his saints.

The features of dispensationalism that go far to explain its notable appeal at certain historical moments take us well beyond these central teachings, however. A number of them are also bound to raise questions in the mind of readers of Girard.

a) *When history and prophecy coincide.* Few of us are not fascinated when there is disclosed to us a remarkable "fit" between contemporary events and an apparently prophetic blueprint laid out at some moment in the past. Marsden observed that on his visits to America Darby made few converts to his Plymouth Brethren, but a host of converts to his scheme of prophetic interpretation.[35] No feature in the entire scenario of end-time events (which are expected to unfold precisely as the ancient writers had choreographed them) is more mind-stretching than the belief that the Antichrist will appear as a new Roman Emperor. From the vision of the great image in Daniel 2, and of the four beasts in Daniel 7, to the ten horns (kings) of Rev 13:3 and 17:12,

---

34 Among numerous works that have documented this point see Vidal, Chap. 8 "Armageddon," in *At Home: Essays 1982–88,* 92–104, and in greater detail Halsell, *Prophecy and Politics,* 40–50.

35 Marsden, *Fundamentalism and American Culture,* 46.

Scripture is seen to point ahead to the advent of a world statesman who will be the leader of a ten-nation European confederacy reincarnating the Empire of the Caesars. It is not difficult to imagine the shivers that must have run down many a prophetically sensitive spine in the 1930s when Benito Mussolini studiously portrayed his achievement as the resurrection of the old Roman Empire.[36]

Unfortunately (or should we say, fortunately) the 'perfect fit' has a habit of disappearing as fast as it appeared in the first place. Hal Lindsey took huge delight in observing in his later books that he had foreseen at the time of his *The Late Great Planet Earth* that the European Common Market would fulfil the prophecy of a ten-nation confederacy, notwithstanding the fact that when he wrote the book (1970) there were only nine. He spoke too soon. It was not long after the tenth entered that the eleventh and twelfth did likewise. History and prophecy seem mostly to coincide like ships that pass in the night.

b) *When the worst is best.* Premillennialist pessimism has been the shadow-side of postmillennialist optimism. The more terrible the earthquakes, floods, pestilences, famines and apostasies the more lively the hope. (These are the "signs of the times" which Girard likewise trusts will make us all realize the lateness of the hour.) Too pragmatic to be a consistent pessimist, Dwight L. Moody nevertheless had a favorite image of disaster which cropped up repeatedly in his sermons.

> I look on this world as a wrecked vessel. God has given me a life-boat, and said to me, "Moody! Save all you can." . . . This world is getting darker and darker; its ruin is coming nearer and nearer. If you have any friends on this wreck unsaved, you had better lose no time in getting them off.[37]

So much did they revel in disaster that Timothy P. Weber, with more than a faint touch of irony, is able to write, "No event in the fifty years after 1875 did more for the morale of American premillennialists than World War I."[38] Whether they have ever consistently lived the creed of world and culture despisers is another question; their leaders have included in every generation some of those most willing to exhaust themselves in the service of their vision of the world that ought to be. Their battles *against* communism, secular humanism, equal rights, and abortion, as their battles *for* rearmament, Israel, and traditional values have been equally unremitting. The other side of the matter is that their scorn for all notions of human betterment have provided a kind of ideology that serves as the flip-side of the traditional American confidence in progress when the going gets tough. Similarly, in the face of a world perched precariously on the brink both of nuclear and ecological suicide, we

---

36   Harrison's *The Resurrection of the Old Roman Empire*, brings this era to life through the eyes of a dispensationalist living through the events.
37   Moody, *New Sermons*, quoted by Weber, *Living in the Shadow of the Second Coming*, 53.
38   Weber, *Living in the Shadow of the Second Coming*, 105.

are understandably chilled by the zeal of those who appear to believe in preparing for war more than in the unremitting struggle for peace with justice and care of the planet.

c) *When the enemy is the Devil*. Andrew McKenna, writing an introduction to the *Semeia* volume on René Girard, superbly summarizes Girard's perspective on the process of mutual polarization between enemies:

> Girard's theory suggests too, on a structural plane, why warring communities regularly sacralize the enemy, dehumanize him and totemize him, making him a monster, allegorizing him as The Force of Evil, as the very Devil, white, black, yellow, or red, Himself. The sacrificial dynamic of war, even as we anticipate it on a global scale, comes to the fore, as just that alienation of violence, in which the enemy fills the role of the scapegoat.[39]

McKenna goes on to affirm that Girard's theory of the religious, which is at the same time a "religious theory of history," draws strength from the very real "prospect of apocalyptic closure" of which he writes so unnervingly.

It is noteworthy that McKenna, in the same context, pays tribute to Robert Jewett's work, *The Captain America Complex*, and its "superbly incisive review of American history as a quest of 'redemption through violence'"[40] At the same time McKenna observes how much Girard's theory would supply theoretical rigor to take Jewett's analysis to a deeper level. Jewett's study is certainly most pertinent to the point we are now making about the fundamentalist's persistent habit of identifying the enemy as Satan, whose two unmistakable minions are communism on the international front and secular humanism on the home front. The combination of scriptural exegesis, in which Russia is "the foe from the North," with the insistence on equating that enemy with none other than Satan, made dispensationalism the implacable and unrelenting foe of communism (or any form of government or welfare even faintly reminiscent of communism) and an ever-reliable friend in demanding massive military build-up.[41] Jewett notes that recent studies have verified a growing credibility of the Devil in America. (This credibility, I might add, is lamentably devoid of the more profound understanding of the demonic such as we see in the work of Girard or Walter Wink.) There is also a striking correlation between all manner of intolerance and belief in a devil.

---

39 McKenna, "René Girard and Biblical Studies," 7. Among Girard's many illuminating treatments of the demons and Satan, the concluding portions of *The Scapegoat*, 165–97 stand out, above all p.166.

40 Jewett, *The Captain America Complex*. Note especially the contention in chap. 8 that there is a prevalent attitude which assumes that, where conversion is not possible, God's next preferred option is to annihilate.

41 Among a host of studies see Wilson, *Armageddon Now*. See also a lucid account of demonism and military thinking by Helgeland, "Civil Religion, Military Religion, Roman and American."

The latter finding is hardly surprising since, when the enemy is the very source of evil, tolerance is anything but a virtue. Rosemary and Herman Ruether have given us a stark picture of this demonizing process in the midst of the ongoing confrontation in Israel: "The face of the enemy takes on more and more untrue proportions. The other become first, animals, then pestilent vermin, and, finally, Satan."[42] One does not need to read one of the classic analyses of the Devil's efficacy throughout history, Gaebelein's *The Conflict of the Ages*, to confirm premillennialism's fixation on Satan as the source of all evil. It can be gleaned from almost any chapter of dispensationalist writing, or more readily from an hour of Televangelism. Scapegoating reigns supreme!

d) *When apocalyptic fundamentalists ally or collide.* We have long thought of the Middle East as an area of special fascination and peril, and rightly so. In the Middle East it is always later than you think. What has been true politically for decades has become true also in the religious sphere. That Islamic fundamentalism has become a potent force in the entire area—and now rapidly in Israel as well—is no longer news. Neither is it surprising that Jewish fundamentalism, of the type that Michael Walzer styles "messianic Zionism"[43] and which he perceives as intensely apocalyptic in origin and goal, should also be active in Israel. But that Christian apocalyptic fundamentalists (that is, premillennialists) have been zealous participants in both the political and religious spheres of life in Lebanon and Israel since 1850, and above all since 1948, seems to be only dimly perceived on this continent.[44] The fact that there exists a close alliance (which is for the most part a marriage of convenience) between Jewish and Christian messianic Zionists to effectuate Israeli control and occupation of the entire biblical Land of Promise (Genesis 17) and to restore the temple and its worship, is scarcely known at all or viewed as too outlandish to be taken seriously. Of course the two agendas will rapidly diverge the moment that the worship of the restored (or third) temple begins. For the Jewish messianic Zionists it will be the moment for the Messiah to come at last. For the Christians, spear-headed by the International Christian Embassy in Jerusalem, it will lead in but three and a half years to the Antichrist's profanation of the temple, a further three and a half years of the Great Tribulation, the war of Armageddon (a mimetic crisis of some proportions) and the triumphant return of Christ.

Jerusalem and the temple mount are naturally the focus of this intense engagement. In the apocalyptic texts, as they are read and, above all, as they are interpreted by these two religious forces Jerusalem is the place where it all

---

42 Ruether and Ruether, *The Wrath of Jonah*, 239.
43 Walzer, *Exodus and Revolution.*
44 The zealous activity of fundamentalist Christian Zionists to provide every possible assistance toward the idea and the reality of the State of Israel in order to further the premillennial end-time agenda was carefully documented by an Israeli senior civil servant and scholar, Yona Malachy, in the 1978 work cited above.

happens—the city of Return, the city of the Messiah, coming for the first or second time, the city at the End of the world where the Last Judgment takes place. Curiously it is the city at the End of the world for Muslims as well. It is a place where the moderate apocalyptic fundamentalists are praying for an earthquake as a "Sign" that the Mosque is to be replaced by the temple, and the most zealous have been trying for some time to assist God by blowing up the Mosque with dynamite. The prophecies tell them the final battle in world history will begin from here. Fundamentalist apocalyptic may succeed in seeing to it that it does.

Conclusion

René Girard possesses a widely acknowledged ability to reformulate the question concerning humankind's age-long enthrallment by violence, and thereby to offer original and profound theses on our endemic captivity to a process of mimetic violence culminating in sacrificial crises and the offering up of a scapegoat. Girard's formulations enable him to recast in a most provocative and challenging manner the entire human story. This ability does not fail him when he comes, mainly in *Things Hidden*, to speak about the future and the prospect even of an ultimate apocalyptic violence. Here, however, serious problems manifest themselves. Unlike his cultured despisers— the devotees of the classics and of modernity, a readiness to hear what might be the last warning before the Judgment could be hoped for among apocalyptic fundamentalists who have gone before him in formulating "a fully fashioned theory of the destruction of all things." Yet a closer look at the origins, goals, and practices of apocalyptic fundamentalism seems to disclose that, except for this one cause in common, the movement is the enemy rather than the friend of the Girardian enterprise.

Works Consulted

Abernathy, Ralph David. *And the Walls Came Tumbling Down*. New York: Harper-Collins, 1990.

Achtemeier, Paul J. *Mark*. Proclamation Commentaries. 2d ed. Philadelphia: Fortress Press, 1986.

———. "Origin and Function of the Pre-Marcan Miracle Catenae." *Journal of Biblical Literature* 91 (1972): 198–221.

———. "Toward the Isolation of Pre-Markan Miracle Catenae." *Journal of Biblical Literature* 89 (1970): 265–91.

Acosta, José de. *Historia natural y moral de las Indias* [1590]. 2d ed. Mexico: Fondo de Cultura Economica, 1962.

———. *De procuranda Indorum salute [1589]*. Trans. Francisco Mateos. Madrid: Coleccion Espana Misionera, 1952.

"Again, The Buddhists." *Time* 83 (June 5, 1964): 27–28.

Allison, Dale C., Jr. "Gnika on Matthew." *Biblica* 70 (1989): 526–38.

Anspach, M. R. "Penser la Vengeance." *Esprit* 128 (1987): 103–11.

Arnold, Edwin. *The Light of Asia*. Boston: Roberts Brothers, 1880.

Atchity, Kenneth John. *Homer's Iliad: The Shield of Memory*. Carbondale and Edwardsville: Southern Illinois University Press, 1978.

Atlan, H., and J. P. Dupuy. "Mimesis and Social Morphogenesis." Pp. 1263–68 in *Applied Systems and Cybernetics (Proceedings of the International Congress on Applied Systems Research and Cybernetics)*. Vol. 3. Ed. G. E. Lasker. New York: Pergamon Press, 1981.

Auerbach, Eric. *Mimesis: The Representation of Reality in Western Literature*. Princeton: Princeton University Press, 1953.

Auerbach, Nina. *Women and the Demon: The Life of a Victorian Myth*. Cambridge: Harvard University Press, 1982.

Bailie, Gil. "Sons of Aaron." Paper presented to Bible, Narrative, and American Culture Seminar, Westar Institute, Sonoma, CA, 1988.

Bal, Mieke. *Lethal Love: Feminist Literary Readings of Biblical Love Stories*. Bloomington: Indiana University Press, 1987.

Barth, Karl, et al. "The Barmen Declaration." Pp. 148–51 in *Karl Barth: Theologian of Freedom*. Ed. Clifford Green. London: Collins, 1989.

Baudrillard, Jean. *Simulations*. New York: Semiotext(e) Inc., 1983.

Beachem, Richard. "Büchner's Use of Sources in *Danton's Death*." Yale/Theatre 3 (1972): 45–55.

"Beat Them." *Newsweek* 62 (August 19, 1963): 46.

Beck, Adolph. *Forschung und Deutung*. Frankfurt a. M. and Bonn: Athenäum, 1966.

Betz, Hans Dieter. *Essays on the Sermon on the Mount*. Philadelphia: Fortress Press, 1985.

Beyer, Stephen, trans. and ed. *The Buddhist Experience*. Encino and Belmont: Dickenson, 1974.

Blanco, Matías Ruiz. *Conversión de Piritu*. Caracas: Academia Nacional de la Historia, 1965.

Blank, Sheldon. *Prophetic Faith in Isaiah*. New York: Harper and Row, 1958.

Bondurant, Joan V. *Conquest of Violence: The Gandhian Philosophy of Conflict*. Revised edition. Berkeley: University of California Press, 1965.

Boring, M. Eugene. "The Spectrum of Eschatological Language." 1989.

Boyd, John. *The Function of Mimesis and Its Decline*. Cambridge: Harvard University Press, 1968.

Boyer, I. H. "Remarks on the Personality of the Shaman. In *The Psychoanalytic Study of Society*. Ed. W. Muensterberger and S. Axelrad. New York: International Universities Press, 1962.

Brichto, Herbert C. "The Worship of the Golden Calf: A Literary Analysis of a Fable on Idolatry." *Hebrew Union College Annual* 54 (1983): 1–44.

Brown, Judith M. *Gandhi and Civil Disobedience*. Cambridge: Cambridge University Press, 1977.

Buber, Martin. *Moses: The Revelation and the Covenant*. New York: Harper and Row, 1958.

Büchner, Georg. *Complete Works and Letters*. Trans. Henry J. Schmidt. New York: Continuum, 1986.

"Buddhists Fight With Sitdowns and Suicides." *Life* 55 (August 2, 1963): 24–25.

Burkert, Walter. *Homo Necans: The Anthropology of Ancient Greek Sacrificial Ritual and Myth*. Trans. Peter Bing. Berkeley: University of California Press, 1983.

Butler, J. P. *Subjects of Desire: Hegelian Reflections in Twentieth-Century France*. New York: Columbia University Press, 1987.

Cassuto, Umberto. *A Commentary on the Book of Exodus*. Jerusalem: Magnes, 1967.

Chatterjee, Margaret. *Gandhi's Religious Thought*. Notre Dame: University of Notre Dame Press, 1983.

Chavannes, Edouard. *Cinq cents contes et apologues extraits du Tripitaka chinois*. Paris: Imprimerie Nationale, 1934.

Chidester, David. "Rituals of Exclusion and the Jonestown Dead." *Journal of the American Academy of Religion* 56 (1988): 681–702.

Christian, Barbara. *Black Feminist Criticism: Perspectives on Black Women Writers*. New York: Pergamon Press, 1985.

———. *Black Women Novelists: The Development of a Tradition 1892–1976*. Westport, CT: Greenwood Press, 1980.

Civrieux, Marc de. *Watunna: Mitología Makiritare*. Caracas: Monte Avila Editores, 1970.

Clifford, Regina T. "The *Dhammadipa* Tradition of Śri Lanka: Three Models Within the Singhalese Chronicles." Pp. 1–12 in *Religion and Legitimation of Power in Śri Lanka*. Ed. Bardwell L. Smith. Chambersburg, PA: Anima Books, 1978.

Coates, George W. *Rebellion in the Wilderness: The Murmuring Motif in the Wilderness Traditions of the Old Testament*. Nashville and New York: Abingdon, 1968.

Coker, Daniel. "A Dialogue Between a Virginian and an African Minister" (1810). In *Negro Protest Pamphlets*. Ed. Dorothy Porter. New York: Arno Press and The New York Times, 1969.

Cone, James H. *God of the Oppressed*. New York: Seabury Press, 1975.

———. *The Spirituals and the Blues: An Interpretation*. New York: Seabury Press, 1972.

Conquest, Robert. *The Great Terror*. Rev. ed. New York: Macmillan, 1973.

"Conversation with a Monk." *Nation* 205 (December 25, 1967): 678–81.

Conze, Edward, trans. and ed. *Buddhist Scriptures*. New York: Penguin, 1959.

Cooper-Lewter, Nicholas C. and Henry H. Mitchell. *Soul Theology: The Heart of American Black Culture*. San Francisco: Harper and Row, 1986.

Courtright, Paul B. "The Fires of Excess: Sati in the Hindu Religious Tradition."

Cross, Frank Moore. *Canaanite Myth and Hebrew Epic: Essays in the History of the Religion of Israel*. Cambridge: Harvard University Press, 1973.

Daim, Wilfried. *Christianity, Judaism, and Revolution*. Trans. P. Tirner. New York: Ungar, 1973.

Davis, Charles. "Sacrifice and Violence." *New Blackfriars* 70 (1989): 311–21.

"Death v. the Family." *Time* 82 (August 16, 1963): 23.

Dennison, Sam. *Scandalize My Name: Black Imagery in American Popular Music*. New York: Garland Publishing, 1982.

Derrida, Jacques. *Dissemination*. Trans. Barbara Johnson. Chicago: University of Chicago Press, 1981.

Des Pres, Terence. *The Survivor: An Anatomy of Life in the Death Camps*. New York: Oxford University Press, 1976.

Devereaux, George. "Shamans as Neurotics." *American Anthropologist* 63 (1961): 1088–90.

Diehl, Wilhelm. *Holy War*. New York: Macmillan, 1984.

Dionysus of Halicarnassus. *The Roman Antiquities*. Vol. 1. Loeb Classical Library. 1937.

Donahue, Phil. "Black Female Authors and Playwrights." Interview by Phil Donahue (New York, 20 July 1989). Multimedia Entertainment, Inc. No. 2733.

Donaldson, Lewis R. "'Do Not Resist Evil' and the Question of Biblical Authority." *Horizons in Biblical Theology* 10 (1988): 33–46.

Doty, William G. *Mythography: The Study of Myths and Rituals*. Tuscaloosa: University of Alabama Press, 1986.

Dozeman, Thomas B. *God on the Mountain: A Study of Redaction, Theology and Canon in Exodus 19–24*. Atlanta: Scholars Press, 1989.

Driver, Samuel Rolles. *Deuteronomy*. International Critical Commentary. Edinburgh: T. & T. Clark, 1902.

Dumouchel, Paul. "Différences et paradoxes: réflexions sur l'amour et la violence dans l'oeuvre de Girard." Pp. 215–24 in *René Girard et le Problem du Mal*. Ed. M. Deguy and J.-P. Depuy. Paris: Bernard Grasset, 1982.

_____, ed. *Violence and Truth: On the Work of René Girard.* Stanford: Stanford University Press, 1988.

Dupuy, J.-P. *Ordres et Désordres, Enquête sur un nouveau Paradigme.* Paris: Grasset, 1982.

Duviols, Pierre. *La destrucción de las religiones andinas: Conquista y Colonia.* Trans. Albor Maruenda. Mexico: Universidad Autóma de México, 1977.

Edwards, Mark W. *Homer: Poet of the Iliad.* Baltimore: Johns Hopkins University Press, 1987.

Eliade, Mircea. *A History of Religious Ideas.* Vol. 2. Chicago: University of Chicago Press, 1982.

_____. *The Sacred and the Profane: The Nature of Religion.* New York: Harper Torchbooks, Cloister, 1961.

_____. *Shamanism: Archaic Techniques of Ecstasy.* Princeton: Princeton University Press, 1964.

_____. *Yoga: Immortality and Freedom.* 2d ed. Princeton: Princeton University Press, 1969.

Eliot, George. *Middlemarch.* New York: W. W. Norton, 1977.

Eliot, T. S. *On Poetry and Poets.* New York: Farrar, Straus and Giroux, 1961.

Elkins, Stanley. *Slavery.* 2d ed. Chicago: University of Chicago Press, 1968.

"End of the Glow." *Time* 82 (December 13, 1963): 32.

"Exploding Power of the Buddhists." *Life* 57 (December 11, 1964): 34–41.

Fackre, Gabriel. "Evangelical Hermeneutics." *Interpretation* 43 (1989): 117–29.

"Suicide Series: The Faith That Lights the Fires." *Time* 82 (July 5, 1963): 33.

Feuer, Lewis S. *Ideology and the Ideologists.* New York: Harper and Row, 1975.

"Fiery Protest." *Newsweek* 61 (June 24, 1963): 63.

"Fiery Rebellion." *Newsweek* 67 (June 13, 1966): 48–49.

Filliozat, Jean. "La mort volontaire par le feu et la tradition bouddhique Indienne." *Journal Asiatique* 252 (1963): 21–51.

Fisher, Walter. Introduction to *Father Henson's Story of His Own Life*, by Josiah Henson. New York: Corinth Books, 1962.

FitzGerald, Frances. *Fire in the Lake: The Vietnamese and the Americans in Vietnam.* New York: Vintage Books, 1973.

Foster, George M. "The Anatomy of Envy: A Study in Symbolic Behavior." *Current Anthropology* 13 (1972): 165–202.

Fox, Michael. "Frame-Narrative and Composition in the Book of Qohelet. *Hebrew Union College Annual* 48 (1977): 83–84.

Francis, H. T. and E. B. Cowell, eds. *The Jātaka.* London: Luzac and Co., 1969.

Freire, Paolo. *Pedagogy of the Oppressed.* New York: Herder & Herder, 1970.

Freud, Sigmund. *Totem and Taboo.* New York: Norton, 1950.

Friedman, Thomas L. "Going For Broke in Lebanon's Proxy War." *New York Times* (August 20, 1989, Section B): 1, 3.

Fromm, Erich. *The Anatomy of Human Destructiveness.* Greenwich, CN: Fawcett, 1973.

Frye, Northrop. *Anatomy of Criticism: Four Essays.* Princeton: Princeton University Press, 1971.

Fuller, Reginald H. "The Decalogue in the New Testament." *Interpretation* 43 (1989): 243–55.

Funk, Robert W., Bernard Brandon Scott, and James R. Butts, eds. *The Parables of Jesus: Red Letter Edition.* Sonoma: Polebridge Press, 1989.

Gadamer, Hans-Georg. *Die Aktualität des Schönen: Kunst als Spiel, Symbol und Fest.* Stuttgart: Philipp Reclam, 1977.

———. "Religious and Poetic Speaking." Pp. 86–98 in *Myth, Symbol and Reality.* Ed. Alan M. Olson. Notre Dame: University of Notre Dame Press, 1980.

———. *Truth and Method.* Trans. Garret Barden and John Cunning. New York: Continuum, 1975.

———. *Wahrheit und Methode.* 2d ed. Tübingen: J. C. B. Mohr (Paul Siebeck), 1965.

Gaebelein, Arno. *The Conflict of the Ages.* New York: Publication Office of Our Hope, 1933.

Gandhi, Mohandas K. *An Autobiography: The Story of My Experiments With Truth.* Boston: Beacon Press, 1957.

Gans, Eric. "Sacred Texts in Secular Culture." Pp. 51–64 in *To Honor René Girard.* Stanford French and Italian Studies 34. Saratoga, CA: Anma Libri, 1986.

Gaster, Theodore H. "Sacrifices and Offerings, OT." Pp. 147–59 in *The Interpreter's Dictionary of the Bible.* Vol. 4. Nashville: Abingdon, 1962.

Gernet, Jacques. "Les suicides par le feu chez les bouddhistes chiniose du Ve au Xe siècle." *Mélanges publiés par des Hautes Études chinoises* 2 (1963): 527–58.

Giáp, Tran-vân. "Le Bouddhisme en Annam: des origines au XIIIe siècle." *Bulletin de l'Ecole Francaise d'Extrême-Orient* 32 (1932): 191–268.

Gilligan, Carol. *In a Different Voice: Psychological Theory and Women's Development.* Cambridge: Harvard University Press, 1982.

Gilligan, Carol and Lawrence Kohlberg. "The Adolescent as a Philosopher: The Discovery of the Self in a Post-Conventional World." *Daedalus* 100 (1971): 1051–86.

Ginzberg, Louis. *The Legends of the Jews.* Vol. 3. Philadelphia: Jewish Publication Society, 1968.

Girard, René. *Deceit, Desire, and the Novel: Self and Other in Literary Structure.* Trans. Yvonne Freccero. Baltimore: The Johns Hopkins University Press, 1965.

———. *Job, the Victim of his People.* Trans. Yvonne Freccero. Stanford: Stanford University Press, 1987.

———. "Levi-Strauss, Frye, Derrida and Shakespearean Criticism." *Diacritics* 3 (Fall 1973): 34–38.

———. "Mimesis and Violence: Perspectives in Cultural Criticism." *The Berkshire Review* 14 (1979): 9–19.

———. *The Scapegoat.* Trans. Yvonne Freccero. Baltimore: The Johns Hopkins University Press, 1986.

———. *Things Hidden Since the Foundation of the World* with Jean-Michel Ourgoulian and Guy Lefort. Trans. Stephen Bann and Michael Metteer. Stanford: Stanford University Press, 1987.

———. *"To Double Business Bound": Essays on Literature, Mimesis, and Anthropology.* Baltimore: The Johns Hopkins University Press, 1978.

_____. *Violence and the Sacred*. Trans. Patrick Gregory. Baltimore: The Johns Hopkins University Press, 1977.

Goodhart, Sandor. "'I am Joseph': René Girard and the Prophetic Law." Pp. 53–74 in *Violence and Truth: On the Work of René Girard*. Ed. Paul Dumochel. Stanford: Stanford University Press, 1988.

Gray, J. Glenn. *The Warriors: Reflections on Men in Battle*. New York: Harcourt Brace and Company, 1959.

Green, Ronald M. "Theodicy." Pp. 430–41 in *The Encyclopedia of Religion*. Vol. 14. Ed. Mircea Eliade. New York: Macmillan, 1987.

Greenberg, Moshe. "Some Postulates of Biblical Criminal Law." Pp. 5–28 in *Yehezkel Kaufmann Jubilee Volume*. Ed. Menaham Haran. Jerusalem: Magnes, 1960.

Greenwald, Alice. "The Relic on the Spear: Historiography and the Saga of Dutt-hagamani." Pp. 13–35 in *Religion and Legitimation of Power in Śri Lanka*. Ed. Bardwell L. Smith. Chambersburg, PA: Anima Books, 1978.

Gurumurthy, S. "Self-Immolation in Ancient South India." *Bulletin of the Institute of Traditional Cultures / Madras* (1969): 44–49.

Haan, Norma. "Hypothetical and Actual Moral Reasoning in a Situation of Civil Disobedience." *Journal of Personality and Social Psychology* 32 (1975): 255–70.

Habel, Norman C. *The Book of Job: A Commentary*. Old Testament Library. Philadelphia: Westminster Press, 1985.

Hahn, Joachim. *Das "Goldene Kalb": Die Jahwe-Verehrung bei Stierbildern in der Geschichte Israels*. Frankfurt a. M. and Bern: Peter Lang, 1981.

Halsell, Grace. *Prophecy and Politics: Militant Evangelists on the Road to Nuclear War*. Westport, CT: Lawrence Hill and Co., 1986.

Hamerton-Kelly, Robert G. "A Girardian Interpretation of Paul: Rivalry, Mimesis and Victimage in the Corinthian Correspondence." *Semeia* 33 (1985): 65–81.

_____. *Sacred Violence: Paul's Hermeneutic of the Cross*. Minneapolis: Fortress Press, 1992.

_____. "Sacred Violence and the Curse of the Law (Galatians 3:13): The Death of Christ as a Sacrificial Travesty." *New Testament Studies* 36 (1990): 98–118.

_____, ed. *Violent Origins: Walter Burkert, René Girard, and Johnathan Z. Smith on Ritual Killing and Social Formation*. Stanford: Stanford University Press, 1987.

Hanigan, James P. *Martin Luther King, Jr. and the Foundations of Nonviolence*. Lanham, MD: University Press of America, 1984.

Harris, Trudier. "On *The Color Purple*, Stereotypes, and Silence." *Black American Literature Forum* 18 (Winter 1984): 155–61.

Harrison, L. Sale. *The Resurrection of the Old Roman Empire*. London: Pickering and Inglis, 1934.

Harvey, David. *The Condition of Postmodernity*. Cambridge: Basil Blackwell, 1989.

"The Heart of Quang Duc." *Time* 82 (July 5, 1963): 33.

Henrichs, Albert. "Loss of Self, Suffering, Violence: The Modern View of Dionysus from Nietzsche to Girard." *Harvard Studies in Classical Philology* 88 (1984): 205–40.

Helgeland, John. "Civil Religion, Military Religion, Roman and American." *Forum* 5,1 (1989): 22–43.

Hendin, Herbert and Ann Pollinger Maas. *Wounds of War: The Psychological Aftermath of Combat in Vietnam.* New York: Basic Books, 1984.

Henninger, Joseph. "Sacrifice." Pp. 544–57 in *The Encyclopedia of Religion.* Vol. 12. Ed. Mircea Eliade. New York: Macmillan, 1987.

Henson, Josiah. *Father Henson's Story of His Own Life.* New York: Corinth Books, 1962.

Hodges, Donald Clark. "Fratricide and Fraternity." Pp. 198–216 in *Guilt: Man and Society.* Ed. Roger W. Smith. Garden City, NY: Anchor Books, 1971.

Holladay, William. *Jeremiah: A Commentary on the Book of the Prophet Jeremiah, chaps. 26–52.* Hermeneia. Philadelphia: Fortress Press, 1989.

Holstein, Constance. "Development of Moral Judgment: A Longitudinal Study of Males and Females." *Child Development* 47 (1976): 51–61.

Homer. *The Iliad.* Trans. Robert Fitzgerald. Garden City: International Collectors Library, 1974.

Horace. *Odes and Epodes.* Trans. Joseph P. Clancy. Chicago: University of Chicago Press, 1960.

Horsley, Richard A. *Jesus and the Spiral of Violence.* San Francisco: Harper and Row, 1987.

Howard, Lillie. "Alice Walker." Pp. 313–15 in *American Women Writers.* Vol. 4. Ed. Lisa Mainiero. New York: Frederick Unger, 1982.

Howard, Richard, ed. *Alone in America.* New York: Atheneum, 1969.

Hughes, Dennis. "Shamanism and Christian Faith." *Religious Education* 71 (1976): 392–404.

"The Human Voice Means More." *Time* 86 (November 19, 1965): 118.

Hurston, Zora Neale. *Moses: Man of the Mountain.* New York: Lippincott, 1939. Reprint. Urbana and Chicago: University of Illinois Press, 1984.

Hurvitz, Leon, trans. *Scripture of the Lotus Blossom of the Fine Dharma.* New York: Columbia University Press, 1976.

Hyatt, J. Philip. *Exodus.* New Century Bible Commentary. Grand Rapids Eerdmans, 1980.

Jacobson, Nolan Pliny. *Buddhism: The Religion of Analysis.* Carbondale and Edwardsville: Southern Illinois University Press, 1966.

Jan Yün-hua. "Buddhist Self-Immolation in Medieval China." *History of Religions* 4 (1964): 243–68.

Jewett, Robert. *The Captain America Complex: The Dilemma of Zealous Nationalism.* Santa Fe, NM: Bear and Co., 1984.

Julliand, Alphonse, ed. *To Honor René Girard.* Stanford French and Italian Studies, 34. Saratoga, CA: Anma Libri, 1986.

Kaptein, R. and P. Tijmes. *Der Andre als Model en Obstakel: Een Inleiding in het Werk van René Girard.* Kampen: Kok, 1986.

"The Karma of Vietnam's Buddhists." *New York Times Magazine* (August 21, 1966): 28–29.

Kern, H., trans. *Saddharma-Puṇḍarīka or The Lotus of the True Law.* New York: Dover, 1963.

Kerr, Malcom. "Political Decision Making in a Confessional Democracy." Pp. 187–212 in *Politics in Lebanon*. Ed. Leonard Binder. New York: John Wiley and Sons, 1966.

Khalaf, Samir. "Communal Conflict in Nineteenth Century Lebanon." Pp. 107–34 in *Christians and Jews in the Ottoman Empire*. Vol. 2. Ed. Benjamin Braude and Bernard Lewis. London: Holmes and Meier, 1982.

King, Martin Luther Jr. "An Experiment in Love." Pp. 16–20 in *A Testament of Hope: The Essential Writings and Speeches of Martin Luther King, Jr*. Ed. James M. Washington. San Francisco: HarperCollins, 1991.

_____. *Stride Toward Freedom: The Montgomery Story*. New York: Harper and Row, 1958.

Kloch, Klaus. *The Rediscovery of Apocalyptic*. London: SCM Press, 1972.

Koestler, Arthur. *Darkness at Noon*. New York: Bantam, 1966.

_____. *The Invisible Writing*. London: Collins, 1954.

_____. *Janus: A Summing Up*. New York: Vintage, 1979.

Kofman, Sarah. "The Narcissistic Woman: Freud and Girard." *Diacritics* 10 (September 1980): 36–45.

Koller, Hermann. *Die Mimesis in Antike: Nachahmung, Darstellung, Ausdruck*. Bern: A. Franke, 1954.

Kroeber, A. L. *Psychosis or Social Sanction: The Nature of Culture*. Chicago: University of Chicago Press, 1952.

Lacoue-Labarthe, Philippe. "Mimesis and Truth." *Diacrtitics* 8 (March 1978): 10–23.

Lacouture, Jean. *Vietnam Between Two Truces*. New York: Random House, Vintage Books, 1966.

Lal, P., ed. *The Dhammapada*. New York: Farrar, Straus and Giroux, 1967.

Lamberton, Robert. *Homer the Theologian*. Berkeley: University of California Press, 1989.

Lamotte, Étienne. *Histoire du Bouddhisme Indien: des origines à l'ère Sáka*. Louvain-la-Neuve: Institut Orientaliste, 1976.

Lasine, Stuart. "Fiction, Falsehood, and Reality in Hebrew Scripture." *Hebrew Studies* 25 (1984): 24–40.

_____. "Guest and Host in Judges 19: Lot's Hospitality in an Inverted World." *Journal for the Study of the Old Testament* 29 (1984): 37–59.

_____." Indeterminacy and the Bible: A Review of Literary and Anthropological Theories and their Application to Biblical Texts." *Hebrew Studies* 27 (1986): 48–80.

_____. "Jehoram and the Cannibal Mothers (2 Kings 6.24–33): Solomon's Judgement in an Inverted World." *Journal for the Study of the Old Testament* 50 (1991): 27–53.

_____. "Judicial Narratives and the Ethics of Reading: The Reader as Judge of the Dispute Between Mephibosheth and Ziba." *Hebrew Studies* 30 (1989): 49–69.

_____. *Justice and Human Nature in the Hebrew Bible*. Semeia Studies. Atlanta: Scholars Press, Forthcoming.

_____. Review of René Girard, *Job: The Victim of His People*. *Hebrew Studies* 32 (1991): 92–104.

Leibowitz, Nehama. *Studies in Bamidbar*. Trans. Aryeh Newman. Jerusalem: World Zionist Organization, 1980.

———. *Studies in Shemot.* 2 vols. Trans. Aryeh Newman. Jerusalem: World Zionist Organization, 1976.

Lifton, Robert Jay. *Home From the War: Vietnam Veterans: Neither Victims not Executioners.* New York: Simon and Schuster, 1973.

———and Richard Falk, eds. *Indefensible Weapons: The Political and Psychological Case Against Nuclearism.* Toronto: CBC Enterprises, 1982.

"The Light That Failed." *Time* 87 (June 10, 1966): 39.

Lingat, H. "Les suicides religieux au Siam." *Felicitation Volumes of Southeast Asian Studies* 1. Bankok: The Siam Society, 1965.

Lipsky, Suzanne. "Internalized Oppression." *Black Re-Emergence* 2 (1977): 5–10.

Livy. *Ab Urbe Condita.* Loeb Classical Library. 1919.

Maccoby, Hyam. *The Sacred Executioner: Human Sacrifice and the Legacy of Guilt.* London: Heinemann, 1982.

Machiavelli, Niccolo. *The Discourses of Niccolo Machiavelli.* Vol. 1. Trans. Leslie J. Walker. London: Routledge and Kegan Paul, 1950.

Mack, Burton. "The Kingdom Sayings in Mark." *Forum* 3,1 (1987): 3–47.

MacQueen, Graeme. "The Conflict Between External and Internal Mastery: An Analysis of the Khantivādi Jātaka." *History of Religions* 20 (1981): 242–52.

Maimonides, Moses. *The Guide for the Perplexed.* Trans. M. Friedländer. 2d ed. London: George Routledge and Sons, 1942.

Malachy, Yona. *American Fundamentalism and Israel: The Relation of Fundamentalist Churches to Zionism and the State of Israel.* Jerusalem: Institute of Contemporary Jewry, Hebrew University, 1978.

Mamani, Gregorio Condori. *De nosotros, los runas: Autobiografia.* Recorded by Ricardo Valderrama Fernandez and Carmen Escalante Guiterrez. Madrid: Ediciones Alfaguara, 1983.

Margalit, Avishai. "Israel: The Rise of the Ultra-Orthodox." *The New York Review of Books* 36 (November 9, 1989): 38–44.

Marsden, George. *Fundamentalism and American Culture.* New York: Oxford University Press, 1980.

———, ed. *Evangelicalism and Modern America.* Grand Rapids: Eerdmans, 1984.

Marx, Karl. *The Class Struggles in France 1849 to 1850.* Moscow: Progress, 1960.

Mathews, Aidan Carl. "Knowledge of Good and Evil." Pp. 17–28 in *To Honor René Girard.* Ed. Alphonse Juilland. Saratoga, CA: Anma, 1986.

McGinn, Bernard. *Visions of the End: Apocalyptic Traditions in the Middle Ages.* New York: Columbia University Press, 1979.

McKenna, Andrew J., ed. *René Girard and Biblical Studies.* Semeia 33 (1985).

Memmi, Albert. *The Colonizer and the Colonized.* Boston: Beacon Press, 1967.

———. *Dominated Man.* New York: Orion Press, 1968.

Mendenhall, George E. *The Tenth Generation: The Origins of the Biblical Tradition.* Baltimore: The Johns Hopkins University Press, 1973.

Michalopoulos, Andre. *Homer.* New York: St. Martin's Press, 1966.

Milgrom, Jacob. *Cult and Conscience.* Leiden: Brill, 1976.

———. "Korah's Rebellion: A Study in Redaction." Pp. 135–46 in *De la Tôrah au Messie.* Ed. Maurice Carrex, Joseph Doré, and Pierre Grelot. Paris: Desclée.

_____. "The Rebellion of Korah, Numbers 16–18: A Study in Tradition History." Pp. 570–73 in *Society of Biblical Literature 1988 Seminar Papers*. Ed. David J. Lull. Atlanta: Scholars Press, 1988.

_____. *Studies in Levitical Terminology, I*. Berkeley and Los Angeles: University of California Press, 1970.

_____. "Wave Offering." Pp. 944–46 in *The Interpreter's Dictionary of the Bible Supplementary Volume*. Ed. Keith R. Crim, et al. Nashville: Abingdon, 1976.

Miller, Nancy, ed. *The Poetics of Gender*. New York: Columbia University Press, 1986.

Miller, Perry. *Errand into the Wilderness*. Cambridge: Harvard University Press, 1956.

Moi, Toril. "The Missing Mother: The Oedipal Rivalries of René Girard." *Diacritics* 12 (1982): 21–31.

Morrison, Karl. *The Mimetic Tradition of Reform in the West*. Princeton: Princeton University Press, 1982.

Moses, Wilson Jeremiah. *Black Messiahs and Uncle Toms: Social and Literary Manipulations of a Religious Myth*. University Park: Pennsylvania State University Press, 1982.

Mowinckel, Sigmund. *He That Cometh*. Trans. G. W. Anderson. New York: Abingdon Press, 1954.

Moyers, Bill. "Facing Evil with Bill Moyers." Interview by Bill Moyers (Salado, Texas, 28 March 1988). Public Affairs Television, Inc., The World of Ideas, No. 1.

Murry, Gilbert. *The Rise of the Greek Epic*. Oxford: Clarendon Press, 1911.

Mus, Paul. *Barabudur*. Hanoi: Imprimerie d'Extrême Orient, 1935.

Nelson, Robert J. "Ritual Reality, Tragic Intention, Mythic Projection." *Diacritics* 6 (Summer 1976): 41–48.

Neumann, Erich. *Depth Psychology and a New Ethic*. New York: Harper and Row, 1973.

Neusner, Jacob. "The Absoluteness of Christianity and the Uniqueness of Judaism." *Interpretation* 43 (1989): 18–31.

Nietzsche, Friedrich. *The Genealogy of Morals*. Trans. H. B. Samuel. New York, 1918.

_____. *Human, All Too Human*. Trans. R. J. Hollingdale. Cambridge: Cambridge University Press, 1986.

Nixon, Will. "Black Male Writers: Endangered Species?" *American Visions: The Magazine of Afro-American Culture* 5 (February 1990): 25–28.

North, Robert. "Violence and the Bible: The Girard Connection." *The Catholic Biblical Quarterly* 47 (1985): 1–27.

Norton, Augustus Richard. *Amal and the Shia: Struggle for the Soul of Lebanon*. Austin: University of Texas Press, 1987.

Novak, David. *The Image of the Non-Jew in Judaism: A Historical and Constructive Study of the Noahide Laws*. New York and Toronto: Edwin Mellen Press, 1983.

"Nuclear Criticism." Special Issue of Diacritics 14 (Summer 1984).

O'Flaherty, Wendy D. *Asceticism and Eroticism in the Mythology of Siva*. Delhi: Oxford University Press, 1973.

_____. *Hindu Myths*. New York: Penguin, 1975.

_____. *Other People's Myths*. Chicago: University of Chicago Press, 1990.

_____. "Sexual Doubles and Sexual Masquerades: The Structures of Sex Symbols." Tempe, AZ: Dept. of Religious Studies, Arizona State University, 1986.

Otto, Rudolf. *The Idea of the Holy.* Trans. John W. Harvey. Oxford: Oxford University Press, 1958.

"The Pacifists." *Time* 86 (November 12, 1965): 68.

Plutarch. *Lives: Theseus and Romulus.* Vol. 1. Loeb Classical Library. 1914.

Philo. *On the Life of Moses.* In *Philo.* Vol. 6. Loeb Classical Library. 1935.

———. *On The Sacrifices of Abel and Cain.* In *Philo.* Vol. 2. Loeb Classical Library. 1929.

Pollack, Susan and Carol Gilligan. "Images of Violence in Thematic Apperception Test Stories." *Journal of Personality and Social Psychology* 42 (1982): 159–67.

Porterfield, Amanda. "Shamanism: A Psychosocial Definition." *Journal of the American Academy of Religion* 55 (Winter 1987): 721–39.

Prebish, Charles S. *American Buddhism.* North Scituate, MA: Duxbury Press, 1979.

———. *Buddhist Monastic Discipline.* University Park: Pennsylvania State University Press, 1975.

Quine, W. V. and J. S. Ullian. *The Web of Belief.* New York: Random House, 1970.

Raboteau, Albert J. *Slave Religion: The "Invisible Institution" in the Antebellum South.* New York: Oxford University Press, 1978.

Rad, Gerhard von. *Old Testament Theology.* 2 vols. Trans. D. M. G. Stalker. New York: Harper and Row, 1965.

Redfield, James. *Nature and Culture in the Iliad: The Tragedy of Hector.* Chicago: University of Chicago Press, 1975.

Rescaniere, Alejandro Ortiz. *De Adaneva a Inkarri: Una Visión Indígena de Peru.* Lima: Ediciones Retablo de Papel, 1973.

Ricoeur, Paul. "Can Fictional Narratives Be True?" *Analecta Husserliana* 14 (1983): 3–19.

———. "Erzählung, Metapher und Interpretationstheorie." *Zeitschrift für Theologie und Kirche* 84 (1987): 232–53.

———. *Essays on Biblical Interpretation.* Ed. Lewis Mudge. Philadelphia: Fortress Press, 1980.

———. "Ethics and Culture." Pp. 243–70 in *Political and Social Essay.* Ed. David Stewart and Joseph Bien. Athens, OH: Ohio University Press, 1974.

———. "The Language of Faith." Pp. 223–38 in *The Philosophy of Paul Ricoeur: An Anthology of His Work.* Ed. Charles E. Regan and David Stewart. Boston: Beacon Press, 1978.

———. "The Metaphorical Process as Cognition, Imagination, and Feeling." *Critical Inquiry* 5 (1978): 143–59.

———. "Naming God." *Union Seminary Quarterly* 34 (1979): 489–508.

———. *The Rule of Metaphor: Multi-Disciplinary Studies of the Creation of Meaning in Language.* Trans. Robert Czerny with K. McLaughlin and J. Costello. Toronto: University of Toronto Press, 1977.

———. *The Symbolism of Evil.* Trans. Emerson Buchanan. Boston: Beacon Press, 1970.

———. *Time and Narrative.* 3 vols. Trans. K. McLaughlin and D. Pellauer. Chicago: The University of Chicago Press, 1984–1986.

Ringgren, Helmer. " ach." Pp. 188–93 in *Theological Dictionary of the Old Testament.* Vol. 1. Ed. Johannes Botterwick and Helmer Ringgren. Grand Rapids: Eerdmans, 1974.

Ruether, Rosemary and Herman Ruether. *The Wrath of Jonah: The Crisis of Religious Nationalism in the Israeli-Palestinian Conflict*. San Francisco: Harper and Row, 1989.

Sagan, Eli. *The Lust to Annihilate: A Psychoanalytic Study of Violence in Ancient Greek Culture*. New York: Psychohistory Press, 1979.

Sandeen, Ernest R. *The Roots of Fundamentalism: British and American Millenarianism 1800–1930*. Chicago: University of Chicago Press, 1970.

Schor, Naomi. *Breaking the Chain: Women, Theory, and French Realist Fiction*. New York: Columbia University Press, 1985.

Schrage, Wolfgang. *Ethics of the New Testament*. Trans. David E. Green. Philadelphia: Fortress Press, 1987.

Schwager, Raymund. *Must There be Scapegoats? Violence and Redemption in the Bible*. Trans. Maria L. Assad. New York: Harper and Row, 1987.

Schweiker, William. "Beyond Imitation: Mimetic Praxis in Gadamer, Ricoeur and Derrida." *Journal of Religion* 68 (1988): 21–38.

_____. *Mimetic Reflections: A Study in Hermeneutics, Theology, and Ethics*. New York: Fordham University Press, 1990.

_____. "Sacrifice, Interpretation and the Sacred: The Import of Gadamer and Girard for Religious Studies." *Journal of the American Academy of Religion* 55 (1987): 791–810.

Scott, Bernard Brandon. *Hear Then the Parable*. Minneapolis: Fortress Press, 1989.

Sedgwick, Eve Kosofsky. *Between Men: English Literature and Male Homosocial Desire*. New York: Columbia University Press, 1985.

Sellew, Philip. "Rules for (or against?) Pious Practice." Paper for Jesus Seminar, Sonoma, CA, March, 1990.

Sherover-Marcuse, Erica. *Emancipation and Consciousness*. New York: Basil Blackwell, 1986.

Shipler, David K. *Arab and Jew: Wounded Spirits in a Promised Land*. New York: Times Books, 1986.

Silberman, Lou H. "Wellhausen and Judaism." *Semeia* 25 (1982): 75–82.

Silkin, John, ed. *The Penguin Book of First World War Poetry*. 2d ed. New York: Penguin Books, 1984.

Silverman, Julian. "Shamans and Acute Schizophrenia." *American Anthropologist* 69 (1967): 21–31.

Skinner, Quentin. *The Return of Grand Theory in the Human Sciences*. Cambridge: Cambridge University Press, 1985.

Sörböm, Goram. *Mimesis in Art: Studies in the Origin and Early Development of an Aesthetic Vocabulary*. Uppasala: Svenska Bokforloget, 1966.

Spariosu, Mihai, ed. *Mimesis in Contemporary Theory*. Philadephia: John Benjamins, 1984.

Staal, Frits. *The Vedic Ritual of the Fire Altar*. 2 vols. Berkeley: Asian Humanities Press, 1983.

Steffens, Lincoln. *Moses in Red: The Revolt of Israel as a Typical Revolution*. Philadelphia: Dorrance, 1926.

Steiner, George. *Language and Silence*. New York: Athenaeum, 1982.

_____. *Nostalgia for the Absolute*. Toronto: CBC Enterprises, 1974.

———. *The Portage to San Cristobal of A. H.* New York: Washington Square Press, 1983.

Stowe, Harriet Beacher. *The Key to Uncle Tom's Cabin: Presenting the Original Fact and Documents upon Which the Story is Founded, Together with Corroborative Statements Verifying the Truth of the Work* (1854). Reprint. New York: Arno Press, 1968.

Strong, John S. *The Legend of King Asóka.* Princeton: Princeton University Press, 1983.

———. "The Legend of the Lion-Roarer: A Study of the Buddhist Arhat Piṇḍola Bhāradvāja." *Numen* 26 (1979): 50–88.

Sully, François. *We the Vietnamese: Voices From Vietnam.* New York: Praeger Publishers, 1971.

Summers, Harry G., Jr. *On Strategy: A Critical Analysis of the Vietnam War.* New York: Dell Publishing Company, 1984.

Swanson, Tod D. *Mission Christs and Indian Christs in South America.* Bloomington: Indiana University Press, forthcoming.

Terzani, Titiano. *Ciai Phong!* New York: Ballantine Books, 1976.

Thakur, Upendra. "Self-Immolation in India (1206–1765 A.D.)." *Journal of the Bihar Research Society* 52 (1966): 117–42.

Thich Nhat-Han. *Vietnam Lotus in a Sea of Fire.* New York: Hill and Wang, 1967.

Thomas, Edward J. *The Life of the Buddha as Legend and History.* 3d ed. London: Routledge and Kegan Paul, 1943.

Tillich, Paul. *Systematic Theology.* 3 vols. Chicago: The University of Chicago Press, 1951, 1957, 1963.

Toulmin, Stephen. *Cosmopolis: The Hidden Agenda of Modernity.* New York: The Free Press, 1990.

"Trial by Fire: Thich Quang Duc." *Time* 81 (June 21, 1963): 32.

Trible, Phyllis. *God and the Rhetoric of Sexuality.* Philadelphia: Fortress Press, 1978.

———. *Texts of Terror: Literary-Feminist Readings of Biblical Narratives.* Philadelphia: Fortress Press, 1984.

Troisfontaines, Claude. "L'identité du social et du religieux selon René Girard." *Revue Philosophique de Louvain* 78 (1980): 71–90.

Tuchman, Barbara. *Bible and Sword: England and Palestine from the Bronze Age to Balfour.* New York: Ballantine Books, 1984.

Turner, F. M. *The Greek Heritage in Victorian Britain.* New Haven: Yale University Press, 1981.

Turner, Victor. *The Ritual Process: Structure and Anti-Structure.* Chicago: Aldine, 1969.

Tuveson, Ernest Lee. *Redeemer Nation: The Idea of America's Millennial Role.* Chicago: University of Chicago Press, 1968.

Valadier, Paul. "Bouc émissaire et Révelation chrétienne selon René Girard." *Etudes* 357 (1982): 251–60.

Valderrama, Ricardo and Carmen Escalante. "El Apu Ausangate en la Narrativa Popular." *Allpanchis* Phuturinga 8 (1975).

Van Den Hengle, John. *The Home of Meaning: The Hermeneutics of the Subject of Paul Ricoeur.* Lanham, MD: University Press of America, 1982.

Vega, Garcilasso de la. *Royal Commentaries of the Incas 1*. Trans. and ed. Clements R. Markham. New York: The Hakluyt Society, 1869.

Verdier, Raymond, ed. *La Vengeance*. 4 vols. Vols. 1 and 2: *La Vengeance dans les sociétiés extra occidentales*. Paris: Cujas, 1980 and 1986; Vol. 3: Raymond Verdier and Jean-Pierre Poly, eds. *Vengeance, pouvoirs et ideologies dans quelques civilisations de l'Antiquite*. Paris: Cujas, 1984; Vol. 4: Gerard Courtois, ed. *La Vengeance dans la pensee occidentale*. Paris: Cujas, 1984.

Vidal, Gore. *At Home: Essays 1982–1988*. New York: Random House, 1988.

Virgil. *The Aneid*. Vol. 1. Ed. T. E. Page. New York: St Martin's Press, 1967.

Voltaire. *Philosophical Dictionary*. Ed. and trans. Theodore Besterman. Harmondsworth: Penguin, 1972.

Walker, Alice. *The Color Purple*. New York: Pocket Books, 1982.

Wallace, Mark I. "Postmodern Biblicism: The Challenge of René Girard for Contemporary Theology." *Modern Theology* 5 (1989): 309–25.

Walzer, Michael. *Exodus and Revolution*. New York: Basic Books, 1985.

Warren, Henry Clarke. *Buddhism in Translations*. New York: Atheneum, 1963.

Webb, Eugene. *Philosophers of Consciousness*. Seattle: University of Washington Press, 1988.

Weber, Timothy. *Living in the Shadow of the Second Coming*. Oxford: Oxford University Press, 1979.

Weinfield, Moshe. *Deuteronomy and the Deuteronomic School*. Oxford: Clarendon, 1972.

Weingreen, Jacob. *From Bible to Mishna: The Continuity of Tradition*. New York: Holmes and Meier, 1976.

Weinsheimer, Joel C. *Gadamer's Hermeneutics: A Reading of Truth and Method*. New Haven: Yale University Press, 1985.

Welbon, Guy Richard. *The Buddhist Nirvana and Its Western Interpreters*. Chicago: University of Chicago Press, 1968.

Westerman, Claus. *Isaiah 40–66: A Commentary*. *Old Testament Library*. Philadelphia: Westminster Press, 1969.

Wetzel, Heinz. "Revolution and the Intellectual: Büchner's Danton and Koestler's Rubashov." *Mosaic* 10 (1977): 23–33.

White, David Gordon. "*Dakkhina and Agnicayana*: An Extended Application of Paul Mus' Typology." *History of Religions* 26 (1986): 188–213.

White, Hayden. "Ethnological 'Lie' and Mythological 'Truth.'" *Diacritics* 8 (March 1978): 2–9.

Wilford, John Noble. "The Big Bang Survives an Onslaught of New Cosmology." *New York Times* (January 21, 1990): IV, 5, 1.

Williams, James G. *The Bible, Violence, and the Sacred: Liberation from the Myth of Sanctioned Violence*. San Francisco: HarperSanFrancisco, 1991.

_____. *Gospel Against Parable*. Decatur and Sheffield: Almond Press, 1985.

_____. "The Innocent Victim: René Girard on Violence, Sacrifice, and the Sacred." *Religious Studies Review* 14 (1988): 320–26.

_____. "Myth, Aphorism and the Christ as Sign." *Forum* 5 (1989): 73–91.

_____. "Neither Here Not There: Between Wisdom and Apocalyptic in Jesus' Kingdom Sayings." *Forum* 5,2 (1989): 7–30.

_____. "Parable and Chreia: From Q to Narrative Gospel." *Semeia* 43 (1988): 85–114.

Wilson, Dwight. *Armageddon Now: The Premillenarian Response to Russia and Israel Since 1917*. Grand Rapids: Baker, 1977.

Windisch, Hans. *The Meaning of the Sermon on the Mount: A Contribution to the Understanding of the Gospels and the Problem of Their True Exegesis*. Trans. S. MacLean Gilmour. Philadelphia: Westminster, 1951.

Winks, Robin, ed. *An Autobiography of the Reverend Josiah Henson*. Reading, MA: Addison-Wesley, 1969.

Wolff, Hans Walter. *Anthropology of the Old Testament*. Trans. Margaret Kohl. Philadelphia: Fortress, 1974.

_____. *Hosea: A Commentary on the Book of the Prophet Hosea*. Hermeneia. Philadelphia: Fortress Press, 1974.

Zimmerli, Walther. *Ezekiel: A Commentary on the Book of the Prophet Ezekiel*. Vol. 1. Hermeneia. Philadelphia: Fortress Press, 1979.

Index of Biblical Passages

321

Index of Authors and Subjects